Computational Intelligent Data Analysis for Sustainable Development

Chapman & Hall/CRC
Data Mining and Knowledge Discovery Series

SERIES EDITOR
Vipin Kumar
University of Minnesota
Department of Computer Science and Engineering
Minneapolis, Minnesota, U.S.A.

AIMS AND SCOPE

This series aims to capture new developments and applications in data mining and knowledge discovery, while summarizing the computational tools and techniques useful in data analysis. This series encourages the integration of mathematical, statistical, and computational methods and techniques through the publication of a broad range of textbooks, reference works, and handbooks. The inclusion of concrete examples and applications is highly encouraged. The scope of the series includes, but is not limited to, titles in the areas of data mining and knowledge discovery methods and applications, modeling, algorithms, theory and foundations, data and knowledge visualization, data mining systems and tools, and privacy and security issues.

PUBLISHED TITLES

ADVANCES IN MACHINE LEARNING AND DATA MINING FOR ASTRONOMY
Michael J. Way, Jeffrey D. Scargle, Kamal M. Ali, and Ashok N. Srivastava

BIOLOGICAL DATA MINING
Jake Y. Chen and Stefano Lonardi

COMPUTATIONAL INTELLIGENT DATA ANALYSIS FOR SUSTAINABLE DEVELOPMENT
Ting Yu, Nitesh V. Chawla, and Simeon Simoff

COMPUTATIONAL METHODS OF FEATURE SELECTION
Huan Liu and Hiroshi Motoda

CONSTRAINED CLUSTERING: ADVANCES IN ALGORITHMS, THEORY, AND APPLICATIONS
Sugato Basu, Ian Davidson, and Kiri L. Wagstaff

CONTRAST DATA MINING: CONCEPTS, ALGORITHMS, AND APPLICATIONS
Guozhu Dong and James Bailey

DATA CLUSTERING IN C++: AN OBJECT-ORIENTED APPROACH
Guojun Gan

DATA MINING FOR DESIGN AND MARKETING
Yukio Ohsawa and Katsutoshi Yada

DATA MINING WITH R: LEARNING WITH CASE STUDIES
Luís Torgo

FOUNDATIONS OF PREDICTIVE ANALYTICS
James Wu and Stephen Coggeshall

GEOGRAPHIC DATA MINING AND KNOWLEDGE DISCOVERY, SECOND EDITION
Harvey J. Miller and Jiawei Han

HANDBOOK OF EDUCATIONAL DATA MINING
Cristóbal Romero, Sebastian Ventura, Mykola Pechenizkiy, and Ryan S.J.d. Baker

INFORMATION DISCOVERY ON ELECTRONIC HEALTH RECORDS
Vagelis Hristidis

INTELLIGENT TECHNOLOGIES FOR WEB APPLICATIONS
Priti Srinivas Sajja and Rajendra Akerkar

INTRODUCTION TO PRIVACY-PRESERVING DATA PUBLISHING:
CONCEPTS AND TECHNIQUES
Benjamin C. M. Fung, Ke Wang, Ada Wai-Chee Fu, and Philip S. Yu

KNOWLEDGE DISCOVERY FOR COUNTERTERRORISM AND LAW ENFORCEMENT
David Skillicorn

KNOWLEDGE DISCOVERY FROM DATA STREAMS
João Gama

MACHINE LEARNING AND KNOWLEDGE DISCOVERY FOR
ENGINEERING SYSTEMS HEALTH MANAGEMENT
Ashok N. Srivastava and Jiawei Han

MINING SOFTWARE SPECIFICATIONS: METHODOLOGIES AND APPLICATIONS
David Lo, Siau-Cheng Khoo, Jiawei Han, and Chao Liu

MULTIMEDIA DATA MINING: A SYSTEMATIC INTRODUCTION TO CONCEPTS AND THEORY
Zhongfei Zhang and Ruofei Zhang

MUSIC DATA MINING
Tao Li, Mitsunori Ogihara, and George Tzanetakis

NEXT GENERATION OF DATA MINING
Hillol Kargupta, Jiawei Han, Philip S. Yu, Rajeev Motwani, and Vipin Kumar

RELATIONAL DATA CLUSTERING: MODELS, ALGORITHMS, AND APPLICATIONS
Bo Long, Zhongfei Zhang, and Philip S. Yu

SERVICE-ORIENTED DISTRIBUTED KNOWLEDGE DISCOVERY
Domenico Talia and Paolo Trunfio

SPECTRAL FEATURE SELECTION FOR DATA MINING
Zheng Alan Zhao and Huan Liu

STATISTICAL DATA MINING USING SAS APPLICATIONS, SECOND EDITION
George Fernandez

SUPPORT VECTOR MACHINES: OPTIMIZATION BASED THEORY, ALGORITHMS,
AND EXTENSIONS
Naiyang Deng, Yingjie Tian, and Chunhua Zhang

TEMPORAL DATA MINING
Theophano Mitsa

TEXT MINING: CLASSIFICATION, CLUSTERING, AND APPLICATIONS
Ashok N. Srivastava and Mehran Sahami

THE TOP TEN ALGORITHMS IN DATA MINING
Xindong Wu and Vipin Kumar

UNDERSTANDING COMPLEX DATASETS:
DATA MINING WITH MATRIX DECOMPOSITIONS
David Skillicorn

Computational Intelligent Data Analysis for Sustainable Development

Edited by

Ting Yu, Nitesh V. Chawla, and Simeon Simoff

CRC Press
Taylor & Francis Group
Boca Raton London New York

CRC Press is an imprint of the
Taylor & Francis Group, an **informa** business

A CHAPMAN & HALL BOOK

CRC Press
Taylor & Francis Group
6000 Broken Sound Parkway NW, Suite 300
Boca Raton, FL 33487-2742

First issued in paperback 2016

© 2013 by Taylor & Francis Group, LLC
CRC Press is an imprint of Taylor & Francis Group, an Informa business

No claim to original U.S. Government works

Version Date: 20130304

ISBN 13: 978-1-138-19869-2 (pbk)
ISBN 13: 978-1-4398-9594-8 (hbk)

Library of Congress Cataloging-in-Publication Data

Computational intelligent data analysis for sustainable development / editors, Ting Yu,
Nitesh Chawla, Simeon Simoff.
pages cm. -- (Chapman & Hall/CRC data mining and knowledge discovery series)
Includes bibliographical references and index.
ISBN 978-1-4398-9594-8 (hardback)
1. Sustainable development--Data processing. 2. Public works--Planning--Data
processing. 3. Social policy--Data processing. 4. Environmental quality--Mathematical
models. 5. Data mining. I. Yu, Ting, 1975-

HC79.E5C61244 2013
338.9'270285--dc23   2012050916

Visit the Taylor & Francis Web site at
http://www.taylorandfrancis.com

and the CRC Press Web site at
http://www.crcpress.com

Contents

Acknowledgments

THIS BOOK WAS INSPIRED BY a series of conferences and workshops, including the IEEE International Conference on Data Mining (ICDM) Workshops on Knowledge Discovery from Climate Data (ClimKD), NASA Conference on Intelligent Data Understanding (CIDU), and the Workshop on Machine Learning and Data Mining for Sustainable Development in conjunction with the Tenth SIAM (Society for Industrial and Applied Mathematics) International Conference on Data Mining (SDM 2010). The organizing committee for the ClimKD included Nitesh Chawla, Auroop Ganguly, Vipin Kumar, Michael Steinbach, and Karsten Steinhaeuser. The general chairs for CIDU were Nitesh Chawla and Ashok Srivastava. The program committee of the Workshop on Machine Learning and Data Mining for Sustainable Development included Manfred Lenzen, Carla P. Gomes, Toby Walsh, Xin Zhou, Jin Fan, Zico Kolter, Zhen Wu, and Ghazi Al-Naymat. Professor Vipin Kumar at the University of Minnesota and Randi Cohen (Taylor & Francis Group) invited us to summarize recent research work on this topic.

No book of this length covering so much ground could ever be the unaided work of just three people. The advisory board includes Professor Manfred Lenzen, Dr. Joy Murray, and Dr. Chris Dey at the University of Sydney, Australia; Dr. Julien Ugon at the University of Ballarat, Australia; Dr. Pohsiang Tsai at the National Formosa University, R.O. China; Professor Volker Wohlgemuth, Industrial Environmental Informatics, HTW Berlin, Germany; and Professor Aditya Ghose at the University of Wollongong, Australia. Other reviewers include Dr. Bin Shen at the Zhejiang University, P.R. China, and Dr. Boda Kang at the University of Technology, Sydney, Australia.

MATLAB® is a registered trademark of The MathWorks, Inc. For product information please contact

The MathWorks, Inc.
3 Apple Hill Drive
Natick, MA 01760-2098 USA
Tel: 508-647-7000
Fax: 508-647-7001
E-mail: info@mathworks.com
Web: www.mathworks.com

About the Editors

Ting Yu, PhD, is an honorary research fellow at the Integrated Sustainability Analysis Group, University of Sydney, Australia. His research interests include machine learning, data mining, parallel computing, applied economics, and sustainability analysis. He has worked on research in machine learning, data mining from environmental data, financial data and transport data, and has published more than 20 journal and conference articles. He is also working as a transport modeler at the Transport for NSW, Australia. Prior to that, he was a quantitative financial analyst at a hedge fund, BCS Capital. He was awarded a PhD in computing science from the University of Technology, Sydney, and received the MSc in distributed multimedia systems from the University of Leeds, United Kingdom, and a BEng from the Zhejiang University, P.R. China.

Nitesh V. Chawla, PhD, is an associate professor in the Department of Computer Science and Engineering, director of the Interdisciplinary Center for Network Science and Applications (iCeNSA), and director of the Data Inference Analysis and Learning Lab (DIAL) at the University of Notre Dame. He started his tenure-track position at Notre Dame in 2007, and was promoted and tenured in 2011. Prior to Notre Dame, he was a senior risk modeling manager at CIBC. His research is focused on machine learning, data mining, and network science. He is at the frontier of interdisciplinary applications with innovative work in healthcare informatics, social networks, analytics, and climate/environmental sciences. He is the recipient of multiple awards for research and teaching innovation, including multiple outstanding teacher awards, a National Academy of Engineers New Faculty Fellowship, and a number of best paper awards and nominations. He is the chair of the IEEE CIS (Computational Intelligence Society) Data Mining Technical Committee. He is associate editor for *IEEE Transactions on Systems, Man and Cybernetics (Part B)* and *Pattern Recognition Letters.*

Simeon J. Simoff, PhD, is currently the dean of the School of Computing, Engineering and Mathematics at the University of Western Sydney. Simeon was previously a professor of information technology at the University of Technology (UTS), Sydney. Prior to UTS, he held academic positions at the University of Sydney, the Middle East Technical University, Ecole Polytechnique–University of Nantes, and Istanbul Technical University. In 2006, he was a BIT Professor at the Free University of Bolzano-Bozen and the University of Trento. He is a founding director and a fellow of the Institute of Analytics Professionals of Australia. Currently, Dr. Simoff is an editor of the Australian Computer Society's (ACS) Conferences in Research and Practice in Information Technology (CRPIT) series in computer science and ICT. Prior to that, he was the associate editor (Australia) of the American Society of Civil Engineering (ASCE) *Journal of Computing in Civil Engineering.* Currently, he serves on the ASCE technical committees on data and information management, and on intelligent computing.

List of Contributors

Francis Alexander
Center for Nonlinear Studies
Los Alamos National Laboratory
Los Alamos, New Mexico

Arindam Banerjee
Department of Computer Science
    and Engineering
and
Institute on the Environment
University of Minnesota
Twin Cities, Minnesota

M. Benno Blumenthal
The International Research Institute
    for Climate and Society
Earth Institute
Columbia University
Palisades, New York

John Boland
School of Mathematics and
    Statistics
and
Barbara Hardy Institute
University of South Australia–
    Mawson Lakes Campus
Adelaide, South Australia

Paolo Cagnoli
ARPA Emilia-Romagna
Bologna, Italy

Varun Chandola
Geographic Information Science
    and Technology Group
Oak Ridge National Laboratory
Oak Ridge, Tennessee

Snigdhansu Chatterjee
School of Statistics
University of Minnesota
Minneapolis, Minnesota

Nitesh V. Chawla
Department of Computer Science
    and Engineering
Interdisciplinary Center
    for Network Science and
    Applications (iCeNSA)
and
Data Inference Analysis and
    Learning Lab (DIAL)
University of Notre Dame
Notre Dame, Indiana

Nathan Eagle
Department of Epidemiology
Harvard University
Cambridge, Massachusetts

Frank Eichinger
SAP Research Karlsruhe
Karlsruhe, Germany

Steven J. Fernandez
Geographic Information Science
and Technology Group
Oak Ridge National Laboratory
Oak Ridge, Tennessee

Jerzy Filar
Information Science & Technology
Flinders University of South
Australia
Adelaide, South Australia

Jacob R. Fooks
Food and Resource Economics
University of Delaware
Newark, Delaware

Auroop R. Ganguly
Civil and Environmental
Engineering
Northeastern University
Boston, Massachusetts

Marco Gavanelli
Engineering department in Ferrara
(EnDIF)
University of Ferrara
Ferrara, Italy

Arne Geschke
Integrated Sustainability Analysis
University of Sydney
New South Wales, Australia

Evan Kodra
Civil and Environmental
Engineering
Northeastern University
Boston, Massachusetts

Manfred Lenzen
Integrated Sustainability Analysis
School of Physics
University of Sydney
Sydney, Australia

Kent D. Messer
Applied Economics and Statistics
University of Delaware
Newark, Delaware

Michela Milano
DEIS
University of Bologna
Bologna, Italy

Claire Monteleoni
Department of Computer Science
George Washington University
Washington, D.C.

Daniel Moran
Integrated Sustainability Analysis
University of Sydney
New South Wales, Australia

Emmanuel Müller
Karlsruhe Institute of Technology
  (KIT)
Karlsruhe, Germany

Habib N. Najm
Sandia National Laboratories
Livermore, California

Alexandru Niculescu-Mizil
NEC Laboratories America Inc.
Princeton, New Jersey

Olufemi Omitaomu
Computational Sciences and
  Engineering Division
Oak Ridge National Laboratory
Oak Ridge, Tennessee

Una-May O'Reilly
Computer Science and Artificial
  Intelligence Laboratory
Massachusetts Institute of
  Technology
Cambridge, Massachusetts

Daniel Pathmaperuma
Karlsruhe Institute of Technology
  (KIT)
Karlsruhe, Germany

Joshua B. Plotkin
Department of Biology
The University of Pennsylvania
Philadelphia, Pennsylvania

Peter Pudney
School of Mathematics and
  Statistics
and
Barbara Hardy Institute
University of South Australia
Adelaide, South Australia

Fabrizio Riguzzi
Engineering Department in
  Ferrara (EnDIF)
University of Ferrara
Ferrara, Italy

Gavin A. Schmidt
NASA Goddard Institute for Space
  Studies
New York, New York

Hiroaki Shirakawa
Graduate School of Environmental
  Studies
Nagoya University
Nagoya, Japan

Simeon Simoff
School of Computing, Engineering
  and Mathematics
University of Western Sydney
New South Wales, Australia

Jason E. Smerdon
Lamont-Doherty Earth
  Observatory
Columbia University
Palisades, New York

Karsten Steinhaeuser
Department of Computer Science
& Engineering
University of Minnesota
Minneapolis, Minnesota

Marco Tedesco
The City College of New York–
CUNY
and
The Graduate Center of the City
University of New York
New York, New York

Michael Tippett
The International Research Institute
for Climate and Society
Earth Institute
Columbia University
Palisades, New York

Jameson L. Toole
Engineering Systems Division
Massachusetts Institute of
Technology
Cambridge, Massachusetts

Kalyan Veeramachaneni
Computer Science and Artificial
Intelligence Laboratory
Massachusetts Institute of
Technology
Cambridge, Massachusetts

Harald Vogt
Acteno Energy
Walldorf, Germany

Xiang Ye
Computer Science and Artificial
Intelligence Laboratory
Massachusetts Institute of
Technology
Cambridge, Massachusetts

Ting Yu
Integrated Sustainability Analysis
University of Sydney
New South Wales, Australia

Xin Zhou
Economy and Environment Group
Institute for Global Environmental
Strategies
Hayama, Japan

CHAPTER 1

Computational Intelligent Data Analysis for Sustainable Development

An Introduction and Overview

Ting Yu, Nitesh V. Chawla, and Simeon Simoff

CONTENTS

1.1 INTRODUCTION TO SUSTAINABLE DEVELOPMENT

T HE CONCEPT OF SUSTAINABILITY received worldwide recognition as a result of a report that was published in 1987 by the World Commission on Environment and Development (known as the Brundtland Commission), titled "Our Common Future." The commission developed today's generally accepted definition of sustainability, stating that sustainable development is development that meets the needs of the present without compromising the ability of future generations to meet their own needs [1]. The three main pillars of sustainable development include economic growth, environmental protection, and sociopolitical sustainability (see Figure 1.1). While many people agree that each of these three ideas contributes to the overall idea of sustainability, it is difficult to find evidence of equal levels of initiatives for the three pillars in governmental policies worldwide [2].

Economic growth is the pillar that most groups focus on when attempting to attain more sustainable efforts and development. In trying to build their economies, many countries focus their efforts on resource extraction, which leads to unsustainable efforts for environmental protection as well as economic growth sustainability. However, recent events indicate that even short-term economic growth has not been managed successfully. The European sovereign debt crisis unleashed that some countries in the Euro area rely too much on borrowing instead of improving the productivity to finance their welfare system. Overwhelming debt burden

FIGURE 1.1   Three pillars of sustainability.

has made it difficult or impossible for these countries to refinance their government debt without the assistance of third parties.

Environmental protection has become more important to government and businesses over the past 20 years, leading to greater improvements in the number of people willing to invest in green technologies. Bloomberg New Energy Finance estimates that a record US$243 billion was invested in 2010, well ahead of traditional energy and up more than 30% from the year before. In Australia, more than $5.2 billion was invested in renewable energy during the 2010–2011 financial year, including approximately $4 billion on household solar power alone. This is more than 60% higher than during 2009–2010 [3].

Until recently, the "sustainability debate" was largely confined to environmental circles, and the social dimensions of sustainability were relatively neglected. *Social sustainability* occurs when the formal and informal processes, systems, structures, and relationships actively support the capacity of current and future generations to create healthy and livable communities. Socially sustainable communities are equitable, diverse, connected, and democratic—and provide a good quality of life [4].

In Figure 1.1, the environment supports human society by providing natural resources and absorbing human wastes. Human society contains not only economic activities, but also includes education, health systems, and communities. A strong economy does necessarily lead to a high standard of living. In many developing countries, high economic growth is built upon the poor standard of living, poor working conditions, and sacrifice of the natural environment. Clearly, a sustainable economic growth must be based on a sustainable society and a sustainable environment. Key issues in the development of policies for sustainable development will entail complex decisions about the management of natural resources and more generally about balancing environmental, economic, and societal needs [5]. With the ratification of the United Nations and ICLEI Triple Bottom Line (TBL) standard for urban and community accounting in early 2007, the triple bottom line captures an expanded spectrum of values and criteria for measuring organizational (and societal) success: economic, ecological, and social. The triple bottom line approach to organizational reporting (also known as "sustainability reporting") coincides with the three pillars of sustainable development.

Technological evolution is a slow process as compared to population growth. It takes a long time to discover new affordable energy sources and new forms of natural resources. Population growth happens more quickly than the evolution of technology. To maintain the health of an ecosystem and human society, a key issue in environmental and economic policy is balancing individual interests and the common good [5, 6].

Here we use "blood tantalum" to illustrate what sustainable development is on a global scale.

A typical Nokia mobile phone contains about 40 milligrams of Tantalum. Tantalum is a rare metal with a melting point of 2,996°C, and it is a superlative thermal conductor. Almost two-thirds of the world's tantalum production ends up in high-quality capacitors that are used in devices such as mobile phones and other electronic gadgets.

However, as the mining company supplying more than 50% of the world's tantalum demand, Australia's Talison Minerals has instead spent the past three years scaling down its operations. The roots of Talison's problems lie in a conflict that is being fought 10,000 kilometers away on the other side of the Indian Ocean.

For much of the past decade, cheap supplies of tantalum derived from mines under the control of various rebel groups based in the northeastern regions of the Democratic Republic of Congo (DRC) have flowed into a long and complex supply chain. Among those groups profiting from this trade are Hutu militia associated with the 1994 Rwandan genocide. Coltan (columbite-tantalite) is found in alluvial deposits or mined in primitive open-cut pits by workers, some of whom are children, enslaved or indentured, using the most basic of tools.

The International Rescue Committee refugee action group says the conflict in the DRC has resulted in the death of over 5.4 million Congolese over the past decade. The investigation was part of an online project called Making a Killing: The Business of War, which explored the world of arms traffickers, resource exploiters, and corrupt politicians who profited from wars and also developed an interest in perpetuating them.

There is pressure being exerted by manufacturers in the electronic industry supply chain to keep prices low, which encourages buyers to seek the cheapest possible sources. If new compliance is created to prohibit the use of "blood tantalum," that type of compliance is going to make life tougher for the likes of Apple®, Sony®, Dell, and Nokia [7].

An ordinary consumer who simply purchases a mobile phone with the lowest price may not only indirectly have sponsored a civil war in Congo and Hutu militia associated with the 1994 Rwandan genocide, but also accelerated the falling of Talison Minerals. However, without this direct information, an ordinary consumer is unable to distinguish a mobile phone with or without "blood tantalum." It is also impossible for an ordinary consumer to track the upper stream of the supply chain to find out where the rare materials of a mobile phone come from. Therefore, ordinary consumers should not be blamed for their actions. The invisible hand of the market seems to lose its magical power because the global supply chain is too complex to indicate where the raw materials come from. Government intervention is necessary to force producers to provide adequate, clear, and accurate information to support ordinary consumers to make ethically correct decisions without any extra costs. This kind of intervention requires adequate analysis tools and practice to take account of all three pillars of sustainable development to give consumers and producers a complete picture. In the meantime, the cost of the extra sustainability analysis should be minimized to avoid disadvantaging producers.

1.2 INTRODUCTION TO COMPUTATIONAL INTELLIGENT DATA ANALYSIS

Over the past 50 years, we have witnessed the creation of high-capacity digital data storage and powerful CPUs (central processing units) to store and process millions and millions of bytes of data. Pens and paper have been replaced by computers; days of mindless calculation have been replaced by a command to the machine, which then effortlessly, accurately, effectively, and instantaneously carries out the calculation. The popularization of computers has enabled modern data analysts to type in a few symbols to complete tasks that have previously taken days to perform.

A possible definition of data analysis is the process of computing various summaries and derived values from the given collection of data [8]. No one sets out simply to analyze data. One always has some objective in mind: one wants to answer certain questions. These questions might be high-level general questions, perhaps exploratory; or the questions might be more specifically confirmatory. Orthogonal to the exploratory/confirmatory distinction, we can also distinguish between descriptive and inferential analysis. A descriptive (or summarizing) analysis is aimed at making a statement about the dataset at hand. In contrast, an inferential analysis is aimed at trying to draw conclusions that have more general validity.

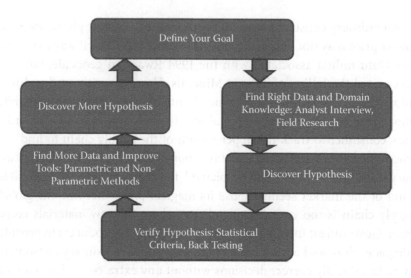

FIGURE 1.2   Iterative process of data analysis.

Often, inferential studies are based on samples from a population, the aim of which is to try to make some general statements about some broader aspect of that population, most (or some) of which has not been observed.

In practice, data analysis is an iterative process (Figure 1.2). After a goal (or a question) is defined to indicate the success of the data analysis, the relevant data is collected. One studies the data, examining it using some analytic techniques. One might decide to look at it another way, perhaps modifying it in the process by transformation or partitioning, and then go back to the beginning and apply another data analytics tool. This can go round and round many times.

Computational intelligent data analysis does computerize the iterative data analysis process by removing tedious and mindless calculations. Computational intelligent data analysis goes beyond this scope. It aims to design algorithms to solve increasingly complex data analysis problems in changing environments. It is the study of adaptive mechanisms to enable or facilitate the data analysis process in complex and changing environments. These mechanisms include paradigms that exhibit an ability to learn or adapt to new situations, to generalize, abstract, discover, and associate [9]. In simple terms, it is the study of how to make computers do things usually associated with human excellence [10]. To a great extent, the ambition of totally autonomous data mining has now been abandoned [11]. Computational intelligent data analysis does not completely replace a human being.

New computing and data storage technologies not only enhance traditional data analysis tools, but also change the landscape of data analysis by raising new challenges. Because computer techniques are able to store and process the latest data and information with milliseconds delay, computational intelligent data analysis addresses a new problem: how do we efficiently and correctly include the latest data, update models, adapt to the new circumstance, and eventually provide sufficient evidence to make timely and correct decisions?

Another motivation for computational intelligent data analysis has been the inability of conventional analytical tools to handle, within reasonable time limits, the quantities of data that are now being stored. Computational intelligent data analysis is thus being seen as a useful method of providing some measure of automated insight into the data being collected. However, it has become apparent that while some useful patterns can be discovered and the discipline has had a number of notable successes, the potential for either logical or statistical error is extremely high. As a result, much of the computational intelligent data analysis is, at best, a set of suggested topics for further investigation [12]. The high unreliability of the results is a major concern to many applications—for example, financial investment. In these fields, the decision must be made prudently and transparently to avoid any catastrophe. Trial and error is unacceptable.

Computational intelligent data analysis has its origins in statistics and machine learning. As a study, it is not a haphazard application of statistical and machine learning tools, and not a random walk through the space of analytics technique, but rather a carefully planned and considered process of deciding what will be most useful and revealing. The process of data analysis can be considered as having two distinct forms: (1) the analytical (or modeling) approach in which the real world is modeled in a mathematical manner, from which predictions can be computed in some way, and (2) pattern matching, or the inductive approach in which prediction is made based on experience [12].

Whereas statistics induction starts with the latter and aims to translate the process into one that is predominately the former, machine learning largely takes place in the latter. Given a set of observations, machine-learning algorithms form the null hypothesis space and search this large hypothesis space to find the optimal hypothesis. This is as close as one can get to achieving the underlying true hypothesis, which may or may not be in the hypothesis space. The fallacy of induction comes into play when the hypothesis developed from the observations resides in a different part of the space from the true solution and yet it is not contradicted by the available data. For example, we could build a regression model to relate one variable to several potential explanatory variables, and perhaps obtain a very accurate predictive model without having any claim or belief that the model in any way represented the causal mechanism.

In most cases of machine-learning algorithms, the null hypothesis space is infinity. Therefore, machine learning is essentially computationally efficient enough to search the space to find the part of space not only to best fit the observations, but also to make correct predictions for the new observations. The latter is critical in addressing the problem of achieving the balance of bias and variance. In terms of mathematical optimization, it is important to find the global optimal instead of the local optimal. However, the design of the search criteria is more important than the optimization process. The criteria directly determine which final optimal solution will achieve the balance of bias and variance to avoid overfitting. The application of machine-learning methods to large databases is called *data mining* or *knowledge discovery* [13].

In the computational intelligent data analysis community, the analyst works via more complex and sophisticated, even semiautomatic, data analysis tools. Given a clearly defined criterion (e.g., sum of squared errors), one can let the computer conduct a much larger search than could have been conducted manually. The program has become a key part of the analysis and has moved the analyst's capabilities into realms that would be impossible unaided. However, one challenge is to find the clearly defined criteria—sometimes not one but a set—to represent the aim of the analysis. The perspective from which the analyst instructs a program to go and do the work is essentially a machine-learning perspective.

Machine-learning algorithms are critical to a range of technologies, including Web search, recommendation systems, personalized Internet advertising, computer vision, and natural language processing. Machine learning has also made significant impacts on the natural sciences, for example, biology; the interdisciplinary field of bioinformatics has facilitated many discoveries in genomics and proteomics [14].

In contrast, modern statistics is almost entirely driven by the notions of hypotheses and models. Prior knowledge is often required to specify a set of null hypotheses and alternative hypotheses and the structure of a model. The data then is used for refutation of a hypothesis, improve the model to better reflect the target problem, and also estimate the coefficients via the calibration process. The nature of machine learning is that it can also yield spurious, logically and statistically erroneous conjectures [12]. The process of modern statistics dramatically reduces the chance of yielding spurious hypotheses by incorporating human knowledge. However, when a large amount of data is continuously collected, more efficient intelligent data analysis methods are required to process the data inflow. This kind of situation occurs more and more often when the Internet and modern sensor networks are widely used for communication and monitoring. Social network mining and data stream mining especially face the completely new phenomena that no theory or even existing research has studied. Nevertheless, as with the dictum of Socrates, "I know one thing, that I know nothing," human knowledge is very limited. Even a lot of knowledge is only true in certain areas and methods.

Data analysis is primarily concerned with numerical data, but other kinds certainly exist. Examples include text data and image data. In text data, the basic symbols are words rather than numbers, and they can be combined in more ways than can numbers. Two major challenges with text data analysis are search and structure.

1.2.1 Process of Computational Intelligent Data Analysis

Traditionally, data analysts have been taught to "familiarize themselves with their data" before beginning to model it or test it against algorithms. This step is basically a descriptive analysis to understand basic characteristics of the data by summarizing and applying simple analysis tools. However, with the large size of modern datasets, this is less feasible (or even entirely impossible in many cases). Here one must rely on computer programs to check data, and also to visualize the data at various aggregated levels.

The first formal step in data analysis is data cleaning and reconciliation. In many cases, a significant proportion of the data used for analysis is collected for other purposes. This results in heterogeneous data sources, and requires that data must be reconciled for the given data analysis tool. The cleaning and reconciliation process aims to handle the missing values and distortions—for example, outliers. These flaws can be caused by misrecordings in the data collection process and inadequate sampling. Missing values can be detected easily, but the distortions are much more difficult to identify. Extreme data does not necessarily mean an outlier. Many extreme events have been observed within the past few years, such as a Japan tsunami, which happens once every hundred years.

The subdisciplines of experimental and survey design have developed over the years and are now very sophisticated [8]. They provide a good illustration of the effort that is necessary to ensure good and accurate data so that effective answers can be obtained in data analysis. However, no matter what analysis tool is being used, the principle is the same: garbage in, garbage out. In many cases, a large dataset is one that has many cases or records. Sometimes, however, the word "large" can refer to the number of variables describing each record. The latter introduces the curse of dimensionality [16]. Artificial neural network and kernel methods map input data into a high-dimensional feature space to convert the nonlinear problem to a linear approximation. The price of doing such mapping is the curse of dimensionality. Dimension reduction is a set of techniques to combine or transform the input data to eliminate less important features.

In scientific communities, the word "experiment" describes an investigation in which (some of) the potentially influential variables can be controlled. Typically, it is not possible to control all the potentially influential variables. To overcome this, subjects (or objects) are randomly assigned to the classes defined by those variables that one wishes to control.

As a summary, there are two main players in the computational intelligent data analysis: (1) computational intelligent data analysis techniques and (2) human analysts. The technique must be efficient enough to process a large amount of data, accurate enough to find the best solution, and reliable enough to resist noise. Human analysts need to understand the problems, define the criteria, and choose the right techniques and analyze the outcomes.

1.3 COMPUTATIONAL INTELLIGENT DATA ANALYSIS FOR SUSTAINABLE DEVELOPMENT

As Section 1.1 states, sustainability is a process that tells of a development of all aspects of human life affecting sustenance. It means resolving the conflict between the various competing goals, and involves the simultaneous pursuit of economic prosperity, environmental quality, and social equity—known as the three dimensions (triple bottom line). Clearly, any thoughtful decision requires the analysis of all three dimensions, and balances their influence to maximize the benefit. This kind of subtle decision-making process demands efficient data collection and analysis methods to provide sufficient evidence to support the rational decision-making process. In the meantime, the characteristics of economic, environmental, and social data provide many unique challenges to the data analysis research community. This has led to the development and consequent application of new methodologies for the automatic processing of economic and environmental data to support the decision-making process for sustainable development. Ness et al. consider that the purpose of a sustainability assessment is to "provide decision-makers with an evaluation of global to local integrated nature-society systems in short and long term perspectives in order to assist decision-makers to determine which actions should or should not be taken in an attempt to make society sustainable" [17].

An ecosystem consists of a biological community together with its abiotic environment, interacting as a system. As human beings, we all live in societies, and interact with other people and surround the environment, including ecosystems. Because sustainable development treats the ecosystem and human society as an integrated system, the analysis of this integrated system unavoidably deals with extremely complex interactions. Due to this complex system, it is difficult to conduct controlled experiments [18]. Intelligent data analysis tools will be useful for sustainable development because of the characteristics of the collected data: large-scale character of environmental, economic, and social data (thousands of state variables); temporal (from milliseconds, seconds, minutes, hours, weeks, year) and statistical nature of the data; existence of a discrete and continuous information mixture; necessity of communication with experts through means of visualization; online operation time restriction for fast decision making; and the existence of uncertainty (noise, outliers, missing information).

First of all, economic, environmental, and social data are often spatial and temporal, because the sustainability problem is often regional or interregional, and evolves over time. Major characteristics of spatial data are its structural complexity and the levels of uncertainty, being inherited from natural systems and the human societies that generate these datasets. New opportunities for machine learning can be integrated into a cohesive and, importantly, scientifically credible knowledge discovery process. This is particularly necessary for spatial and spatio-temporal discovery, as the opportunity for meaningless and expensive diversions is high.

Secondly, over the past two decades, long periods of environmental observation, monitoring of pollution, rare and extreme events, and recent remote sensing technologies generate large databases and allow for the use of new analytical and processing tools. Observation only provides identification of the necessary datasets, but a correct interpretation of the monitored phenomena requires a process of knowledge extraction from data aimed at the detection of spatial patterns and the underlying relationships among the measured variables. This is possible only through a careful data analysis process. On the other hand, many ecological researchers collect over a very limited amount of historical time, the series of which only extend back 100 years. The oldest continuous dataset at HJ Andrews Experimental Forest is 1909–present; they only began their data collection in 1990 [18].

Third, in most cases, economic and environmental data manifolds are subject to strong noise and nonlinearity. The relationships among the involved variables are often not very clear or are distorted by the noise. Low signal-to-noise ratios cause the high variance in the resultant models. In the classical machine-learning application, variance can be decreased by including more training data. In many cases, disregarding the abundant supply of data, many economic and environmental phenomena are time evolving, which shortens the time span of the data and limits its relevance to the present decision making. More real time and coverage data analysis is required to process data across a large area promptly.

1.3.1 Spatio-Temporal Data Analysis

The geographic information system (GIS) recognizes a complex system (natural or urban) by having multiple representations of geography. For example, in the transport modeling tool EMME, a completed transport system is recorded as multiple layers of networks and matrices: geographical surface, road and rail networks, trip flows, and centroids. Geographical surface is encoded as latitude/longitude, and trip flows are often represented as an origin–destination matrix based on a given spatial unit, such as Statistical Local Area (SLA). For example, the Australian Standard Geographical Classification (ASGC) is used to collect and disseminate a broad range of Australian Bureau of Statistics (ABS) social, demographic, and economic statistics. The ASGC has five hierarchical levels comprising, in ascending order: Census Collection District (CD), Statistical Local Area, Statistical Subdivision (SSD), Statistical Division (SD), and State and Territory (S/T) [19].

One of the most important tasks of spatial analysis is to determine the spatial unit. Each spatial unit has a group of homogeneous populations regarding the given purpose. For example, in transport modeling, a strong assumption is that the population within each travel zone has uniform travel behaviors. Of course, different applications may result in different spatial units. Heterogeneous data is integrated via the map overlay.

David O'Sullivan and David Unwin have listed the pitfalls of spatial data. Most important among them: conventional statistics assumes that all observations are independent and identically distributed, that is the I.I.D. assumption. Clearly, the spatial data violates this assumption by having spatial autocorrelation. "Spatial autocorrelation" is a term referring to the obvious fact that data from locations near one another in space is more likely to be similar than data from locations remote from one another [20].

The uncertainty of the boundary introduces the modifiable areal unit problem (MAUP). The aggregation units used are arbitrary with respect to the phenomena under investigation, yet the aggregation units used will affect statistics determined on the basis of data reported in this way. The choice of geographical scale also introduces ecological fallacy. This arises when a statistical relationship observed at one level of aggregation is assumed to hold because the same relationship holds when looking at a more detailed level.

A final significant issue distinguishing spatial analysis from conventional statistics is that space is not uniform. A particular type of nonuniformity of space problem is due to edge effects. These effects arise where an artificial boundary is imposed on a study, often just to keep it manageable. The problem is that sites in the center of the study area can have nearby observations in all directions, whereas sites at the edges of the study area only have neighbors toward the center of the study area.

One of the goals of temporal analysis is to provide evidence to make correct and timely decisions. Temporal analysis (or time-series analysis) faces several dilemmas and difficulties. First, because a natural system, or human society, constantly evolves either slowly or rapidly, data analysts have to decide (1) whether to update the current model, that is, whether the new data is pure noise or contains useful new information; and (2) how to update the current model, if it is useful new information. Updates will cause a structural change or simple parameter updates.

Another related issue is the relevance of historical data. Because the goal of temporal analysis is to predict the future, analysts often assume that historical data reflects a part of the future—if not the entire future—in order to build a reasonable model based on the historical data. However, which historical period should one use to collect the data? It depends on the degree of relevance between a historical and future period. The Hidden Markov Process provides a mechanism to deal with region change, but we still need to determine multiple relevant time periods [21]. More recently, the Internet and sensor networks have generated abundant amounts of evolving and streaming data [22]. A powerful computational data analysis method is required to process extracted knowledge structures from continuous, rapid data records. Also, due to the data collection process, multifrequency time series often coexist, such as daily, weekly, monthly, and yearly time series. It is relatively easy to aggregate the high-frequency time series from the lower-frequency ones, such as daily data from monthly data. However, vice versa, lower to higher, is extremely difficult.

Finally, an extreme event occurs much more often than what normal distribution indicates. We have already witnessed the impact of extreme cases (e.g., the "Global Financial Crisis" and natural disasters)—profound enough to completely derail so-called normal life. The "black swan theory" indicates that the frequency and impact of totally unexpected events is generally underestimated. Unfortunately, the disproportionate role of high-impact, hard-to-predict, and rare events are beyond the realm of normal expectations in history, science, finance, and technology. The probability of consequential rare events is small [23]. A significant proportion of sustainable analysis aims to predict, prevent, or recover from these kinds of extreme events, such as natural disease or social unrest.

1.3.2 Integrated Sustainability Analysis

There are a multitude of tools that can be used to describe and/or quantify the structure of a technical society and its interactions with the environment [24]. Ness et al. divide them in three main groups: (1) regional or national sustainability indicators and indices, (2) product-related tools, and (3) integrated assessment tools [17]. The first group represents measurements of the economic, social, or environmental state of a region or nation. The indicators and indices are continuously measured and calculated and therefore allow for describing long-term sustainability trends from a retrospective point of view. The second group is more specific, as it focuses on the flows related to the production and consumption of goods and services. The goal of these tools is to evaluate the consumption of natural resources and emission of environmental loads along the production or consumption chains or throughout the life cycle of a product or service. Examples from this group include the Life-Cycle Assessment (LCA). The third group, integrated assessment tools, includes in the analysis the three pillars of sustainability and allows analyses at the regional level. Integrated sustainability analysis captures the complexities and interdependencies of our social, economic, and environmental support systems.

The LCA is the investigation and evaluation of the environmental impacts of a given product or service caused or necessitated by its existence, and an evaluation of the environmental impacts of a product or process over its entire life cycle. Environmental LCA is often thought of as "cradle-to-grave" and therefore is the most complete accounting of the environmental costs and benefits of a product or service [25]. For example, the CO_2 footprint of a paper shopping bag might be the sum of CO_2 emitted by logging vehicles, the paper factory, the transport from the factory to the shop, and the decomposition of the bag after it has been used.

Among the various LCA methods, the Economic Input-Output Life-Cycle Assessment (EIO-LCA) method uses information about industry transactions—purchases of materials by one industry from other industry, and the information about direct environmental emissions of industries—to estimate the total emissions throughout the supply chain [25]. In the EIO-LCA method, the input-output table acts as the key engine. The input-output table simply uses a matrix representing the intra-industry flows and the flow between industrial sections and consumption, or the flow between the value-added section and the industrial section. As the economy constantly evolves, the input-output table must be updated at least annually to reflect the new circumstance. A typical input-output table for the Australian economy is represented in the format of seven 2800-by-2800 matrices.

More than 100 countries worldwide regularly publish input-output tables according to guidelines governed by the UN Department of Economic and Social Affairs Statistics Division [26]. Unfortunately, in most countries, including Australia, the input-output table is released every three to four years, due to the large amounts of monetary and human costs involved. The Integrated Sustainability Analysis (ISA) group at the University of Sydney has developed large-scale computational modeling methods comprehensively covering the process of estimating and updating the input-output tables for different levels of economy, and following reporting phases based on the estimated input-output tables.

Globalization, combined with an increasing human population and increased consumption, means that the ecological footprint is now falling more widely and more heavily across the planet. The environmental impact is increasing, and lengthening supply chains mean that consumers are often far removed from the impacts they drive. To manage and reduce our footprint, we must first be able to measure it. The ISA group calculated the net trade balances of 187 countries in terms of implicated commodities to construct a high-resolution global trade input-output table. Using a high-resolution global trade input-output table, they traced the implicated commodities from the country of their production, often through several intermediate trade and transformation steps, to the country of final consumption [27]. The international trade in biodiversity-implicated commodities can be visualized using global trade-flow maps.*

Chapter 2 expands the input-output table from the national scale to the multinational scale in order to measure the footprint covering the whole supply chain. The multiregional input-output table is a 1,000-by-1,000 matrix, and this requires estimating multimillion variables. Chapter 2 provides a mathematical optimization approach to address a few critical issues of estimating, such as conflicting information. One of the difficulties of spatial analysis is the impact of the scale on the estimation results. In the application of multiregional models to environmental analysis, sector reclassification and aggregation are often needed to match environmental data and economic data. Therefore, sector aggregation is a practical and important task for environmentally extended analysis using Multi-Regional Input-Output (MRIO) models. Chapter 3 quantifies the error or dispersion between different reclassification and aggregation schemas, and discovers that aggregation errors have a high concentration over specific regions and sectors, which indicates that these regions and sectors are more influential at the level of aggregation errors.

1.3.3 Computational Intelligent Data Analysis for Climate Change

The Kyoto Protocol was initially adopted on 11 December 1997 in Kyoto, Japan, and entered into force on 16 February 2005. As of May 2012, 192 states have signed and ratified the protocol. In 2005, the European Union Emissions Trading System (EU ETS) was the first large emissions trading scheme in the world. It was launched to combat climate change and is a major pillar of EU climate policy. The EU ETS currently covers more than 10,000 installations with a net heat excess of 20 MW (megawatts) in the energy and industrial sectors, which are collectively responsible for close to half of the EU's emissions of CO_2 and 40% of its total greenhouse gas emissions [28]. In the meantime, numerous debates and research efforts occur at government, academic, and community levels. The National Science Foundation (NSF) funds the project "Understanding Climate Change, a Data Driven Approach," led by Professor Vipin Kumar, University of Minnesota, to provide an improved understanding of the complex nature of the Earth system and the mechanisms contributing to

---

* The ISA group provides an interactive global trade-flow map: http://www.worldmrio.com/biodivmap.

the adverse consequences of climate change, such as increased frequency and intensity of hurricanes, and the propensity for extreme weather events that result in environmental disasters [29].

Climate Informatics 2011, the First International Workshop on Climate Informatics, was organized by a group of data-mining and machine-learning researchers. As one of the outcomes of this workshop, Chapter 4 summarizes the latest progress of the contribution of the data analysis community to climate change. This chapter aims to inspire future work in the nascent field of climate informatics. A profuse amount of climate data of various types is available, providing a rich and fertile playground for future data-mining and machine-learning research. Even exploratory data analysis could prove useful for accelerating discovery in climate informatics.

Based on the introduction of climate informatics, Chapter 5 pays special attention to the climate extremes and uncertainty. In the extreme value theory, extreme events are at the tail of the probability distribution, as the frequency of occurrence is very low. However, many natural extreme events, such as hurricanes and heat waves, have profound impacts that relate to human discomfort and possible loss of life. Due to their rarity, classical data analysis tools, which require sufficient data, may not well explain and predict them. Chapter 5 presents several critical challenges in the science of climate extremes that are not handled by the current generation of climate models. These long standing challenges may not be solved in the near future by improvements in physics-based modeling, and delta-driven computational methods may offer novel solutions.

1.3.4 Computational Intelligent Data Analysis for Biodiversity and Species Conservation

The reduction and fragmentation of natural habitats as a result of deforestation, agriculture, urbanization, and land development are a leading cause of species decline and extinction [5]. Ando et al. have shown that a large number of endangered species are contained within a relatively small number of countries and concluded that if conservation efforts and funds can be expanded in a few key areas, it should be possible to conserve endangered species with great efficiency [30]. They compared two versions of the reserve site selection problem—the set coverage problem (SCP) and the maximal coverage problem (MCP)—to underline the importance of considering both ecological and economic factors in efficient species conservation.

Three leading research groups have done pioneer work on understanding ecosystem structure and function. At the Institute for Computational Sustainability (ICS) at Cornell University, Carla Gomes recently formulated this problem mathematically as a so-called "connection sub-graph problem" [31, 32]. The goal was to design wildlife corridors for grizzly bears in the U.S. northern Rockies to enable movement between three core ecosystems—Yellowstone, Salmon-Selway, and Northern Continental Divide Ecosystems—that span 64 counties in Idaho, Wyoming, and Montana. This large-scale optimization problem places significant demands on current computational methods.

At Oregon State University, Thomas Dietterich has pointed out many opportunities to apply advanced computer science and artificial intelligence methods in the data pipeline. Sensors capture data to create datasets. These are then analyzed to produce models that can support the design of policies. Models also guide the formation of hypotheses, which can then be tested by designing and executing experiments [18]. One of Dietterich's projects is rapid throughput arthropod identification to measure ecosystem functioning. Arthropod counting provides convenient measures of biodiversity and ecosystem health, and it is an important dependent variable for understanding and restoring ecosystems. Another project is automated data cleaning for sensor networks. Sensors fail, particularly when they are placed in challenging environments (e.g., glaciers, mountaintops, and seafloor). When data is collected on a large scale, it is no longer feasible for people to manually detect and diagnose sensor failures. Automated data cleaning methods are needed that can detect and correct sensor failures in real time.

At the AT&T® Lab, Steven Phillips leads the Computational and Mathematical Research in Conservation Biology group; they have developed a software package based on the maximum-entropy approach for species habitat modeling [33, 34]. Government and nonprofit organizations throughout the world are the major funding sources of programs to conserve ecologically valuable land and ensure environmental services. The project selection strategies typically used by conservation organizations rely on a parcel-rating scheme that involves expert panels or standardized scoring systems. Chapter 6 presents Multiple-Objective Linear Programming (MOLP), which is an alternative to the widely used Benefit Targeting (BT) selection process. A case study on the Pennsylvania Dirt and Gravel Roads Program demonstrates that MOLP not only addresses the inefficiency of the BT approach, but also provides a more versatile approach such as handling in-kind cost share, etc.

1.3.5 Computational Intelligent Data Analysis for Smart Grid and Renewable Energy

The ultimate objective of renewable energy and the smart grid is to supply affordable, reliable, clean electricity. The new energy sources should have a reasonable price to final consumers, and switching to new energy should not lower the current living standard. This requires improving current renewable energy technologies to generate the electricity at a lower than or equivalent price to the current fossil-fuel generator, thus optimizing assets, and operating efficiently to distribute the electricity efficiently. The reliable renewable electricity supply provides quality power for the economy and society without chronic power shortages, automatically anticipates and responds to system disturbances, and operates resiliently in the event of attacks or natural disasters.

Renewable energy does not mean zero environmental impact. The development of renewable energy can have an unexpected negative environmental impact in addition to increasing energy efficiency. For example, the greenhouse gas benefits of bioenergy have recently been questioned, partly on the basis of economic modeling of indirect land-use changes. The actual emissions due to both direct and indirect land-use change depend heavily on where and how agriculture expands or intensifies. For example, the conversion of tropical forests, peatlands, and savannas to agricultural land releases large amounts of carbon into the atmosphere [35]. It has been reported that U.S. incentives for biofuel production are promoting land conversion and deforestation in Southeast Asia and the Amazon. The massive subsidies to promote American corn production for ethanol have shifted soy production to Brazil, where large areas of cerrado grasslands are being torn up for soybean farms. The expansion of soy in the region is contributing to deforestation in the Amazon [36].

Another example is the impact of wind power, a promising renewable energy source that has raised concerns about damage to bird and bat populations [5]. Chapter 7 demonstrates that ongoing transformation to a sustainable energy system relying on renewable sources leads to a paradigm shift from demand-driven generation to generation-driven demand. In particular, renewable energies challenge the electricity grid, which needs to be stable and should allow everybody at any point in time to consume energy. Due to the hard-to-store nature of electrical energy, it is required to permanently maintain a constant balance between demand and supply. The maintenance of this balance is becoming more difficult as the share of renewable energy sources rises, due to their unsteady and fluctuating generation. This calls for so-called *smart grids*.

Chapter 8 forecasts the short-term supply, which may be frustrating due to the changing environment. Renewable energy heavily relies on the surrounding environment. For example, the productivity of solar energy reaches its daily peak around the lunchtime. From its monthly pattern, solar energy presents an alternative seasonality pattern, and reaches its peak during the summer period. Chapter 8 demonstrates that maximizing the penetration of renewable energy sources for supplying electricity can be achieved through two disparate techniques: building a supergrid or mixing the renewable sources with demand management and storage.

Chapter 9 provides intelligent data analysis for real-time detection of disruptive events from power system frequency data collected using an existing Internet-based frequency monitoring network. Early detection of supply disturbances within a power grid enables the grid operator to maintain a continuous balance between generation and load with impressive levels of efficiency and reliability.

Based on 2011 data from the World Wind Energy Association, wind power now has the capacity to generate 239 gigawatts, compared with 197 gigawatts in 2010, which is enough to cover 3% of the world's electricity demand [37]. Between 2005 and 2010, the average annual growth in new installations of wind power was 27.6%. Electricity production from wind does not depend on customer demand; it depends on wind speed around the wind farmers. Chapter 10 evaluates a set of computationally intelligent techniques for long-term wind resource assessment. It provides a general approach—Measure, Correlate, and Predict (MCP)—to estimate the joint distribution of wind speeds at the site and publicly available neighboring sources.

1.3.6 Computational Intelligent Data Analysis for Sociopolitical Sustainability

Sociopolitical sustainability focuses on the sustainability of human-built social systems, including transportation systems; cities; buildings; agriculture; health information and health in its environmental, cultural, economic, and social contexts; tax information; levels of governance: sustainability at local, regional, national, and international levels; planning for sustainability; population growth and its consequences; theories of complexity and uncertainty; and knowledge sources, information resources, and data collection processes.

Nathan Eagle uses mobile phone data to gain an in-depth look into and understanding of the slum dweller population toward quantitative results measuring slum dynamics [38]. Because slums are informally established, unplanned, and unrecognized by the government, scientists have a very limited understanding of the 200,000 slums worldwide and the billion individuals living in them. Chris Barrett of the ICS has studied the socio-economic interrelationship between poverty, food security, and environmental stress in Africa, particularly the links between resource dynamics and the poverty trap in smallholder agrarian systems [39].

Chapter 11 gives an excellent example of how temporal and spatial data analysis tools are used to get insight into behavioral data and address important social problems such as criminal offense. Over the past several years, significant amounts of data have been collected from all aspects of human society. As Chapter 11 reveals, there were nearly 1 million theft-related crimes from year 1991 through 1999, and data on 200,000 reported crimes within the City of Philadelphia were collected. This amount of data was unimaginable before the invention of digital data storage systems.

Regional planning is the science of efficient placement of activities and infrastructures for the sustainable growth of a region [40]. On the regional plan, the policy maker must take into account the impact on the environment, the economy, and the society. Chapter 12 presents an application of Constraint Logic Programming (CLP) to a planning problem, the environmental and social impact assessment of the regional energy plan of the Emilia-Romagna region of Italy.

1.4 CONCLUSION AND RESEARCH CHALLENGES

Both computational intelligent data analysis and sustainable development are relatively new research areas. However, both of them have experienced rapid development within the past two decades. Over the past few years, we have witnessed increasing interest from the data analysis community. Sustainable development has become an important application area of intelligent data analysis. For example, three international conferences on computational sustainability have been held in the United States and Europe. The *IEEE International Conference on Data Mining (ICDM)* has continuously hosted a *Workshop on Knowledge Discovery from Climate Data: Prediction, Extremes and Impacts* since 2009. The *ACM SIGKDD Conference on Knowledge Discovery and Data Mining* (KDD) started its *Workshop on Data Mining Applications in Sustainability* in 2011. The *SIAM Data Mining Conference* hosted a *Workshop on Machine Learning and*

Data Mining for Sustainable Development in 2010. The Neural Information Processing Systems (NIPS) had a Mini Symposia, *Machine Learning for Sustainability*, in 2009. Katharina Morik, Kanishka Bhaduri, and Hillol Kargupta [41] presented a brief listing of ten projects and groups who are performing active research pertaining to the field of sustainable systems.

Modern sensor networks, mobile devices, and society networks deliver an explosive amount of environmental, economic, and social data. Indeed, history has never had such a large amount of data to analyze and process. In the meantime, a changing human society urgently needs comprehensive, systematic, and immediate action to address various kinds of sustainable development issues, such as global warming, overpopulation, poverty, and pollution. None of these issues are independently or easily solved. Very often, we have to balance individual interests with the common good [6]. Invisible hands are not the ultimate solution to these problems. Intelligent data analysis cannot solve these problems by itself, but it provides powerful tools to get insight into these problems to support rational decision making. In the meantime, the data provided by sustainable development problems creates opportunities and challenges to data analysis researchers in that they can create and apply powerful technologies to real-life problems. It presents the need for a new approach to study such challenging problems, one in which computational problems are viewed as "natural" phenomena, amenable to a scientific methodology in which principled experimentation, to explore problem parameter spaces and hidden problem structure, plays as prominent a role as formal analysis. It is therefore important to develop new approaches to identify and exploit this real-world structure, combining principled experimentation with mathematical modeling, which will lead to scalable and practical effective solutions [42]. This book is one of the early attempts to explore this new topic. We hope this book will attract more researchers to contribute to developing new methods and applications in this young but promising field.

REFERENCES

1. UNEP, *Report of the World Commission on Environment and Development, General Assembly Resolution 42/187*, United Nations, Editor. 1987.
2. UNCED, *Agenda 21, The Rio Declaration on Environment and Development*, U.N.D.o.E.a.S.A. The United Nations Division for Sustainable Development (DSD), Editor. 1992: Rio de Janerio, Brazil.
3. CEC, *Clean Energy Australia 2011*, C.E. Council, Editor. 2012.

4. Partridge, E., Social sustainability: A useful theoretical framework?, in *Australasian Political Science Association Annual Conference*. 2005. Dunedin, New Zealand.
5. Gomes, C.P., Computational sustainability—Computational methods for a sustainable environment, economy, and society. *The Bridge*, 2009. 39(4). p. 5–13.
6. Hardin, G., The tragedy of the commons. *Science*, 1968. 162(3859): 1243–1248.
7. Hutcheon, S., Out of Africa: The Blood Tantalum in Your Mobile Phone, in *Sydney Morning Herald*. May 8, 2009: FairFax Media: Sydney, Australia.
8. Berthold, M., and D.J. Hand, *Intelligent Data Analysis: An Introduction*. 2003. Berlin, New York: Springer.
9. Engelbrecht, A.P., *Computational Intelligence: An Introduction, 2nd ed.* 2007. New York: Wiley.
10. Rich, E., and K. Knight, *Artificial Intelligence*. 1991, New York: McGraw-Hill.
11. Roddick, J.F., Data warehousing and data mining: Are we working on the right things?, in *Advances in Database Technologies. Lecture Notes in Computer Science*. 1999. New York: Springer. p. 1552–1556.
12. Roddick, J.R., and B.G. Lees, Spatio-temporal data mining paradigms and methodologies, in *Geographic Data Mining and Knowledge Discovery*, H.J. Miller and J. Han, Editors. 2009. Boca Raton, FL: CRC Press. p. 27–44.
13. Akbani, R., S. Kwek, and N. Japkowicz. Applying support vector machines to imbalanced datasets, in *15th European Conference on Machine Learning (ECML)*. 2004.
14. Bishop, C.M., *Pattern Recognition and Machine Learning*. 2006. New York: Springer.
15. Ness, B. et al., Categorizing tools for sustainability assessment. *Ecological Economics*, 2007. 60: 498–508.
16. Dietterich, T.G., Machine learning in ecosystem informatics and sustainability, in *Proceedings of the 21st International Joint Conference on Artifical Intelligence*. 2009. Pasadena, CA.
17. ABS, 1216.0—*Australian Standard Geographical Classification (ASGC)*, Australian Bureau of Statistics, Editor. 2011. Canberra.
18. O'Sullivan, D., and D. Unwin, *Geographic Information Analysis, 1st ed.* 2002. New York: Wiley.
19. Hamilton, J.D., *Time Series Analysis, 1st ed.* 1994. Princeton, NJ: Princeton University Press.
20. Gaber, M.M., A. Zaslavsky, and S. Krishnaswamy. Mining data streams: A review. *ACM Sigmod Record*, 2005. 34(2): 18–26.
21. Taleb, N.N., *The Black Swan: The Impact of the Highly Improbable, 1st ed.* 2007. New York: Random House.
22. Butnar, I., Input-Output Analysis for Use in Life Cycle Assessment: Introduction to Regional Modelling, in *Department of Chemical Engineering*. 2007, the Rovira i Virgili University: Tarragona, in Spanish.
23. Hendrickson, C.T., L.B. Lave, and H.S. Matthews, *Environmental Life Cycle Assessment of Goods and Services: An Input-Output Approach*. 2006. Resources for the Future, Washington, D.C.

24. Murray, J., R. Wood, and M. Lenzen, Input-output analysis—Strengths and limitations, in *The Sustainability Practitioner's Guide to Input-Output Analysis*, J. Murray and R. Wood, Editors. 2010. Champaign, IL: Common Ground Publishing LLC. p. 165–176.

25. Lenzen, M. et al., International trade drives biodiversity threats in developing nations. *Nature*, 2012. 486: 109.

26. Ellerman, D., and B.K. Buchner, The European Union emissions trading scheme: Origins, allocation, and early results. *Review of Environmental Economics and Policy*, 2007. 1(1): 66–87.

27. Kawale, J. et al., Data guided discovery of dynamic climate dipoles, in *NASA Conference on Intelligent Data Understanding*. 2011.

28. Ando, A. et al., Species distributions, land values, and efficient conservation. *Science*, 1998. 279(27): 2126–2128.

29. Conrad, J. et al., Connections in networks: Hardness of feasibility versus optimality?, in *Fifth International Conference on Integration of AI and OR Techniques in Constraint Programming for Combinatorial Optimization Problems (CPAIOR 2008)*. 2008.

31. Conrada, J.M. et al., Wildlife corridors as a connected subgraph problem. *Journal of Environmental Economics and Management*, 2012. 63: 1–18.

32. Phillips, S.J., M. Dudík, and R.E. Schapire, A maximum entropy approach to species distribution modeling, in *Twenty-First International Conference on Machine Learning*. 2004.

33. Elith, J. et al., A statistical explanation of MaxEnt for ecologists. *Diversity and Distributions*, 2011. 17: 43–57.

34. Kline, K. et al., *Workshop on Land-Use Change and Bioenergy*. 2009. Vonore, TN.

35. Butler, R.A. *U.S. Biofuels Policy Drives Deforestation in Indonesia, the Amazon*. 2008 [cited 12 May 2012]; Available from: http://news.mongabay.com/2008/0117-biofuels.html.

36. WWEA, *WWEA Quarterly Bulletin: Wind Energy Around the World*. 2012. World Wind Energy Association.

37. Wesolowski, A.P., and N. Eagle. Parameterizing the dynamics of slums, in *AAAI Spring Symposium 2010 on Artificial Intelligence for Development (AI-D)*. 2010.

38. Barrett, C.B., P. Little, and M. Carter, Eds. *Understanding and Reducing Persistent Poverty in Africa*. 2007. New York: Routledge.

39. Isard, W. et al., *Methods of Interregional and Regional Analysis*. 1998. Hants, England: Ashgate.

40. Morik, K., K. Bhaduri, and H. Kargupta, Introduction to data mining for sustainability. *Data Mining and Knowledge Discovery*, 2012. 24(2): 311–324.

41. Gomes, C.P., *Challenges for Constraint Reasoning and Optimization in Computational Sustainability in Principles and Practice of Constraint Programming—CP 2009*. 2009. New York: Springer.

I

Integrated Sustainability Analysis

I

Integrated Sustainability Analysis

CHAPTER 2

Tracing Embodied CO$_2$ in Trade Using High-Resolution Input–Output Tables

Daniel Moran and Arne Geschke

CONTENTS

Tʜɪꜱ ᴄʜᴀᴘᴛᴇʀ ɪꜱ ʀᴇᴘʀᴏᴅᴜᴄᴇᴅ ꜰʀᴏᴍ *Ecological Footprints and International Trade* (D. Moran, University of Sydney, 2012) with the author's permission. The section titled "Reconciling Conflicting Constraints: Eora as a Solution of a Constrained Optimization Problem" is excerpted from AISHA: *A Tool to Construct Large-Scale Contingency Matrices* (A. Geschke, University of Sydney, 2012) with the author's permission.

2.1 SUMMARY

Input-output (IO) tables document all the flows between sectors of an economy. IO tables are useful in sustainability applications for tracing connections between consumers and upstream environmental or social harms in secondary and primary industries. IO tables have historically been difficult to construct because they are so data intensive. The Eora multi-region IO (MRIO) table is a new high-resolution table that records the bilateral flows between 15,000 sectors in 187 countries. Such a comprehensive, high-resolution model is advantageous for analysis and implementation of sustainability policy. This chapter provides an overview of how the Eora IO table was built. A custom data processing language was developed to read, aggregate, disaggregate, and translate raw data from a number of government sources into a harmonized tensor. These raw data often conflict and do not result in a balanced matrix. A custom optimization algorithm was created to reconcile conflicting data and balance the table. Building and balancing the Eora MRIO is computationally intensive: it requires approximately 20 hours of compute time per data year on a cluster with 66 cores, 600 GB of RAM, and 15Tb of storage. We conclude by summarizing some sustainability applications of high-resolution MRIO tables, such as calculating carbon footprints.

Globalization combined with an increasing human population and increased consumption means that our ecological footprint is now falling more widely and more heavily across the planet. Our environmental impact is increasing. And lengthening supply chains mean that consumers are often far removed from the impacts they drive. In order to manage and reduce our footprint we must first be able to measure it. This is the aim of environmentally extended input-output analysis.

We want to identify which countries and sectors are directly causing, and which are ultimately benefiting from, environmental harms. We want to link individuals, households, and companies to the upstream environmental harms they ultimately drive. This principle is called *consumer responsibility*: the idea that consumers, not producers, should be responsible for pollution. Successful sustainability policies will consider both producer and consumer responsibilities, and will need to address different challenges at the production, trade, and consumption points along the supply chain.

There are two approaches to measuring footprints: bottom-up and top-down. Bottom-up approaches add up the various components of the footprint. For example, the CO$_2$ footprint of a paper shopping bag might be the sum of CO$_2$ emitted by logging vehicles, the pulp mill, the transport from the factory to the shop, and the decomposition of the bag after it has been used. Top-down approaches consider the total footprint first and then allocate to different products; for example, of total CO$_2$ emissions, how much is from paper products, and what fraction of paper products are paper shopping bags.

Life-cycle analysis (LCA) is the main methodology for bottom-up analysis. LCA traces inputs, processes, and outputs at all points along a production-use-disposal chain. LCA studies are complex, data hungry, and often involve difficult boundary issues where it is hard to extract a single flow without undercounting (missing some input or output flows) or double-counting (when two stocks or flows overlap so the sum of the parts exceeds the sum of the whole).

Input-output analysis takes a top-down approach. Generally, the problem with top-down approaches is that they are low resolution. A top-down analysis may be able to tell you the CO$_2$ footprint of the average passenger vehicle, but cannot differentiate between an SUV and a hybrid sedan.

The Eora project uses sophisticated data processing to keep original data in its native form, resulting in an IO table that has substantially higher resolution than any other produced to date. Most multi-region IO tables to date have settled on a common low-resolution sector classification and harmonized all input tables to that classification. The Eora MRIO employs many correspondence matrices to link together data in different classifications. The Eora high-resolution table enables better top-down analysis, and makes it easier to combine with bottom-up approaches in a so-called *hybrid LCA*. IO analysis is comprehensive, does not suffer boundary issues, and is increasingly accurate.

Input-output tables were originally conceived by Wasily Leontief as an economic tool to analyze the flows between sectors of the American economy. Using IO tables, Leontief could estimate how shocks to one sector might affect others. A variety of modern economic models, including widely used Computable General Equilibrium (CGE) models, are built upon IO tables. Most national statistical bureaus produce IO tables and use them as the basis of their national accounts, following the UN standard System of National Accounts. A multi-region IO table brings together many national IO tables into one large, whole-world IO table. MRIOs are not built by national governments but instead by a small number of academic research teams. They are a powerful tool for international policy analysis, and environmentally extended IO tables are extremely useful for sustainability analysis. IO-based analysis has become increasingly popular in recent years as greater data availability and computational power enable the creation of higher resolution, more accurate tables. The Eora multi-region IO table is the largest and most detailed IO table yet assembled. It has been made feasible by using sophisticated data processing automation, modern computer hardware, and mathematical rather than manual procedure to balance and resolve data conflict.

2.2 STRUCTURE OF IO TABLES

This section provides a brief overview of the structure of IO tables for readers unfamiliar with input-output analysis. To learn more, the authoritative text by Miller and Blair (2009) is recommended.

The elements of an IO matrix are the sum of sales from one sector to another. Each row in the matrix represents the goods and services produced by one sector, that is, that sector's output. The columns along that row are the various sectors that consume those products. Each element in the matrix thus represents the total value of transactions between sector A and sector B. In a single-country IO table, the rows and columns represent sectors within that economy.

Figure 2.1 shows the layout of a single-country IO table and illustrates the element of the transaction matrix recording the total value of Steel sector inputs to the Vehicles Production sector. This transaction's matrix T is the main block of an IO table. Appended to it on the right is another block of columns Y representing final consumption by households, government, inventories, and so on. Also added below is a block of rows V for so-called "primary inputs." The most important of these is value added. By treating value added as an input to production, a sector can sell its output for more than the sum of its other inputs.

In a multi-region IO table, the sectors represent each country's sectors. For example, instead of one Steel sector, Japanese Steel and Australian Steel are two separate rows and two columns. This is illustrated in Figure 2.2. It is possible to construct an MRIO where the regions are not countries but

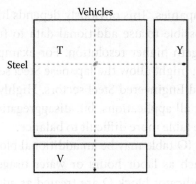

FIGURE 2.1   A basic IO table with annotation showing where in the transactions matrix the total value of outputs from the Steel sector to the Vehicle Production sector is recorded.

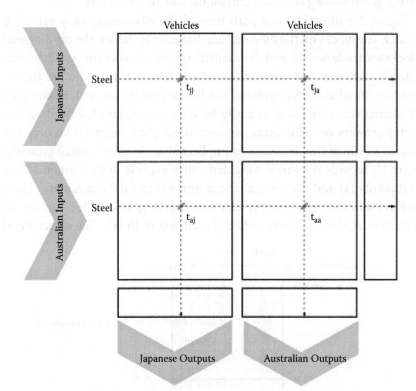

FIGURE 2.2   A two-country MRIO. The transactions t_{jj}, t_{ja}, t_{aj}, and t_{aa} record the value of steel used in domestic vehicle industries and exported to another country's vehicle industry.

states, cities, or companies. This obviously depends highly on data availability. It is also possible to use additional data to further disaggregate the table and thus gain higher resolution. For example, additional sales and purchasing data might allow the Japanese Steel sector to be split into Traditional Steel and Engineered Steel sectors. Highly detailed tables are desirable for almost all applications, but disaggregation is data intensive and often makes the table more difficult to balance.

Resting below an IO table may be an additional block of rows for non-monetary inputs such as labor hours or water usage. The rows of this so-called satellite indicator block Q are treated as additional inputs into production. In IO analysis, pollution, too, is regarded not as a consequence of production but as a necessary input, and thus added as an indicator row. The Eora model has nearly 2,000 indicator rows covering nonmonetary inputs such as energy use, water use, land area required (ecological footprint), greenhouse gas (GHG) emissions, and air pollutants.

Figure 2.3 illustrates one path through an environmentally extended MRIO. The blocks on the diagonal are domestic IO tables, the off-diagonal blocks are trade blocks, and the shaded bottom row contains satellite indicator blocks. The data point at (1) records how many species are threatened by Brazilian coffee growers. Satellite accounts can contain any type of metric; this could just as easily be tons of CO_2 emitted by Brazilian coffee growers or cubic liters of water used. Data point (2) records the degree to which this indicator is implicated in Brazilian coffee growing; point (3) records the threat-weighted coffee exports to the United States, and points (4) and (5) connect those imports to final consumers. These five points make up a supply chain connecting U.S. coffee consumers with species threats due to coffee plantations in Brazil. The structure of

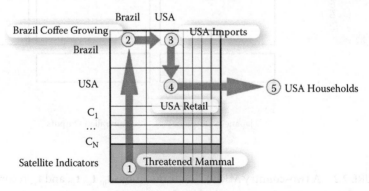

FIGURE 2.3   Diagram of an MRIO with satellite accounts for threatened species.

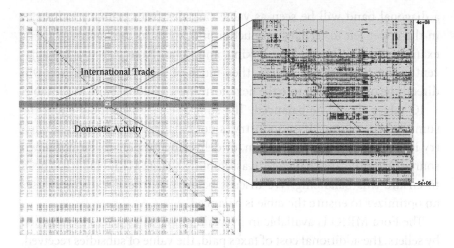

FIGURE 2.4 Heatmap of Eora and zoom-in on the Korean IO table. Each pixel represents one element in the transaction matrix, with darker cells representing larger transaction values.

environmentally extended IO tables is outlined by the United Nations System of Environmental-Economic Accounts (SEEA). In this structure, every environmental indicator (the satellite account row sums) is allocated among the various sectors (columns) that directly cause that impact.

The Eora MRIO covers 187 countries with a total of over 15,000 sectors. Heatmaps help visualize and validate IO tables. Figure 2.4 shows a heatmap visualization of Eora with a zoom-in on the Korea IO table. The Eora MRIO is not homogeneous. Some countries have large, high-resolution IO tables while other countries have small tables where the sectors are broadly defined. In order to offer the highest resolution and data integrity, Eora maintains each national IO table in the national economic classification of the country providing it.

The strong downward diagonal band is a notable feature in Figure 2.4. One reason for the diagonal band is that transactions between companies within the same sector can be large, particularly if the sectors are broadly defined, for example, if the Vehicles Production sector includes companies selling automotive components as well as assembled vehicles. Same-sector transactions account for much of the diagonal band. The band also arises from the structure of common economic classification systems. Most sector classifications start with basic industries, ascend through intermediate processing industries, and end with final production and retail industries. To the extent that economic value creation follows this same stepwise path, a diagonal band will be seen as value cascades from primary industries in the upper left to tertiary production industries in the lower right. For example, if the Wheat, Flour, Baking, and Retail Bakery sectors are adjacent in the classification system, then much of the output from each will directly be used as input into the next, forming a diagonal band in the table.

IO tables should be balanced. The sum of each row should equal the sum of each column. If an industry is not balanced, it means the industry is either receiving inputs from, or delivering outputs to, an unknown source. A significant challenge in assembling a large MRIO table has been to ensure this balancing. We discuss below how the Eora project uses an optimizer to ensure the table is balanced.

The Eora MRIO is available in five valuations: sales prices as recorded by sellers, the additional cost of taxes paid, the value of subsidies received, transportation costs, and retail and distribution costs. These margins allow distinction of the several types of middleman price markups between producers and purchasers. Taxes, subsidies, transportation, and retail and distribution costs are added to the producer's price to arrive at the purchaser's price. These markups are represented by four additional sheets on top of the basic price IO table (Figure 2.5). Separating these markups into separate sheets is useful for analyzing the effects of policy changes on taxes, subsidies, and transportation costs, and how these changes differentially affect sellers and purchasers.

Structurally, Eora is a tensor. In the most intuitive representation, it is a three-dimensional tensor: a vertical stack of five matrices. However, we address it as an eight-dimensional tensor. The rows and columns have a logical hierarchical grouping illustrated in Figure 2.6.

To quickly locate a particular element in the tensor, we use an eight-dimensional address of the form:

Input country/block/sector index
Output country/block/sector index
Sheet
Year

The two "block" dimensions group sectors as value-add sectors, final demand sectors, industries, commodities, or satellite (Q block) sectors. This eight-dimensional addressing is used in the AISHA (An Automated Integration System for Harmonised Accounts) data processing language to specify regions of the Eora tensor.

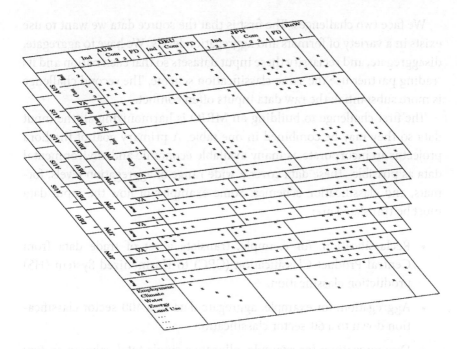

FIGURE 2.5 An MRIO with five valuation sheets; structurally, a three-dimensional tensor.

Australia									Japan						Country N
Industries			Commodities			Final Demand				Industries			Final Demand		Industries
Industry 1	Industry 2	Industry N	Commodity 1	Commodity 2	Commodity N	Households	Government	Inventories	Other	Industry 1	Industry 2	Industry N	Households	Government	Inventories	Industry 1	...

FIGURE 2.6 Rows and columns on the sheets follow a tree structure hierarchy.

2.3 POPULATING THE MRIO

2.3.1 Data Processing Language, Distributed Database Server

We want to populate the Eora tensor using data from a variety of sources (e.g., United Nations, national economic bureau, etc.). The task is essentially the reverse of a database query. SQL and MDX are languages that help users easily address and aggregate subsections of a multidimensional tensor. We want to do the opposite: populate subsections of the tensor.

We face two challenges. The first is that the source data we want to use exists in a variety of formats and aggregation levels. We have to aggregate, disaggregate, and reclassify these input datasets so that each nation and its trading partner use the same classification scheme. The second challenge is more substantial: the raw data inputs often conflict.

The first challenge to building an MRIO is harmonizing all the input data so they may be combined in one table. A primary goal of the Eora project is to incorporate as many available economic and environmental data as possible. These data cover a wide range of aggregation levels, formats, and classification schemes. Some examples of how the input data must be translated are:

- Reclassification: for example, translate a set of trade data from Central Product Classification (CPC) to Harmonized System (HS) production classification.

- Aggregation: for example, aggregate data in a 400-sector classification down to a 60-sector classification.

- Disaggregation: for example, allocate a single total value to sectors according to each sector's contribution to gross domestic product (GDP).

We created a data processing language to help with this task. This language assists with aggregation and disaggregation and facilitates addressing and populating areas of the tensor. A disaggregation command in the processing language could specify a total value of steel sector sales that should be allocated proportionally, or equally, among a number of metal manufacturing industries.

Tightly integrated with the language is a large library of correspondence matrices. Correspondence matrices contain a weighted mapping that reallocates values in a source vector into a different destination vector. A correspondence matrix maps a source vector of length N to a destination vector of length M using an N × M matrix. Each row contains a set of weights that sum to 1. The first element of the source vector is allocated to the destination vector using the weights specified in the first row, the second element added to the destination vector using the weights of the second row, and so on. Correspondence matrices are an especially convenient tool for aggregating and disaggregating data and projecting data in one classification scheme into another scheme.

For each data source (each table from all the agencies supplying data, e.g., UN, national agencies, environmental agencies, and so on), we wrote a processing language script to populate the tensor with the contents of that source. The scripts specify which concordance matrix/matrices to use to translate the data into the classification used in the Eora table. The scripts also specify the destination address in the Eora tensor where the reclassified data should be placed.

The data processing language interpreter is called AISHA (*An Automated System for Harmonised Accounts*). AISHA is essentially a database server. It reads data processing scripts in batch and populates the tensor. Our implementation uses a distributed architecture. A number of workers process these scripts autonomously, and then the master process aggregates the results.

This would be the end of the story if data sources did not overlap and conflict. AISHA does not actually populate a tensor but rather populates an initial estimate and constraint matrix, which are run through an optimization package to produce the final tensor.

2.4 RECONCILING CONFLICTING CONSTRAINTS: EORA AS A SOLUTION OF A CONSTRAINED OPTIMIZATION PROBLEM

The MRIO should satisfy several constraints. One basic constraint is a balancing constraint: the total outputs of a sector must equal the total inputs of a sector. Published data provided by statistical agencies adhere to this condition. But when constructing a large MRIO like Eora, data from a number of different sources have to be combined into one table. This newly combined table will most likely not fulfill this balancing constraint. Some elements of the table must be slightly adjusted in order to ensure that the balancing condition is fulfilled.

Another common problem during the construction of an MRIO is that of conflicting data. Consider the following situation: We have an IO table from the U.S. government, detailing the sector-wise composition of GDP. We also have a figure for total U.S. GDP, provided from the UN. The two total GDP figures are not equal. These two figures define lower and upper bounds to the final value, and the realized final value must lie in between. To reconcile these conflicting constraints, we determine the reliability of each datum and ask the optimizer to find a solution value that maximally satisfies these two reliability-weighted constraints.

To build Eora, the problem of generating a table that adheres to all specified constraints (balancing, conflicting data and/or others) was taken in one step. Reconciling the data in order to fulfill any given external condition was achieved by interpreting this problem as a mathematically constrained optimization problem.

We begin the process of building Eora by constructing an initial version of the table using raw data from a number of different sources. Let's call this version of MRIO the *Raw Data Table*. If all these different data sources coincided, the MRIO would be finished. But most likely, the challenges described in the previous section will hold: the MRIO will violate our specified constraints.

2.4.1 Reliability Information

In order to approach the problem, we first have to introduce reliability data. The Maximum Entropy Principle introduced by Jaynes (1957) asserts that an IO-transaction is a random variable with a best guess and an associated reliability. IO tables are assembled carefully by statistical bureaus but still the individual inter-sectoral transaction values are not 100% certain. Hence, both elements of the MRIO and external conditions are subject to a certain, individual reliability. Additionally, the elements of an MRIO can be assumed to be normally distributed and statistically independent from one another. Therefore, each transaction can be interpreted as the best guess of the corresponding variable, and the reliability is expressed in the standard deviation of this random variable. A transaction value with large reliability corresponds to a very small standard deviation; a less reliable transaction value corresponds to a larger standard deviation. Usually, reliability information is not provided for every transaction of an MRIO. In this case, the standard deviation values can be estimated. In general, it can be assumed that larger values are far more reliable than smaller values. A good approximation is to define the standard deviation of the largest value in an MRIO to be 3% of its own absolute value, and 200% for the smallest value of the MRIO. The standard deviation of the remaining values can then be calculated by a logarithmic function whose coefficients must be calculated by the user. Lenzen et al. (2010) give a detailed motivation and explanation of this strategy. Additionally the reliability of some constraints might be known. For example, the balancing condition must be exact; otherwise an MRIO cannot represent an economy appropriately (see Leontief, 1986). This means that the corresponding standard deviation of the balancing constraints is 0. Constraints with a standard deviation of

0 are called *hard constraints*. Other hard constraints include upper and lower bounds, specifying that transactions may never be negative, or the constraint that subsidies (recorded as negative values) may never be positive. Therefore, these constraints also have standard deviations of 0. Other constraints like the previous example of the U.S. GDP might be less reliable and have positive standard deviation values. These are *soft constraints*. Clearly, if the same piece of information from two different sources states different facts, at least one of the two must be incorrect. In reality, this will most likely hold for both. But one of the data sources might be more reliable than the other one. In this case, for example, the data for the total U.S. GDP provided by a national statistical agency could be far more reliable than what the UN reported. Hence, an external condition that is not 100% reliable does not have to be 100% fulfilled by the MRIO.

This concept holds for the elements in the MRIO. Each transaction value in the MRIO is subject to a certain reliability. That means that every element in the Raw Data Table can be adjusted (within a certain range determined by its reliability) and still represent the real transaction value reasonably well.

Reliability data is usually not published by statistical agencies. In these cases, the reliability information can be estimated. We use a variety of heuristics to estimate the reliability of various datasets. Large transaction values are typically well-measured and thus more reliable than small values (Lenzen et al., 2010). We assign a higher reliability to national statistical agency data than to UN data, and higher reliability to UN economic data than to trade data. The published Eora results include the information about our reliability estimates of every dataset. Because the final MRIO table is a composite of these data, we also provide reliability figures for the final table showing how reliable each value in the table is, based on the combined reliability of the various input data informing that result.

2.4.2 The Concept of Constrained Optimization

The basic idea of constrained optimization is the following:

Obtain the Final MRIO by reconciling the elements of Raw Data Table according to their reliability in such a way that

1. All hard external conditions are fulfilled exactly.
2. All soft external conditions are well satisfied, the degree of fulfillment being determined by their reliability.
3. The original Raw Data Table is minimally disturbed.

Or in short: Find a Final MRIO that fulfills all external conditions while minimally disturbing the Raw Data Table.

2.4.3 Mathematical Interpretation of an MRIO

In order to apply constrained optimization to the reconciliation problem, we have to see the MRIO from a mathematical perspective. Consider a small MRIO:

$$T = \begin{matrix} t_{11} & t_{12} & y_1 \\ t_{21} & t_{22} & y_1 \\ v_1 & v_2 \end{matrix}$$

In mathematical terminology, the Raw Data Table is called the *initial estimate*. The term *initial estimate* sometimes causes confusion as the Raw Data Table was sourced from an officially published dataset; hence it is not an estimate at all. But from a mathematical point of view, the Final MRIO is the solution of an optimization problem and the Raw Data Table is the initial estimate of what the solution will be.

In order to fulfill the balancing condition, the sum over all elements of the first row of the table must equal the sum over all elements of the first column of the table. The same must hold for the second row and second column. The equations for the balancing constraints (or balancing condition) for the table T are given by

$$t_{11} + t_{12} + y_1 = t_{11} + t_{21} + v_1$$

$$t_{21} + t_{22} + y_2 = t_{12} + t_{22} + v_2$$

Trivial manipulation of these two equations yields

$$t_{11} + t_{12} + y_1 - t_{11} - t_{21} - v_1 = 0$$

$$t_{21} + t_{22} + y_2 - t_{12} - t_{22} - v_2 = 0$$

The diagonal elements t_{11} and t_{22} appear with altering signs in the equations; hence they cancel each other out. The final equations for the balancing constraints are thus

$$t_{12} + y_1 - t_{21} - v_1 = 0$$

$$\text{(2.1)}$$

$$t_{21} + y_2 - t_{12} - v_2 = 0$$

All variables and values of these two equations have a corresponding reliability. We know from the definition of IO that the balancing constraints must be fulfilled. Hence, the 0-values on the right-hand side of the equations cannot be violated. That means that the 0-values have standard deviations of $\sigma = 0$. Balancing constraints are hard constraints and hard constraints have a standard deviation of $\sigma = 0$. An example of a soft constraint could be the following. Consider a data source is available that provides information that the total final demand of the MRIO M is equal to a value a. The corresponding equation for this information is

$$y_1 + y_2 = a$$

In this case, we can be almost certain that the value a is not totally reliable. Hence, the standard deviation for the value a would not be equal to zero, that is, $\sigma > 0$. This equation can be violated by the Final MRIO that is to be computed. The acceptable amount of violation is determined by the standard deviation σ of the value a.

2.4.4 Summarizing the Balancing Constraints in a Single Matrix Equation

Now that the constraints are already available as equations, the first step to a mathematical interpretation has been taken. In order to more easily work with the MRIO as an optimization problem, we vectorize the transactions matrix **T** and call the resulting vector **a**

$$\mathbf{T} = \begin{matrix} t_{11} & t_{12} & y_1 \\ t_{21} & t_{22} & y_1 \\ v_1 & v_2 & \end{matrix} \quad \text{becomes} \quad \mathbf{a} = \begin{pmatrix} t_{11} \\ t_{12} \\ y_1 \\ t_{21} \\ t_{22} \\ y_2 \\ v_1 \\ v_2 \end{pmatrix}$$

This allows us to reformulate the first balancing constraint

$$t_{12} + y_1 - t_{21} - v_1 = 0$$

as a vector-by-vector equation:

$$\underbrace{\begin{pmatrix} 0 & 1 & 1 & -1 & 0 & 0 & -1 & 0 \end{pmatrix}}_{=:g^T} \underbrace{\begin{pmatrix} t_{11} \\ t_{12} \\ y_1 \\ t_{21} \\ t_{22} \\ y_2 \\ v_1 \\ v_2 \end{pmatrix}}_{a} = 0.$$

This gives the balancing constraint equation the form

$$\mathbf{g}^T \mathbf{a} = 0 \tag{2.2}$$

The vector $\mathbf{g}$ is the so-called *coefficients vector* holding the corresponding coefficients for the elements of the vector p to represent the balancing equation.

Every constraint can be formulated in the form of (Equation 2.2). Hence, each constraint provides a constraint vector $\mathbf{g}$. These constraint vectors can now be summarized in a constraint matrix $\mathbf{G}$. Every row of this constraints matrix represents one constraint. For the three constraint examples previously used in this section, the coefficients matrix $\mathbf{G}$ is

$$\underbrace{\begin{pmatrix} 0 & 1 & 1 & -1 & 0 & 0 & -1 & 0 \\ 0 & -1 & 0 & 1 & 0 & 1 & -1 & 0 \\ 0 & 0 & 1 & 0 & 0 & 1 & 0 & 0 \end{pmatrix}}_{G} \underbrace{\begin{pmatrix} t_{11} \\ t_{12} \\ y_1 \\ t_{21} \\ t_{22} \\ y_2 \\ v_1 \\ v_2 \end{pmatrix}}_{a} = \underbrace{\begin{pmatrix} 0 \\ 0 \\ a \end{pmatrix}}_{=1c} \tag{2.3}$$

The values on the right-hand side of the corresponding constraints equations are summarized in the vector c.

With the concepts of Equation (2.3) we can write the complete set of external constraints that an MRIO must adhere to elegantly as

$$Ga = c$$

The corresponding reliability data for the vectorized MRIO **a** and the right-hand side values c can be stored in two separate vectors σ_a and σ_c that have the same sizes as the vectors whose reliability information they hold, namely **a** and **c**.

2.4.5 Formulating the Constrained Optimization Problem

Let us call the Raw Data Table $\mathbf{T}^0$ and the Final MRIO (that is yet to be calculated) $\mathbf{T}$. Let a^0 be the vectorization of $\mathbf{T}^0$ and let a be the vectorization of $\mathbf{T}$ and let a be the vectorization of $\mathbf{T}$.

Recall the concept of the optimization problem that was stated before:

Find a Final MRIO that fulfills all external conditions while minimally disturbing the Raw Data Table.

With the concepts that were developed so far, the mathematical expression of the statement *"MRIO that fulfills all external conditions"* is simply given by

$$Ga = c$$

This system of equation is usually underdetermined, which means that there are more unknowns (in this case, the number of elements in the MRIO) than constraints. Hence, there is usually more than one solution that adheres to the constraints (i.e., the Final MRIO is not uniquely defined by the constraints).

What remains to be interpreted mathematically is what it actually means to *"consider the Raw Data Table as well as possible."*

As a^0 and **a** are vectorized representations of the Raw Data Table and the Final Table, the change applied to the Raw Data Table a^0 in order to adhere to the given constraints can be "measured" by a so-called objective function $f(a^0, a)$. Because the system of constraints equation allows more than one solution, the optimizer is designed to find that solution which minimizes the objective function subject to the constraints. The optimization problem is therefore given by

$$\min f\left(\mathbf{a}^0, \mathbf{a}\right) \text{ subject to } \mathbf{Ga} = \mathbf{c}$$

For the Eora model, the objective function was based on Byron's (1978) approach, which uses a quadratic Lagrange function of the form

$$f = \left(a^0 - a\right) \sum_a{}^{-1} \left(a^0 - a\right) + \lambda'\left(\mathbf{Ga} - \mathbf{c}\right)$$

where Σ_a denotes a diagonal matrix with the σ_a values of the vector as the main diagonal. First-order conditions then must be applied in order to find the Lagrange multiplier and then the Final MRIO.

To calculate the Lagrange multiplier, a matrix inversion must be calculated, which would have proven to be calculation intensive and possibly numerically unstable for a very large problem like the Eora problem. To avoid the explicit calculation of the Lagrange multipliers and matrix inversion, Van der Ploeg (1982) elegantly reformulates Byron's approach using the following ideas:

1. Reorder the rows of matrix **G** and the right-hand side vector **c** such that all rows for hard constraints are at the top, followed by the rows belonging to soft constraints. Let $\mathbf{G}_{hard}$ and $\mathbf{G}_{soft}$ denote the block of constraint lines that belongs to the hard constraints and the soft constraints, respectively. Then **G** and **c** can take the form

$$\mathbf{G} = \begin{pmatrix} \mathbf{G}_{hard} \\ \mathbf{G}_{soft} \end{pmatrix} \text{ and } \mathbf{c} = \begin{pmatrix} \mathbf{c}_{hard} \\ \mathbf{c}_{soft} \end{pmatrix}$$

Because soft constraints are not completely reliable, they may be violated to some extent. These violations are taken care of by introducing a disturbance ε_i for each soft constraint (note that there are no disturbances introduced for hard constraints, as they must be adhered to exactly). Let ε be the vector of all disturbances; then the system of soft constraints becomes

$$\mathbf{G}_{soft}\mathbf{a} = \mathbf{c}_{soft} + \varepsilon \Leftrightarrow \mathbf{G}_{soft}\mathbf{a} - \varepsilon = \mathbf{c}_{soft}$$

2. Defining

$$p = \begin{pmatrix} a \\ \varepsilon \end{pmatrix}$$

the system of equation for the soft constraints can then be rewritten as

$$[G_{soft} \quad -I]p = c_{soft}$$

Here, I denotes the unity matrix of appropriate dimensions. For the hard constraints, we simply obtain

$$[G_{hard} \quad 0]p = c_{hard}$$

Here, 0 denotes an all-zero matrix of appropriate dimensions. Hence, despite the introduction of disturbances for the soft constraints, the equations for the hard constraints have not changed.

By summarizing soft and hard constraints again into one equation, we obtain

$$\underbrace{\begin{bmatrix} G_{hard} & 0 \\ G_{soft} & -I \end{bmatrix}}_{C} p = \begin{pmatrix} c_{hard} \\ c_{soft} \end{pmatrix}$$

The diagonal matrix of standard deviations for the vector p then becomes

$$\Sigma_p = \begin{bmatrix} \Sigma_a & 0 \\ 0 & \Sigma_c \end{bmatrix}$$

Here, Σ_a is defined as before and Σ_c is the diagonal matrix of σ_c values of c_{soft}. Because hard constraints do not obtain a disturbance variable, Σ_p does not contain σ values that are equal to zero.

With these concepts, the optimization problem can be rewritten as

$$\min_p (p^0 - p) \sum\nolimits_p^{-1} (p^0 - p) \text{ subject to } Cp = c$$

$$\mathbf{p}^0 = \begin{pmatrix} \mathbf{a}^0 \\ 0 \end{pmatrix}$$

The advantage of Van der Ploeg's approach is that the reliability information of the right-hand side vector $\mathbf{c}$ has shifted to the iterate, which is now called $\mathbf{p}$. The disadvantage is that the iterate (formerly $\mathbf{a}$ now $\mathbf{p}$ grows by as many variables as there are soft constraints and, hence, the problem becomes significantly bigger). However, the number of constraints remains the same. The solution of this problem is the Final MRIO and the vector of disturbances of the soft constraints. The Final MRIO adheres to all constraints and considers the reliability of the raw data and the constraints during the calculation process.

Often, certain values of the MRIO must stay within certain boundaries. Transaction values of the basic price table, for example, must be positive values. Values in the subsidies sheet can only be negative values. Hence, each element p_i can be subject to an upper or lower bound, that is, $l_i \le p_i \le u_i$. By allowing positive or negative infinity as a feasible value for the upper or lower bound, a bound equation can be formulated for each element p_i. The upper bound and lower bound values can be summarized in vectors of equal size to the size of $\mathbf{p}$. The boundary conditions for the whole MRIO can then be summarized as

$$\mathbf{l} \le \mathbf{p} \le \mathbf{u}$$

Adding these boundary conditions to the optimization problem, we obtain

$$\min_{\mathbf{p}} \left(\mathbf{p}^0 - \mathbf{p} \right) \sum \left(\mathbf{p}^0 - \mathbf{p} \right) \text{ subject to } \mathbf{Gp} = \mathbf{c}, \mathbf{l} \le \mathbf{p} \le \mathbf{u} \qquad (2.4)$$

The Eora model was generated based on the optimization problem given by Equation (2.4).

For the Eora project, the total MRIO held roughly 10^9 elements that were subject to 10^6 constraints. The total amount of data that was considered during the optimization process was approximately 40 GB. During the calculation process, more than 250 GB of RAM were used by the algorithm. As commercial algorithms were not able to solve a problem of this size, a custom parallelized optimization algorithm was developed. The frequency of iterations, the heavy communication load, and the fact that every worker requires **G** (the 30-GB constraints matrix) together recommended the use of a large shared memory multiprocessor system. To build Eora for one year, the optimizer runs for several hours on a commercial 24-core system with 288 GB of memory. Solving the constrained optimization problem is tractable but pushes the limits of current computing hardware.

Because the raw data table and conflicting data are specified as soft constraints, the optimizer is also able to generate an estimate of the standard deviation of each element in the result table.

Estimating the standard deviation values of the resulting MRIO is— much like the reconciliation of the table itself—an undetermined optimization problem. Assume that the standard deviations of the initial raw data table and the constraints values are known. Let $\mathbf{p}^0$ be the vectorized raw data MRIO and **c** the constraints values. Let **p** be the reconciled MRIO so that

$$\mathbf{Gp} = \mathbf{c}$$

holds. Then the standard deviations of **dp** of **p** and **dc** of **c** must fullfill

$$\sqrt{\mathbf{G\,dp}\ \#\ \mathbf{G\,dp}} = \left\{ \sqrt{\sum_j \left(g_{ij} dp_j^0 \right)^2} \right\}_i = \mathbf{dc}$$

The standard deviations **dp** were part of the input to the optimization process and are therefore known. The standard deviations **dp** are unknown. However, the shift that each element of the MRIO experiences during the optimization process to obtain **p** from $\mathbf{p}^0$ are known. Using the distance vector $\mathbf{p} - \mathbf{p}^0$ as the initial guess for the standard deviations **dp** the algorithm SDRAS can solve the underdetermined optimization problem

$$\sqrt{\mathbf{G\,dp}\ \#\ \mathbf{G\,dp}} = \mathbf{dc}$$

to obtain **dp**. SDRAS was first presented in Lenzen et al. (2010).

Figure 2.7 illustrates how the optimizer reconciles two conflicting data points, both purporting to report the same value. The optimizer would report the estimated standard deviation of the solution S as larger than the standard deviation of D$_1$ but smaller than the standard deviation of D$_2$.

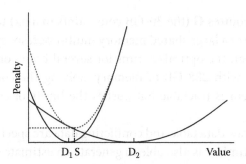

FIGURE 2.7   Schematic of how the optimizer reconciles conflicting constraints. Data point D_1 has a high confidence and data point D_2, purporting to report the same value, has a low confidence. The optimal solution S minimizes the violation of the conflicting constraints and thus lies closer to the higher reliability constraint D_1.

Eora is the first large MRIO to provide results along with an estimate of the confidence of those results. Eora provides users with transaction-level reliability estimates and comprehensive reporting on which constraints (from the various input data sources) are best and least respected in the final table.

2.5 THE LEONTIEF INVERSE

Now we have a complete balanced, harmonized MRIO table. Nearly all environmental applications will proceed by calculating the Leontief inverse of the MRIO. The Leontief inverse answers the question: How much total input, both directly in the product and indirectly required for its production, is in a given unit of output? This calculation is the foundation for determining consumer-responsibility footprints, as it makes it possible to calculate the *total* environmental impact, including all impacts upstream in the supply chain, required to produce one unit of output.

The Leontief inverse is calculated as follows. Normalizing the transactions matrix **T** by gross output converts each element into a coefficient such that each column sums to one; that is, each coefficient represents the relative contribution of each input per unit of output. This matrix is called **A**, the technical coefficients matrix, or direct requirements matrix. A car, for example, contains steel directly (chassis, engine, etc.), but it also requires steel indirectly as an input to its production. The factory, car carrier, and showroom all use some steel as well, some fraction of which is needed for the provision of that car. This total requirement matrix **L** (in contrast to the direct requirement matrix) is the sum of an infinite series starting with the identity matrix I:

$$L = I + A + A^2 + A^3 + \ldots = \sum_{n=0}^{\infty} A^n$$

Leontief realized that this is simply the matrix inversion

$$L = (I - A)^{-1}$$

Each element of the matrix Leontief inverse matrix L thus reports the total quantity input required to produce one unit of output. The inputs can be weighted by their environmental load, using the satellite indicators, in order to find the environmentally weighted total input required for each unit product produced.

Structural Path Analysis (SPA) can be used to selectively perform this series expansion on individual elements and trace out supply chains. SPA is commonly used to search the top-ranked (largest flow) supply chain or chains, starting or ending at sectors of interest. The idea of SPA is not difficult but implementation is an art. SPA algorithms must essentially search a 15,000 * 15,000 = 225,000,000-branch tree whose leaf node values asymptotically approach zero with depth. In the worst case, a single input could visit every single sector in the world before being finally consumed. In practice, evaluating each supply chain to 10 to 15 steps captures 99% of the chain's value. Still, intelligent heuristics for pruning and sorting are mandatory. The Leontief inverse and SPA are used complementarily. Footprints calculated using the Leontief inverse report the total footprint of products and sectors and SPA algorithms search for the individual supply chains involved.

2.6 APPLICATIONS OF THE EORA MRIO

The Eora MRIO provides a time series of MRIO tables with matching environmental and social satellite accounts for the entire world economy at a high level of sector and country detail. Some 187 countries are represented at resolutions of 25 to 500 sectors, depending on raw data availability, tracing over 5 billion supply chains. The time series covers 1990 to 2010. The Eora MRIO presents a completely harmonized and balanced world MRIO table, incorporating millions of raw data points from major sources such as the UN System of National Accounts (SNA), UN COMTRADE, Eurostat, Institute of Developing Economies (IDE)/Japan External Trade Organization (JETRO), and many national input-output tables. Every MRIO element comes with an accompanying estimate of reliability.

The Eora MRIO table tracks nearly 2,000 sustainability indicator line items covering

- Energy

- GHG emissions

- Air pollutants

- Ecological footprint (hectares)

- Human appropriated net primary productivity (grams of carbon)

- Water use (liters)

- Material flow (kilograms of materials)

The Eora MRIO has also been used for studies on the footprint of biodiversity, linking 30,000 species threat records from the International Union for Conservation of Nature (IUCN) Red List to production industries and final consumers, and to study conflict mineral (coltan and rare earth metals) supply chains originating in Africa and Asia.

The power of IO analysis to distinguish and link producers, supply chains, and consumers makes it useful for developing sustainability policies. IO analysis can quantify the links between producers and consumers, and systematically identify and quantify supply chains of interest. This data-rich resource can be used to inform sustainability policies for producers, traders, and consumers.

Most environmental legislation is currently designed to control the footprint of production. The footprint of production can be constrained with regulation requiring cleaner production, protection and conservation measures, better enforcement of existing legislation, and by buyers demanding high environmental standards from suppliers.

Trade flows in environmentally deleterious products can be constrained. For example, the Convention on International Trade in Endangered Species of Wild Fauna and Flora (CITES) broadly restricts any trade in endangered species and derived products. Proposed carbon taxes function similarly, effectively restricting trade of an undesirable good.

Sustainability certificates such as those issued by the Forest Stewardship Council and Marine Stewardship Council serve to constrain trade in illegal and irresponsibly sourced forest and marine products. Currently, high-risk tradeflows are discovered and investigated opportunistically, not systematically. IO analysis systematically and comprehensively quantifies supply chain paths. This is useful for identifying and ranking at-risk supply chains. To constrain consumer demand, sustainability labels, such as dolphin-safe tuna, organic produce, and fair trade coffee, can be used to shift consumer demand away from high-impact products toward more responsibly sourced products. Corporate and government buyers can use footprint data to help build sustainable procurement policies ensuring those organizations consume products with a lower environmental footprint. One major motivation of environmental footprinting is to provide more information on helping consumers understand their ecological footprint. The Eora MRIO table uses sophisticated computational techniques to provide data-rich answers that inform sustainability policy.

REFERENCES

Byron, R. 1978. The estimation of large social account matrices. *Journal of the Royal Statistical Society Series A*, 141(3): 359–367.

Jaynes, E.T. 1957. Information theory and statistical mechanics. *Physical Review*, 106: 620–630.

Lenzen, M., R. Wood, and T. Wiedman. 2010. Uncertainty analysis for Multi-Region Input-Output models—A case study of the UK's carbon footprint. *Economic Systems Research*, 22: 43–63.

Leontief, W. 1986. *Input-Output Economics*. New York: Oxford University Press.

Miller, R.E. and P.D. Blair. 2009. *Input-Output Analysis: Foundations and Extensions 2nd ed.* Cambridge, UK: Cambridge University Press.

Van der Ploeg, F. 1982. Reliability and the adjustment of sequences of large economic accounting matrices. *Journal of the Royal Statistical Society Series A*, 145(2): 169–194.

CHAPTER **3**

Aggregation Effects in Carbon Footprint Accounting Using Multi-Region Input–Output Analysis

Xin Zhou, Hiroaki Shirakawa, and Manfred Lenzen

CONTENTS

3.1 INTRODUCTION

IN PRACTICE, ENVIRONMENTAL IMPACT ASSESSMENT and emissions accounting are generally conducted at the firm level, project level, or product level, where the firsthand data is available. Since the early 1990s, input-output analysis (IOA) has been widely used for environmental accounting, such as carbon footprint assessment and the calculations of embodied emissions and virtual water at the sectoral level for a nation, a region, or multiple regions, depending on the purpose of the research. One of the advantages of using IOA is that not only direct emissions, but also indirect emissions from various upstream processes in a supply chain can be taken into account systematically. Every empirical input-output (IO) table rests on the definition of industries, which is usually given by aggregating similar products into one sector. For each defined industry, firm-level data is collected and the input coefficients in an IO table can represent an average of the production functions of many different sample firms. Therefore, the usefulness of published IO tables for practical environmental assessment is challenged by the robustness of the results, which can be influenced by different classifications of firms, products, or processes into sectors (Gibbons et al., 1982; Wiedmann, 2009a).

The aggregation problem is not new to the society of IOA, which has intensively discussed the issue since the 1950s. Fisher (1958, 1962, and 1966) provided rich theoretical thinking on the optimization of aggregation. Ara (1959) provided theoretical proof of the necessary and sufficient condition for sector aggregation that is acceptable for IOA. Unlike conventional methods aiming to reduce the size of an IO model, Leontief (1967) alternatively presented a systematic procedure to eliminate certain goods and processes from an existing IO table. Doeksen and Little (1968) tested the aggregation with both hypothetical models and actual regional IO models. They concluded that the model size (level of aggregation) has little impact on the multipliers of unaggregated sectors when the remaining sectors were highly aggregated. A useful implication is that even with a small regional model, it could be possible to determine the impacts of a new plant on local employment and income. By using the survey data and other information for Philadelphia, Karaska (1968) tested the variations of Leontief coefficients in a regional IO table. He found that variation increases with the level of aggregation from the detailed four-digit level to the two-digit level defined in the Standard Industrial Classification (SIC) system, and the variations of the local coefficients are greater than the variations of technological coefficients. Hewings (1974) examined various methods for the identification of key sectors in a regional economy and tested with different aggregation levels. He concluded that various methods lack the consistency in identifying key sectors and are sensitive to the level of aggregation. Gibbons and colleagues (Gibbons et al., 1982) developed an iterative process for disaggregating a sector, by which the magnitude of aggregation errors can be reduced to a level that satisfies any desired tolerance. Blair and Miller (1983) examined aggregation bias by aggregating regions in a multi-region IO system and concluded that spatial aggregation does not necessarily lead to unacceptable errors.

In environmentally extended IOA, the aggregation problem will be more complicated. Not only will the input and output structure of sectors to be aggregated influence the results, but also the environmental nature of heterogeneous sectors (usually presented as environmental pressures per unit of output) will have certain impacts. Based on our best knowledge, there are few experiments exploring the aggregation problem in environmentally extended IOA. Lenzen (2007) discussed the effect of aggregation on environmental analysis based on shared producer and consumer responsibility. He (2011) also provided a theoretical analysis on aggregation versus disaggregation in IOA of the environment and suggested that disaggregating economic IO data is superior to aggregating environmental data in determining IO multipliers. Andrew and colleagues (2009) used a multi-region input-output (MRIO) model based on the dataset provided by the Global Trade Analysis Project (GTAP) to quantify the errors introduced by various approximations of the full MRIO model. Su and his colleagues (Su et al., 2010) analyzed the effects of sector aggregation on the calculation of CO_2 embodied in exports for China and Singapore, respectively, based on single-country IO models. Su and Ang (2010) also analyzed the effects of spatial aggregation of intra-national IO models on the calculation of CO_2 embodied in a country's exports, in particular for a large economy like China.

In this chapter, we examine the aggregation effect in carbon footprint (CF) accounting using an MRIO model. "Carbon footprint" is increasingly being recognized as a valuable indicator in the field of greenhouse gas emissions management, which aims to measure all the direct and indirect carbon emissions caused by consumption. There are widespread applications of IO models in the estimation of the CFs of nations (e.g., Wyckoff and Roop, 1994; Munksgaard and Pedersen, 2001; Peters and

Hertwich, 2008; Hertwich and Peters, 2009; Zhou et al., 2010). For reviews in this area, see Wiedmann (2009b) and Minx et al. (2012).

The MRIO model used is Asian Input-Output (AIO) Table 2000 (AIO, 2000), which is published by the Institute of Developing Economies (2006). The AIO 2000 is a Chenery-Moses type of model (Chenery, 1953; Moses, 1955), including 76 sectors for ten Asian-Pacific economies (Indonesia, Malaysia, the Philippines, Singapore, Thailand, Mainland China, Taiwan, the Republic of Korea, Japan, and the United States). By aggregating sectors randomly, we tested the magnitude of aggregation errors and analyzed them as random variables.

3.2 TEST OF AGGREGATION EFFECT

A typical MRIO model for the supply-and-demand equilibrium among sectors and regions can be expressed as follows:

$$x_i^r = \sum_s \sum_j t_{ij}^{rs} + \sum_s f_i^{rs} \tag{3.1}$$

where r and s are regions, i and j are sectors, x_i^r is sector i's outputs in region r, t_{ij}^{rs} is sector i's outputs in region r that are used as inputs to sector j in region s (intermediate demand), and f_i^{rs} is final demand of product i in region s that is supplied by region r.

By defining the input coefficients $a_{ij}^{rs} = t_{ij}^{rs}/x_j^s$, Equation (3.1) for a k-region model can be expressed in a matrix format as follows:

$$
\begin{pmatrix} x^1 \\ x^2 \\ \vdots \\ x^k \end{pmatrix} =
\begin{pmatrix} A^{11} & A^{12} & \cdots & A^{1k} \\ A^{21} & A^{22} & \cdots & A^{2k} \\ \vdots & \vdots & \ddots & \vdots \\ A^{k1} & A^{k2} & \cdots & A^{kk} \end{pmatrix}
\begin{pmatrix} x^1 \\ x^2 \\ \vdots \\ x^k \end{pmatrix} +
\begin{pmatrix} \sum_s f^{1s} \\ \sum_s f^{2s} \\ \vdots \\ \sum_s f^{ks} \end{pmatrix} \tag{3.2}
$$

Introduced by Wassily Leontief in the early 1940s (Leontief, 1941), IOA has been widely used to predict a change in sectoral output that is driven by a change in final demand (Equation (3.3)). At regional levels, IOA can help predict the impacts of the establishment of a new factory on regional economy. At multi-region levels, IOA can analyze the trade relations among different regions.

TABLE 3.1   Definitions

	Unaggregated Model	Aggregated Model
Intermediate demand	$T = [T^{rs}] = [t_{ij}^{rs}]$	$\bar{T} = [\bar{T}^{rs}] = [\bar{t}_{ij}^{rs}]$
Final demand	$f = [f^{rs}] = [f_i^{rs}]$	$\bar{f} = [\bar{f}^{rs}] = [\bar{f}_i^{rs}]$
Total output	$x = \{x^r\} = \{x_i^r\}$	$\bar{x} = \{\bar{x}^r\} = \{\bar{x}_i^r\}$
Input coefficients	$A = [A^{rs}] = [a_{ij}^{rs}]$	$\bar{A} = [\bar{A}^{rs}] = [\bar{a}_{ij}^{rs}]$
Leontief inverse	$L = [L^{rs}] = [l_{ij}^{rs}]$	$\bar{L} = [\bar{L}^{rs}] = [\bar{l}_{ij}^{rs}]$
Carbon intensity (emissions per unit output)	$c = \{c^r\} = \{c_i^r\}$	$\bar{c} = \{\bar{c}^r\} = \{\bar{c}_i^r\}$
Carbon footprint	$w = \{w^s\} = \{w_j^s\}$	$\bar{w} = \{\bar{w}^s\} = \{\bar{w}_j^s\}$

$$x = (I - A)^{-1} f \tag{3.3}$$

where I is an identity matrix and $(I - A)^{-1}$ is called the Leontief inverse, indicating the amount of outputs required directly (by the final demand) or indirectly (via intermediate demand in the upstream production) to satisfy one unit of final demand.

The convention for matrices and vectors used for the unaggregated model and the aggregated model (letters with a bar) is provided in Table 3.1. Matrices are expressed in capital letters, while vectors and scalars are expressed in lowercase letters.

Consider there are n sectors and k regions. The size of matrix T before aggregation is therefore $nk \times nk$, with the size of each block matrix T^{rs} being $n \times n$. The aggregation rules are defined as follows:

1. Sectors within one region can be aggregated but sectors in different regions cannot.

2. More than one aggregation within a region is allowed (such as the aggregation of Sectors 1 and 2, and the aggregation of Sectors 3, 4, and 5 in Region 1 at the same time).

3. Aggregations in several regions simultaneously are allowed (such as the aggregation of Sectors 1 and 2 in Region 1 and the aggregation of Sectors 1, 2, and 3 in Region 2 at the same time). Assume that n sectors in Region r are grouped into $n(r) \le n$ sectors.

Define

$$m = \left[\sum_{r=1}^{k} n(r) \right] \le nk$$

as the size of the aggregate model. The intermediate demand after aggregation, $\bar{T}$, is an $m \times m$ square matrix. Each block on the diagonal, $\bar{T}^{rr}$, is an $n(r) \times n(r)$ square matrix. Off-diagonal matrices are basically rectangular, depending on the size of the supply region r and the size of the demand region s after aggregation. For example, the size of $\bar{T}^{rs}$ is $n(r) \times n(s)$.

We define the aggregation matrix as follows:

$$Z = \begin{bmatrix} z(1) & 0 & 0 & 0 \\ 0 & z(2) & 0 & 0 \\ 0 & 0 & \ddots & 0 \\ 0 & 0 & 0 & z(k) \end{bmatrix}$$

Each $z(r)$ on the diagonal is an $n(r) \times n$ block aggregation matrix. Each column of $z(r)$ must have one and only one "1," with other entries being "0"; and each row must have at least one "1" (can be more than one "1"), with other entries being "0." The locations of "1"s in a row indicate which sectors in the unaggregated model will be combined into a new sector in the aggregate model. If a matrix is pre-multiplied by $z(r)$, then the rows—but not the columns—of the original matrix are grouped into $n(r)$ sectors. A prime represents the transpose of a matrix or vector. Post-multiplying a matrix by $z'(r)$ will therefore aggregate the columns into $n(r)$ sectors.

The relationships for intermediate demand, final demand, total output, and carbon intensity before and after aggregation are presented as follows:

$$ZTZ' = \bar{T} \tag{3.4}$$

$$Zx = \bar{x} \tag{3.5}$$

$$ZF = \bar{F} \tag{3.6}$$

$$[Z(c \otimes x)] \otimes (Zx)^{-1} = \bar{c} \tag{3.7}$$

$\otimes$ is the multiplication of corresponding elements. c is a diagonal matrix of carbon intensity for the detailed model with c^1, c^2, ... and c^k on the diagonal. $\bar{c}$ is the corresponding diagonal matrix of carbon intensity after aggregation.

Based on Equation (3.3), we have the following relations for the unaggregated model:

$$x = (I - A)^{-1} F = Lf \tag{3.8}$$

The calculation of CFs using MRIO is as follows:

$$C \otimes x = C \otimes Lf \tag{3.9}$$

For a particular region s, the carbon footprints, $w = \{w_j^s\}$, are calculated as follows:

$$w_j^s = \sum_q \left[\left(\sum_r \sum_i c_i^r l_{ij}^{rq} \right) f_j^{qs} \right] \tag{3.10}$$

For the aggregate model, there are two alternative ways for the calculation of CFs:

Procedure 1:

$$\bar{w} = Zw \tag{3.11}$$

where w is the CFs calculated from the unaggregated model. Because all the information of the unaggregated system is known and Procedure 1 is only a summation of relevant sectoral CFs in the original model, there is no aggregation bias. We define $\bar{w}$ as the "true" value.

Procedure 2:
In another procedure, we first aggregate the MRIO model based on Equations (3.4) through (3.7). From the aggregated model, we then calculate the CFs:

$$\bar{x} = (I - \bar{A})^{-1} \bar{f} = \bar{L}\bar{f} \tag{3.12}$$

$$\bar{C} \otimes \bar{x} = \bar{C} \otimes \bar{L}\bar{f} \tag{3.13}$$

$$\hat{w}_j^s = \sum_q \left[\left(\sum_r \sum_i \bar{c}_i^r \bar{l}_{ij}^{rq} \right) \bar{f}_j^{qs} \right] \tag{3.14}$$

where $\hat{w}$ is the CFs calculated from the aggregate model. Procedure 2 is the question at issue in which aggregation bias will occur in the calculations of CFs. We define the discrepancy between $\hat{w}$ and $\bar{w}$ as aggregation error. At region-sectoral level, this is $(\hat{w}_j^s - \bar{w}_j^s)$. In addition, we use error rate, $(\hat{w}_j^s - \bar{w}_j^s)/\bar{w}_j^s$, to assess the relative, rather than the absolute, effects of aggregation. Error rate is used because the magnitude of aggregation errors can be extremely large due to the different economic scales of sectors in a national economy. The aggregation errors of some small sectors, although important to the sectors themselves, can be overlooked when compared with the aggregation errors of large-scale sectors.

3.3 RESULTS

To examine aggregation bias, we set aggregation schemes, determined by Z, randomly using Monte Carlo simulation. The procedure includes the following:

1. Randomly determine the number of regions in which aggregation will be conducted.

2. Randomly determine which regions are selected for conducting aggregation.

3. Randomly determine the number of sectors for each selected region.

4. Randomly determine which sectors are selected for aggregation in each selected region.

We repeated this procedure 100,000 times and obtained 100,000 randomly determined aggregation matrices Zs. For each Z^i, we calculate $\hat{w}^{Z^i}$ = $\{(\hat{w}_j^s)^{Z^i}\}$, $\bar{w}^{Z^i} = \{(\bar{w}_j^s)^{Z^i}\}$, $(\hat{w}_j^s)^{Z^i} - (\bar{w}_j^s)^{Z^i}$, and $[(\hat{w}_j^s)^{Z^i} - (\bar{w}_j^s)^{Z^i}]/(\bar{w}_j^s)^{Z^i}$. Because aggregation is conducted randomly many times, aggregation errors and error rates can be considered random variables.

The unaggregated MRIO model we used for this experiment is the AIO 2000. Because the inputs and outputs of Malaysian "unclassified sector" are all "0"s, which can cause a problem in the calculation of the Leontief inverse, we combined the "unclassified sector" with the "public administration" sector and named it the "unclassified" sector in the new MRIO system. For the calculation of carbon intensity, we used the GTAP-E Database Version 6 (Dimaranan, 2006). The GTAP Database Version 6 is the global database representing the world economy for 87 regions and 57 commodities for the year 2001. GTAP-E Database Version 6 provides the emissions data for corresponding regions and sectors in 2001.

We first match sectors in the GTAP Database with those in the AIO 2000 (see Appendix 3A), based on which we recalculate the carbon intensity for 75 sectors.

3.3.1 Magnitude of Aggregation Effect

Because cross-region aggregation is not allowed, we analyzed the results based on individual regions. For each simulation, samples were divided into two groups: (1) new sectors after aggregation are grouped as "aggregated sectors," and (2) sectors that remain the same as in the original model are grouped as "unaggregated sectors." The probability distribution of the error rates is depicted in Figure 3.1. Most distributions did not show a perfectly symmetric normal distribution, but were skewed either to the left or to the right. The distribution of unaggregated sectors was more concentrated than the distribution of aggregated sectors.

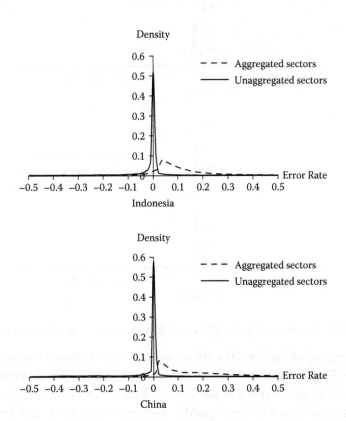

FIGURE 3.1   Probability distribution of error rates in ten economies.

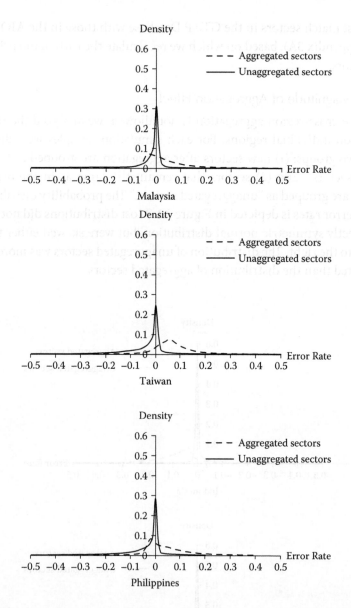

FIGURE 3.1 (continued) Probability distribution of error rates in ten economies.

For aggregated sectors, the error rates of samples showed a wide range, from −479 (aggregation of three sectors in China, i.e., "crude petroleum and natural gas," "iron and steel," and "finance and insurance") to 166 (aggregation of two sectors, "paddy" and "synthetic resins and fiber" in Thailand) (Table 3.2). The mean of error rates ranged from 0.029 (for Korea) to 0.167 (for China). This indicates that, in general, aggregation of

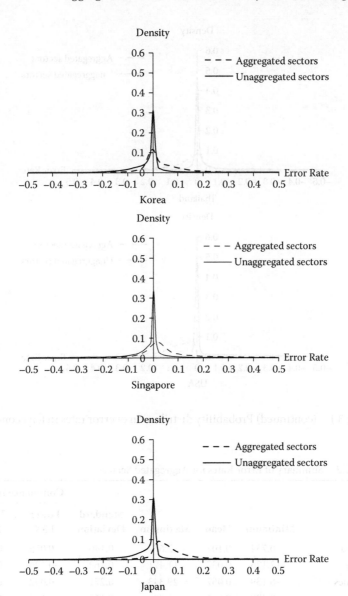

FIGURE 3.1 (continued) Probability distribution of error rates in ten economies.

the AIO 2000 will have moderate effects on CF accounting; however, the aggregation of some sectors can cause considerable bias. For unaggregated sectors, the range of error rates were from −0.876 (for Singapore) to more than 16 (for Indonesia) (Table 3.3), with mean levels between −2% and −5%. The confidence interval showed that, for example, for Indonesia, 95% of the error rates fell in the interval of −0.055 and 0.465 for aggregated

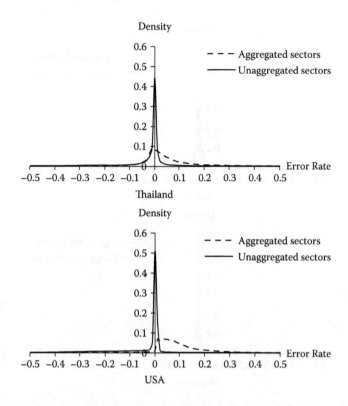

FIGURE 3.1 (continued) Probability distribution of error rates in ten economies.

TABLE 3.2 Summary of Error Rates for Aggregated Sectors

Region	Minimum	Mean	Maximum	Standard Deviation	Confidence Interval Lower 2.5%	Upper 2.5%
Indonesia	−0.734	0.107	2.677	0.140	−0.055	0.465
Malaysia	−12.176	0.037	11.471	0.162	−0.126	0.377
Philippines	−8.139	0.057	29.343	0.271	−0.092	0.380
Singapore	−0.438	0.066	1.885	0.162	−0.102	0.536
Thailand	−2.941	0.044	165.589	0.713	−0.099	0.326
Mainland China	−478.753	0.167	119.134	2.149	−0.013	0.746
Taiwan	−1.384	0.072	8.798	0.119	−0.080	0.311
Korea	−0.527	0.029	6.869	0.100	−0.096	0.235
Japan	−7.846	0.065	4.558	0.100	−0.043	0.289
USA	−0.355	0.092	1.574	0.088	−0.007	0.310

TABLE 3.3 Summary of Error Rates for Unaggregated Sectors

Region	Minimum	Mean	Maximum	Standard Deviation	Confidence Interval Lower 2.5%	Confidence Interval Upper 2.5%
Indonesia	−0.733	−0.023	16.585	0.162	−0.398	0.113
Malaysia	−0.758	−0.040	5.779	0.118	−0.399	0.105
Philippines	−0.669	−0.042	5.309	0.100	−0.318	0.108
Singapore	−0.876	−0.049	3.349	0.127	−0.506	0.074
Thailand	−0.772	−0.030	6.237	0.107	−0.335	0.085
Mainland China	−0.806	−0.036	3.548	0.115	−0.383	0.073
Taiwan	−0.595	−0.031	5.072	0.094	−0.234	0.140
Korea	-0.681	-0.025	4.338	0.066	−0.175	0.075
Japan	-0.694	-0.038	2.906	0.074	−0.247	0.034
USA	-0.826	-0.043	3.596	0.106	−0.353	0.017

sectors. The range of confidence intervals were between −0.102 and 0.746 for aggregated sectors, and between −0.506 and 0.14 for unaggregated sectors.

Comparing results for the two groups, and except for a few cases, the range of error rates was larger and the mean levels were higher for the aggregated sectors than for the unaggregated sectors. This indicates that aggregation has more impact on aggregated sectors than on unaggregated sectors. In addition, positive mean values for aggregated sectors indicate that, on average, aggregation of the AIO 2000 led to overestimation of CFs for aggregated sectors. Negative mean values indicate that there is a tendency of underestimation of the CFs for the nonaggregated sectors when other sectors are aggregated.

For individual economies, aggregation of sectors, on average, may influence CF accounting of China, Indonesia, and the USA more than other economies. From the range of error rates and the standard deviation of aggregated sectors, we can find that the aggregation of some sectors in China, Thailand, and the Philippines will have considerable impacts. For Indonesia, the aggregation of sectors within the country will have large effects on some specific unaggregated sectors (Table 3.3).

3.3.2 Factors Influencing the Aggregation Effect

As inferred by the ranges and standard deviations of error rates, the aggregation of some specific sectors may have significant impacts on the certainty of CF accounting using the AIO 2000. By ranking the absolute value of error rates for aggregated sectors, we identified those sectors whose aggregation may cause large bias (an example of top 30 results are shown in Appendix 3B).

Among the top 300 samples, with the absolute value of error rates ranging from 479 down to 1.85, 140 occurred in Mainland China (accounting for 46.7% of top 300 aggregation results), 105 in the Philippines (35%), 22 in Indonesia (7.3%), 14 in Malaysia (4.7%), 13 in Korea (4.3%), and 3 (1%) in Japan and Singapore, respectively. Among 140 top aggregation errors in Mainland China, 87 aggregation schemes included the sector of "iron and steel" and 25 aggregation schemes included the sector of "chemical fertilizers and pesticides." For the Philippines, 104 results out of 105 top-error aggregation schemes included the sector of "crude petroleum and natural gas." For Indonesia, 20 out of 22 top-error aggregation schemes included the sector of "iron and steel." For Malaysia, 13 out of 14 top-error aggregation schemes included the sector of "non-metallic ore and quarrying." Korea did not show such high concentrations over particular sectors. Among 13 top-error aggregation schemes, sector "timber" appeared 5 times. For Japan, sector "cement and cement products" appeared twice out of 3 top-error aggregation schemes. For Singapore, sector "electricity and gas" and sector "building construction" occurred twice (nonexclusively) among 3 top-error aggregation schemes.

For unaggregated sectors, we conducted similar experiments by ranking the absolute value of error rates. Among the top 300 results, with the range from 16.585 down to 4.16, sector "milled grain and flour" in Indonesia (occurred 282 times) was influenced the most by different aggregations of other sectors in the region.

We compared the minimum value, maximum value, mean, and standard deviation for all the simulations with and without the 300 top-error results (see Table 3.4 and Table 3.5). It can be found that the absolute levels of the minimum value and the maximum value decreased sharply, in particular for China, Thailand, the Philippines, Indonesia, Malaysia, and Japan, which have high occurrence in 300 top-error results. Because of the large number of samples, the mean levels did not have obvious changes. Standard deviations, also because of the large number of samples, did not change for most of the regions, except for China and Thailand, for which levels decreased considerably.

TABLE 3.4   Summary of Error Rates for All Simulation Results

Region	Minimum	Average	Maximum	Standard Deviation	Number of Samples
Indonesia	−0.734	−0.051	16.585	0.260	2,081,316
Malaysia	−12.176	−0.090	11.471	0.177	2,092,685
Philippines	−8.139	−0.086	29.343	0.147	2,089,085
Singapore	−0.876	−0.102	3.349	0.186	2,088,507
Thailand	−2.941	−0.067	165.589	0.199	2,105,087
Mainland China	−478.753	−0.087	119.134	0.390	2,082,398
Taiwan	−1.384	−0.047	8.798	0.142	2,093,642
Korea	−0.681	−0.045	6.869	0.094	2,094,986
Japan	−7.846	−0.078	4.558	0.104	2,095,602
USA	−0.826	−0.107	3.596	0.152	2,089,001

TABLE 3.5   Summary of Error Rates for the Simulation Results Excluding 300 Top-Error Results

Region	Minimum	Average	Maximum	Standard Deviation	Number of Samples
Indonesia	−0.734	−0.052	4.335	0.253	2,081,086
Malaysia	−0.779	−0.090	3.991	0.176	2,092,676
Philippines	−0.897	−0.086	4.289	0.142	2,089,059
Singapore	−0.876	−0.102	3.349	0.186	2,088,507
Thailand	−2.941	−0.067	4.278	0.163	2,105,083
Mainland China	−4.199	−0.087	3.883	0.179	2,082,374
Taiwan	−1.384	−0.047	4.280	0.142	2,093,638
Korea	−0.681	−0.045	3.875	0.094	2,094,985
Japan	−0.694	−0.078	2.906	0.103	2,095,600
USA	−0.826	−0.107	3.596	0.152	2,089,001

3.4 CONCLUSIONS

The construction of MRIO tables is both time-consuming and expensive. There are still very few MRIO tables available for practical applications. MRIO tables are generally constructed based on national IO tables and bilateral trade data. Different countries have different key sectors and national priorities that can influence sector classification and the level of aggregation in their national IO tables. In constructing MRIO tables, reclassification and aggregation are usually necessary to adjust the differences among national IO tables. In the application of MRIO models to environmental analysis, sector reclassification and aggregation are needed again to match environmental data and economic data. Therefore, sector aggregation is a practical and important task for environmentally extended analysis using MRIO models. By examining the magnitude of aggregation bias in carbon footprint accounting using an empirical MRIO model for Asian-Pacific economies, we have several conclusions.

1. On average, aggregation of the AIO 2000 had moderate effects on carbon footprint accounting (with the absolute value of the mean error rates less than 20%). However, the aggregation of some sectors can cause considerable bias (with extremely high absolute value of error rates, e.g., 479).

2. Aggregation exerted more impacts on aggregated sectors than on unaggregated sectors. There is a tendency for the AIO 2000 that aggregation will cause overestimation of CFs for aggregated sectors and underestimation for unaggregated sectors.

3. Different from other empirical literature to which concluded that aggregation bias increases with the level of aggregation (e.g., as suggested by Karaska (1968) and Hewings (1974)), we found that for the AIO 2000, the level of aggregation is not the key factor, but some specific sectors in specific regions do play a key role in affecting aggregation bias. The range of error rates can be narrowed sharply by excluding limited top-errors, for example, decreased from (−479, 166) to (−4, 4) when the top 300 results are excluded. For those who will excise the aggregation of the AIO 2000 for environmental analysis, the exclusion of specific sectors in their aggregation schemes can greatly improve the certainty of the accounting results.

4. Although we identified some sectors that, if aggregated, generate a large aggregation error, identifying them by *a priori* approach is still lacking. Because sectoral carbon intensity, Leontief multiplier, and the level of final demand influence the aggregation errors simultaneously and nonlinearly based on Equations (3.12) through (3.14), it is difficult to provide a simple method to check, *a priori*, which sectors will have potential impacts. It is not included in the scope of this work but can form an important agenda for future research.

ACKNOWLEDGMENTS

Xin Zhou would like to thank the Ministry of the Environment, Japan, for its financial support of the project on the Assessment of the Environmental, Economic, and Social Impacts of Resource Circulation Systems in Asia, under the Policy Study on Environmental Economics (PSEE). Hiroaki Shirakawa would like to thank the Ministry of the Environment, Japan, for supporting the project on Development and Practice of Advanced Basin Model in Asia: Towards Adaptation of Climate Change (FY2011–FY2013) under its Environment Research & Technology Development Fund (E-1104).

REFERENCES

Andrew, R., Peters, G.P., and Lennox, J., 2009. Approximation and regional aggregation in multi-regional input-output analysis for national carbon footprint accounting. *Economic Systems Research,* 21(3), 311–335.

Ara, K., 1959. The aggregation problem in input-output analysis. *Econometrica,* 27, 257–262.

Blair, P., and Miller, R.E., 1983. Spatial aggregation in multiregional input-output models. *Environment and Planning A,* 15, 187–206.

Chenery, H.B., 1953. Regional Analysis. In Chenery, H.B., Clark, P.G., and Pinne, V.C., Eds., *The Structure and Growth of the Italian Economy*: 97–129, U.S. Mutual Security Agency, Rome.

Dimaranan, B.V., 2006. Global Trade, Assistance, and Production: GTAP 6 Data Base, 2-8, 2-9. Center for Global Trade Analysis, Purdue University, West Lafayette, IN.

Doeksen, G.A., and Little, C.H., 1968. Effect of size of the input-output model on the results of an impact analysis. *Agricultural Economics Research,* 20(4), 134–138.

Fisher, W.D., 1958. Criteria for aggregation in input-output analysis. The *Review of Economics and Statistics,* 40, 250–260.

Fisher, W.D., 1962. Optimal aggregation in multi-equation prediction models. *Econometrica,* 30, 744–769.

Fisher, W.D., 1966. Simplification in economic models. *Econometrica,* 34, 563–584.

Gibbons, J.C., Wolsky, A.M., and Tolley, G., 1982. Approximate aggregation and error in input-output models. *Resources and Energy,* 4, 203–230.

Hertwich, E.G., and Peters, G.P., 2009. Carbon footprint of nations: A global, trade-linked analysis. *Environmental Science & Technology,* 43, 6416–6420.

Hewings, G.J.D., 1974. The effect of aggregation on the empirical identification of key sectors in a regional economy: A partial evaluation of alternative techniques. *Environment and Planning A,* 6, 439–453.

Institute of Developing Economies, Japan External Trade Organization, 2006. *Asian International Input-Output Table 2000, Volume 1, Explanatory Notes.* Institute of Developing Economies, Tokyo.

Karaska, G.J., 1968. Variation of input-output coefficients for different levels of aggregation. *Journal of Regional Science*, 8(2), 215–227.

Lenzen, M., 2007. Aggregation (in-variance) of shared responsibility: A case study of Australia. *Ecological Economics*, 64, 19–24.

Lenzen, M., 2011. Aggregation versus disaggregation in input-output analysis of the environment. *Economic Systems Research*, 23(1), 73–89.

Leontief, W., 1941. *The Structure of American Economy: 1919–1929.* Oxford University Press, New York.

Leontief, W., 1967. An alternative to aggregation in input-output analysis and national accounts. *The Review of Economics and Statistics*, 49, 412–419.

Minx, J.C., Wiedmann, T., Wood, R., Peters, G.P., Lenzen, M., Owen, A., Scott, K., Barrett, J., Hubacek, K., Baiocchi, G., Paul, A., Dawkins, E., Briggs, J., Guan, D., Suh, S., and Ackerman, F., 2012. Input–output analysis and carbon footprinting: An overview of applications. *Economic Systems Research*, 21(3), 187–216.

Moses, L.N., 1955. The stability of interregional trading patterns and input-output analysis. *American Econmic Review*, 45, 803–832.

Munksgaard, J., and Pedersen, K.A., 2001. CO_2 accounts for open economies: Producer or consumer responsibility. *Energy Policy*, 29, 327–334.

Peters, G.P., and Hertwich, E.G., 2008. CO_2 embodied in international trade with implications for global climate policy. *Environmental Science & Technology*, 42, 1401–1407.

Su, B. and Ang, B.W., 2010. Input-output analysis of CO_2 emissions embodied in trade: The effects of spatial aggregaton. *Ecological Economics*, 70(1), 10–18.

Su, B., Huang, H.C., Ang, B.W., and Zhou, P., 2010. Input-output analysis of CO_2 emissions embodied in trade: The effects of sector aggregation. *Energy Economics*, 32(1), 166–175.

Wiedmann, T., 2009a. A review of recent multi-region input–output models used for consumption-based emission and resource accounting. *Ecological Economics*, 69, 211–222.

Wiedmann, T., 2009b. Editorial: Carbon footprint and input-output analysis—An introduction. *Economic Systems Research*, 21 (3), 175–186.

Wyckoff, A.W., and Roop, J.M., 1994. The embodiment of carbon in imports of manufactured products. *Energy Policy*, 23(3), 187–194.

Zhou, X., Liu, X.B., and Kojima, S., Eds., 2010. Carbon Emissions Embodied in International Trade: An Assessment from the Asian Perspective. Institute for Global Environmental Strategies (IGES), Hayama, Japan. Retrieved from http://enviroscope.iges.or.jp/modules/envirolib/upload/2719/attach/embodied_emissions_whole_sf_publication.pdf.pdf.

APPENDIX 3A: SECTOR CLASSIFICATION IN THE AIO 2000 AND GTAP6 DATABASE

Code	Sectors in the AIO 2000	Corresponding Sector Classification in the GTAP6 Database
001	Paddy	Paddy rice (pdr)
002	Other grain	Wheat (wht); cereal grains (gro)
003	Food crops	Vegetables (v_f); oil seeds (osd); sugar cane, sugar beet (c_b)
004	Non-food crops	Plant-based fibers (pfb); crops (ocr)
005	Livestock and poultry	Cattle, sheep, goats, houses (ctl); animal products (oap); raw milk (rmk); wool, silk-worm cocoons (wol)
006	Forestry	Forestry (frs)
007	Fishery	Fishing (fsh)
008	Crude petroleum and natural gas	Oil (oil); gas (gas)
009	Iron ore	Minerals (omn); coal (coa)
010	Other metallic ore	
011	Non-metallic ore and quarrying	
012	Milled grain and flour	Processed rice (pcr); vegetable oils and fats (vol); sugar (sgr); food products (ofd)
013	Fish products	Meat of cattle, sheep, goat and horse (cmt); meat products (omt); dairy products (mil)
014	Slaughtering, meat products and dairy products	
015	Other food products	
016	Beverage	Beverages and tobacco products (b_t)
017	Tobacco	
018	Spinning	Textiles (tex)
019	Weaving and dyeing	
020	Knitting	
021	Wearing apparel	Wearing apparel (wap)
022	Other made-up textile products	
023	Leather and leather products	Leather products (lea)
024	Timber	Wood products (lum)
025	Wooden furniture	
026	Other wooden products	
027	Pulp and paper	Paper products, publishing (ppp)
028	Printing and publishing	
029	Synthetic resins and fiber	Chemical, rubber, plastic products (crp)
030	Basic industrial chemicals	

continued

Code	Sectors in the AIO 2000	Corresponding Sector Classification in the GTAP6 Database
031	Chemical fertilizers and pesticides	
032	Drugs and medicine	
033	Other chemical products	
034	Refined petroleum and its products	Petroleum, coal products (p_c)
035	Plastic products	
036	Tires and tubes	
037	Other rubber products	
038	Cement and cement products	Non-metallic mineral product (nmm)
039	Glass and glass products	
040	Other non-metallic mineral products	
041	Iron and steel	Ferrous metals (i_s)
042	Non-ferrous metal	Non-ferrous metals (nfm)
043	Metal products	Metal products (fmp)
044	Boilers, engines and turbines	Other machinery and equipment (ome)
045	General machinery	
046	Metal working machinery	
047	Specialized machinery	
048	Heavy electrical equipment	
049	Television sets, radios, audios and communication equipment	Electronic equipment (ele)
050	Electronic computing equipment	
051	Semiconductors and integrated circuits	
052	Other electronics and electronic products	
053	Household electrical equipment	Other manufactures (omf)
054	Lighting fixtures, batteries, wiring and others	
055	Motor vehicles	Motor vehicles and parts (mvh)
056	Motorcycles	Other transport equipment (otn)
057	Shipbuilding	
058	Other transport equipment	
059	Precision machines	
060	Other manufacturing products	
061	Electricity and gas	Electricity (ely), gas manufacture, distribution (gdt)
062	Water supply	Water (wtr)
063	Building construction	Construction (cns)
064	Other construction	
065	Wholesale and retail trade	Trade (trd)

Code	Sectors in the AIO 2000	Corresponding Sector Classification in the GTAP6 Database
066	Transportation	Sea transport (wtp); air transport (atp); other transport (otp)
067	Telephone and telecommunication	Communication (cmn)
068	Finance and insurance	Other financial services (ofi); insurance (isr)
069	Real estate	Other business services (obs)
070	Education and research	Recreation and other services (ros); public administration, defense, health and education (osg)
071	Medical and health service	
072	Restaurants	
073	Hotel	
074	Other services	
075	Unclassified	

APPENDIX 3B: RANKING OF TOP 30 AGGREGATION ERRORS

(See table on next page.)

Rank	Country	No. of Sectors Aggregated	Error Rate	Aggregated Sectors	Carbon Intensity (After)	Carbon Intensity (Before)	Leontief Multiplier (After)	Leontief Multiplier (Before)	Carbon Multiplier (After)	Carbon Multiplier (Before)	Final Demand (After)	Final Demand (Before)
1	China	3	−478.753	Crude petroleum and natural gas, Iron and steel, Finance and insurance	0.907	0.735, 1.544, 0.030	2.116	1.739, 2.813, 1.529	2.892	2.228, 5.191, 0.477	18614524	6068602, −4162585, 16708507
2	Thailand	2	165.589	Paddy, Synthetic resins and fiber	0.202	0.090, 0.499	1.626	1.437, 2.145	0.612	0.249, 1.563	−113935	−135191, 21256
3	China	3	119.134	Iron and steel, Telephone and telecommunication, Finance and insurance	0.759	1.544, 0.033, 0.030	2.221	2.813, 2.175, 1.529	2.738	5.191, 1.597, 0.477	21389644	−4162585, 8843722, 16708507
4	China	5	65.765	Paddy, Iron ore, Fish products, Chemical fertilizers and pesticides, Iron and steel	0.911	0.062, 1.330, 0.060, 0.472, 1.544	2.496	1.921, 2.648, 2.419, 2.878, 2.813	3.499	1.240, 5.361, 1.342, 3.964, 5.191	19615881	19813723, 330883, 6907401, −3273541, −4162585
5	China	3	−35.293	Other rubber products, Iron and steel, Electronic computing equipment	1.145	0.472, 1.544, 0.019	2.724	2.737, 2.813, 2.573	3.883	2.386, 5.191, 0.804	15144006	2761198, −4162585, 1654539
6	Philippines	2	29.343	Crude petroleum and natural gas, Leather and leather products	13.812	284.147, 0.304444107	2.103	1.486, 2.173	20.454	284.258, 0.695395	41118	−3, 41121
7	Philippines	3	17.572	Crude petroleum and natural gas, Other rubber products, Other transport equipment	7.608	284.147, 0.172, 0.002	2.079	1.486, 2.142, 1.793	8.429	284.258, 0.5140, 0.222	117223	−3, 95972, 21254

#	Country		Sector								
8	Philippines	17.112	Crude petroleum and natural gas, Spinning	8.125	284.147, 0.257	1.877	1.486, 1.845	8.523	284.258, 0.485	57846	−3, 57849
9	China	14.761	Spinning, Iron and steel, Electronic computing equipment	0.915	0.173, 1.544, 0.019	2.714	2.702, 2.813, 2.573	3.286	1.48, 5.191, 0.804	20904509	8521701, −4162585, 16545393
10	Philippines	13.586	Crude petroleum and natural gas, Other wooden products	5.191	284.147, 0.036	1.900	1.486, 1.912	5.562	284.258, 0.388	123587	−3, 123590
11	China	−12.576	Crude petroleum and natural gas, Refined petroleum and its products, Iron and steel, Non-ferrous metal	0.887	0.735, 0.472, 1.544, 0.482	2.462	1.734, 2.154, 2.813, 2.804	3.631	2.228, 2.195, 5.191, 4.239	2819996	6068602, −1628065, −4162585, 2542044
12	China	12.186	Weaving and dyeing, Iron and steel	0.985	0.173, 1.544	2.808	2.801, 2.813	3.664	1.471, 5.191	12973490	17136075, −4162585
13	Malaysia	−12.176	Non-food crops, Non-metallic ore and quarrying	0.459	0.015, 1.346	1.683	1.676, 1.695	0.845	0.286, 1.829	196598	242665, −46067
14	Malaysia	−11.934	Non-metallic ore and quarrying, Metal working machinery	0.936	1.346, 0.124	1.746	1.695, 1.839	1.356	1.829, 0.449	110919	−46067, 156986
15	Malaysia	11.471	Non-metallic ore and quarrying, Shipbuilding	0.861	1.346, 0.188	1.780	1.695, 1.891	1.261	1.829, 0.485	161021	−46067, 207088
16	China	10.847	Iron and steel, Real estate	1.184	1.544, 0.175	2.498	2.813, 1.862	3.865	5.191, 1.148	20476625	−4162585, 24639210
17	China	10.322	Crude petroleum and natural gas, Iron and steel, Metal working machinery	1.215	0.735, 1.544, 0.229	2.399	1.739, 2.813, 2.819	3.943	2.228, 5.191, 2.598	5795736	6068602, −4162585, 3889719

continued

Rank	Country	Error Rate	No. of Sectors Aggregated	Aggregated Sectors	Carbon Intensity (After)	Carbon Intensity (Before)	Leontief Multiplier (After)	Leontief Multiplier (Before)	Carbon Multiplier (After)	Carbon Multiplier (Before)	Final Demand (After)	Final Demand (Before)
18	Philippines	9.983	2	Crude petroleum and natural gas, Hotel	3.648	284.147, 0.039	1.841	1.486, 1.849	3.946	284.258, 0.361	477794	−3,477797
19	Philippines	9.982	2	Crude petroleum and natural gas, Hotel	3.648	284.147, 0.039	1.842	1.486, 1.849	3.945	284.258, 0.361	477794	−3,477797
20	Philippines	9.973	3	Crude petroleum and natural gas, Spinning, Heavy electrical equipment	4.817	284.1478, 0.257, 0.005	1.999	1.486, 1.845, 2.236	5.257	284.258, 0.485, 0.4826	200030	−3,57849, 142184
21	Philippines	9.565	3	Crude petroleum and natural gas, Tobacco, Cement and cement products	1.664	284.147, 0.077, 0.707	1.963	1.486, 1.826, 2.077	2.424	284.258, 0.197, 1.296	576358	−3,558643, 17718
22	China	9.119	3	Non-metallic ore and quarrying, Chemical fertilizers and pesticides, Electronic computing equipment	0.621	1.330, 0.472, 0.019	2.505	2.125, 2.878, 2.573	2.788	3.516, 3.964, 0.804	14299005	1027153, −3273541, 16545393
23	Taiwan	8.798	2	Synthetic resins and fiber, Finance and insurance	0.029	0.100, 0.002	1.479	2.428, 1.153	0.128	0.472, 0.010	14145348	85884, 14059464
24	Philippines	8.513	3	Crude petroleum and natural gas, Chemical fertilizers and pesticides, Other manufacturing products	3.783	284.147, 0.172, 0.003	2.055	1.486, 2.041, 2.106	4.240	284.258, 0.624, 0.390	155193	−3,40441, 114755

25	Philippines	3	8.198	Forestry, Crude petroleum and natural gas, Electronic computing equipment	1.603	0.426, 284.147, 0.002	2.280	1.319, 1.486, 2.580	1.853	0.584, 284.258, 0.195	655956	13838, −3, 642121
26	Philippines	3	−8.139	Crude petroleum and natural gas, Knitting, Non-ferrous metal	3.084	284.147, 0.2571, 0.020	2.259	1.486, 2.275, 2.280	4.084	284.258, 0.6918, 0.527	−2702	−3, 23284, −25983
27	Philippines	2	8.049	Crude petroleum and natural gas, Glass and glass products	10.308	284.147, 0.707	2.186	1.486, 2.215	12.620	284.258, 1.422	30573	−3, 30576
28	Philippines	2	8.039	Crude petroleum and natural gas, Glass and glass products	10.308	284.147, 0.707	2.184	1.486, 2.215	12.606	284.258, 1.422	30573	−3, 30576
29	Japan	2	−7.846	Crude petroleum and natural gas, Non-metallic ore and quarrying	0.096	0.001, 0.102	2.021	1.651, 2.048	0.174	0.060, 0.183	−6197	−10486, 4289
30	China	4	7.833	Fish products, Slaughtering, Other rubber products, Iron and steel	1.159	0.060, 0.060, 0.472, 1.544	2.751	2.419, 2.769, 2.737, 2.813	3.923	1.34, 1.119, 2.386, 5.191	17640078	6907401, 12134064, 2761198, −4162585

II

Computational Intelligent Data Analysis for Climate Change

II

Computational Intelligent Data
Analysis for Climate Change

CHAPTER 4

Climate Informatics

Claire Monteleoni, Gavin A. Schmidt,
Francis Alexander, Alexandru Niculescu-Mizil,
Karsten Steinhaeuser, Michael Tippett,
Arindam Banerjee, M. Benno Blumenthal,
Auroop R. Ganguly, Jason E. Smerdon,
and Marco Tedesco

CONTENTS

4.1 INTRODUCTION

THE IMPACTS OF PRESENT and potential future climate change will be one of the most important scientific and societal challenges in the 21st century. Given observed changes in temperature, sea ice, and sea level, improving our understanding of the climate system is an international priority. This system is characterized by complex phenomena that are imperfectly observed and even more imperfectly simulated. But with an ever-growing supply of climate data from satellites and environmental sensors, the magnitude of data and climate model output is beginning to overwhelm the relatively simple tools currently used to analyze them. A computational approach will therefore be indispensable for these analysis challenges. This chapter introduces the fledgling research discipline *climate informatics*: collaborations between climate scientists and machine learning researchers in order to bridge this gap between data and understanding. We hope that the study of climate informatics will accelerate discovery in answering pressing questions in climate science.

Machine learning is an active research area at the interface of computer science and statistics, concerned with developing automated techniques, or algorithms, to detect patterns in data. Machine learning (and data mining) algorithms are critical to a range of technologies, including Web search, recommendation systems, personalized Internet advertising, computer vision, and natural language processing. Machine learning has also made significant impacts on the natural sciences, for example, in biology; the interdisciplinary field of bioinformatics has facilitated many discoveries in genomics and proteomics. The impact of machine learning on climate science promises to be similarly profound.

The goal of this chapter is to define *climate informatics* and to propose some grand challenges for this nascent field. Recent progress on climate informatics, by the authors as well as by other groups, reveals that collaborations with climate scientists also open up interesting new problems for machine learning. There are a myriad of collaborations possible at the intersection of these two fields. This chapter uses both top-down and bottom-up approaches to stimulate research progress on a range of problems in climate informatics, some of which have yet to be proposed. For the former, we present challenge problems posed by climate scientists, and discussed with machine learning, data mining, and statistics researchers at *Climate Informatics 2011*, the *First International Workshop on Climate Informatics*, the inaugural event of a new annual workshop in which all co-authors participated. To spur innovation from the bottom-up, we also describe and discuss some of the types of data available. In addition to summarizing some of the key challenges for climate informatics, this chapter also draws on some of the recent climate informatics research of the co-authors.

The chapter is organized as follows. First, we discuss the types of climate data available and outline some challenges for climate informatics, including problems in analyzing climate data. Then we go into further detail on several key climate informatics problems: seasonal climate forecasting, predicting climate extremes, reconstructing past climate, and some problems in polar regions. We then discuss some machine learning and statistical approaches that might prove promising (and that were not mentioned in previous sections). Finally, we discuss some challenges and opportunities for climate science data and data management. Due to the broad coverage of the chapter, related work discussions are interspersed throughout the sections.

4.2 MACHINE LEARNING

Over the past few decades, the field of machine learning has matured significantly, drawing on ideas from several disciplines, including optimization, statistics, and artificial intelligence [4, 34]. Application of machine learning has led to important advances in a wide variety of domains ranging from Internet applications to scientific problems. Machine learning methods have been developed for a wide variety of predictive modeling as well as exploratory data analysis problems. In the context of predictive modeling, important advances have been made in linear classification and regression, hierarchical linear models, nonlinear models based on kernels, as well as ensemble methods that combine outputs from different predictors. In the context of exploratory data analysis, advances have been made in clustering and dimensionality reduction, including nonlinear methods to detect low-dimensional manifold structures in the data. Some of the important themes driving research in modern machine learning are motivated by properties of modern datasets from scientific, societal, and commercial applications. In particular, the datasets are extremely large scale, running into millions or billions of data points; are high-dimensional, going up to tens of thousands or more dimensions; and have intricate statistical dependencies that violate the "independent and identically distributed" assumption made in traditional approaches. Such properties are readily observed in climate datasets, including observations, reanalysis, as well as climate model outputs. These aspects have led to increased emphasis on scalable optimization methods [94], online learning methods [11], and graphical models [47], which can handle large-scale data in high dimensions with statistical dependencies.

4.3 UNDERSTANDING AND USING CLIMATE DATA

Profuse amounts of climate data of various types are available, providing a rich and fertile playground for future data mining and machine learning research. Here we discuss some of the varieties of data available, and provide some suggestions on how they can be used. The discussion opens up some interesting problems. There are multiple sources of climate data, ranging from single-site observations scattered in an unstructured way across the globe to climate model output that is global and uniformly gridded. Each class of data has particular characteristics that should be appreciated before it can be successfully used or compared. We provide here a brief introduction to each, with a few examples and references for further information. Common issues that arise in cross-class syntheses are also addressed.

4.3.1 *In-Situ* Observations

In-situ measurements refer to raw (or only minimally processed) measurements of diverse climate system properties that can include temperatures, rainfall, winds, column ozone, cloud cover, radiation, etc., taken from specific locations. These locations are often at the surface (e.g., from weather stations), but can also include atmospheric measurements from radiosonde balloons, subsurface ocean data from floats, data from ships, aircraft, and special intensive observing platforms.

Much of this data is routinely collected and made available in collated form from National Weather Services or special projects such as AEROCOM (for aerosol data), International Comprehensive Ocean-Atmosphere Data Set (ICOADS) (ocean temperature and salinity from ships), Argo (ocean floats), etc. Multivariate data related to single experiments (e.g., the Atmospheric Radiation Measurement (ARM) program or the Surface Heat Budget of the Arctic (SHEBA)), are a little less well organized, although usually available at specialized websites.

This kind of data is useful for looking at coherent multivariate comparisons, although usually on limited time and space domains, as input to weather model analyses or as the raw material for processed gridded data (see next subsection). The principal problem with this data is their sparseness spatially and, in time, inhomogeneities due to differing measurement practices or instruments and overall incompleteness (not all variables are measured at the same time or place) [45, 62].

4.3.2 Gridded/Processed Observations

Given a network of raw *in-situ* data, the next step is synthesizing those networks into quality-controlled regularly gridded datasets. These have a number of advantages over the raw data in that they are easier to work with, are more comparable to model output (discussed below), and have fewer nonclimatic artifacts. Gridded products are usually available on 5° latitude by 5° longitude grids or even higher resolution. However, these products use interpolation, gap-filling in space and time, and corrections for known biases, all of which affect the structural uncertainty in the product. The resulting error estimates are often dependent upon space and time. Different products targeting the same basic quantity can give some idea of the structural uncertainty in these products, and we strongly recommend using multiple versions. For example, for different estimates of the global mean surface temperature, anomalies can be found from the National Climatic Data Center (NCDC), the Hadley Centre, and NASA [6, 33, 90] that differ in processing and details but show a large amount of agreement at the large scale.

4.3.3 Satellite Retrievals

Since 1979, global and near-global observations of the Earth's climate have been made from low-earth orbit and geostationary satellites. These observations are based either on passive radiances (either emitted directly from the Earth, or via reflected solar radiation) or by active scanning via lasers or radars. These satellites, mainly operated by U.S. agencies (NOAA, NASA), the European Space Agency, and the Japanese program (JAXA), and data are generally available in near-real-time. There are a number of levels of data, ranging from raw radiances (Level 1), processed data as a function of time (Level 2), and gridded averaged data at the global scale (Level 3).

Satellite products do have specific and particular views of the climate system, which requires that knowledge of the "satellite-eye" view be incorporated into any comparison of satellite data with other products. Many satellite products are available for specific instruments on specific platforms; synthesis products across multiple instruments and multiple platforms are possible, but remain rare.

4.3.4 Paleoclimate Proxies

In-situ instrumental data only extends on a global basis to the mid-19th century, although individual records can extend to the 17th or 18th century. For a longer term perspective, climate information must be extracted from so-called "proxy" archives, such as ice cores, ocean mud, lake sediments, tree rings, pollen records, caves, or corals, which retain information that is sometimes highly correlated to specific climate variables or events [41].

As with satellite data, appropriate comparisons often require a forward model of the process by which climate information is stored and that incorporates the multiple variables that influence any particular proxy [75]. However, the often dramatically larger signals that can be found in past climates can overcome the increase in uncertainty due to spatial sparseness and nonclimatic noise, especially when combined in a multi-proxy approach [58]. Problems in paleoclimate are discussed in further detail in Section 4.8.

4.3.5 Reanalysis Products

Weather forecast models use as much observational data (*in-situ*, remote sensing, etc.) as can be assimilated in producing 6-hour forecasts (the "analyses"), which are excellent estimates of the state of the climate at any one time. However, as models have improved over time, the time series of weather forecasts can contain trends related only to the change in model rather than changes in the real world. Thus, many of the weather forecasting groups have undertaken "reanalyses" that use a fixed model to reprocess data from the past in order to have a consistent view of the real world (see reanalyses.org for more details). This is somewhat equivalent to a physics-based interpolation of existing datasets and often provides the best estimate of the climate state over the instrumental period (e.g., ERA-Interim [16]).

However, not all variables in the reanalyses are equally constrained by observational data. Thus, sea-level pressure and winds are well characterized, but precipitation, cloud fields, and surface fluxes are far more model dependent and thus are not as reliable. Additionally, there remain unphysical trends in the output as a function of changes in the observing network over time. In particular, the onset of large-scale remote sensing in 1979 imparts jumps in many fields that can be confused with real climate trends [105].

4.3.6 Global Climate Model (GCM) Output

Global climate models are physics-based simulations of the climate system, incorporating (optionally) components for the atmosphere, ocean, sea ice, land surface, vegetation, ice sheets, atmospheric aerosols and chemistry, and carbon cycles. Simulations can either be transient in response to changing boundary conditions (such as hindcasts of the 20th century), or time slices for periods thought to be relatively stable (such as the mid-Holocene 6,000 years ago). Variations in output can depend on initial conditions (because of the chaotic nature of the weather), the model used, or variations in the forcing fields (due to uncertainties in the time history, say, of aerosol emissions). A number of coordinated programs, notably the Coupled Model Intercomparison Project (CMIP), have organized coherent model experiments that have been followed by multiple climate modeling groups around the world and which are the dominant source for model output [96].

These models are used to define fingerprints of forced climate change that can be used in the detection and attribution of climate change [39], for hypothesis generation about linkages in the climate system, as test-beds for evaluating proposed real-world analyses [24], and, of course, future predictions [61]. Quantifying the structural uncertainty in model parameterizations or the model framework, the impact of known imperfections in the realizations of key processes, and the necessity of compromises at small spatial or temporal scales are all important challenges.

4.3.7 Regional Climate Model (RCM) Output

Global models necessarily need to compromise on horizontal resolution. In order to incorporate more details at the local level (particularly regional topography), output from the global models or the global reanalyses can be used to drive a higher-resolution, regional climate model. The large-scale fields can then be transformed to higher resolution using physical principles embedded in the RCM code. In particular, rainfall patterns that are very sensitive to the detailed topography are often far better modeled within the RCM than in the global-scale driving model. However, there are many variables to consider in RCMs—from variations in how the boundary field forcing is implemented and in the physics packages—and the utility of using RCMs to improve predictions of change is not yet clear. A coordinated experiment to test these issues is the North American Regional Climate Change Assessment Program (NARCCAP) [60].

4.4 SCIENTIFIC PROBLEMS IN CLIMATE INFORMATICS

There are a number of different kinds of problems that climate scientists are working on where machine learning and computer science techniques may make a big impact. This is a brief description of a few examples (with discussion of related work in the literature) that typify these ideas, although any specific implementation mentioned should not be considered the last word. This section provides short descriptions of several challenging problems in climate informatics broadly defined. In Section 4.5 we present problems in climate data analysis. In subsequent sections we delve into more detail on some specific problems in climate informatics.

4.4.1 Parameterization Development

Climate models need to deal with the physics that occurs at scales smaller than any finite model can resolve. This can involve cloud formation, turbulence in the ocean, land surface heterogeneity, ice floe interactions, chemistry on dust particle surfaces, etc. This is dealt with by using parameterizations that attempt to capture the phenomenology of a specific process and its sensitivity in terms of the (resolved) large scales. This is an ongoing task, and is currently driven mainly by scientists' physical intuition and relatively limited calibration data. As observational data become more available, and direct numerical simulation of key processes becomes more tractable, there is an increase in the potential for machine learning and data mining techniques to help define new parameterizations and frameworks. For example, neural network frameworks have been used to develop radiation models [50].

4.4.2 Using Multimodel Ensembles of Climate Projections

There are multiple climate models that have been developed and are actively being improved at approximately 25 centers across the globe. Each model shares some basic features with at least some other models, but each has generally been designed and implemented independently and has many unique aspects. In coordinated Model Intercomparison Projects (MIPs) (most usefully, the Coupled MIP (CMIP3, CMIP5), the Atmospheric Chemistry and Climate MIP (ACCMIP), the PaleoClimate MIP (PMIP3), etc.), modeling groups have attempted to perform analogous simulations with similar boundary conditions but with multiple models. These "ensembles" offer the possibility of assessing what is robust across models, what are the roles of internal variability, structural uncertainty, and scenario uncertainty in assessing the different projections at different time and space scales, and multiple opportunities for model-observation comparisons. Do there exist skill metrics for model simulations of the present and past that are informative for future projections? Are there weighting strategies that maximize predictive skill? How would one explore this? These are questions that also come up in weather forecasts, or seasonal forecasts, but are made more difficult for the climate problem because of the long timescales involved [40, 97]. Some recent work has applied machine learning to this problem with encouraging results [63].

4.4.3 Paleoreconstructions

Understanding how climate varied in the past before the onset of widespread instrumentation is of great interest—not least because the climate changes seen in the paleo-record dwarf those seen in the 20th century and hence may provide much insight into the significant changes expected this century. Paleo-data is, however, even sparser than instrumental data and, moreover, is not usually directly commensurate with the instrumental record. As mentioned in Section 4.3, paleo-proxies (such as water isotopes, tree rings, pollen counts, etc.) are indicators of climate change but often have nonclimatic influences on their behavior, or whose relation to what would be considered more standard variables (such as temperature or precipitation) is perhaps nonstationary or convolved. There is an enormous challenge in bringing together disparate, multi-proxy evidence to produce large-scale patterns of climate change [59], or from the other direction build enough "forward modeling" capability into the models to use the proxies directly as modeling targets [76]. This topic is discussed in further detail in Section 4.8.

4.4.4 Data Assimilation and Initialized Decadal Predictions

The primary way in which sparse observational data are used to construct complete fields is through data assimilation. This is a staple of weather forecasts and various reanalyses in the atmosphere and ocean. In many ways, this is the most sophisticated use of the combination of models and observations, but its use in improving *climate* predictions is still in its infancy. For weather timescales, this works well; but for longer term forecasts (seasons to decades), the key variables are in the ocean, not the atmosphere, and initializing a climate model so that the evolution of ocean variability models the real world in useful ways is very much a work in progress [44, 90]. First results have been intriguing, if not convincing, and many more examples are slated to come online in the new CMIP5 archive [61].

4.4.5 Developing and Understanding Perturbed
Physics Ensembles (PPEs)

One measure of structural uncertainty in models is the spread among the different models from different modeling groups. But these models cannot be considered a random sample from the space of all possible models. Another approach is to take a single model and, within the code, vary multiple (uncertain) parameters in order to generate a family of similar models that nonetheless sample a good deal of the intrinsic uncertainty that arises in choosing any specific set of parameter values. These "Perturbed Physics Ensembles" (PPEs) have been used successfully in the climateprediction. net and Quantifying Uncertainty in Model Predictions (QUMP) projects to generate controlled model ensembles that can be compared systematically to observed data and make inferences [46, 64]. However, designing such experiments and efficiently analyzing sometimes thousands of simulations is a challenge, but one that will increasingly be attempted.

4.5 CLIMATE DATA ANALYSIS: PROBLEMS AND APPROACHES

Here we discuss some additional challenge problems in analyzing climate data. The rate of data acquisition via satellite network and reanalyses projects is very rapid. Similarly, the amount of model output is equally fast growing. Model-observation comparisons based on processes (i.e., the multivariate changes that occur in a single event [or collection of events], such as a North Atlantic storm, an ocean eddy, an ice floe melting event, a hurricane, a jet stream excursion, a stratospheric sudden warming, etc.) have the potential to provide very useful information on model credibility, physics, and new directions for parameterization improvements. However, data services usually deliver data in single-variable, spatially fixed, time-varying formats that make it very onerous to apply space and time filters to the collection of data to extract generic instances of the process in question. As a first step, algorithms for clustering data streams will be critical for clustering and detecting the patterns listed. There will also be the need to collaborate with systems and database researchers on the data challenges mentioned here and in Section 4.11. Here we present several other problems to which cutting-edge data analysis and machine learning techniques are poised to contribute.

4.5.1 Abrupt Changes

Earth system processes form a nonlinear dynamical system and, as a result, changes in climate patterns can be abrupt at times [74]. Moreover, there is some evidence, particularly in glacial conditions, that climate tends to remain in relatively stable states for some period of time, interrupted by sporadic transitions (perhaps associated with so-called *tipping points*) that delineate different climate regimes. Understanding the causes behind significant abrupt changes in climate patterns can provide a deeper understanding of the complex interactions between Earth system processes. The first step toward realizing this goal is to have the ability to detect and identify abrupt changes from climate data.

Machine learning methods for detecting abrupt changes, such as extensive droughts that last for multiple years over a large region, should have the ability to detect changes with spatial and temporal persistence, and should be scalable to large datasets. Such methods should be able to detect well-known droughts such as the Sahel drought in Africa, the 1930s Dust Bowl in the United States, and droughts with similar characteristics where the climatic conditions were radically changed for a period of time over an extended region [23, 37, 78, 113]. A simple approach for detecting droughts is to apply a suitable threshold to a pertinent climate variable, such as precipitation or soil moisture content, and label low-precipitation regions as droughts. While such an approach will detect major events like the Sahel drought and dust bowls, it will also detect isolated events, such as low precipitation in one month for a single location that is clearly not an abrupt change event. Thus, the number of "false positives" from such a simple approach would be high, making subsequent study of each detected event difficult.

To identify drought regions that are spatially and temporally persistent, one can consider a discrete graphical model that ensures spatiotemporal smoothness of identified regions. Consider a discrete Markov Random Field (MRF) with a node corresponding to each location at each time step and a meaningful neighborhood structure that determines the edges in the underlying graph $G = (V,E)$ [111]. Each node can be in one of two states: "normal" or "drought." The maximum a posteriori (MAP) inference problem in the MRF can be posed as

$$x^* = \underset{x \in \{0,1\}^N}{\arg\max} \left\{ \sum_{x \in V} \theta_u(x_u) + \sum_{(u,v) \in E} \theta_{uv}(x_u, x_v) \right\}$$

where θ_u, θ_{uv} are node-wise and edge-wise potential functions that, respectively, encourage agreement with actual observations and agreement among neighbors; and is the state (i.e., "normal" or "drought") at node $u \in V$. The MAP inference problem is an integer programming problem often solved using a suitable linear programming (LP) relaxation [70, 111].

Figure 4.1 shows results on drought detection over the past century based on the MAP inference method. For the analysis, the Climatic Research

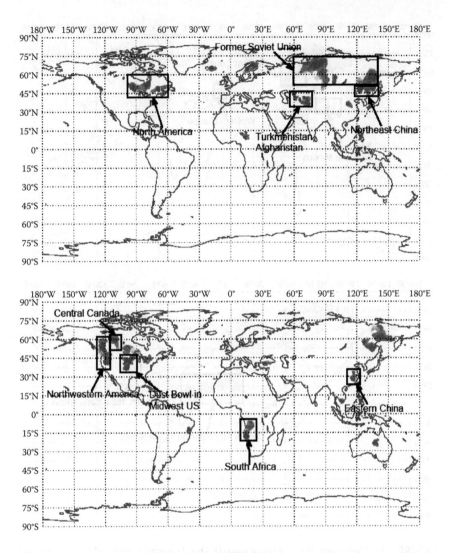

FIGURE 4.1 (*See color insert.*) The drought regions detected by our algorithm. Each panel shows the drought starting from a particular decade: 1905–1920 (top left), 1921–1930 (top right), 1941–1950 (bottom left), and 1961–1970 (bottom right). The regions in black rectangles indicate the common droughts found by [63].

Unit (CRU) precipitation dataset was used at 0.5° × 0.5° latitude-longitude spatial resolution from 1901 to 2006. The LP involved approximately 7 million variables and was solved using efficient optimization techniques. The method detected almost all well-known droughts over the past century. More generally, such a method can be used to detect and study abrupt changes for a variety of settings, including heat waves, droughts,

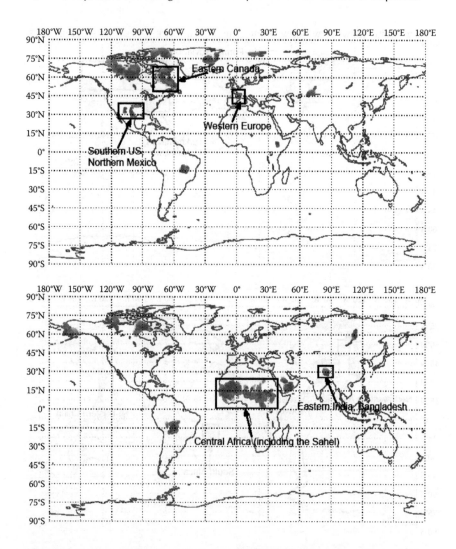

FIGURE 4.1 (*See color insert.*) (continued) The drought regions detected by our algorithm. Each panel shows the drought starting from a particular decade: 1905–1920 (top left), 1921–1930 (top right), 1941–1950 (bottom left), and 1961–1970 (bottom right). The regions in black rectangles indicate the common droughts found by [63].

precipitation, and vegetation. The analysis can be performed on observed data, reanalysis data, as well as model outputs as appropriate.

4.5.2 Climate Networks

Identifying dependencies between various climate variables and climate processes form a key part of understanding the global climate system. Such dependencies can be represented as climate networks [19, 20, 106, 107], where relevant variables or processes are represented as nodes and dependencies are captured as edges between them. Climate networks are a rich representation for the complex processes underlying the global climate system, and can be used to understand and explain observed phenomena [95, 108].

A key challenge in the context of climate networks is to construct such networks from observed climate variables. From a statistical machine learning perspective, the climate network should reflect suitable dependencies captured by the joint distribution of the variables involved. Existing methods usually focus on a suitable measure derived from the joint distribution, such as the covariance or the mutual information. From a sample-based estimate of the pairwise covariance or mutual information matrix, one obtains the climate network by suitably thresholding the estimated matrix. Such approaches have already shown great promise, often identifying some key dependencies in the global climate system [43] (Figure 4.2).

Going forward, there are a number of other computational and algorithmic challenges that must be addressed to achieve more accurate representations of the global climate system. For instance, current network construction methods do not account for the possibility of time-lagged correlations, yet we know that such relationships exist. Similarly, temporal autocorrelations and signals with varying amplitudes and phases are not explicitly handled. There is also a need for better balancing of the dominating signal of spatial autocorrelation with that of possible teleconnections (long-range dependencies across regions), which are often of high interest. In addition, there are many other processes that are well known and documented in the climate

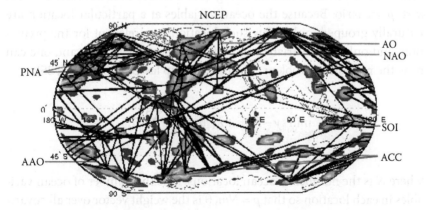

FIGURE 4.2 (*See color insert.*) Climate dipoles discovered from sea-level pressure (reanalysis) data using graph-based analysis methods (see [42] for details).

science literature, and network representations should be able to incorporate this *a priori* knowledge in a systematic manner. One of the initial motivations and advantages of these network-based approaches is their interpretability, and it will be critical that this property be retained as these various aspects are integrated into increasingly complex models and analysis methods.

4.5.3 Predictive Modeling: Mean Processes and Extremes

Predictive modeling of observed climatic phenomena can help in understanding key factors affecting a certain observed behavior. While the usual goal of predictive modeling is to achieve high accuracy for the response variable, for example, the temperature or precipitation at a given location, in the context of climate data analysis, identifying the covariates having the most significant influence on the response is often more important. Thus, in addition to getting high predictive accuracy, feature selection will be a key focus of predictive modeling. Further, one needs to differentiate between mean processes and extremes, which are rather different regimes for the response variable. In practice, different covariates may be influencing the response variable under different regimes and timescales.

In recent literature, important advances have been made in doing feature selection in the context of high-dimensional regression [66, 101]. For concreteness, consider the problem of predicting the mean temperature in Brazil based on multiple ocean variables over all ocean locations. While the number of covariates p runs into tens of thousands, the number of samples n based on monthly means over a few decades are a few hundred to a few thousand. Standard regression theory does not extend to this $n \ll p$ scenario. Because the ocean variables at a particular location are naturally grouped, only a few such locations are relevant for the prediction, and only a few variables in each such location are relevant, one can pose the regression problem as a sparse group lasso problem [24, 25]:

$$\min_{\theta \in \mathbb{R}^{Nm}} \|y - X\theta\|^2 + \lambda_1 \|\theta\|_1 + \lambda_2 \sum_{g=1}^{N} \|\theta_g\|_2$$

where N is the number of ocean locations, m is the number of ocean variables in each location so that $p = Nm$, θ is the weight vector over all covariates to be estimated, θ_g is the set of weights over variables at location g, and λ_1, λ_2 are nonnegative constants. The sparse group lasso regularizer

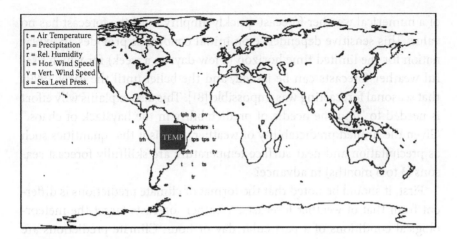

FIGURE 4.3 Temperature prediction in Brazil: Variables chosen through cross-validation.

ensures that only few locations get non-zero weights, and even among these locations, only a few variables are selected. Figure 4.3 shows the locations and features that were consistently selected for the task of temperature prediction in Brazil.

4.6 SEASONAL CLIMATE FORECASTING

Seasonal climate forecasts are those beyond the time frame of standard weather forecasts (e.g., 2 weeks) out to a season or two ahead (up to 6 months). Fundamental questions concern what is (and is not) predictable and exactly how predictable it is. Addressing these questions also often gives a good indication of how to make a prediction in practice. These are difficult questions because much in the climate system is unpredictable and the observational record is short. Methods from data mining and machine learning applied to observations and data from numerical climate prediction models provide promising approaches. Key issues include finding components of the climate state-space that are predictable, and constructing useful associations between observations and corresponding predictions from numerical models.

4.6.1 What Is the Basis for Seasonal Forecasting?

The chaotic nature of the atmosphere and the associated sensitivity of numerical weather forecasts to their initial conditions is described by the well-known "butterfly effect"—that the flap of a butterfly's wings in Brazil could set off a tornado in Texas. Small errors in the initial state of a numerical weather forecast quickly amplify until the forecast has no value. This sensitive dependence on initial conditions provides an explanation for the limited time horizon (a few days to a week) for which useful weather forecasts can be issued, and the belief until the early 1980s that seasonal forecasting was impossible [81]. This also explains why effort is needed to "find the needle of predictability in the haystack of chaos." Given the limited predictability of weather, how is it that quantities such as precipitation and near-surface temperature are skillfully forecast seasons (3 to 6 months) in advance?

First, it should be noted that the format of climate predictions is different from that of weather forecasts. Weather forecasts target the meteorological conditions of a particular day or hour. Climate predictions are made in terms of weather statistics over some time range. For instance, the most common quantities in current climate forecasts are 3-month (seasonal) averages of precipitation and near-surface temperature. Two fundamental facts about the Earth system make climate forecasts possible. First, the oceans evolve on timescales that are generally slower than those of the atmosphere, and some ocean structures are predictable several months in advance. The outstanding predictable ocean structure is associated with the El Niño–Southern Oscillation (ENSO) and is manifest in the form of widespread, persistent departures (anomalies) of equatorial Pacific sea surface temperature (SST) from its seasonally adjusted long-term value. The first ENSO forecasts were made in the late 1980s [10]. The second fact is that some components of the atmosphere respond to persistent SST anomalies. The atmospheric response to SST on any given day tends to be small relative to the usual weather variability. However, because the SST forcing and the associated atmospheric response may persist for months or seasons, the response of a seasonal average to SST forcing may be significant [82]. For instance, ENSO has impacts on temperature, precipitation, tropical cyclones, human health, and perhaps even conflict [31, 38, 49, 72]. Early seasonal forecasts constructed using canonical correlation analysis (CCA) between antecedent SST and climate responses [3] took advantage of this persistence of SST. Such statistical (or empirical, in the sense of not including explicit fundamental physical laws) forecasts remain attractive because of their generally low dimensional and cost relative to physical process-based models (typically general circulation models; GCMs) with many millions of degrees of freedom.

4.6.2 Data Challenges

Here we introduce some challenges posed by the available data. Data challenges are further discussed in Section 4.11. Serious constraints come from the dimensions of the available data. Reliable climate observations often do not extend more than 40 or 50 years into the past. This means that, for example, there may be only 40 or 50 available observations of January–March average precipitation. Moreover, the quality and completeness of that data may vary in time and space. Climate forecasts from GCMs often do not even cover this limited period. Many seasonal climate forecast systems started hindcasts in the early 1980s when satellite observations, particularly of SST, became available. In contrast to the sample size, the dimension of the GCM state-space may be of the order 10^6, depending on spatial grid resolution. Dimension reduction (principal component analysis [PCA] is commonly used) is necessary before applying classical methods like canonical correlation analysis to find associated features in predictions and observations [5]. There has been some use of more sophisticated dimensionality reduction methods in seasonal climate prediction problems [53]. Methods that can handle large state-spaces and small sample size are needed. An intriguing recent approach that avoids the problem of small sample size is to estimate statistical models using long climate simulations unconstrained by observations and test the resulting model on observations [18, 115]. This approach has the challenge of selecting GCMs whose climate variability is "realistic," which is a remarkably difficult problem given the observational record.

4.6.3 Identifying Predictable Quantities

The initial success of climate forecasting has been in the prediction of seasonal averages of quantities such as precipitation and near-surface temperature. In this case, time averaging serves as a filter with which to find predictable signals. A spatial average of SST in a region of the equatorial Pacific is used to define the NINO3.4 index, which is used in ENSO forecasts and observational analysis. This spatial average serves to enhance the large-scale predictable ENSO signal by reducing noise. The Madden-Julian Oscillation (MJO) is a sub-seasonal component of climate variability that is detected using time and space filtering. There has been some work on constructing spatial filters that were designed to optimize measures of predictability [17] and there are opportunities for new methods that incorporate optimal time and space filtering and that optimize more general measures of predictability.

While predicting the weather of an individual day is not possible in a seasonal forecast, it may be possible to forecast statistics of weather such as the frequency of dry days or the frequency of consecutive dry days. These quantities are often more important to agriculture than seasonal totals. Drought has a complex time-space structure that depends on multiple meteorological variables. Data mining and machine learning (DM/ML) methods can be applied to observations and forecasts to identify drought, as discussed in Section 4.5.

Identification of previously unknown predictable climate features may benefit from the use of DM/ML methods. Cluster analysis of tropical cyclone tracks has been used to identify features that are associated with ENSO and MJO variability [9]. Graphical models, the nonhomogeneous Hidden Markov Model in particular, have been used to obtain stochastic daily sequences of rainfall conditioned on GCM seasonal forecasts [32].

The time and space resolution of GCM forecasts limits the physical phenomena they can resolve. However, they may be able to predict proxies or large-scale antecedents of relevant phenomena. For instance, GCMs that do not resolve tropical cyclones (TCs) completely do form TC-like structures that can be used to make TC seasonal forecasts [8, 110]. Identifying and associating GCMs "proxies" with observed phenomena is also a DM/ML problem.

Regression methods are used to connect climate quantities to associated variables that are either unresolved by GCMs or not even climate variables. For instance, Poisson regression is used to relate large-scale climate quantities with hurricanes [104], and generalized additive models are used to relate heat waves with increased mortality [68]. Again, the length of the observational record makes this challenging.

4.6.4 Making the Best Use of GCM Data

Data from multiple GCM climate forecasts are routinely available. However, converting that data into a useful forecast product is a nontrivial task. GCMs have systematic errors that can be identified (and potentially corrected) through regression-like procedures with observations. Robust estimates of uncertainty are needed to construct probabilistic forecasts. Because forecasts are available from multiple GCMs, another question is how best to combine information from multiple sources, given the relatively short observation records with which to estimate model performance.

4.7 CLIMATE EXTREMES, UNCERTAINTY, AND IMPACTS

4.7.1 The Climate Change Challenge

The Fourth Assessment Report of the Intergovernmental Panel on Climate Change (IPCC, AR4) has resulted in wider acceptance of global climate change caused by anthropogenic drivers of emission scenarios. However, earth system modelers struggle to develop precise predictions of extreme events (e.g., heat waves, cold spells, extreme rainfall events, droughts, hurricanes, and tropical storms) or extreme stresses (e.g., tropical climate in temperate regions or shifting rainfall patterns) at regional and decadal scales. In addition, the most significant knowledge gap relevant for policy makers and stakeholders remains the inability to produce credible estimates of local-to-regional scale climate extremes and change impacts. Uncertainties in process studies, climate models, and associated spatiotemporal downscaling strategies may be assessed and reduced by statistical evaluations. But a similar treatment for extreme hydrological and meteorological events may require novel statistical approaches and improved downscaling. Scenario uncertainty for climate change impacts is fundamentally intractable, but other sources of uncertainty may be amenable to reduction. Regional impacts need to account for additional uncertainties in the estimates of anticipatory risks and damages, whether on the environment, infrastructures, economy, or society. The cascading uncertainties from scenarios, to models, to downscaling, and finally to impacts, make costly decisions difficult to assess. This problem grows acute if credible attributions must be made to causal drivers or policy impacts.

4.7.2 The Science of Climate Extremes

One goal is to develop quantifiable insights on the impacts of global climate change on weather or hydrological extreme stresses and extreme events at regional to decadal scales. Precise and local predictions, for example, the likelihood of an extreme event on a given day of any given year a decade later, will never be achievable, owing to the chaotic nature of the climate system as well as the limits to precision of measurements and our inability to model all aspects of the process physics. However, probability density functions of the weather and hydrology, for example, likelihoods of intensity-duration-frequency (IDF) of extreme events or of mean change leading to extreme stress, may be achievable targets. The tools of choice range from the two traditional pillars of science: theory (e.g., advances in physical understanding and high-resolution process models of atmospheric or oceanic climate, weather, or hydrology) to experimentation (e.g., development of remote and *in-situ* sensor systems as well as related cyber-infrastructures to monitor the Earth and environmental systems). However, perhaps the most significant breakthroughs are expected from the relatively new pillars: computational sciences and informatics. Research in the computational sciences for climate extremes science include the computational data sciences (e.g., high-performance analytics based on extreme value theory and nonlinear data sciences to develop predictive insights based on a combination of observations and climate model simulations) and computational modeling (e.g., regional scale climate models, models of hydrology, improvements in high-resolution processes within general circulation models, as well as feedback to model development based on comparisons of simulations with observations), while the informatics aspects include data management and discovery (e.g., development of methodologies for geographic data integration and management, knowledge discovery from sensor data, and geospatial-temporal uncertainty quantification).

4.7.3 The Science of Climate Impacts

The study of climate extremes is inextricably linked to the study of impacts, including risks and damage assessments as well as adaptation and mitigation strategies. Thus, an abnormally hot summer or high occurrence of hurricanes in unpopulated or remote regions of the world, which do not otherwise affect resources or infrastructures, have little or no climate impact on society. On the other hand, extreme events such as the aftereffects of Hurricane Katrina have extreme impacts owing to complex interactions among multiple effects: a large hurricane hitting an urban area, an already vulnerable levee breaking down because of the flood waters, as well as an impacted society and response systems that are neither robust nor resilient to shocks. In general, climate change mitigation (e.g., emission policies and regulations to possible weather modification and geoengineering strategies) and adaptation (e.g., hazards and disaster preparedness, early warning and humanitarian assistance or the management of natural water, nutritional and other resources, as well as possible migration and changes in regional population growth or demographics) must be based on actionable predictive insights that consider the interaction of climate extremes science with the critical infrastructures and key resources, population, and society. While the science of impacts can be challenging and relatively difficult to quantify, given recent advances in machine learning, geospatial modeling, data fusion, and Geographic Information Systems (GIS), this is a fertile area for progress on climate informatics.

4.8 RECONSTRUCTING PAST CLIMATE

The most comprehensive observations of Earth's climate span only the past one to two hundred years [105]. This time period includes the establishment of long-term and widespread meteorological stations across the continental landmasses [6], ocean observing networks from ships and buoys [114] and, within the more recent past, remote sensing from satellites [109]. Much of our understanding about the climate system and contemporary climate change comes from these and related observations and their fundamental role in evaluating theories and models of the climate system. Despite the valuable collection of modern observations, however, two factors limit their use as a description of the Earth's climate and its variability: (1) relative to known timescales of climate variability, they span a brief period of time; and (2) much of the modern observational interval is during an emergent and anomalous climate response to anthropogenic emissions of greenhouse gases [36]. Both of these factors limit assessments of climate variability on multi-decadal and longer timescales, or characterizations of climatic mean states under different forcing[*] scenarios (e.g., orbital configurations or greenhouse gas concentrations). Efforts to estimate climate variability and mean states prior to the instrumental period are thus necessary to fully characterize how the climate can change and how it might evolve in the future in response to increasing greenhouse gas emissions.

Paleoclimatology is the study of Earth's climate history and offers estimates of climate variability and change over a range of timescales and climate regimes. Among the many time periods of relevance, the Common Era (CE; the past two millennia) is an important target because the abundance of high-resolution paleoclimatic proxies (e.g., tree rings, ice cores, cave deposits, corals, and lake sediments) over this time interval allows seasonal-to-annual reconstructions on regional-to-global spatial

---

[*] A "forcing" is a specific driver of climate change, external to the climate models—for instance, changes in the composition of well-mixed greenhouse gases (e.g., CO_2 or CH_4), changes in the land surface due to deforestation or urbanization, changes in air pollution, changes in the sun's input, or the impact of large volcanic eruptions. Each forcing can be usefully characterized by the impact it has on the radiative balance at the top of the atmosphere: positive forcings increase the energy coming into the climate system and hence warm the planet, while negative forcings cool the climate.

scales [40]. The CE also spans the rise and fall of many human civilizations, making paleoclimatic information during this time period important for understanding the complicated relationships between climate and organized societies [7, 15].

Given the broad utility and vast number of proxy systems that are involved, the study of CE climate is a wide-ranging and diverse enterprise. The purpose of the following discussion is not meant to survey this field as a whole, but instead to focus on a relatively recent pursuit in CE paleoclimatology that seeks to reconstruct global or hemispheric temperatures using syntheses of globally distributed multi-proxy networks. This particular problem is one that may lend itself well to new and emerging data analysis techniques, including machine learning and data mining methods. The motivation of the following discussion therefore is to outline the basic reconstruction problem and describe how methods are tested in synthetic experiments.

4.8.1 The Global Temperature Reconstruction Problem

It is common to separate global or hemispheric (large-scale) temperature reconstruction methods into two categories. The first involves index methods that target large-scale indices such as hemispheric mean temperatures [13, 35, 51, 58]; the second comprises climate field reconstruction (CFR) methods that target large-scale patterns, that is, global maps of temperature change [21, 55, 56, 59, 88]. Although both of these approaches often share common methodological foundations, the following discussion focuses principally on the CFR problem.

Large-scale temperature CFRs rely on two primary data sets. The first is monthly or annual gridded (5° latitude × 5° longitude) temperature products that have near-global coverage beginning in the mid-to-late 19th century. These gridded temperature fields have been derived from analyses of land- and sea-based surface temperature measurements from meteorological stations, and ship- and buoy-based observing networks [6, 42]. The second dataset comprises collections of multiple climate proxy archives [58], each of which has been independently analyzed to establish their sensitivity to some aspect of local or regional climate variability. These proxy records are distributed heterogeneously about the globe (Figure 4.4), span variable periods of time, and each is subject to proxy-specific errors and uncertainties.

The basic premise of CFR techniques is that a relationship can be determined between observed climate fields and multi-proxy networks during

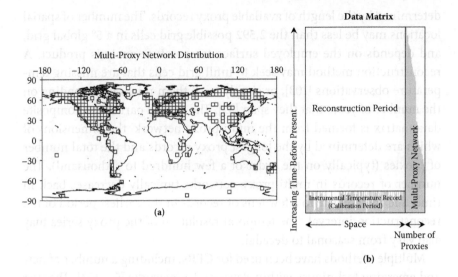

FIGURE 4.4 (a) Representation of the global distribution of the most up-to-date global multi-proxy network used by Mann et al. [58]. Grey squares indicate the 5° grid cells that contain at least one proxy in the unscreened network from ref. [58]. (b) Schematic of the data matrix for temperature field reconstructions spanning all or part of the CE. Grey regions in the data matrix are schematic representations of data availability in the instrumental temperature field and the multi-proxy matrix. White regions indicate missing data in the various sections of the data matrix.

their common interval of overlap. Once defined, this relationship can be used to estimate the climate fields prior to their direct measurement using the multi-proxy network that extends further into the past. Figure 4.4 represents this concept schematically using a data matrix that casts the CFR formalism as a missing data problem. Note that this missing data approach was originally proposed for CFRs using regularized expectation maximization [77], and has since become a common method for reconstructions targeting the CE [56, 57, 59]. The time-by-space data matrix in Figure 4.4 is constructed first from the instrumental data, with rows corresponding to years and columns corresponding to the number of grid cells in the instrumental field. For a typical CFR targeting an annual and global 5° × 5° temperature field, the time dimension is several centuries to multiple millennia, and the space dimension is on the order of one to two thousand grid cells. The time dimension of the data matrix is determined by the length of the calibration interval during which time the temperature observations are available, plus the reconstruction interval that is determined by the length of available proxy records. The number of spatial locations may be less than the 2,592 possible grid cells in a 5° global grid, and depends on the employed surface temperature analysis product. A reconstruction method may seek to infill grid cells that are missing temperature observations [103], or simply leave them missing, depending on the number of years that they span [59]. The second part of the composite data matrix is formed from the multi-proxy network, the dimensions of which are determined by the longest proxy records and the total number of proxies (typically on the order of a few hundred to a thousand). The number of records in multi-proxy networks typically decreases back in time, and may reduce to a few tens of records in the earliest period of the reconstruction interval. The temporal resolution of the proxy series may also vary from seasonal to decadal.

Multiple methods have been used for CFRs, including a number of new and emerging techniques within Bayesian frameworks [52, 103]. The vast majority of CFRs to date, however, have applied forms of regularized, multivariate linear regression, in which a linear regression operator is estimated during a period of overlap between the temperature and proxy matrices. Such linear regression approaches work best when the time dimension in the calibration interval (Figure 4.4) is much larger than the spatial dimension, because the covariance between the temperature field and the proxies is more reliably estimated. The challenge for CFR methods involves the manner in which the linear regression operator is estimated in practical situations when this condition is not met. It is often the case in CFR applications that the number of target variables exceeds the time dimension, yielding a rank-deficient problem. The linear regression formalism therefore requires some form of regularization. Published linear methods for global temperature CFRs vary primarily in their adopted form of regularization (see [88, 102] for general discussions on the methodological formalism). Matrix factorizations such as Singular Value Decomposition [29] of the temperature and proxy matrices are common first steps. If the squared singular values decrease quickly, as is often the case in climatological data where leading climate patterns dominate over many more weakly expressed local patterns or noise, reduced-rank representations of the temperature and proxy matrices are typically good approximations of the full-rank versions of the matrices. These reduced-rank temperature and proxy matrices therefore are used to estimate a linear regression operator during the calibration interval using various multivariate regression techniques. Depending on the method used, this regression operator may be further regularized based on analyses of the cross-covariance or correlation of the reduced temperature and proxy matrices. Multiple means of selecting rank reductions at each of these steps have been pursued, such as selection rules based on analyses of the singular value (or eigenvalue) spectrum [57] or minimization of cross-validation statistics calculated for the full range of possible rank-reduction combinations [88].

4.8.2 Pseudoproxy Experiments

The literature is replete with discussions of the variously applied CFR methods and their performance (see [29] for a cogent summary of many employed methods). Given this large number of proposed approaches, it has become important to establish means of comparing methods using common datasets. An emerging tool for such comparisons is millennium-length, forced transient simulations from Coupled General Circulation Models (CGCMs) [1, 30]. These model simulations have been used as synthetic climates in which to evaluate the performance of reconstruction methods in tests that have been termed pseudoproxy experiments (see [85] for a review). The motivation for pseudoproxy experiments is to adopt a common framework that can be systematically altered and evaluated. They also provide a much longer, albeit synthetic, validation period than can be achieved with real-world data, and thus methodological evaluations can extend to lower frequencies and longer timescales. Although one must always be mindful of how the results translate into real-world implications, these design attributes allow researchers to test reconstruction techniques beyond what was previously possible and to compare multiple methods on common datasets.

The basic approach of a pseudoproxy experiment is to extract a portion of a spatiotemporally complete CGCM field in a way that mimics the available proxy and instrumental data used in real-world reconstructions. The principal experimental steps proceed as follows: (1) pseudoinstrumental and pseudoproxy data are subsampled from the complete CGCM field from locations and over temporal periods that approximate their real-world data availability; (2) the time series that represent proxy information are added to noise series to simulate the temporal (and in some cases spatial) noise characteristics that are present in real-world proxy networks; and (3) reconstruction algorithms are applied to the model-sampled pseudo-instrumental data and pseudoproxy network to produce a reconstruction of the climate simulated by the CGCM. The culminating fourth step is to compare the derived reconstruction to the known model target as a means of evaluating the skill of the applied method and the uncertainties expected to accompany a real-world reconstruction product. Multi-method comparisons can also be undertaken from this point.

Multiple datasets are publicly available for pseudoproxy experiments through supplemental Websites of published papers [57, 87, 89, 103]. The Paleoclimate Reconstruction Challenge is also a newly established online portal through the Paleoclimatology Division of the National Oceanographic and Atmospheric Administration that provides additional pseudoproxy datasets.* This collection of common datasets is an important resource for researchers wishing to propose new methodological applications for CFRs, and is an excellent starting point for these investigations.

4.8.3 Climate Reconstructions and the Future

More than a decade of research on deriving large-scale temperature reconstructions of the CE has yielded many insights into our past climate and established the utility of such efforts as a guide to the future. Important CFR improvements are nevertheless still necessary and leave open the potential for new analysis methods to have significant impacts on the field. Broad assessments of the multivariate linear regression framework have shown the potential for variance losses and mean biases in reconstructions on hemispheric scales [13, 51, 86], although some methods have demonstrated significant skill for reconstructions of hemispheric and global indices [57]. The spatial skill of CFRs, however, has been shown in pseudoproxy experiments to vary widely, with some regions showing significant errors [89]. Establishing methods with improved spatial skill is therefore an important target for alternative CFR approaches. It also is critical to establish rigorous uncertainty estimates for derived reconstructions by incorporating a more comprehensive characterization of known errors into the reconstruction problem. Bayesian and ensemble approaches lend themselves well to this task and constitute another open area of pursuit for new methodological applications. Process-based characterizations of the connection between climate and proxy responses also are becoming more widely established [2, 22, 76, 100]. These developments make it possible to incorporate physically based forward models as constraints on CFR problems and further open the possibility of methodological advancement. Recent Bayesian studies have provided the groundwork

---

* http://www.ncdc.noaa.gov/paleo/pubs/pr-challenge/pr-challenge.html.

for such approaches [52, 103], while paleoclimatic assimilation techniques have also shown promise [112].

In the context of machine learning, the problem of reconstructing parts of a missing data matrix has been widely studied as the matrix completion problem (see Figure 4.4). A popular example of the problem is encountered in movie recommendation systems, in which each user of a given system rates a few movies out of tens of thousands of available titles. The system subsequently predicts a tentative user rating for all possible movies, and ultimately displays the ones that the user might like. Unlike traditional missing value imputation problems where a few entries in a given data matrix are missing, in the context of matrix completion, one works with mostly missing entries (e.g., in movie recommendation systems, 99% or more of the matrix is typically missing). Low-rank matrix factorization methods have been shown to be quite successful in such matrix completion problems [48, 73]. Further explorations of matrix completion methods for the paleoclimate reconstruction problem therefore are fully warranted. This includes investigations into the applicability of existing methods, such as probabilistic matrix factorization [73] or low-rank and sparse decompositions [114], as well as explorations of new methods that take into account aspects specific to the paleoclimate reconstruction. Methods that can perform completions along with a confidence score are more desirable because uncertainty quantification is an important desideratum for paleoclimate.

Finally, it is important to return to the fact that extensive methodological work in the field of CE paleoclimatology is aimed, in part, at better constraining natural climate variability on decadal-to-centennial timescales. This timescale of variability, in addition to expected forced changes, will be the other key contribution to observed climate during the 21st century. Whether we are seeking improved decadal predictions [93] or refined projections of 20th century regional climate impacts [28], these estimates must incorporate estimates of both forced and natural variability. It therefore is imperative that we fully understand how the climate naturally varies across a range of relevant timescales, how it changes when forced, and how these two components of change may couple together. This understanding cannot be achieved from the modern instrumental record alone, and the CE is a strategic paleoclimate target because it provides both reconstructions with high temporal and spatial resolution and an interval over which CGCM simulations are also feasible. Combining these two sources of information to assess model projections of future climate therefore is itself an important future area of discovery. Analyses that incorporate both the uncertainties in paleoclimatic estimates and the ensemble results of multiple model simulations will be essential for these assessments and is likely a key component of climate informatics as the field evolves into the future.

4.9 APPLICATIONS TO PROBLEMS IN POLAR REGIONS

Another potential application of machine learning concerns the impact of climate change at the poles and the interaction between the poles and climate in general. Because of the difficulty in collecting data from polar regions, the relatively expensive costs, and logistics, it is important to maximize the potential benefit deriving from the data. The paucity of surface-measured data is complemented by the richness and increasing volume of either satellite/airborne data and model outputs. In this regard, powerful tools are needed—not only to analyze, manipulate, and visualize large datasets, but also to search and discover new information from different sources—in order to exploit relationships between data and processes that are not evident or captured by physical models.

The number of applications of machine learning to study polar regions is not high although it has been increasing over the past decade. This is especially true in those cases when data collected from spaceborne sensors are considered. For example, Tedesco and colleagues [98, 99] use artificial neural networks (ANNs) or genetic algorithms to estimate snow parameters from spaceborne microwave observations. Soh and Tsatsoulis [91] use an Automated Sea Ice Segmentation (ASIS) system that automatically segments Synthetic Aperture Radar (SAR) sea ice imagery by integrating image processing, data mining, and machine learning methodologies. The system is further developed by Soh et al. [92], where an intelligent system for satellite sea ice image analysis called Advanced Reasoning using Knowledge for Typing Of Sea ice (ARKTOS) "mimicking the reasoning process of sea ice experts" is presented. Lu and Leen [54] use semi-supervised learning to separate snow and non-snow areas over Greenland using a multispectral approach. Reusch [71] applies tools from the field of ANNs to reconstruct centennial-scale records of West Antarctic sea-ice variability using ice-core datasets from 18 West Antarctic sites and satellite-based records of sea ice. ANNs are used as a nonlinear tool to ice-core predictors to sea-ice targets such as sea salt chemistry to sea ice edge. One of the results from this study is that, in general, reconstructions are quite sensitive to predictor used, and not all predictors appear to be useful. Finally, Gifford [27] shows a detailed study of team learning, collaboration, and decision applied to ice-penetrating radar data collected in Greenland in May 1999 and September 2007 as part of a model-creation effort for subglacial water presence classification.

The above-mentioned examples represent a few cases where machine learning tools have been applied to problems focusing on studying the polar regions. Although the number of studies appears to be increasing, likely because of both the increased research focusing on climate change and the poles and the increased computational power allowing machine learning tools to expand in their usage, they are still relatively rare compared to simpler but often less efficient techniques.

Machine learning and data mining can be used to enhance the value of the data by exposing information that would not be apparent from single-dataset analyses. For example, identifying the link between diminishing sea ice extent and increasing melting in Greenland can be done through physical models attempting to model the connections between the two through the exchange of atmospheric fluxes. However, large-scale connections (or others at different temporal and spatial scales) might be revealed through the use of data-driven models or, in a more sophisticated fashion, through the combination of both physical and data-driven models. Such an approach would, among other things, overcome the limitation of the physical models that, even if they represent the state-of-the-art in the corresponding fields, are limited by our knowledge and understanding of the physical processes. ANNs can also be used in understanding not only the connections among multiple parameters (through the analysis of the neurons connections), but also to understand potential temporal shifts in the importance of parameters on the overall process (e.g., increased importance of albedo due to the exposure of bare ice and reduced solid precipitation in Greenland over the past few years). Applications are not limited to a pure scientific analysis but also include the management of information, error analysis, missing linkages between databases, and improving data acquisition procedures.

In synthesis, there are many areas in which machine learning can support studies of the poles within the context of climate and climate change. These include climate model parameterizations and multimodel ensembles of projections for variables such as sea ice extent, melting in Greenland, and sea-level rise contribution, in addition to those discussed in previous sections.

4.10 TOWARD A CLIMATE INFORMATICS TOOLBOX

Recent additions to the toolbox of modern machine learning have considerable potential to contribute to and greatly improve the prediction and inference capability for climate science. Climate prediction has significant challenges, including high dimensionality, multiscale behavior, uncertainty, and strong nonlinearity, and also benefits from having historical data and physics-based models. It is imperative that we bring all available, relevant tools to bear on the climate arena. In addition to the methods cited in Section 4.2 and in subsequent sections, here we briefly describe several other methods (some proposed recently) that one might consider to apply to problems in climate science.

We begin with CalTech and Los Alamos National Laboratory's recently developed Optimal Uncertainty Quantification (OUQ) formalism [67, 79]. OUQ is a rigorous, yet practical, approach to uncertainty quantification that provides optimal bounds on uncertainties for a given, stated set of assumptions. For example, OUQ can provide a guarantee that the probability that a physical variable exceeds a cutoff is less than some value ϵ. This method has been successfully applied to assess the safety of truss structures to seismic activity. In particular, OUQ can provide the maximum and minimum values of the probability of failure of a structure as a function of earthquake magnitude. These probabilities are calculated by solving an optimization problem that is determined by the assumptions in the problem. As input, OUQ requires a detailed specification of assumptions. One form of assumption may be (historical) data. The method's potential for practical use resides in a reduction from an infinite-dimensional, nonconvex optimization problem to a finite- (typically low) dimensional one. For a given set of assumptions, the OUQ method returns one of three answers: (1) Yes, the structure will withstand the earthquake with probability greater than p; (2) No, it will not withstand it with probability p; or (3) Given the input, one cannot conclude either (i.e., undetermined). In the undetermined case, more/different data/assumptions are then required to say something definite. Climate models are typically infinite-dimensional dynamical systems, and a given set of assumptions will reduce this to a finite-dimensional problem. The OUQ approach could address such questions as whether (given a potential scenario) the global mean temperature increase will exceed some threshold T, with some probability ϵ.

To improve the performance (e.g., reduce the generalization error) in statistical learning problems, it sometimes helps to incorporate domain knowledge. This approach is particularly beneficial when there is limited data from which to learn, as is often the case in high-dimensional problems (genomics is another example). This general philosophy is described in a number of approaches such as learning with side information, Universum Learning [84], and learning from non-examples [83]. Learning with the Universum and learning from non-examples involve augmenting the available data with related examples from the same problem domain, but not necessarily from the same distribution. Quite often, the generalization error for predictions can be shown to be smaller for carefully chosen augmented data, but this is a relatively uncharted field of research and it is not yet known how to use this optimally. One can imagine using an ensemble of climate models in conjunction with data from model simulations to improve predictive capacity. How to optimally select Universum or non-examples is an open problem.

Domain knowledge in the form of competing models provides the basis of a game-theoretic approach of model selection [11]. This relates to recent work in applying algorithms for online learning with experts to combining the predictions of the multimodel ensemble of GCMs [63]. On historical data, this online learning algorithm's average prediction loss nearly matched that of the best performing climate model. Moreover, the performance of the algorithm surpassed that of the average model prediction, which is a common state-of-the-art method in climate science. A major advantage of these approaches, as well as game-theoretic formulations, is their robustness, including the lack of assumptions regarding linearity and noise. However, because future observations are missing, algorithms for unsupervised or semi-supervised learning with experts should be developed and explored.

Conformal prediction is a recently developed framework for learning based on the theory of algorithmic randomness. The strength of conformal prediction is that it allows one to quantify the confidence in a prediction [80]. Moreover, the reliability of the prediction is never overestimated. This is, of course, very important in climate prediction. To apply the suite of tools from conformal prediction, however, one needs to have iid (independent, identically distributed) or exchangeable data. While this is a serious restriction, one can imagine using iid computer simulations and checking for robustness. Conformal prediction is fairly easy to use and can be implemented as a simple wrapper to existing classifiers or regression algorithms. Conformal prediction has been applied successfully in genomics and medical diagnoses. It is likely worthwhile to apply conformal prediction to other complex problems in computational science.

Statistical Relational Learning [26] offers a natural framework for inference in climate. Included within this set of methods are graphical models [47], a flexible and powerful formalism with which to carry out inference for large, highly complex systems (some of which were discussed in Sections 4.5 and 4.6). At one extreme, graphical models can be derived solely from data. At the other extreme, graphical models provide a generalization of Kalman filters or smoothers, where data are integrated with a model. This general approach is quite powerful but requires efficient computation of conditional probabilities. As a result, one might explore how to adapt or extend the current suite of belief propagation methods to climate-specific problems.

Finally, for all of the above methods, it would be helpful if the learning algorithm could automatically determine which information or data it would be useful to get next. The "optimal learning" formalism addresses this question [69]. This gradient learning approach can be applied to a whole host of problems for learning where one has limited resources to allocate for information gathering. Optimal learning has been applied successfully to experiment design, in particular in the pharmaceutical industry, where it has the potential to reduce the cost (financial, time, etc.) of the drug discovery process. Optimal learning might be applied to climate science in order to guide the next set of observations and/or the next simulations.

To conclude, there is a suite of recently developed machine learning methods whose applicability and usefulness in climate science should be explored. At this point, we have only begun to scratch the surface. If these methods prove successful in climate studies, we would expect them to apply elsewhere—where one has a model of the physical system and can access data.

4.11 DATA CHALLENGES AND OPPORTUNITIES IN CLIMATE INFORMATICS

Here we discuss additional challenges and important issues in analyzing climate data.

4.11.1 Issues with Cross-Class Comparisons

There is often a need to compare across different classes of data, whether to provide ground truth for a satellite retrieval or to evaluate a climate model prediction or to calibrate a proxy measurement. But because of the different characteristics of the data, comparing "apples to apples" can be difficult.

One of the recurring issues is the difference between internal variability (or weather) and climate responses tied to a specific external forcing. The internal variability is a function of the chaotic dynamics in the atmosphere and cannot be predicted over time periods longer than 10 days or so (see Section 4.6). This variability, which can exist on all timescales, exists also in climate models; but because of the sensitive dependence on initial conditions, any unique simulation will have a different realization of the internal variability. Climate changes are then effectively defined as the ensemble mean response (i.e., after averaging out any internal variability). Thus, any single realization (such as the real-world record) must be thought of as a forced signal (driven by external drivers) combined with a stochastic weather component.

The internal variability increases in relative magnitude as a function of decreasing time or spatial scale. Thus, comparisons of the specific time evolution of the climate system need to either take the variability into account or use specific techniques to minimize the difference from the real world. For instance, "nudged" simulations use observed winds from the reanalyses to keep the weather in the model loosely tied to the observations. Simulations using the observed ocean temperatures as a boundary condition can do a good job of synchronizing the impacts of variability in the ocean on the atmospheric fields. Another way to minimize the impact of internal variability is to look for property-to-property correlations to focus on specific processes that, although they may occur at different points in time or space, can nonetheless be compared across models and observations.

Another issue is that model output does not necessarily represent exact topography or conditions related to an *in-situ* observation. The average height of a specific grid box might not correspond to the height of a mountain-based observing platform, or the resolved shape of the coastline might make a difference of 200 kilometers or so in the distance of a station to the shore. These issues can be alleviated to some extent if comparisons focus on large-scale gridded data. Another technique is to "downscale" the model output to specific locations, either statistically (based on observed correlations of a local record to larger-scale features of the circulation) or dynamically (using an embedded RCM). These methods have the potential to correct for biases in the large-scale model, but many practical issues remain in assessing by how much.

Finally, observations are a function of a specific observing methodology that encompasses technology, practice, and opportunity. These factors can impart a bias or skewness to the observation relative to what the real world may nominally be doing. Examples in satellite remote sensing are common—for example, a low cloud record from a satellite will only be able to see low clouds when there are no high clouds. Similarly, a satellite record of "mid-tropospheric" temperatures might actually be a weighted integral of temperatures from the surface to the stratosphere. A paleo-climate record may be of a quantity that while related to temperature or precipitation, may be a complex function of both, weighted towards a specific season. In all these cases, it is often advisable to create a 'forward model' of the observational process itself to post-process the raw simulation output to create more commensurate diagnostics.

4.11.2 Climate System Complexity

A further issue arises in creating statistical models of the climate system because both the real world and dynamical models have a large number of different physical variables.

Even simplified models can have hundreds of variables, and while not all of them are essential to determining the state of the system, one variable is frequently not sufficient. Land, atmosphere, and ocean processes all have different dominant timescales, and thus different components are essential at different scales. Some physical understanding is thus necessary to make the proper variable/data choices, even with analysis schemes that extract structure from large datasets. Furthermore, these systems are chaotic, that is, initial conditions that are practically indistinguishable from each other in any given observing system will diverge greatly from each other on some short timescale. Thus, extracting useful predictions requires more than creating more accurate models—one needs to determine which aspects are predictable and which are not.

4.11.3 Challenge: Cloud-Computing-Based Reproducible
Climate Data Analysis

The study of science requires reproducible results: science is a body of work where the community strives to ensure that results are not from the unique abilities and circumstances of one particular person or group. Traditionally, this has been done in large part by publishing papers, but the scale of modern climate modeling and data analysis efforts has far outstripped the ability of a journal article to convey enough information to allow reproducibility. This is an issue both of size and of complexity: model results are much larger than can be conveyed in a few pages, and both models and analysis procedures are too complex to be adequately described in a few pages.

The sheer size of GCMs and satellite datasets is also outstripping our traditional data storage and distribution methods: frequently, only a few variables from a model's output are saved and distributed at high resolution, and the remaining model output is heavily averaged to generate datasets that are sufficiently small.

One promising approach to addressing these problems is cloud-computing-based reproducible climate data analysis. Having both the data and the analyses resident in the computational cloud allows the details of the computation to be hidden from the user; so, for example, data-intensive portions of the computation could be executed close to where the data resides. But these analyses must be reproducible, which brings not only technical challenges of archiving and finding, describing, and publishing analysis procedures, but also institutional challenges of ensuring that the large datasets that form the basis of these analyses remain accessible.

4.11.3.1 Data Scale

The size of datasets is rapidly outstripping the ability to store and serve the data. We have difficulty storing even a single copy of the complete archive of the CMIP3 model results, and making complete copies of those results and distributing them for analysis becomes both a large undertaking and limits the analysis to the few places that have data storage facilities of that scale. Analysis done by the host prior to distribution, such as averaging, reduces the size to something more manageable, but currently those reductions are chosen far in advance, and there are many other useful analyses that are not currently being done.

A cloud-based analysis framework would allow such reductions to be chosen and still executed on machines with fast access to the data.

4.11.3.2 Reproducibility and Provenance Graphs

A cloud-based analysis framework would have to generate reproducible documented results; that is, we would not only need the ability to rerun a calculation and know that it would generate the same results, but also know precisely what analysis had been done. This could be achieved, in part, by having standardized analysis schemes, so that one could be sure precisely what was calculated in a given data filter, and also important is systematically tracking the full provenance of the calculation. This *provenance graph*, showing the full network of data filters and initial, intermediate, and final results, would provide the basis of both reproducibility and communication of results. Provenance graphs provide the information necessary to rerun a calculation and get the same results; they also provide the basis of the full documentation of the results. This full network would need to have layers of abstraction so that the user could start with an overall picture and then proceed to more detailed versions as needed.

4.12 CONCLUSION

The goal of this chapter is to inspire future work in the nascent field of climate informatics. We hope to encourage work not only on some of the challenge problems proposed here, but also on new problems. A profuse amount of climate data of various types is available, providing a rich and fertile playground for future machine learning and data mining research. Even exploratory data analysis could prove useful for accelerating discovery. To that end, we have prepared a climate informatics wiki as a result of the *First International Workshop on Climate Informatics*, which includes climate data links with descriptions, challenge problems, and tutorials on machine learning techniques [14]. We are confident that there are myriad collaborations possible at the intersection of climate science and machine learning, data mining, and statistics. We hope our work will encourage progress on a range of emerging problems in climate informatics.

ACKNOWLEDGMENTS

The First International Workshop on Climate Informatics (2011) served as an inspiration for this chapter, and some of these topics were discussed there. The workshop sponsors included Lamont-Doherty Earth Observatory (LDEO)/Goddard Institute for Space Studies (GISS) Climate Center, Columbia University; Information Science and Technology Center, Los Alamos National Laboratory; NEC Laboratories America, Department of Statistics, Columbia University; Yahoo! Labs; and The New York Academy of Sciences.

KS was supported in part by National Science Foundation (NSF) Grant 1029711. MKT and MBB are supported by a grant/cooperative agreement from the National Oceanic and Atmospheric Administration (NOAA. NA05OAR4311004). The views expressed herein are those of the authors and do not necessarily reflect the views of NOAA or any of its subagencies. AB was supported, in part, by NSF grants IIS-1029711, IIS-0916750, and IIS-0812183, and NSF CAREER award IIS-0953274. ARG's research reported here has been financially supported by the Oak Ridge National Laboratory and Northeastern University grants, as well as the National Science Foundation award 1029166, in addition to funding from the U.S. Department of Energy and the Department of Science and Technology of the Government of India. The work of JES was supported in part by NSF grant ATM0902436 and by NOAA grants NA07OAR4310060 and NA10OAR4320137. MT would like to acknowledge NSF grant ARC 0909388. GAS is supported by the NASA Modeling and Analysis Program.

REFERENCES

1. C.M. Ammann, F. Joos, D.S. Schimel, B.L. Otto-Bliesner, and R.A. Tomas. Solar influence on climate during the past millennium: Results from transient simulations with the NCAR Climate System Model. *Proc. U.S. Natl. Acad. Sci.,* 104(10): 3713–3718, 2007.

2. K.J. Anchukaitis, M.N. Evans, A. Kaplan, E.A. Vaganov, M.K. Hughes, and H.D. Grissino-Mayer. Forward modeling of regional scale tree-ring patterns in the southeastern United States and the recent influence of summer drought. *Geophys. Res. Lett.,* 33, L04705, DOI:10.1029/2005GL025050.

3. A.G. Barnston and T.M. Smith. Specification and prediction of global surface temperature and precipitation from global SST using CCA. *J. Climate,* 9: 2660–2697, 1996.

4. C.M. Bishop. *Machine Learning and Pattern Recognition.* New York: Springer, 2007.

5. C.S. Bretherton, C. Smith, and J.M. Wallace. An intercomparison of methods for finding coupled patterns in climate data. *J. Climate,* 5: 541–560, 1992.

6. P. Brohan, J.J. Kennedy, I. Harris, S.F.B. Tett, and P.D. Jones. Uncertainty estimates in regional and global observed temperature changes: A new dataset from 1850. *J. Geophys. Res.,* 111, D12106, 2006.

7. B.M. Buckley, K.J. Anchukaitis, D. Penny et al. Climate as a contributing factor in the demise of Angkor, Cambodia. *Proc. Nat. Acad. Sci. USA,* 107: 6748–6752, 2010.

8. S.J. Camargo and A.G. Barnston. Experimental seasonal dynamical forecasts of tropical cyclone activity at IRI. *Wea. Forecasting,* 24: 472–491, 2009.

9. S.J. Camargo, A.W. Robertson, A.G. Barnston, and M. Ghil. Clustering of eastern North Pacific tropical cyclone tracks: ENSO and MJO effects. *Geochem. Geophys. and Geosys.,* 9:Q06V05, 2008. doi:10.1029/2007GC001861.

10. M.A. Cane, S.E. Zebiak, and S.C. Dolan. Experimental forecasts of El Niño. *Nature,* 321: 827–832, 1986.

11. N. Cesa-Bianchi and G. Lugosi. *Prediction, Learning and Games.* Cambridge (UK) and New York: Cambridge University Press, 2006.

12. V. Chandrasekaran, S. Sanghavi, P. Parril, and A. Willsky. Rank-sparsity incoherence for matrix decomposition. *SIAM Journal of Optimization,* 21(2): 572–596, 2011.

13. B. Christiansen, T. Schmith, and P. Thejll. A surrogate ensemble study of climate reconstruction methods: Stochasticity and robustness. *J. Climate*, 22(4): 951–976, 2009.

14. Climate Informatics wiki: http://sites.google.com/site/1stclimateinformatics/

15. E.R. Cook, R. Seager, M.A. Cane, and D.W. Stahle. North American drought: Reconstructions, causes, and consequences. *Earth Science Reviews*, 81: 93–134, 2007.

16. D.P. Dee, S.M. Uppala, A.J. Simmons et al. The ERA-Interim reanalysis: Configuration and performance of the data assimilation system. *Quart. J. Roy. Meteorol. Soc.*, 137: 553–597, 2011.

17. T. DelSole and M.K. Tippett. Average Predictability Time: Part I. Theory. *J. Atmos. Sci.*, 66: 1188–1204, 2009.

18. T. DelSole, M.K. Tippett, and J. Shukla. A significant component of unforced multidecadal variability in the recent acceleration of global warming. *J. Climate*, 24: 909–926, 2011.

19. J.F. Donges, Y. Zou, N. Marwan, and J. Kurths. The backbone of the climate network. *Eur. Phys. Lett.*, 87(4): 48007, 2007.

20. R. Donner, S. Barbosa, J. Kurths, and N. Marwan. Understanding the earth as a complex system—Recent advances in data analysis and modeling in earth sciences. *Eur. Phys. J. Special Topics*, 174: 1–9, 2009.

21. M.N. Evans, A. Kaplan, and M.A. Cane. Pacific sea surface temperature field reconstruction from coral $\delta^{18}O$ data using reduced space objective analysis. *Paleoceanography*, 17: 7, 10.1029/2000PA000590, 2002.

22. M.N. Evans, B.K. Reichert, A. Kaplan, K.J. Anchukaitis, E.A. Vaganov, M.K. Hughes, and M.A. Cane. A forward modeling approach to paleoclimatic interpretation of tree-ring data. *J. Geophys. Res.*, 111(G3): G03008, 2006.

23. J.A. Foley, M.T. Coe, M. Scheffer, and G. Wang. Regime shifts in the Sahara and Sahel: Interactions between ecological and climatic systems in Northern Africa. *Ecosystems*, 6: 524–532, 2003.

24. G. Foster, J.D. Annan, G.A. Schmidt, and M.E. Mann. Comment on "Heat capacity, time constant, and sensitivity of Earth's climate system" by S.E. Schwartz. *J. Geophys. Res.*, 113, D15102, 2008.

25. J. Friedman, T. Hastie, and R. Tibshirani. A note on the group lasso and a sparse group lasso. Preprint, 2010.

26. L. Getoor and B. Tasker (Eds.). *Introduction to Statistical Relational Learning*. MIT Press, Cambridge, MA, 2007.

27. C.M. Gifford. Collective Machine Learning: Team Learning and Classification in Multi-Agent Systems. Ph.D. dissertation, University of Kansas, 2009.

28. F. Giorgi and N. Diffenbaugh. Developing regional climate change scenarios for use in assessment of effects on human health and disease. *Clim. Res.*, 36: 141–151, 2008.

29. G.H. Golub and C.F. Van Loan. *Matrix Computations, third edition*. The Johns Hopkins University Press, Washington, D.C., 1996.

30. J.F. González-Rouco, H. Beltrami, E. Zorita, and H. Von Storch. Simulation and inversion of borehole temperature profiles in surrogate climates: Spatial distribution and surface coupling. *Geophys. Res. Lett.*, 33(1): L01703, DOI:10.1029/2005GL024693.2006.

31. W.M. Gray. Atlantic seasonal hurricane frequency. Part I: El-Niño and 30-MB quasi-biennial oscillation influences. *Mon. Wea. Rev.*, 112: 1649–1688, 1984.

32. A.M. Greene, A.W. Robertson, P. Smyth, and S. Triglia. Downscaling forecasts of Indian monsoon rainfall using a nonhomogeneous hidden Markov model. *Quart. J. Royal Meteor. Soc.*, 137: 347–359, 2011.

33. J. Hansen, R. Ruedy, M. Sato, and K. Lo. Global surface temperature change. *Rev. Geophys.*, 48: RG4004, 2010.

34. T. Hastie, R. Tibshirani, and J. Friedman. *The Elements of Statistical Learning: Data Mining, Inference, and Prediction*. Springer, New York, 2001.

35. G.C. Hegerl, T.J. Crowley, M. Allen et al. Detection of human influence on a new, validated 1500-year temperature reconstruction. *J. Climate*, 20: 650–666, 2007.

36. G.C. Hegerl, F.W. Zwiers, P. Braconnot et al. Understanding and attributing climate change. *Climate Change 2007: The Physical Science Basis*. Contribution of Working Group I to the Fourth Assessment Report of the Intergovernmental Panel on Climate Change, S. Solomon et al. (Eds.), Cambridge University Press, Cambridge (UK) and New York, 2007.

37. M. Hoerling, J. Hurrell, J. Eischeid, and A. Phillips. Detection and attribution of twentieth-century Northern and Southern African rainfall change. *J. Climate*, 19(16): 3989–4008, August 2006.

38. S.M. Hsiang, K.C. Meng, and M.A. Cane. Civil conflicts are associated with the global climate. *Nature*, 476: 438–441, 2011.

39. IDAG (International ad hoc Detection and Attribution Group). Detecting and attributing external influences on the climate system: A review of recent advances. *J. Clim.*, 18: 1291–1314, 2005.

40. IPCC (Intergovernmental Panel on Climate Change). Expert Meeting on Assessing and Combining Multi Model Climate Projections: Good Practice Guidance Paper on Assessing and Combining Multi Model Climate Projections, R. Knutti et al., 2010.

41. P.D. Jones, K.R. Briffa, T.J. Osborn et al. High-resolution palaeoclimatology of the last millennium: A review of current status and future prospects. *The Holocene*, 19: 3–49, 2009.

42. A. Kaplan, M.A. Cane, and Y. Kushnir. Reduced space approach to the optimal analysis interpolation of historical marine observations: Accomplishments, difficulties, and prospects. In *Advances in the Applications of Marine Climatology: The Dynamic Part of the WMO Guide to the Applications of Marine Climatology*, p. 199–216, Geneva, Switzerland, 2003. World Meteorological Organization.

43. J. Kawale, S. Liess, A. Kumar et al. Data guided discovery of dynamic dipoles. In *Proceedings of the NASA Conference on Intelligent Data Understanding*, 2011.

44. N.S. Keenlyside, M. Latif, J. Jungclaus, L. Kornblueh, and E. Roeckner. Advancing decadal-scale climate prediction in the North Atlantic Sector. *Nature,* 453: 84–88, 2008.

45. J.J. Kennedy, N.A. Rayner, R.O. Smith, D.E. Parker, and M. Saunby. Reassessing biases and other uncertainties in sea surface temperature observations measured in situ since 1850. 1. Measurement sampling uncertainties. *J. Geophys. Res.,* 116: D14103, 2011.

46. R. Knutti, G.A. Meehl, M.R. Allen, and D.A. Stainforth. Constraining climate sensitivity from the seasonal cycle in surface temperature. *J. Clim.,* 19: 4224–4233, 2006.

47. D. Koller and N. Friedman. *Probabilistic Graphical Models: Principles and Techniques.* MIT Press, Cambridge, MA, 2009.

48. Y. Koren, R.M. Bell, and C. Volinsky. Matrix factorization techniques for recommender systems. *IEEE Computer,* 42(8): 30–37, 2009.

49. R.S. Kovats, M.J. Bouma, S. Hajat, E. Worrall, and A. Haines. El Niño and health. *The Lancet,* 362: 1481–1489, 2003.

50. V.M. Krasnopolsky and M.S. Fox-Rabinovitz. Complex hybrid models combining deterministic and machine learning components for numerical climate modeling and weather prediction. *Neural Networks,* 19(2): 122–134, 2006.

51. T.C.K. Lee, F.W. Zwiers, and M. Tsao. Evaluation of proxy-based millennial reconstruction methods. *Climate Dyn.,* 31: 263–281, 2008.

52. B. Li, D.W. Nychka, and C.M. Ammann. The value of multiproxy reconstruction of past climate. *J. Am. Stat. Assoc.,* 105: 883–895, 2010.

53. C.H.R. Lima, U. Lall, T. Jebara, and A.G. Barnston. Statistical prediction of ENSO from subsurface sea temperature using a nonlinear dimensionality reduction. *J. Climate,* 22: 4501–4519, 2009.

54. Z. Lu and T.K. Leen. Semi-supervised learning with penalized probabilistic clustering. In *Advances of Neural Information Processing System,* MIT Press, Cambridge, MA, 2005.

55. M.E. Mann, R.S. Bradley, and M.K. Hughes. Northern hemisphere temperatures during the past millennium: Inferences, uncertainties, and limitations. *Geophys. Res. Lett.,* 26: 759–762, 1999.

56. M.E. Mann, S. Rutherford, E. Wahl, and C. Ammann. Testing the fidelity of methods used in proxy-based reconstructions of past climate. *J. Climate,* 18: 4097–4107, 2005.

57. M.E. Mann, S. Rutherford, E. Wahl, and C. Ammann. Robustness of proxy-based climate field reconstruction methods. *J. Geophys. Res.,* 112(D12109), 2007.

58. M.E. Mann, Z. Zhang, M.K. Hughes et al. Proxy-based reconstructions of hemispheric and global surface temperature variations over the past two millennia. *Proc. Nat. Acad. Sci. USA,* 105: 13252–13257, 2008.

59. M.E. Mann, Z. Zhang, S. Rutherford et al. Global signatures and dynamical origins of the Little Ice Age and Medieval Climate Anomaly. *Science,* 326: 1256–1260, 2009.

60. L.O. Mearns, W.J. Gutowski, R. Jones et al. A regional climate change assessment program for North America. *EOS,* 90: 311–312, 2009.

61. G.A. Meehl, T.F. Stocker, W.D. Collins et al. Global climate projections. *Climate Change 2007: The Physical Science Basis.* Contribution of Working Group I to the Fourth Assessment Report of the Intergovernmental Panel on Climate Change, S. Solomon et al. (Eds), Cambridge University Press, Cambridge (UK) and New York, 2007.

62. M.J. Menne, C.N. Williams Jr., and M.A. Palecki. On the reliability of the U.S. surface temperature record. *J. Geophys. Res.,* 115: D11108, 2010.

63. C. Monteleoni, G.A. Schmidt, S. Saroha, and E. Asplund. Tracking climate models. *Statistical Analysis and Data Mining,* 4: 372–392, 2011.

64. J.M. Murphy, B.B. Booth, M. Collins et al. A methodology for probabilistic predictions of regional climate change from perturbed physics ensembles. *Phil. Trans. Roy. Soc. A,* 365: 2053–2075, 2007.

65. G.T. Narisma, J.A. Foley, R. Licker, and N. Ramankutty. Abrupt changes in rainfall during the twentieth century. *Geophys. Res. Lett.,* 34: L06710, March 2007.

66. S. Negahban, P. Ravikumar, M.J. Wainwright, and B. Yu. A unified framework for high-dimensional analysis of m-estimators with decomposable regularizers. Arxiv, 2010. http://arxiv.org/abs/1010.2731v1.

67. H. Owhadi, J.C. Scovel, T. Sullivan, M. McKems, and M. Ortiz. Optimal uncertainty quantification, *SIAM Review,* 2011 (submitted).

68. R.D. Peng, J.F. Bobb, C. Tebaldi, L. McDaniel, M.L. Bell, and F. Dominici. Toward a quantitative estimate of future heat wave mortality under global climate change. *Environ. Health Perspect.,* 119: 701–706, 2010.

69. W.B. Powell and P. Frazier. Optimal learning. In *Tutorials in Operations Research: State-of-the-Art Decision Making Tools in the Information Age.* Hanover, MD, 2008.

70. P. Ravikumar, A. Agarwal, and M.J. Wainwright. Message-passing for graph-structured linear programs: Proximal projections, convergence and rounding schemes. *J. Machine Learning Res.,* 11: 1043–1080, 2010.

71. D.B. Reusch. Ice-core reconstructions of West Antarctic Sea-Ice variability: A neural network perspective. *Fall Meeting of the American Geophysical Union,* 2010.

72. C.F Ropelewski and M.S. Halpert. Global and regional scale precipitation patterns associated with the El Niño/Southern Oscillation. *Mon. Wea. Rev.,* 115: 1606–1626, 1987.

73. R. Salakhutdinov and A. Mnih. Probabilistic matrix factorization. In *Advances in Neural Information Processing Systems 20,* 2008.

74. M. Scheffer, S. Carpenter, J.A. Foley, C. Folke, and B. Walker. Catastrophic shifts in ecosystems. *Nature,* 413(6856): 591–596, October 2001.

75. G.A. Schmidt. Error analysis of paleosalinity calculations. *Paleoceanography,* 14: 422–429, 1999.

76. G.A. Schmidt, A. LeGrande, and G. Hoffmann. Water isotope expressions of intrinsic and forced variability in a coupled ocean-atmosphere model. *J. Geophys. Res.,* 112, D10103, 2007.

77. T. Schneider. Analysis of incomplete climate data: Estimation of mean values and covariance matrices and imputation of missing values. *J. Climate,* 14: 853–871, 2001.

78. S.D. Schubert, M.J. Suarez, P.J. Pegion, R.D. Koster, and J.T. Bacmeister. On the cause of the 1930s dust bowl. *Science*, 303: 1855–1859, 2004.

79. C. Scovel and I. Steinwart. Hypothesis testing for validation and certification. *J. Complexity*, 2010 (submitted).

80. G. Shafer and V. Vovk. A tutorial on conformal prediction. *J. Mach. Learn. Res.*, 9: 371–421, 2008.

81. J. Shukla. Dynamical predictability of monthly means. *Mon. Wea. Rev.*, 38: 2547–2572, 1981.

82. J. Shukla. Predictability in the midst of chaos: A scientific basis for climate forecasting. *Science*, 282: 728–731, 1998.

83. F.H. Sinz. *A Priori Knowledge from Non-Examples*. Diplomarbeit (thesis), Universität Tübingen, Germany, 2007.

84. F.H. Sinz, O. Chapelle, A. Agrawal, and B. Schölkopf. An analysis of inference with the universum. In *Advances in Neural Information Processing Systems*, 20, 2008.

85. J.E. Smerdon. Climate models as a test bed for climate reconstruction methods: Pseudoproxy experiments. Wiley Interdisciplinary Reviews Climate Change, in revision, 2011.

86. J.E. Smerdon and A. Kaplan. Comment on "Testing the Fidelity of Methods Used in Proxy-Based Reconstructions of Past Climate": The Role of the Standardization Interval. *J. Climate*, 20(22): 5666–5670, 2007.

87. J.E. Smerdon, A. Kaplan, and D.E. Amrhein. Erroneous model field representations in multiple pseudoproxy studies: Corrections and implications. *J. Climate*, 23: 5548–5554, 2010.

88. J.E. Smerdon, A. Kaplan, D. Chang, and M.N. Evans. A pseudoproxy evaluation of the CCA and RegEM methods for reconstructing climate fields of the last millennium. *J. Climate*, 24: 1284–1309, 2011.

89. J.E. Smerdon, A. Kaplan, E. Zorita, J.F. González-Rouco, and M.N. Evans. Spatial performance of four climate field reconstruction methods targeting the Common Era. *Geophys. Res. Lett.*, 38, 2011.

90. D.M. Smith, S. Cusack, A.W. Colman et al. Improved surface temperature prediction for the coming decade from a global climate model. *Science*, 317: 769–799, 2007.

91. L.-K. Soh and C. Tsatsoulis. Unsupervised segmentation of ERS and Radarsat sea ice images using multiresolution peak detection and aggregated population equalization. *Int. J. Remote S.*, 20: 3087–3109, 1999.

92. L.-K. Soh, C. Tsatsoulis, D. Gineris, and C. Bertoia. ARKTOS: An intelligent system for SAR sea ice image classification. *IEEE T. Geosci. Remote S.*, 42: 229–248, 2004.

93. A. Solomon, L. Goddard, A. Kumar, J. Carton, C. Deser, I. Fukumori, A. Greene, G. Hegerl, B. Kirtman, Y. Kushnir, M. Newman, D. Smith, D. Vimont, T. Delworth, J. Meehl, and T. Stockdale. Distinguishing the roles of natural and anthropogenically forced decadal climate variability: Implications for prediction. *Bull. Amer. Meteor. Soc.*, 92: 141–156, 2010.

94. S. Sra, S. Nowozin, and S. Wright. *Optimization for Machine Learning*. MIT Press, 2011.

95. K. Steinhaeuser, A.R. Ganguly, and N.V. Chawla. Multivariate and multiscale dependence in the global climate system revealed through complex networks. *Climate Dynamics*, doi:10.1007/s00382-011-1135-9, in press, 2011.

96. K.E. Taylor, R. Stouffer, and G. Meehl. The CMIP5 experimental design. *Bull Amer. Meteorol. Soc.*, 2011 (submitted).

97. C. Tebaldi and R. Knutti. The use of the multi-model ensemble in probabilistic climate projections. *Phil. Trans. Roy. Soc. A*, 365: 2053–2075, 2007.

98. M. Tedesco and E.J. Kim. A study on the retrieval of dry snow parameters from radiometric data using a dense medium model and genetic algorithms. *IEEE T. Geosci. Remote S.*, 44: 2143–2151, 2006.

99. M. Tedesco, J. Pulliainen, P. Pampaloni, and M. Hallikainen. Artificial neural network based techniques for the retrieval of SWE and snow depth from SSM/I data. *Remote Sens. Environ.*, 90: 76–85, 2004.

100. D.M. Thompson, T.R. Ault, M.N. Evans, J.E. Cole, and J. Emile-Geay. Comparison of observed and simulated tropical climate trends using a forward model of coral δ^{18}O. *Geophys. Res. Lett.*, in review, 2011.

101. R. Tibshirani. Regression shrinkage and selection via the lasso. *Journal of Royal Statistical Society B*, 58: 267–288, 1996.

102. M.P. Tingley, P.F. Craigmile, M. Haran, B. Li, E. Mannshardt-Shamseldin, and B. Rajaratnam. Piecing Together the Past: Statistical Insights into Paleoclimatic Reconstructions. Technical report 2010-09, Department of Statistics, Stanford University, 2010.

103. M.P. Tingley and P. Huybers. A Bayesian algorithm for reconstructing climate anomalies in space and time. Part I: Development and applications to paleoclimate reconstruction problems. *J. Climate*, 23(10): 2759–2781, 2010.

104. M.K. Tippett, S.J. Camargo, and A.H. Sobel. A Poisson regression index for tropical cyclone genesis and the role of large-scale vorticity in genesis. *J. Climate*, 24: 2335–2357, 2011.

105. K.E. Trenberth, P.D. Jones, P. Ambenje et al. Observations: Surface and atmospheric climate change. *Climate Change 2007: The Physical Science Basis*. Contribution of Working Group I to the Fourth Assessment Report of the Intergovernmental Panel on Climate Change, S. Solomon et al. (Eds.), Cambridge (UK) and New York: Cambridge University Press, 2007.

106. A.A. Tsonis, K.L. Swanson, and P.J. Roebber. What do networks have to do with climate? *Bulletin of the American Meteorological Society*, 87(5): 585–595, 2006.

107. A.A. Tsonis and P.J. Roebber. The architecture of the climate network. *Physica A*, 333: 497–504, 2004.

108. A.A. Tsonis and K.L. Swanson. Topology and predictability of El Niño and La Niña networks. *Physical Review Letters*, 100(22): 228502, 2008.

109. K.Y. Vinnikov, N.C. Grody, A. Robok et al. Temperature trends at the surface and in the troposphere. *J. Geophys. Res.*, 111: D03106, 2006.

110. F.D. Vitart and T.N. Stockdale. Seasonal forecasting of tropical storms using coupled GCM integrations. *Mon. Wea. Rev.*, 129: 2521–2537, 2001.

111. M.J. Wainwright and M.I. Jordan. Graphical models, exponential families, and variational inference. *Foundations and Trends in Machine Learning*, 1(1–2): 1–305, 2008.

112. M. Widmann, H. Goosse, G. van der Schrier, R. Schnur, and J. Barkmeijer. Using data assimilation to study extratropical northern hemisphere climate over the last millennium. *Clim. Past*, 6: 627–644, 2010.

113. C.A. Woodhouse and J.T. Overpeck. 2000 years of drought variability in the central United States. *Bull. Am. Meteorologic. Soc.*, 79: 2693–2714, 1998.

114. S.D. Woodruff, S.J. Worley, S.J. Lubker et al. ICOADS Release 2.5: Extensions and enhancements to the surface marine meteorological archive. *J. Geophys. Res.*, 31: 951–967, 2011.

115. Qiaoyan Wu and Dake Chen. Ensemble forecast of Indo-Pacific SST based on IPCC twentieth-century climate simulations. *Geophys. Res. Lett.*, 37: 2010.

CHAPTER 5

Computational Data Sciences for Actionable Insights on Climate Extremes and Uncertainty

Auroop R. Ganguly, Evan Kodra, Snigdhansu Chatterjee, Arindam Banerjee, and Habib N. Najm

CONTENTS

5.1   OVERVIEW AND MOTIVATION

5.1.1 Climate Extremes: Definitions and Concepts

THE INTERGOVERNMENTAL PANEL ON Climate Change (IPCC) SREX (IPCC, 2011) summary for policymakers defines climate extremes as follows:

> The occurrence of a value of a weather or climate variable above (or below) a threshold value near the upper (or lower) ends of the range of observed values of the variable. For simplicity, both extreme weather events and extreme climate events are referred to collectively as "climate extremes."

Climate extremes in this chapter are defined as extreme weather events, or those that may last from several hours to several days. Thus, they may include heat waves and cold snaps, rainfall patterns in space and time potentially leading to floods and droughts, tropical cyclones, tornadoes, and storm surges. Figure 5.1 provides an overview.

There is evidence that statistical attributes of certain climate extremes have been growing steadily and significantly worse as a result of human influence, and these changes can be projected from analysis of physics-based computational climate model simulations as well as observations from remote or *in-situ* sensors. However, climate science cannot predict any particular event at decadal to centennial scales or assign a specific cause, and the confidence in statistical projections differs by the variable considered, the extent of spatial or temporal aggregation, regional and seasonal characteristics, and other considerations. Thus, we have relatively higher confidence in projections of temperature-related extremes, followed by extremes of precipitation and tropical cyclones. The climates of the extra-tropics are often relatively easier to project than that of the tropics, while statistical properties of extremes and change are typically better projected at aggregate space-time scales compared to finer resolutions.

5.1.2 Societal and Stakeholder Priorities

Stakeholder communities across multiple sectors such as water and food security, natural hazards preparedness and humanitarian aid, or

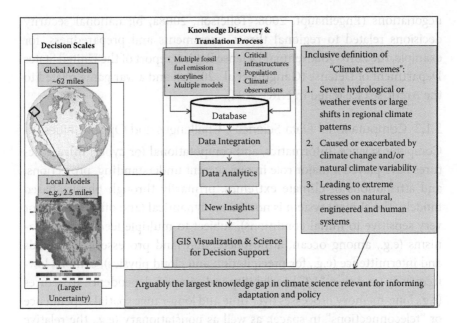

Decision Scales

Global Models
~62 miles

Local Models
~e.g., 2.5 miles

(Larger
Uncertainty)

**Knowledge Discovery &
Translation Process**

- Multiple fossil fuel emission storylines
- Multiple models

- Critical infrastructures
- Population
- Climate observations

Database

Data Integration

Data Analytics

New Insights

GIS Visualization & Science
for Decision Support

Inclusive definition of
"Climate extremes":

1. Severe hydrological or weather events or large shifts in regional climate patterns

2. Caused or exacerbated by climate change and/or natural climate variability

3. Leading to extreme stresses on natural, engineered and human systems

Arguably the largest knowledge gap in climate science relevant for informing
adaptation and policy

FIGURE 5.1 Uncertainty quantification for climate extremes, which are broadly construed in this context, represents one of the largest knowledge gaps in terms of translating the physical science basis of climate to information relevant for impacts assessments and adaptation decisions, and eventually to mitigation policy. However, the cascade of uncertainties is difficult to quantify. The societal costs of action and inaction are both potentially large for climate adaptation and mitigation policies; hence, uncertainties in climate are important to effectively characterize and communicate. Climate extremes may broadly include large shifts in regional climate patterns or severe weather or hydrological events caused or exacerbated by natural climate variability or climate change. This chapter primarily focuses on the statistical attributes of severe events, or, changes in tail behavior.

management of natural and engineered infrastructures, as well as policy makers dealing with urbanization, population growth, or migration, land use or energy and water sustainability, and energy or emissions control, require actionable insights about climate extremes at local to regional scales. The costs of action and inaction can both be large, as adaptation and mitigation strategies designed for climate extremes may be costly for the current generation and potentially even more costly for future generations. Specific examples of prior work that demonstrated the importance of climate extremes to the stakeholder community include the following: an international climate change policy related to global emissions negotiations (Engelhaupt, 2008; Tollefson, 2008a, b); national security decisions related to regional threat assessments and preparedness, for example, the 2010 Quadrennial Defense Review report of the United States Department of Defense (Ganguly et al., 2009a); and a war game related to the Arctic sea ice (cited in NRC, 2011).

5.1.3 Computational Data Sciences: Challenges and Opportunities

Computer science, informatics, and computational (or cyber) infrastructures have played a major role in our current understanding, projections, and attributions of climate extremes, primarily through physics-based models. The climate system is nonlinear, dynamical (and often chaotic, or very sensitive to initial conditions), subject to multiple feedback mechanisms (e.g., among ocean, atmosphere, and land processes), thresholds and intermittence (e.g., for precipitation and cloud physics), exhibits low-frequency (and even "$1/f$") variability and complex dependence structures (e.g., long-memory processes over time and long-range spatial dependence or "teleconnections" in space), as well as nonstationary (e.g., the relative dominance of processes generating extremes may change in a warmer world). Thus, purely data-driven extrapolation may not be adequate or even appropriate, especially for long lead time projections (e.g., decadal to centennial scales), where data assimilation methods may also have limited value. State-of-the-art physical climate models are based on fundamental physical laws (e.g., laws of motion and conservation of mass and momentum). Physical approximations and mathematical discretization techniques (e.g., strategically chosen finite difference equation system formulations) are applied to these laws, resulting in complex systems encapsulated in hundreds of thousands or millions of lines of low-level source code (Christensen et al., 2005). Current global climate models are composed of multiple interacting components, including atmospheric, oceanic, and often land and sea ice models (IPCC, 2007). Such physics-based models, whether global climate or Earth system models or regional climate models used to downscale the outputs of global models, are more credible for variables such as mean temperature at continental to global scales. The same models are less reliable for climate extremes; for example, they are inadequate for precipitation extremes and tropical cyclones, especially at the precision required for making informed decisions.

The research opportunities for computational data sciences are three-fold: (1) improved characterization, projections, and attribution of climate extremes; (2) characterization of uncertainties, especially at local to regional scales for annual or seasonal projections over decades and centuries; and (3) enhanced predictive insights over and above what may be obtained from direct extrapolation of historical trends or analysis of climate model simulations. The volume of the data (e.g., hundreds of terabytes going on petabytes for archived climate model simulations, and gigabytes going on terabytes for remotely sensed observations) and the complexity of the methods (Lozano et al., 2009a, b; Steinhaeuser et al., 2011a, b) require data-intensive computational methods. A schematic is shown in Figure 5.2.

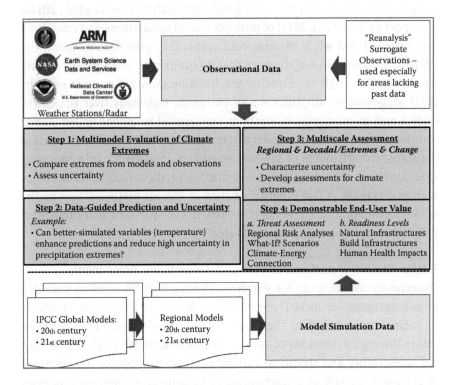

FIGURE 5.2 Remote or *in-situ* sensor observations and climate model simulations can be investigated through computational data science methods for multimodel evaluations, enhanced projections, and multiscale assessments to inform decisions and policy. The growth in climate data from models and observations is expected to grow exponentially over the next several decades (Overpeck et al., 2011), providing a vast set of challenges and opportunities for data science communities.

5.1.3.1 Overview of Research Areas: 1. Extremes Characterization

Extremes may be characterized based on their relevance to impacts (e.g., heat waves based on nighttime minima, which relate to human discomfort and possible loss of lives: Meehl and Tebaldi, 2004) or through statistical distributions (e.g., extreme value theory for precipitation extremes: Kharin et al., 2007). Thus, our analysis (Ganguly et al., 2009b) of model simulations and surrogate observations (reanalysis data generated by assimilating weather data from disparate sensors into a numerical weather prediction model) pointed to higher trends but larger uncertainty in heat waves in this century based on a plausible but high emissions scenario, which in turn implies greater urgency but caution in adaptation or mitigation decisions. On the other hand, our analysis (Kodra et al., 2011a; see report by Tollefson, 2011) of multiple model simulations and reanalysis data revealed that while extreme cold events may grow less frequent, the intensity and duration of the ones that do occur may often persist at current levels. Our analysis of intense precipitation events (Kao and Ganguly, 2011) suggested an amplification of extremes, especially over the extra-tropics and in an aggregate sense at continental to global scales. Major community-wide efforts are necessary to comprehensively characterize the statistical attributes of gradual or sudden changes in extremes over space and time, including less well-defined or predictable climate extremes such as droughts. A combination of state-of-the-art methods, new methodological adaptations, and novel approaches in spatial or spatiotemporal statistics and data mining are motivated.

5.1.3.2 Overview of Research Areas: 2. Uncertainty Assessments

Uncertainty assessments for extremes (Wehner, 2010) need to consider knowledge-gaps in model physics (e.g., based on statistical methods to balance model skill in the past and multimodel convergence in the future through extensions of approaches such as Smith et al., 2009), and the applicability and statistical validity of the definitions or distributions of extremes, as well as uncertainties in parameter estimation processes (e.g., through the bootstrap as in Kharin et al., 2007 or Kao and Ganguly, 2011). The potential differences in the nature of the insights and uncertainties based on definitions of extremes become obvious by comparing our recent work (Ghosh et al., 2011) with a previous approach (Goswami et al., 2006). Current methods for attribution of extremes, e.g., for intense precipitation events, include statistical techniques (Min et al., 2011) or numerical simulations (Pall et al., 2011): these methods can benefit from rigorous uncertainty quantification approaches. New mathematical methods for uncertainty are critically needed in these areas.

5.1.3.3 Overview of Research Areas: 3. Enhanced Predictions

Large gaps continue to exist in our scientific understanding and projections of certain crucial variables, often related to climate extremes, and fine-scale or aggregate processes that drive the extremes. There have been claims that *the sad truth of climate science is that the most crucial information is the least reliable* (Schiermeier, 2010). One question relevant for enhanced projections of climate extremes is the extent to which the variables that are relatively better predicted (e.g., sea surface temperature or ocean meteorology in general, atmospheric temperature or humidity profiles over land) may have information content about the variables that may be more crucial (e.g., precipitation extremes or intensity and frequency of hurricanes), and whether such information can be utilized for developing predictive models. There is evidence of information content; for example, Liu et al. (2009) and others have reported on temperature dependence of precipitation extremes. And there is literature attempting to develop physics-based relations; for example, O'Gorman and Schneider (2009), Sugiyama et al. (2010), as well as Muller and O'Gorman (2011), have sought to develop a better understanding of precipitation processes related to extremes based on atmospheric covariates, while Emanuel et al. (2008) have attempted to produce projections of the statistical attributes of hurricanes based on climate model-simulated oceanic variables. While data-driven methods should be explored to develop novel and actionable predictive insights, the methods have to be able to handle nonlinear processes as well as complex dependence patterns, yet remain physically interpretable and able to generalize to nonstationary conditions. This area may represent a steep challenge for computational data sciences, and perhaps motivate truly interdisciplinary approaches conceived from traditionally disparate methods ranging from computational statistics, signal processing, and econometrics, to nonlinear dynamics, graph-based methods, data mining, and machine learning. Our recent efforts (Steinhaeuser et al., 2011a, b and Chatterjee et al., 2012) for improved regional predictions over land based on ocean meteorological variables or Kawale et al., 2011 for understanding climate dipoles) are only initial steps in an area that may well represent a grand challenge for data-intensive sciences.

5.2 EXTREMES CHARACTERIZATION

There are several challenges in characterizing and analyzing data related to climate extremes. One of the first challenges is the nature of the data: observational data are of relatively short duration and typically do not allow for many important extreme conditions to be manifest, they are unevenly spread spatially, and data quality is also uneven. Climate model outputs and reanalysis data do not have several of these problems, but Mannshardt-Shamseldin et al. (2011) demonstrate that the nature of extremes from gridded data differ considerably from observed data. Moreover, as Wehner (2010) observes:

> ...to the extent that climate models can be tuned to reproduce the recent past, model developers focus on the mean values of climatic observations, not the tails of their distributions.

Several other studies (O'Gorman and Schneider, 2009; Sugiyama et al., 2010; Wehner, 2010; Min et al., 2011) have pointed out that our current understanding of precipitation extremes has room for improvement and that the current generation of climate models probably fails to reflect reality. Recent studies (O'Gorman and Schneider, 2009; Sugiyama et al., 2010) suggest a deficiency in our understanding of the relationship between precipitation extremes and atmospheric moisture content. Wehner (2010) suggests that climate models might actually be able to emulate extreme events if they were run at sufficiently high resolution; that is not the case for models run at the typical resolution level adopted for the "International Panel on Climate Change's Fourth Assessment Report" (AR4, a landmark assessment report on the state of climate change science) (IPCC, 2007), and higher-resolution runs are computationally expensive. Min et al. (2011) point to the possible underestimation of trends in precipitation from a potential lack of accounting for anthropogenic effects on future precipitation extreme events. All of these suggest that there is room for improvement in the quality of data, and in the development of methodology to analyze available extreme data.

Another challenge for statistical and data-driven analysis of climate extremes is that the definition of *what* is extreme should be guided by various stakeholders and users. For example, in the case of rainfall, (1) the amount of rainfall in a given unit of time, (2) the total amount of rainfall, (3) the duration of rainfall, (4) the time gaps between rainfall events,

(5) the spatial pattern of rainfall, and several other variables can be of interest. Accordingly, the definition and the notion of an extreme may be different. The trifecta of intensity, duration, frequency (IDF), which is often characterized using extreme value theory (Kao and Ganguly, 2011) is useful in many cases, but not all. Another example is that of cold temperatures, which are important for crop production and food security. The variables of interest in this example could be the number of days of a certain level of frost, consecutive frost days, and time spent below a temperature threshold (Kodra et al., 2011a). Not all such definitions of "extremes" lend themselves to common, theoretically satisfying statistical analysis (Coles, 2001).

Another potential problem is that of identification of *extreme* events versus *rare* events, which are not always the same; in other words, an event might be extreme in impact but not rare, and vice versa. The definition of an extreme event may often be determined by its impact, and this definition will, in turn, often determine its rarity. The rarity of the defined events, along with other data properties, will dictate which statistical inference approaches may be appropriate. In some cases, summary measures have been used to obtain conclusions about extreme events (Goswami et al., 2006), although subsequent uses of the extreme-value model have provided different conclusions on similar data (Ghosh et al., 2011). Also, as Ferro and Segers (2003) observe, extremes can be clustered, which may present additional challenges related to the independence assumed by some extreme value statistical approaches.

From a purely statistical perspective, there is a gap between finite sample data-based extreme events and the general asymptotic theory that is used for extreme event analysis. Classic extreme-value statistical approaches attempt to extrapolate the extreme behavior of variables by fitting distributions to tail observations, such as annual maxima or exceedances above or below some predetermined (quantile) threshold (Coles, 2001; Kharin et al., 2007). Note that the generalized extreme value distribution or the generalized Pareto distribution, which have been used in the climate extremes literature (Kharin and Zwiers, 2000; Perkins et al., 2009; Kao and Ganguly, 2011), are asymptotic limits of probabilities relating to finite-sample size extreme events, and need not be exact characterizations. Also, most real data are temporally and spatially correlated, a fact that is often ignored in computing return-level characteristics, quantifying uncertainty, or making inference. There is no consensus about the best parameter estimation and inference technique for extreme-value distributions (Hosking and Wallis, 1997; Kharin and Zwiers, 2000; Coles and Dixon, 1999; Kharin and Zwiers, 2005), and approaches for including information from covariables are still in development (Hall and Tajvidi, 2000).

The bootstrap, broadly speaking, is a class of resampling techniques that can be employed to quantify sampling variability (uncertainty) in parameter estimation, among other uses (Efron, 1979). Parametric bootstrap and the traditional nonparametric bootstrap approaches of Efron (1979) were used in conjunction with the L-moments method and the maximum likelihood method for studying climate extremes in Kharin and Zwiers (2000; 2005; 2007), who also compared various estimation techniques and listed several caveats. Inference for climate extremes may benefit from a better understanding of the limits and appropriateness of popular statistical inference procedures (such as extreme value theory), as well as the application and/or creation of other approaches that relax assumptions or are robust to limitations of available extreme data.

5.3 UNCERTAINTY ASSESSMENTS

5.3.1 Statistical Modeling of Uncertainty in Multimodel Ensembles

Here we discuss the state-of-the-art in uncertainty quantification (UQ) for situations where ensembles of global climate models or Earth system models (GCMs/ESMs) are used to assess regional climate change. While statistical and dynamical (regional climate models) downscalings are often used for regional assessments, they are in turn driven by ESMs, and hence UQ in ESMs remains an important challenge. UQ is often inundated with a sense of urgency, and ensembles of ESMs are tools from which practical and timely uncertainty assessments can be readily formed.

Structural uncertainty, or that which arises from variations in the mathematical mechanics of climate models, is the principal focus of UQ in approaches discussed in this section; it has been studied in several forms with multimodel ensembles where weights are assigned to individual models as a measure of their reliability. We distinguish the ensemble approaches discussed here from other UQ methodologies—for example, physics perturbed ensembles—that have been used to explore parameter uncertainty within single climate models (Stainforth et al., 2005), and approaches based on or similar to polynomial chaos expansion (see Section 5.3.2). It is important to be aware of all approaches for

UQ to understand the scope and limitations of multimodel ensembles for climate UQ: to date, no statistical multimodel ensemble UQ methodology explicitly incorporates uncertainty within climate models (e.g., to understand the uncertainties contributed by parameterizations of climate processes and the propagation of these uncertainties along the rest of the model components). The ensemble methods discussed here, however, provide a basis for exploring inter-model (i.e., structural) uncertainty.

While the use of multimodel ensembles for prediction has been studied extensively in data science disciplines (Seni and Elder, 2010), an important distinction must be made for the climate science domain. In many typical time series and classification applications, for example, a forecast horizon of interest is often one or two (or a few) periods ahead, or the binary classification is for the next observation (Seni and Elder, 2010). In such cases, there is the potential for a predictive model to learn from an ensemble of predictions and recalibrate its next prediction upon validation (Fern and Givan, 2003). Several key challenges, however, distinguish climate forecasting from more typical problem settings: long prediction lead times (multidecadal to centennial scales), potential nonstationarity (where the validity of processes embedded within a GCM may change), the difficulty in selecting metrics that are meaningful for model training (Knutti, 2010), and finally the impossibility of true validation for the prediction horizons of interest. Many of the methods developed in data sciences, while valuable on their own and across applications, do not directly translate well to climate prediction. For example, even in the case where past data are segmented into multiple training samples in order to rigorously develop a multimodel ensemble prediction formula founded on well-chosen, physically meaningful error metrics, there is no guarantee that nonstationarity will not invalidate the prediction formula in the future, given the lead time. Thus, while mature data science ensemble methodologies may be valuable as foundational approaches, novel and creative methods are needed to solve the problem of UQ in climate with multimodel ensembles.

One persisting notion in the climate literature is that the multimodel average (MMA), or the average of spatial, temporal, or spatiotemporal fields of climate outputs from multiple GCMs, is a robust approach for making "most likely" projections; this robustness is largely based on alleged bias (noise) cancellation and orthogonal skills of GCMs (Knutti et al., 2010). The concept of its potential utility in climate may have followed from success in weather forecasting (Krishnamurti et al., 1999; Hagedorn et al.,

2005) and has been empirically justified in climate attribution studies (Pierce et al., 2009; Santer et al, 2009); in fact, the latter studies implicitly suggest that the MMA of a random selection of an adequate number of GCMs will form a reliable projection, at least for anthropogenic attribution. Equal-weighted MMAs may represent a more conservative approach, as optimum model weighting may hold less potential benefit than risk compared to equal weighting (Weigel et al., 2010). The MMA has been a default in some climate stakeholder assessment reports (Karl et al., 2009), where they are sometimes displayed visually without clear reference to uncertainty. This may be a questionable practice, as averaging of dynamically consistent spatial fields or time series may lead to physically meaningless signals, and the exclusion of individual model results may serve to obscure plausible lower and upper bounds of climate change (Knutti et al., 2010). A recent case study (Perkins et al., 2009) has also implicitly questioned the notion of *a priori* use of MMAs and inclusion of demonstrably poor GCMs. Work with historical (20th century) observations and simulations of Indian monsoon climatology (Kodra et al., 2012) may suggest that the MMA should not be a default choice, and that all models within an ensemble should be evaluated carefully.

Given this debate surrounding MMAs, the display of worst and best cases as derived from archived GCM outputs may be advisable as the bare minimum requirement for communicating uncertainty. However, because multimodel ensembles are not true random samples of independent GCMs from a larger population, they should not be considered formal probability distributions (Tebaldi and Knutti, 2007). More rigorous and statistically grounded approaches may be desired; recently, several notable probabilistic approaches have been developed: Giorgi and Mearns (2002) proposed the Reliability Ensemble Average (REA) method for assigning reliability to simulations of regional mean temperature from GCMs; this method has since been expanded and developed into a more formal Bayesian framework that has become perhaps the most prominent method for UQ using multimodel ensembles. Essentially, the REA method attempts to weight GCMs based on their alleged reliability, which is a balance of (1) historical model bias relative to observations and (2) future multimodel consensus (convergence), or model distance from the center of the ensemble spread. Giorgi and Mearns (2002) define bias and convergence as the following, respectively:

$$\lambda_{B,j} = \min\left(1, \frac{1}{|x_j - \mu|}\right), \tag{5.1}$$

$$\lambda_{C,j} = \min\left(1, \frac{1}{|y_j - \tilde{Y}|}\right), \tag{5.2}$$

where X_j is a historical (20th century) temperature output from climate model j, and μ is observed ("true") temperature from the same time period; Y_j and $\tilde{Y}$ are, respectively, the same for a future time period. If the arguments

$$\frac{1}{|X_j - \mu|} \quad \text{or} \quad \frac{1}{|Y_j - \tilde{Y}|}$$

are more than 1, then 1 is chosen as $\lambda_{B,j}$ or $\lambda_{C,j}$, with the notion that $|X_j - \mu|$ or $|Y_j - \tilde{Y}|$ could have been small just by chance. "$\tilde{Y}$" is an unknown and thus must be estimated using the following weights:

$$\lambda_j = \left(\lambda_{B,j}^m \lambda_{C,j}^n\right)^{1/mn}, \tag{5.3}$$

$$\tilde{Y} = \frac{\Sigma_j \lambda_j Y_j}{\Sigma_j \lambda_j}. \tag{5.4}$$

In practice, Giorgi and Mearns (2002) arbitrarily set $m = n = 1$ so that bias and consensus received equal favor. Because $\tilde{Y}$ and $\lambda_{C,j}$ are both unknowns but depend on each other, a recursive procedure was used to compute both (Giorgi and Mearns, 2002).

These two criteria suggest that information on the credibility (weights) of models can be estimated by performance compared to observed data, as well as degree of convergence; if a model falls far from the center of the ensemble, it may be treated more like an outlier than a likely outcome. The consensus criterion may have been borne at least partially from the ideas of bias cancellation and orthogonal skills of MMAs discussed previously (Krishnamurti et al., 1999; Hagedorn et al., 2005), and strong criticisms of the criterion have been acknowledged (Tebaldi and Knutti,

2007). Additionally, the criterion of GCM skill (*bias* in most recent work) is difficult to define and evaluate; in most cases, it is difficult to determine whether metrics measuring past GCM skill will translate to the future (Tebaldi and Knutti, 2007; Knutti et al., 2010).

The REA was admittedly ad hoc; however, its two notions of GCM skill and consensus (Giorgi and Mearns, 2002) have formed the foundation for a prominent line of work, beginning with Tebaldi et al., (2004), that formalized them in a Bayesian model. One of the most recent versions of this statistical model can be found in Smith et al. (2009), which also allows for the joint consideration of multiple regions. Specifically, using this model, a posterior distribution for past or current temperature μ and future temperature υ can be simulated from a Markov Chain Monte Carlo (MCMC) sampler using a weight λ_j for each GCM j. Next, each λ_j can be simulated from a posterior by considering the bias and consensus of GCM j. The weights λ_j then inform a new estimate of μ and υ, which informs a new estimate of each λ_j, and so on. Specifically, λ_j follows a Gamma posterior distribution with the following expectation:

$$E\left[\lambda_j\middle|\bullet\right]=\frac{a+1}{b+0.5\left(X_j-\mu\right)^2+0.5\theta\left(Y_j-\upsilon-\beta\left(X_j-\mu\right)\right)^2} \quad (5.5)$$

where a and b are prior parameters (usually uninformative), β is an unknown quantity representing the correlation between historical and future model outputs, and θ is a random quantity that allows future climate variance to differ from that of the past. The conditionality serves to illustrate the fact that the expectation of λ_j is contingent upon the values of all other random parameters and data. Thus, the value of λ_j is a function of the random quantities μ, υ, θ, and β, which in turn have their own posterior conditional distributions. In general, it is notable that under this formulation all of these random quantities are conditionally independent and cannot be readily analyzed marginally.

An initial post-hoc analysis (Kodra et al., 2011b) of simulation results from the latest model (Smith et al., 2009) suggested it may rely more on consensus and less on bias (i.e., skill), and that the bias criterion may not be adequate in representing model skill. Conceptually, in the state-of-the-art statistical model, holding all else constant, the posterior distribution for $\upsilon-\mu$ will "shrink" toward the multimodel mean, even if all GCMs exhibit poor skill with respect to past data; in such circumstances, it might

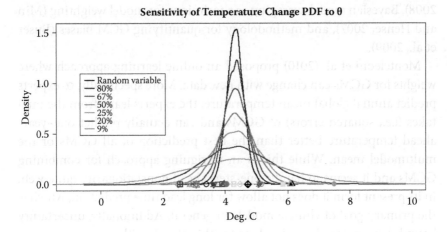

FIGURE 5.3 The univariate (one region) Bayesian model from Smith et al. (2009) illustrates the importance of the parameter θ in dictating the spread of the probability density function (PDF) for change in regional mean temperature. This particular set of PDFs is obtained for spatiotemporally averaged Greenland temperature change from 1970 to 1999 to 2070 to 2099. The horizontal axis measures change in degrees Celsius, while the vertical axis measures frequency. The legend indicates the condition of θ and from top to bottom corresponds to PDFs from narrow to wide: "random" is the narrowest density, and treats θ as a random unknown quantity as in Smith et al. (2009). For the remaining PDFs, values of θ are fixed at different quantities that come to represent the relative importance of convergence versus bias (where the importance of bias is 100% minus that of θ). Notably, treating θ as a random quantity yields a result where convergence is favored much more than bias.

make sense that that uncertainty should actually increase. The degree of shrinkage toward the mean is dictated by the parameter θ. Its importance is stressed in Figure 5.3 and clear from Equation 5.1: if $\theta \gg 1$, then holding all else constant, consensus is favored by the statistical model. Indeed, an earlier work by Tebaldi et al. (2004) featured a slight variant of their statistical model with a provision that, through a prior distribution, restricted the influence of θ; this provision was not included later by Smith et al. (2009). While the above represents the most prominent line of work on combining multimodel ensembles for quantifying uncertainty in regional climate, a few other initial approaches have been developed. These approaches have extended the broad multimodel UQ line of work by integrating methodology for quantifying inter-model covariance (Greene et al., 2006) and spatial variability structure (Furrer et al., 2007; Sain et al.,

2008), Bayesian model averaging as a technique for model weighting (Min and Hense, 2007), and methodology for quantifying GCM biases (Buser et al., 2009).

Monteleoni et al. (2010) proposed an online learning approach where weights for GCMs can change with new data. More specifically, α-experts predict annual global mean temperature; the experts learn from the mistakes (i.e., squared errors) of GCMs and can actually predict one–year-ahead temperature better than the best prediction of all GCMs or the multimodel mean. While this is an intriguing approach for combining GCMs and it seems to handle one-step-ahead nonstationarity quite well, in its present form it does not allow for long lead time prediction, which is the primary goal of climate models in general. Additionally, uncertainty bounds have not yet been developed within the algorithm.

The regional climate UQ research area is still relatively nascent and may benefit from new approaches (Knutti et al., 2010). Methods must be developed that simultaneously accommodate long lead times as well as potential nonstationarity, where conditions (e.g., relationships between variables) could change. In addition, there may be value in considering physical relationships between multiple variables to encourage robustness and interpretation in the GCM weighting process, as is discussed in Section 5.4. Recent UQ work (Tebaldi and Sanso, 2009), along the same line as Smith et al. (2009), developed a hierarchical Bayesian model for joint projections of mean temperature and precipitation; this model attempted to statistically utilize correlation between the two variables. Extending this type of statistical model to one that considers climate extremes would be valuable to the climate community. For instance, O'Gorman and Schneider (2009) developed a relatively simple conceptual physical model for an increase in precipitation extremes under anthropogenic climate change, while Kao and Ganguly (2011) explored conceptual physical bases in their characterization of 21st century precipitation extremes. Careful statistical utilization of such insights could lead to novel multimodel ensemble UQ methodology for extremes, which could be useful for informing various impact sectors.

5.3.2 Parametric Uncertainties in Individual Climate Models

While approaches for quantifying structural uncertainty were discussed in Section 5.3.1, accounting for parametric uncertainty is important for understanding intrinsic model variability, especially because archived global models do not traverse the entire space of plausible prediction space

(Stainforth et al., 2005). Climate models employ a wide range of parameterizations in land, ocean, atmosphere, and ice sub-model components. These parameters are typically calibrated based on data. Bayesian methods are useful for parameter estimation with quantified uncertainty, as they provide estimation of the joint posterior density of the parameters. While Bayesian methods have been used for parameter estimation in climate model components (Jackson et al., 2003, 2004, 2008; Annan and Hargreaves, 2006; Govaerts and Lattanzio, 2007; Villagran et al., 2008), much more remains to be done in general for estimating the wide variety of climate model parameters. One key challenge is the construction of effective climate model surrogates for facilitating the Bayesian/inverse problem solution. Gaussian processes, as well as other surrogate models, have been used for representing climate data (Jackson et al., 2004; Banerjee et al., 2008; Cressie and Johannesson, 2008; Sanso et al., 2008; Villagran et al., 2008; Drignei et al., 2009; Furrer and Sain, 2009). High dimensionality, in the present context largely embodied in the large number of uncertain parameters, is a significant challenge for surrogate construction and for uncertainty quantification in general. Global sensitivity analysis methods (Morris, 1991; Saltelli et al., 2000) have been used to identify a small subset of parameters that are critical to the climate system outputs of interest. Alternatively, compressed sensing (CS) methods have been developed to provide means of constructing sparse representations of high-dimensional information (Donoho, 2006; Candès and Wakin, 2008). Bayesian CS methods have been used for discovering sparsity in land models (S. Babacan et al. 2010).

With parameters calibrated using Bayesian methods, and described using a posterior density, one can estimate the forward propagation of uncertainty in model observables resulting from the input parametric uncertainty. While this can be done via random sampling, employing the parameter posterior density, model complexity, and computational cost render this an infeasible task due to the large number of random samples needed for convergence of Monte Carlo methods (Caflisch, 1998). In recent years, Polynomial Chaos (PC) UQ methods have been developed and used to great advantage in representing uncertain/random variables, and in accelerating forward uncertainty propagation in computational models (Ghanem and Spanos, 1991; Xiu and Karniadakis, 2002; Debusschere et al., 2004; Le Maitre et al., 2004; Soize and Ghanem, 2004). PC methods rely on a representation of random variables as truncated expansions in terms of orthogonal functions of a given random basis. Thus, an uncertain model parameter χ can be written as a PC expansion (PCE) in terms of an n-dimensional basis:

$$\chi \approx \sum_{k=0}^{P} \alpha_k \Psi_k \left(\xi_1, \xi_2, \ldots, \xi_n \right) \tag{5.6}$$

The key task is then the propagation of uncertainty from parameter χ to climate model output Z, where $Z = \mathcal{H}(\chi)$ (Najm, 2009). Generally, PC methods come in two variants (Najm, 2009): (1) intrusive methods, where the governing equations are transformed employing Galerkin projection, arriving at a new set of equations for the PC mode coefficients; and (2) nonintrusive methods, where the original model is employed as a black box in a sampling context. The former approach requires changing the source code/forward solvers of the underlying physical model. The latter is the more practical, given established legacy codes. In this approach, the mode coefficients in the PCE for a model output of interest Z are evaluated employing a chosen set of N samples of the basis ξ, $\{\xi^j\}_{j=1}^{N}$ and associated model output values Z^j. Adaptive anisotropic deterministic sampling methods, employing sparse-quadrature evaluations of projection integrals for the PC coefficients, are highly effective in this regard (Nobile et al., 2008).

The outcome of the PC forward UQ problem is a PCE for the uncertain model outputs of interest, which can be employed to generate corresponding probability density functions, or moments of interest. Note that the PCE, being a functional representation of model outputs over the range of uncertainty in input parameters, is also useful simply as a surrogate for the dependence of model outputs on the parameters. PC surrogates have been used, very much like GP surrogates, for accelerating Bayesian inference (Marzouk and Najm, 2009).

The use of PC UQ methods in the global scale climate-modeling context is feasible in principle employing a nonintrusive formalism, although it is severely challenged by the high dimensionality of the stochastic input space, particularly given the computational expense of a single model run. Presuming known uncertainties of model parameters, targeted studies exploring small subsets of parameters are quite feasible. Sparsification via sensitivity analysis or CS methods, as well as utilization of known parameter correlations, and the hierarchical structure of climate models, is useful to reduce the effective dimensionality of the uncertain input space, thereby rendering the overall problem more feasible.

Finally, given that the most damaging consequences of climate change are associated with climate extremes, it is worthwhile to discuss the prediction of extreme behavior under uncertainty in model parameters. This is a more challenging pursuit than that of estimating means/moments of uncertain climate predictions when extreme events of interest are also rare. Capturing the tails of probability distributions accurately in a computational setting is challenging when there is small probability of sampling the tail region, and hence implies the need for a very large number of samples overall. While PC methods can avoid random sampling, the accuracy of the PC representation for modeling the tail-behavior of the underlying random variable requires particular attention. In principle, using high-order expansions may help; however, that renders the problem even more computationally challenging, requiring, for example, a large number of samples in a nonintrusive setting. It is also feasible to use a PC basis that is tailored to achieve higher accuracy in the tail region than conventional constructions. This can be done, for example, by choosing a basis that has a density with fat-tail behavior. This approach, however, still requires further development to be implemented practically with climate models.

5.4 ENHANCED PREDICTIONS

The key desiderata from predictive models in the context of extremes include accurate and uncertainty-quantified projections of crucial variables related to extremes as well as succinct characterizations of covariates and climate processes collectively influencing extremes. Such characterizations must be cognizant of complex and possibly nonlinear dependency patterns while staying physically interpretable, thereby yielding scientific understanding of extremes and the processes driving them. While uncertainty quantification methods were discussed in Section 5.3, we now briefly introduce some methodology that could be useful in enhancing predictions and perhaps reducing uncertainty in crucial climate variables that are not captured well by current-generation physical models.

Standard predictive models, such as least squares or logistic linear regression, fall short of such desiderata in multiple ways. The number p of covariates and fine-scale climate processes potentially influencing key variables such as extreme precipitation far surpass the number of examples n of such extreme events. In the $n \ll p$ regime for regression, consistency guarantees from standard theory breakdown, implying that the model inferred is not even statistically meaningful (Girko, 1995; Candès and Tao, 2007). Moreover, such standard models will assign nonzero regression coefficients to all covariates and processes provided as input without any model selection (Tibshirani, 1996; Zhao and Yu, 2006). The corresponding model is not likely to have a meaningful physical interpretation or to aid hypothesis generation by identifying a small number of covariates or processes potentially influencing the key response variable(s).

Sparse regression, a relatively recent development in statistics and machine learning, may be a promising approach toward building enhanced prediction models. Preliminary studies in the context of multivariate autoregressive models and Granger causality have shown promise for modeling both normal as well as extreme behavior (Lozano et al., 2009a, b; Liu et al., 2009). Sparse regression models attempt to identify a small set of predictors out of a large space of candidates by balancing model fit and parsimony. Regularization (penalty) terms are combined with error minimization criteria to encourage predictive models that are accurate while choosing a relatively small subset of covariates with nonzero coefficients. Penalty terms could enforce temporal, spatial, and/or covariate sparsity (Lozano et al., 2009a, b), which may be needed to obtain physically sensible solutions. The models can be shown to be statistically consistent even in the $n \ll p$ regime, along with rigorous finite sample rates of convergence (Meinshausen and Bühlmann, 2006; Zhao and Yu 2006; Candès and Tao, 2007; Meinshausen and Yu, 2009; Negahban et al. 2009; Ravikumar et al. 2010; Negahban and Wainwright, 2011; Obozinski et al. 2011). While the number of samples n for extremes will be rather small, sparse regression methods will still be able to do model selection in a statistically consistent way. There are, however, a few key assumptions made while developing statistical consistency guarantees, which need not be true for climate data, especially extremes. A typical linear model of the form $y = X \theta + w$ assumes that (1) y has a linear dependence on the covariates, (2) the noise w is Gaussian or sub-Gaussian, and (3) samples are independently drawn from a fixed but unknown distribution. Such assumptions can often be violated in the context of extremes. In particular, (1) the extremes may have a nonlinear dependence on the covariates (Koltchinskii and Yuan, 2008; Raskutti et al., 2010), (2) the noise component may be non-Gaussian and may be even heavy tailed (Falk et al., 2010; Embrechts et al., 2011), and (3) the samples (y_i, X_i) may be dependent or even from a nonstationary distribution, violating the independence assumptions (Meir, 2000; Mohri and Rostamizadeh, 2010). The ability to accommodate such nonlinear, non-Gaussian, nonstationary behavior using advanced predictive models will determine the success of enhanced prediction for extremes.

An alternative promising approach for regression of unreliable variables, especially extremes, can be based on correlated but more reliable variables, or those that are currently better predicted. For example, although rainfall extremes may be difficult to characterize directly in terms of a set of covariates, given that rainfall extremes may be correlated with temperature in some way (O'Gorman and Schneider, 2009; Sugiyama et al., 2010), and temperature can be effectively characterized using suitable (sparse) regression models, one then obtains an indirect but reliable way to model rainfall extremes. The above idea is a prominent theme in multivariate or multiple output regression, especially in the context of spatial and geostatistics, where such models are studied as Linear Models of Coregionalization (LMC) (Wackernagel, 2003; Gelfand and Banerjee, 2010) and related spatiotemporal models (Higdon, 2002; Mardia and Goodall, 1993). In recent years, correlated multiple-output, nonlinear, nonparametric regression models have been studied in statistical machine learning using Gaussian Processes (Agovic et al., 2011; Álvarez and Lawrence, 2011). In particular, our recent work on Probabilistic Matrix Addition (Agovic et al., 2011) has two additional capabilities that may be useful in this context: (1) the ability to utilize a nonlinear covariance function (kernel) K_x among the covariates, as well as a nonlinear covariance function K_y among the multivariate output (e.g., precipitation and temperature); and (2) the ability to handle data matrices with missing entries. Recent literature has shown evidence that reliable auxiliary variables may contain valuable information on crucial variables that are currently difficult to physically model (e.g., O'Gorman and Schneider, 2009; Sugiyama et al., 2010), and the ideas outlined above may lead to a systematic way to leverage such signals. Such an accomplishment might not only enhance predictability of such key variables, but also augment physical understanding, which could inform future efforts in the climate modeling community.

5.5 CONCLUSIONS AND FUTURE RESEARCH

Computational data sciences may offer a path forward to one of the key science challenges relevant for stakeholders, resources managers, and policy makers—specifically, the consequences on statistical attributes of extreme events as a consequence of climate change. This chapter presented several critical challenges in the science of climate extremes that are not handled by the current generation of climate models, represent long-standing challenges in scientific understanding, may not be solved in the near future by improvements in physics-based modeling, and where data-driven computational methods may offer novel solutions. The chapter presented specific details on three interrelated problem areas—*extremes characterization, uncertainty quantification*, and *enhanced prediction*—as well as several potential conceptual and methodological directions for the interdisciplinary computational and data sciences communities to advance the science in these areas.

The close integration between physical understanding, or physics-based modeling, and data-driven insights is emphasized from three interrelated perspectives.

1. Data-driven insights from observations inform model diagnostics and uncertainty quantification.

2. Enhanced projections rely on data-guided functional mappings (e.g., between precipitation extremes and temperature), which in turn may be derived from both observations and model-simulations but remain conditioned on physics-based, model-simulated results in the future (e.g., future data-driven insights on precipitation extremes may be conditioned on projected temperatures in the future from models).

3. New insights from massive data on multivariate associations derived from observed or model-simulated data not only improve our understanding of relevant processes but also may inform the physical formulation and parameter choices within global or regional climate models.

This chapter made no attempt to comprehensively address two important research directions. The first area, on attribution of climate extremes, has been primarily motivated by prior and ongoing work led by the climate science community but has witnessed recent progress by the computer science community. The second area, on graphical models and complex networks in climate, has been motivated by nonlinear dynamics communities within the geosciences as well as more recently by the interdisciplinary data science communities. Attribution of climate extremes to global warming and anthropogenic emissions, regional changes in urbanization and land use, as well as other plausible causal factors, is a key concern for policy makers. The corresponding methods include data-driven approaches such as Granger causality and optimal fingerprinting, that, for example, may be used for attribution of global and regional changes in rainfall extremes (Min et al., 2011). Numerical modeling techniques have attempted to generate a range of simulations at specific locations and time periods to delineate what may be caused by natural variability versus what may have to be attributed to climate change, for example, with application to location-based precipitation extremes in a given season (Pall et al., 2011). While data science communities have developed (Lozano et al., 2009b) innovative approaches, new developments are motivated. Nonlinear dynamics methods have been used in climate for a while (e.g., to relate climate oscillators to the variability of river flows: Khan et al., 2006, 2007). Correlation-based complex networks have been used in climate to capture multivariate dependence (Steinhaeuser et al., 2011b), diagnose model performance through their ability to capture ocean-based oscillators (Kawale et al., 2011), relate ocean-based oscillators to regional climate (Steinhaeuser et al., 2011a; Chatterjee et al., 2012), as well as for abrupt change (Tsonis et al., 2007) and extremes processes (Malik et al., 2011). Further developments may make these emerging approaches important tools for climate extremes.

ACKNOWLEDGMENTS

This research was primarily supported by the National Science Foundation through their Expeditions in Computing program; grant number 1029166. ARG and EK were supported in part by a Northeastern University grant, as well as by the Nuclear Regulatory Commission. HNN acknowledges support by the U.S. Department of Energy (DOE), Office of Basic Energy Sciences (BES) Division of Chemical Sciences, Geosciences, and Biosciences. Sandia National Laboratories is a multi-program laboratory operated by Sandia Corporation, a Lockheed Martin Company, for the United States Department of Energy under contract DE-AC04-94-AL85000.

REFERENCES

Agovic, A., Banerjee, A., and Chatterjee, S. 2011. Probabilistic Matrix Addition. *International Conference on Machine Learning (ICML)*.

Álvarez, M.A., and Lawrence, N.D. 2011. Computationally efficient convolved multiple output Gaussian processes. *Journal of Machine Learning Research*, 12: 1425–1466.

Annan, J.D., and Hargreaves, J.C. 2006. Using multiple observationally-based constraints to estimate climate sensitivity. *Geophysical Research Letters*, 33, L06704, doi: http://dx.doi.org/10.1029/2005GL025259.

Babacan, S., Molina, R., and Katsaggelos, A., 2010. Bayesian comprehensive sensing using LaPlace priors. *IEEE Transactions on Image Processing*, 19(1): 53–63.

Banerjee, S., Gelfand, A.E., Finley, A.O., and Sang, H. 2008. Gaussian predictive process models for large spatial data sets. *Journal of the Royal Statistical Society B*, 70(4): 825–848.

Buser, C.M., Künsch, H.R., Lüthi, D., Wild, M., and Schär, C. 2009. Bayesian multi-model projection of climate: Bias assumptions and interannual variability. *Climate Dynamics*, 33: 849–868, doi:10.1007/s00382-009-0588-6.

Caflisch, R. 1998. Monte Carlo and quasi-Monte Carlo methods. *Acta Numerica*, 7: 1–49.

Candès, E., and Tao, T. 2007. The Dantzig selector: Statistical estimation when p is much larger than n. *Annals of Statistics*, 35(6): 2313–2351.

Candès, E.J., and Wakin, M.B., 2008. An introduction to compressive sampling. *IEEE Signal Processing Magazine*, 25(2), 21–30.

Chatterjee, S., Banerjee, A., Chatterjee, S., Steinhaeuser, K., and Ganguly, A.R. 2012. Sparse group lasso: Consistency and climate applications. *Proceedings of the SIAM International Conference on Data Mining* (in press).

Christensen, C., Aina, T., and Stainforth, D. 2005. The challenge of volunteer computing with lengthy climate model simulations. *First International Conference on e-Science and Grid Computing*. doi: 10.1109/E-SCIENCE.2005.76.

Coles, S.G. 2001. *An Introduction to Statistical Modeling of Extreme Values*. New York: Springer, 208 pp.

Coles, S.G., and Dixon, M.J. 1999. Likelihood-based inference for extreme value models. *Extremes*, 2(1): 5–23.

Cressie, N., and Johannesson, G. 2008. Fixed rank kriging for very large spatial data sets. *Journal of the Royal Statistical Society B*, 70(1): 209–226.

Debusschere, B., Najm, H., Pebay, P., Knio, O., Ghanem, R., and Le Maitre, O. 2004. Numerical challenges in the use of polynomial chaos representations for stochastic processes. *SIAM Journal of Scientific Computing*, 26: 698–719.

Donoho, D.L. 2006. Compressed Sensing. *IEEE Transactions on Information Theory*, 52(4): 1289–1306.

Drignei, D., Forest, C.E., and Nychka, D. 2009. Parameter estimation for computationally intensive nonlinear regression with an application to climate modeling. *Annals of Applied Statistics*, 2(4): 1217–1230.

Efron, B. 1979. Bootstrap methods: Another look at the jackknife. *Annals of Statistics*, 7: 101–118.

Emanuel, K., Sundararajan, R., and Williams, J. 2008. Hurricanes and global warming: Results from downscaling IPCC AR4 simulations. *Bulletin of the American Meteorological Society*, 89(3): 347–368.

Embrechts, P., Klüppelberg, C., and Mikosch, T. 2011. *Modelling Extremal Events for Insurance and Finance*. New York: Springer.

Engelhaupt, E. 2008. Climate change: A matter of national security. *Environmental Science & Technology*, 42(20): 7458–7549.

Falk, M., Hüsler, J., and Reiss, R. 2010. *Laws of Small Numbers: Extremes and Rare Events*. New York and Berlin: Springer.

Fern, A., and Givan, R. 2003. Online ensemble learning: An empirical study. *Machine Learning*, 53: 71–109.

Ferro, C.A.T., and Segers, J. 2003. Inference for clusters of extreme values. *Journal of the Royal Statistical Society, Series B*, 65(2): 545–556.

Furrer, R., and Sain, S.R. 2009. Spatial model fitting for large datasets with applications to climate and microarray problems. *Statistics and Computing*, 19: 113–128, doi: http://dx.doi.org/10.1007/s11222-008-9075-x.

Furrer, R., Sain, S.R., Nychka, D., and Tebaldi, C. 2007. Multivariate Bayesian analysis of atmosphere-ocean general circulation models. *Environmental and Ecological Statistics*, 14: 249–266.

Ganguly, A.R., Steinhaeuser, K., Erickson, D.J., Branstetter, M., Parish, E.S., Singh, N., Drake, J.B., and Buja, L. 2009b. Higher trends but larger uncertainty and geographic variability in 21st century temperature and heat waves. *Proceedings of the National Academy of Sciences of the United States of America*, 106(37): 15555–15559.

Ganguly, A.R., Steinhaeuser, K., Sorokine, A., Parish, E.S., Kao, S.-C., and Branstetter, M. 2009a. Geographic analysis and visualization of climate extremes for the Quadrennial Defense Review. *Proceedings of the 17th ACM SIGSPATIAL International Conference on Advances in Geographic Information Systems*, p. 542–543.

Gelfand, A.E., and Banerjee, S. 2010. Multivariate spatial process models. In A.E. Gelfand, P. Diggle, P. Guttorp, and M. Fuentes (Eds.), *Handbook of Spatial Statistics*. Boca Raton, FL: CRC Press.

Ghanem, R., and Spanos, P. 1991. *Stochastic Finite Elements: A Spectral Approach*. New York and Berlin: Springer.

Ghosh, S., Das, D., Kao, S.-C., and Ganguly, A.R. 2011. Lack of uniform trends increasing spatial variability in observed Indian rainfall extremes. *Nature Climate Change*. (In press—available online). 2, 86–91, DOI: 1038/nclimate1377.

Giorgi, F., and Mearns, L.O. 2002. Calculation of average, uncertainty range, and reliability of regional climate changes from AOGCM simulations via the "Reliability Ensemble Averaging" (REA) method. *Journal of Climate*, 15: 1141–1158.

Girko, V.L. 1995. *Statistical Analysis of Observations of Increasing Dimension*. New York: Kluwer Academic.

Goswami, B.N., Venugopal, V., Sengupta, D., Madhusoodanan, M.S., and Xavier, P.K. 2006. Increasing trend of extreme rain events over India in a warming environment. *Science*, 314(5804): 1442–1445.

Govaerts, Y.M., and Lattanzio, A. 2007. Retrieval error estimation of surface albedo derived from geostationary large band satellite observations: Application to Meteosat-2 and Meteosat-7 data. *Journal of Geophysical Research*, 112 D05102, doi: http://dx.doi.org/10.1029/2006JD007313.

Greene, A.M., Goddard, L., and Lall, U. 2006. Probabilistic multimodel regional temperature projections. *Journal of Climate*, 19: 4326–4343.

Hagedorn, R.F., Doblas-Reyes, F.J., and Palmer T.N. 2005. The rationale behind the success of multi-model ensembles in seasonal forecasting. I. Basic concept. *Tellus A,* 57: 219–233.

Hall, P., and Tajvidi, N. 2000. Nonparametric analysis of temporal trend when fitting parametric models to extreme value data. *Statistical Science,* 15(2): 153–167.

Higdon, D.M. 2002. Space and space-time modelling using process convolutions. In *Quantitative Methods for Current Environmental Issues,* p. 37–56. Berlin: Springer-Verlag.

Hosking, J.R.M., and Wallis, J.R. 1997. *Regional Frequency Analysis: An Approach Based on L-Moments.* Cambridge: Cambridge University Press.

IPCC. 2007. Fourth Assessment Report (AR4), Working Group I, Chapter 8.

IPCC. 2011. Summary for Policymakers. In Intergovernmental Panel on Climate Change Special Report on Managing the Risks of Extreme Events and Disasters to Advance Climate Change Adaptation, Field, C.B., Barros, V., Stocker, T.F., Qin, D., Dokken, D., Ebi, K.L., Mastrandrea, M.D., Mach, K.J., Plattner, G.-K., Allen, S., Tignor, M., and Midgley, P.M. (Eds.). Cambridge (UK) and New York: Cambridge University Press.

Jackson, C., Sen, M., and Stoffa, P. 2004. An efficient stochastic Bayesian approach to optimal parameter and uncertainty estimation for climate model predictions. *Journal of Climate,* 17(14): 2828–2841.

Jackson, C., Xia, Y., Sen, M., and Stoffa, P. 2003. Optimal parameter and uncertainty estimation of a land surface model: A case example using data from Cabauw. *Netherlands Journal of Geophysical Research,* 108 (D18): 4583 http://dx.doi.org/10.1029/2002JD002991.

Jackson, C.S., Sen, M.K., Huerta, G., Deng, Y., and Bowman, K.P. 2008. Error reduction and convergence in climate prediction. *Journal of Climate,* 21: 6698–6709, doi: 10.1175/2008JCLI2112.1.

Kao, S.-C., and Ganguly, A.R. 2011. Intensity, duration, and frequency of precipitation extremes under 21st-century warming scenarios. *Journal of Geophysical Research,* 116(D16119): 14 pages. DOI: 10.1029/2010JD015529.

Karl, T.R., Melillo, J.M., and Peterson, T.C. Eds. 2009. *Global Climate Change Impacts in the United States.* Cambridge (UK) and New York: Cambridge University Press, 196 pp.

Kawale, J., Liess, S., Kumar, A., Steinbach, M., Ganguly, A., Samatova, N.F., Semazzi, F., Snyder, P., and Kumar, V. 2011. Data guided discovery of dynamic climate dipoles. *Proceedings of the 2011 NASA Conference on Intelligent Data Understanding (CIDU).*

Khan, S., Bandyopadhyay, S., Ganguly, A.R., Saigal, S., Erickson, D.J., Protopopescu, V., and Ostrouchov, G. 2007. Relative performance of mutual information estimation methods for quantifying the dependence among short and noisy data. *Physical Review,* E 026209.

Khan, S., Ganguly, A.R., Bandyopadhyay, S., Saigal, S., Erickson, D.J., Protopopescu, V., and Ostrouchov, G. 2006. Nonlinear statistics reveals stronger ties between ENSO and the tropical hydrological cycle. *Geophysical Research Letters,* 33: L24402.

Kharin, V.V., and Zwiers, F.W. 2000. Changes in the extremes in an ensemble of transient climate simulations with a coupled atmosphere-ocean GCM. *Journal of Climate*, 13: 3760–3788.

Kharin, V.V., and Zwiers, F.W. 2005. Estimating extremes in transient climate change simulations. *Journal of Climate*, 18: 1156–1173.

Kharin, V.V., Zwiers, F.W., Zhang, X., and Hegerl, G.C. 2007. Changes in temperature and precipitation extremes in the IPCC ensemble of global coupled model simulations. *Journal of Climate*, 20: 1419–1444.

Knutti, R. 2010. The end of model democracy? *Climatic Change*, 102(3-4): 395–404.

Knutti, R., Furrer, R., Tebaldi, C., Cermak, J., and Meehl, G.A. 2010. Challenges in combining projections from multiple climate models. *Journal of Climate*, 23(10): 2739–2758.

Kodra, E., Chatterjee, S., and Ganguly, A.R. 2011b. Challenges and opportunities toward improved data-guided handling of global climate model ensembles for regional climate change assessments. *ICML Workshop on Machine Learning for Global Challenges*.

Kodra, E., Ghosh, S., and Ganguly, A.R. 2012. Evaluation of global climate models for Indian monsoon climatology. *Environmental Research Letters*, 7, 014012, 7 pp., doi: 10.1088/1748-9326/7/1/014012.

Kodra, E., Steinhaeuser, K., and Ganguly, A.R. 2011a. Persisting cold extremes under 21st-century warming scenarios. *Geophysical Research Letters*, 38(L08705): 5 pages. DOI: 10.1029/2011GL047103.

Koltchinskii, V., and Yuan, M. 2008. Sparse recovery in large ensembles of kernel machines. *Conference on Learning Theory (COLT)*.

Krishnamurti, T.N. et al. 1999. Improved weather and seasonal climate forecasts from multimodel superensemble. *Science*, 285(5433): 1548–1550.

Le Maitre, O., Najm, H., Ghanem, R., and Knio, O. 2004. Multi-resolution analysis of Wiener-type uncertainty propagation schemes. *Journal of Computational Physics*, 197: 502–531.

Liu, S.C., Fu, C., Shiu, C.-J., Chen, J.-P., and Wu, Fu. 2009. Temperature dependence of global precipitation extremes. *Geophysical Research Letters*, 36(L17702): 4 pages. DOI: 10.1029/2009GL040218.

Lozano, A.C., Abe, N., Liu, Y., and Rosset, S. 2009b. Grouped graphical Granger modeling methods for temporal causal modeling. *ACM SIGKDD Conference on Knowledge Discovery and Data Mining (KDD) 2009*, p. 577–586.

Lozano, A.C., Li, H., Niculescu-Mizil, A., Liu, Y., Perlich, C., Hosking, J., and Abe, N. 2009a. Spatial-temporal causal modeling for climate change attribution. *Proceedings of the 15th ACM SIGKDD International Conference on Knowledge Discovery and Data Mining*, p. 587–596.

Malik, N., Bookhagen, B., Marwan, N., and Kurths, J. 2011. Analysis of spatial and temporal extreme monsoonal rainfall over South Asia using complex networks. *Climate Dynamics* 39(3–4), 971–987, DOI: 10,1007/500382-011-1156-4.

Mannshardt-Shamseldin, E.C., Smith, R.L., Sain, S.R., Mearns, L.O., and Cooley, D. 2011. Downscaling extremes: A comparison of extreme value distributions in point-source and gridded precipitation data. *Annals of Applied Statistics*, 4(1), 486–502.

Mardia, K.V., and Goodall, C.R. 1993. Spatial-temporal analysis of multivariate environmental monitoring data. In *Multivariate Environmental Statistics*, pp. 347–386. Elsevier Science Publishers B.V., North Holland.

Marzouk, Y.M., and Najm, H.N. 2009. Dimensionality reduction and polynomial chaos acceleration of Bayesian inference in inverse problems. *Journal of Computational Physics*, 228(6): 1862–1902.

Meehl, G.A., and Tebaldi, C. 2004. More intense, more frequent, and longer lasting heat waves in the 21st-century. *Science*, 305(5686): 994–997.

Meinshausen, N., and Bühlmann, P. 2006. High-dimensional graphs and variable selection with the Lasso. *Annals of Statistics*, 34: 1436–1462.

Meinshausen, N., and Yu, B. 2009. Lasso-type recovery of sparse representations for high-dimensional data. *Annals of Statistics*, 37(1): 246–270.

Meir, R. 2000. Nonparametric time series prediction through adaptive model selection. *Machine Learning*, 39: 5–34.

Min, S.-K., and Hense, A. 2007. Hierarchical evaluation of IPCC AR4 coupled climate models with systematic consideration of model uncertainties. *Climate Dynamics*, 29: 853–868.

Min, S.-K., Zhang, X., Zwiers, F.W., and Hegerl, G.C. 2011. Human contribution to more-intense precipitation extremes. *Nature*, 470: 378–381.

Mohri, M., and Rostamizadeh, A. 2010. Stability bounds for stationary φ-mixing and β-mixing processes. *Journal of Machine Learning Research*, 11: 789–814.

Monteleoni, C., Schmidt, G., and Saroha, S. 2010. Tracking climate models. *NASA Conference on Intelligent Data Understanding*.

Morris, M. 1991. Factorial sampling plans for preliminary computer experiments. *Technometrics*, 33(2): 161–174.

Muller, C.J., and O'Gorman, P.A. 2011. An energetic perspective on the regional response of precipitation to climate change. *Nature Climate Change*, 1: 266–271.

Najm, H.N. 2009. Uncertainty quantification and polynomial chaos techniques in computational fluid dynamics. *Annual Reviews of Fluid Mechanics*, 41: 35–52.

Negahban, S., Ravikumar, P.D., Wainwright, M.J., and Yu, B. 2009. A unified framework for high-dimensional analysis of M-estimators with decomposable regularizers. *NIPS*, 2009: 1348–1356.

Negahban, S., and Wainwright, M.J. 2011. Simultaneous support recovery in high-dimensional regression: Benefits and perils of L_1-L_∞-regularization. *IEEE Transactions on Information Theory*, 57(6): 3841-3863, June 2011.

Nobile, F., Tempone, R., and Webster, C. 2008. A sparse grid stochastic collocation method for partial differential equations with random input data. *SIAM Journal of Numerical Analysis*, 46(5): 2411–2442.

NRC. 2011. *National Security Implications of Climate Change for U.S. Naval Forces*. Committee on National Security Implications of Climate Change for U.S. Naval Forces. National Research Council of the National Academies. National Academies Press. 172 pp.

Obozinski, G., Wainwright, M.J., and Jordan, M.I. 2011. Union support recovery in high-dimensional multivariate regression. *Annals of Statistics*, 39(1): 1–47.

O'Gorman, P.A., and Schneider, T. 2009. The physical basis for increases in precipitation extremes in simulations of 21st-century climate change. *Proceedings of the National Academy of Sciences of the United States of America,* 106(35): 14773–14777.

Overpeck, J.T., Meehl, G.A., Bony, S., and Easterling, D.R. 2011. Climate data challenges in the 21st century. *Science,* 331: 700-702. doi: 10.1126/science.1197869.

Pall, P., Aina, T., Stone, D.A., Stott, P.A., Nozawa, T., Hilberts, A.G.J., Lohmann, D., and Allen, M.R. 2011. Anthropogenic greenhouse gas contribution to flood risk in England and Wales in autumn 2000. *Nature,* 470: 382–385.

Perkins, S.E., Pitman, A.J., and Sisson, S.A. 2009. Smaller projected increases in 20-year temperature returns over Australia in skill-selected climate models. *Geophysical Research Letters,* 36: L06710, doi:10.1029/2009GL037293.

Pierce, D.W., Barnett, T.P., Santer, B.D., and Gleckler, P.J. 2009. Selecting global climate models for regional climate change studies. *Proceedings of the National Academy of Sciences USA,* 106(21): 8441–8446.

Raskutti, G., Wainwright, M.J., and Yu, B. 2010. Minimax-Optimal Rates for Sparse Additive Models over Kernel Classes via Convex Programming. Technical report, http://arxiv.org/abs/1008.3654, UC Berkeley, Department of Statistics, August.

Ravikumar, P., Wainwright, M.J., and Lafferty, J. 2010. High-dimensional Ising model selection using L1 regularized logistic regression. *Annals of Statistics,* 38(3): 1287–1319.

Sain, S., Furrer, R., and Cressie, N. 2008. Combining Ensembles of Regional Climate Model Output via a Multivariate Markov Random Field Model. Technical report, Department of Statistics, The Ohio State University.

Saltelli, A., Chan, K., and Scott, E.M. 2000. *Sensitivity Analysis.* Wiley Series in Probability and Statistics New York.

Sanso, B., Forest, C.E., and Zantedeschi, D. 2008. Inferring climate system properties using a computer model. *Bayesian Analysis,* 3(1): 1–38.

Santer, B.D. et al. 2009. Incorporating model quality information in climate change detection and attribution studies. *Proc. Natl. Acad. Sci. USA,* 106(35): 14778–14783.

Schiermeier, Q. 2010. The real holes in climate science. *Nature,* 463: 284–287.

Seni, G., and Elder, J.F. 2010. Ensemble methods in data mining: Improving accuracy through combining predictions. *Synthesis Lectures on Data Mining and Knowledge Discovery.*

Smith, R.L., Tebaldi, C., Nychka, D., and Mearns, L.O. 2009. Bayesian modeling of uncertainty in ensembles of climate models. *Journal of the American Statistical Association,* 104(485): 97–116. doi:10.1198/jasa.2009.0007.

Soize, C., and Ghanem, R. 2004. Physical systems with random uncertainties: Chaos representations with arbitrary probability measure. *SIAM Journal of Scientific Computing,* 26: 395–410.

Stainforth, D.A. et al. 2005. Uncertainty in predictions of the climate response to rising levels of greenhouse gases. *Nature,* 433: 403–406.

Steinhaeuser, K., Chawla, N.V., and Ganguly, A.R. 2011a. Complex networks as a unified framework for descriptive analysis and predictive modeling in climate science. *Statistical Analysis and Data Mining,* 4(5): 497–511.

Steinhaeuser, K., Ganguly, A.R., and Chawla, N. 2011b. Multivariate and multiscale dependence in the global climate system revealed through complex networks. *Climate Dynamics,* DOI: 10.1007/s00382-011-1135-9. 39(3–4), 889–895

Sugiyama, M., Shiogama, H., and Emori, S. 2010. Precipitation extreme changes exceeding moisture content increases in MIROC and IPCC climate models. *Proceedings of the National Academy of Sciences of the United States of America,* 107(2): 571–575.

Tebaldi, C., and Knutti, R. 2007. The use of the multimodel ensemble in probabilistic climate projections. *Philosophical Transactions of the Royal Society A,* 365, 2053–2075.

Tebaldi, C., Mearns, L.O., Nychka, D., and Smith, R.L. 2004. Regional probabilities of precipitation change: A Bayesian analysis of multimodel simulations. *Geophysical Research Letters,* 31, L24213, doi:10.1029/2004GL021276.

Tebaldi, C., and Sanso, B. 2009. Joint projections of temperature and precipitation change from multiple climate models: A hierarchical Bayesian approach. *Journal of the Royal Statistical Society A,* 172(1): 83–106.

Tibshirani, R. 1996. Regression shrinkage and selection via the lasso. *Journal of the Royal Statistical Society, Series B,* 58(1): 267–288.

Tollefson, J. 2008a. Climate war games. *Nature,* 454(7205): 673. August 7.

Tollefson, J. 2008b. Climate war games: The "Angry Red Chart." Nature Blogs. 30 July: http://blogs.nature.com/news/blog/events/climate_war_game/.

Tollefson, J. 2011. Climate change: Cold spells in a warm world. *Nature,* 139. Research Highlights. 14 April. DOI:10.1038/472139d.

Tsonis, A.A., Swanson, K., and Kravtsov, S. 2007. A new dynamical mechanism for major climate shifts. *Geophysical Research Letters,* 34: L13705, 5 pp., doi:10.1029/2007GL030288.

Villagran, A., Huerta, G., Jackson, C.S., and Sen. M.K. 2008. Computational methods for parameter estimation in climate models. *Bayesian Analysis,* 3: 823–850, doi: http://dx.doi.org/10.1214/08-BA331.

Wackernagel, H. 2003. *Geostatistics: An Introduction with Applications.* Berlin: Springer-Verlag.

Wehner, M. 2010. Source of uncertainty in the extreme value statistics of climate data. *Extremes,* 13(2): 205–217.

Weigel, A.P., Knutti, R., Linger, M.A., and Appenzeller, C. 2010. Risks of model weighting in multimodel climate projections. *Journal of Climate,* 23: 4175–4191.

Xiu, D., and Karniadakis, G. 2002. The Wiener-Askey polynomial chaos for stochastic differential equations. *SIAM Journal on Scientific Computing,* 24: 619–644.

Zhao, P., and Yu, B. 2006. On model selection consistency of lasso. *Journal of Machine Learning Research,* 7: 2541–2567.

III

**Computational Intelligent Data Analysis
for Biodiversity and Species Conservation**

III

Mathematical Programming Applications to Land Conservation and Environmental Quality

Jacob R. Fooks and Kent D. Messer

CONTENTS

6.1 INTRODUCTION

PROGRAMS TO CONSERVE ECOLOGICALLY valuable land and ensure environmental services are major sources of government and nonprofit spending in the United States and throughout the world. At the federal level, the U.S. Department of Agriculture (USDA) Conservation Reserve Program planned to spend upward of $1.8 billion in 2010 (USDA, 2009), while the most recent Farm Bill (2008–2012) included $11.7 billion for conservation purposes (Claassen, 2009). State and county programs have spent more than $2 billion on permanent agricultural conservation easements in a recent 25-year period (American Farmland Trust, 2010), and open-space referenda for all of the United States authorized $31 billion between 1996 and 2009 (Trust for Public Lands, 2009). As of 2005, private land trusts had protected 37 million acres (Aldrich and Wyerman, 2006). The European Union (EU) anticipated spending €35.4 billion on "agri-environmental" programs between 2007 and 2013 (EU, 2009), while China's Sloping Land Conversion Program has a budget estimated at $48 billion (Xu et al., 2010).

Despite the substantial sums available for conservation efforts, programs typically identify more potential projects than they can fund. Given such budgetary constraints among conservation organizations, economists have long argued that consideration should be given to maximizing the value achieved with public funds when selecting projects (Underhill, 1994; Babcock et al., 1997). The strategies typically used by conservation organizations rely on a parcel-rating scheme that involves expert panels or standardized scoring systems. Commonly used systems include the USDA's Natural Resource Conservation Service (NRCS) Land Evaluation and Site Assessment (LESA) score for agricultural land and the Environmental Benefit Index (EBI), which was originally designed for the Conservation Reserve Program. These ratings are used in a Benefit Targeting (BT) selection process to rank potential projects from highest to lowest. Projects are then sequentially selected for funding based on their rank until the budget is exhausted. Numerous studies report that this "greedy" algorithm is highly inefficient when compared to alternative mathematical optimization approaches (see, for example, Babcock et al. (1997), Wu et al. (2000), and Polasky et al. (2001)).

6.1.1 Background of Optimization in Conservation Planning

Two approaches commonly advocated as better alternatives to the BT selection process are Cost-Effectiveness Analysis (CEA) and Binary Linear

Programming (BLP). CEA ranks and selects in a manner similar to BT, but project rankings are based on the ratio of the benefit score per dollar of cost. Consequently, CEA can achieve a greater value per dollar spent. It typically performs much better than BT and has the added advantage of being intuitive, easy to explain, and relatively easy to sell to program managers. On the other hand, it achieves suboptimal results under many conditions (Messer, 2006) and is difficult to extend to problems with complex constraint structures or nonlinear benefit functions.

BLP (sometimes referred to as Binary Integer Programming (BIP)) is an extension of linear programming in which the decision variables take binary values that represent the decision to fund (given a value of zero) or not fund a project (given a value of one). An advantage of the binary formation of this problem is that the objective function can be represented as a vector of benefit scores multiplied by the binary decision variables. This objective function is maximized subject to a budget constraint and potentially under additional program-specific constraints. A BLP model typically is solved with a branch-and-bound algorithm and is a reliable algorithm as it will always identify the true optimum when feasible. Its performance vis-à-vis CEA ranges from a marginal improvement to, at most, twice the level of benefit achieved by CEA (Dantzig, 1957).

Conservation programs generally have been slow to adopt either of these methods. Despite the promise of a substantial increase in environmental benefit offered by either CEA or BLP, the only conservation organization known to be using either one is the Baltimore County Division of Environmental Protection and Resource Management (DEPRM), which has used CEA for its agricultural protection program since 2007. During the first 3 years that DEPRM used CEA, it protected 680 more acres of land worth $5.4 million than its previous BT process would have under the same budgets (Kaiser and Messer, 2011).

Researchers have studied this lack of adoption (e.g., Prendergast et al., 1999; Messer, Allen, and Chen, 2011; Pressey and Cowling, 2001) and identified several barriers in the conservation decision process. For example, Prendergast et al. (1999), through an informal interview process involving a sampling of ecologists and land managers, identified three main barriers to adoption: (1) lack of knowledge of the alternative methods, (2) lack of resources, and (3) real and perceived shortcomings in the methods. A recent survey of Maryland's county-level conservation program administrators suggested not only that managers were not familiar with either

BLP or CEA, but also that these managers did not consider that being cost-effective was a major priority, and also reported lacking incentives to adopt alternative selection approaches (Messer, Allen, and Chen, 2011).

A common concern identified in these studies was a "black-box" perception of BLP. Program managers' duties can include more than merely maximizing benefit scores. They also must defend the "value" achieved from donor, funding agency, and taxpayer money; ensure that participants get a fair deal from a transparent decision mechanism; and distribute funds in a manner that is perceived as equitable. BLP, as classically implemented, has been seen as lacking transparency and the flexibility necessary to address many of these duties, which can be thought of as secondary or operational objectives. These objectives may not immediately impact the primary goal of protecting high-quality land but still may be important factors in the decision-making process and thus significant barriers to the adoption of new approaches. Operational objectives can be incorporated as constraints, as was done by Önal et al. (1998), who used an optimization model to address both environmental and equity concerns in a watershed management scenario. Their model maximized total profit across a watershed with a chance constraint on chemical runoff levels to account for the stochastic nature of rainfall and a constraint on the equity of the program's impact that was measured by an index of deviation from a uniform loss-sharing level. The study varied these constraints to examine trade-offs among income, pollution, and equity losses. This approach, however, still offered little ability to consider the sensitivity of the single solution provided or alternatives to it.

A second option is to format the process as a Multiple-Objective Linear Programming (MOLP) problem (also referred to as Goal Programming) with the secondary objectives included as weighted goals. MOLP has been applied to several conservation programs: a balancing of economic and biological objectives over short-term and long-term time frames in fishery management (Drynan and Sandiford, 1985; Mardle and Pascoe, 1999; Mardle et al., 2000), an optimization of environmental, social, and economic goals in energy production (Silva and Nakata, 2009); and management of public water resources (Neely et al., 1977; Ballestero et al., 2002). Önal (1997) considered an approach similar to MOLP in a forest management setting; he employed a model that, instead of minimizing deviations from a goal as is done in MOLP, used constrained deviations from a goal to maximize the discounted future harvest value while maintaining a minimum value for a species diversity index.

6.1.2 An Overview of the Pennsylvania Dirt and Gravel Roads Program

As an example of how an optimization approach incorporating MOLP could be applied in a nonpoint source pollution context, we present the case of the Pennsylvania Dirt and Gravel Roads Program (DGRP).[*] DGRP is an innovative program established in conjunction with Trout Unlimited to reduce sediment pollution and improve water quality in sensitive rainbow trout habitats in Pennsylvania streams, where sediment is the largest, single source of pollution. Sediment pollution has immediate effects on the health of fish and other aquatic wildlife that lead to long-term ecosystem disruption and compositional changes downstream in estuaries such as the Chesapeake and Delaware Bays. Programs have been developed that regulate easily identified point sources of sediment pollution such as large, confined animal operations and construction sites with some degree of success, but a significant nonpoint source remains: Pennsylvania's 27,000 miles of dirt roads. The DGRP was established in 1997 as part of the Pennsylvania Vehicle Code to reduce dust and sediment pollution in the state's streams by funding improvements for dirt roads. As part of the program, the state annually distributes a fund of $4 million to 63 county conservation districts that, in turn, administer the program within a county and distribute funds for that county as grants to municipalities. Funds are assigned to a county based primarily on the number of miles of dirt road it contains, how many miles of those roads traverse specifically protected watersheds maintained by the county, and local material costs.

The Pennsylvania DGRP has had some success with more than 1,827 projects representing 982 miles of road protected as of 2008 (Center for Dirt and Gravel Road Studies, 2009). However, because the decision process used by many counties is essentially a modified benefit ranking scheme, there is likely some room for improvement in efficiency. In this chapter, we evaluate the results of a BLP model to determine the maximum potential environmental benefit available to the DGRP over several years. Those results can then be compared to the results of the current ranking method. Once a baseline model is developed, it can be extended to address specific questions related to the overall efficiency of a program. In the DGRP case, the model is extended to improve how the value of in-kind contributions is internalized in the decision process, assess the

---

[*] The authors would like to acknowledge the generous assistance of Wayne Kober, Robb Piper, and Barry Scheetz associated with the state of Pennsylvania's Dirt and Gravel Roads program.

effect of uncertainty about the actual cost of each project and in-kind contributions on the optimal solution, and investigate how the distribution of funds among counties influences the overall statewide benefit.

Several characteristics of the DGRP are important. First, the program focuses on local administration, with all allocation and auditing administration done at the county level. The state is involved only in training county program managers, reporting overall program results, and establishing basic project standards. The state also sets environmentally sustainable method (ESM) standards that dictate the methods and materials that may be used to ensure that each project represents an environmentally sustainable fix over the long term. All grant recipients must have an employee who has received ESM training within the previous 5 years to be eligible. Sites are ranked in terms of potential environmental impact based on a set of 12 criteria relating to road topology, proximity to a stream, stability of the drainage infrastructure, and the amount of canopy cover, among other considerations. The individual scores from each criterion are totaled to generate an overall environmental rank that ranges from 0 to 100, and the ranking is used to assign funding priorities. Additionally, in-kind contributions from grant applicants play a significant role in the program. Those contributions, typically in the form of in-kind equipment and labor, are not required by the state, but counties may enact minimum contribution levels or use the level of these in-kind contributions to adjust the ranking scores. Over the past several years, in-kind support for the program has been in the range of 40% ton 50% of program money spent. Also, counties often enact regulations that limit the total number of contracts or projects that can be awarded to a township simultaneously, or stipulate that all applicants must have received at least one funded project before any applicant can be considered for multiple projects. Further details on state-level administration of the program are available from Penn State University Center for Dirt and Gravel Road Studies (CDGRS), which was created to provide technical services for the program (CDGRS, 2009).

The inclusion of in-kind cost sharing and matching funds is a common practice in conservation programs and is designed to leverage additional resources from partner agencies and individuals to achieve their conservation objectives (Kotani, Messer, and Schulze, 2010). Implementation schemes vary, but most require the participating organization to cover some percentage of the project's cost. The numerous other federal, state, and private conservation funding programs that require some sort of cost sharing include the USDA Conservation Reserve Program (USDA, 2010), the U.S. Forest Service's Forest Legacy Program (Fooks and Messer, 2012), and the U.S. Fish and Wildlife Service National Wetlands Conservation Grant Program.

In the literature, in-kind cost sharing has been considered a type of matching grant program where the agency requesting a grant agrees to pay some percentage of the total project cost. Theoretically, matching grants are seen as a mechanism that corrects for externalities and "spillovers" in federalized agency structures. Oates (1999) pointed out that the local benefits from a project under consideration might not justify funding it for the local agency. However, a project may offer additional nonlocal benefits, and those spillover benefits could make it attractive to society as a whole. The matching grant offered by an outside body would represent a sort of "Pigouvian subsidy" to pay the local agency for the external benefits obtained in other jurisdictions. On the other hand, Bucovetsky et al. (1998) have offered an informational argument for matching grants, starting with the assumption that a government should distribute funds to the regions that value public services the most, then justifying a matching grant mechanism as revealing the level of commitment of the potential grant recipients—in other words, requiring to demonstrate the true benefits of the program by having them "put their money where their mouth is." Thus, the matching grant serves as a mechanism by which the funder can reveal the private value of funding to the participants.

The evidence thus far offered on the effect of matching grants and cost sharing has been mixed.* Baker et al. (1999) found that instituting a matching grant system in the Canada Assistance Plan lowered expenditure growth by eight to nine percentage points as provinces became responsible for a portion of program costs. Using simulations, Borge and Rattsø (2008) found that matching grants decreased expenses more than block grants but led to unstable service provision over time. Chernick (1995) found that conversions from matching to fixed block grants by U.S. federal welfare programs varied substantially across states but generally led to a reduction in benefits.

---

* For an in-depth discussion of matching grants and their implementation, see Boadway and Shah (2007).

The project selection literature generally does not address issues associated with the incorporation of in-kind requirements into the selection process. In-kind contributions are implicitly accounted for by the reduction in the project cost to the government, but that measure fails to take full advantage of the additional information potentially provided by the size of the in-kind cost share, such as the degree of commitment of the partner organization, and the political benefits of using program funds to leverage resources from other organizations, agencies, and individuals. In this chapter, we incorporate that additional information into an optimization approach by developing a MOLP model that seeks to optimize both conservation outcomes and partner in-kind cost sharing contributions. Results from the models show that MOLP offers results that are superior to approaches currently used by the DGRP while yielding cost-effective outcomes that are likely to be more practical than solutions generated by the standard BLP approach.

For the DGRP case study, datasets were available for three Pennsylvania counties: Bradford, Cambria, and Carbon (displayed in Figure 6.1). Bradford County is the largest and most rural of the three. It has the second largest dirt road network in the state and has been granted an average of $246,000 per year in funding over the course of the program. Carbon and Cambria Counties both have a smaller area and are more densely populated. Carbon County has received, on average, $24,000 per year over

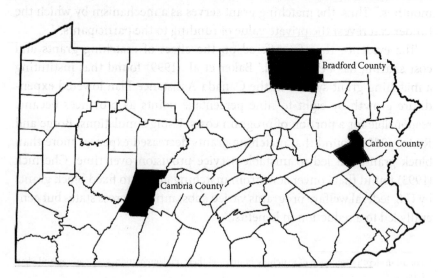

FIGURE 6.1   Map of Pennsylvania counties.

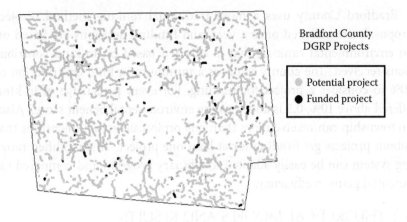

FIGURE 6.2   Map of Bradford County projects.

the course of the program, while Cambria County has received $17,000 annually. These three counties were recommended by state program personnel for analysis because the local officials were most willing to cooperate by sharing their data, and these counties were the most representative of the range of counties participating in the program. Data on the completed projects and fund distributions were provided by the Center for Dirt and Gravel Road Studies (CDRGS, 2009). Data on the submitted projects and procedures for Bradford County by year were obtained from the Bradford County Conservation District (BCCD) (M. Lovegreen, BCCD Director, personal communication, November 2, 2009). A map of potential and funded projects is displayed in Figure 6.2.

Because Cambria and Carbon Counties receive limited funds each year (less than $30,000, while many projects cost more than $50,000), their project choices are limited and they use less-complex decision criteria. Cambria County issued a call for projects when the program was first initiated and has since worked its way through the initial applicants and funded all of the projects that met the state's criteria. Carbon County does not officially advertise the program, and it funds any appropriate project that the conservation district manager comes across during the course of his duties. These processes are difficult to approach with a binary program as the counties have maintained no data on projects that were not funded. That is not to say that the selection processes they use are in any way optimal; but because there is little data on alternative projects, it is impossible to say how much opportunity was missed by not soliciting new projects on a regular basis.

Bradford County uses a more traditional ranking method. Project proposals are solicited once a year, and funding decisions are based on an environmental ranking that is adjusted based on in-kind contributions received. The county requires a minimum in-kind contribution of 10% to consider a project for funding. For every percentage of in-kind offered above 10%, 0.5 is added to the environmental benefit score.[*] Also, no township can receive more than one project unless all townships that submit projects get funding for at least one project. This modified ranking system can be easily adapted to a binary program and compared for potential gains in efficiency.

6.2 THEORETICAL MODELS AND RESULTS

The basic template used for this case is BLP. In its most general form, it can be expressed as

$$\text{Max: } Z = c^T x$$

$$\text{Subject to: } Ax \leq b$$

$$x_i \in \{0, 1\}$$

where Z is the total amount of environmental benefit obtainable from the county's funds and is the sum of the individual project's environmental scores, c is a vector of the environmental scores for the projects, x is a vector of binary variables indicating whether a given project is chosen (1 if selected; 0 if not selected), A is a matrix of constraining factors such as project costs, and b is a vector of the total endowment for each constraining factor, such as total budget. The basic model maximizes environmental scores subject only to budget constraints. However, there are several additional factors that must be considered in this case. Specifically, any conditions on funding of multiple projects for the same applicant and consideration of in-kind contributions must be part of the model. To capture funding restrictions, we can include a constraint that is the sum of all the

---

[*] Projects are occasionally specially designated as "Trout Unlimited" based on being located in sensitive watersheds. Those projects always get first priority for all funds. Recall that the Trout Unlimited organization originally helped organize the DGRP. However, Trout Unlimited projects are sufficiently rare (there was only one for 2002 through 2008) so they are left out of this analysis.

projects in a township. When set to greater than or equal to 1, this constraint ensures that all townships receive at least one funded project. Setting this constraint to less than 1, it prevents funding of more than one project for each township. One of these conditions must be true for the constraint to hold. This can be achieved using a logical condition or a binary switch variable; however, those techniques would make the program nonlinear, which complicates solving it. As an alternative, because there generally is insufficient funding for townships to obtain multiple projects, the first condition can be omitted with the caveat that the model must be altered slightly if there were ever sufficient funding for at least one project for each township. In-kind contributions are considered in depth in the following subsection. Thus, for an initial base model, we use the following:

$$\text{Max: } Z = \sum_{i=1}^{n} x_i e_i$$

$$\text{Subject to: } \sum_{i=1}^{n} x_i p_i \leq B$$

$$\sum_{i=1}^{n} x_i^j \leq 1$$

$$x_i \in \{0,1\}$$

where x_i is a binary variable indicating whether project i is chosen, x_i^j is x_i for projects submitted by township j, e_i is the environmental score for project i, p_i is the requested grant amount for project i, and B is the total budget for the year.

Table 6.1 outlines the results from the model in terms of the total benefit to Bradford County offered by the two methods for 2002 through 2008. The key observation here is that BIP offers a significant improvement. Specifically, BIP selects a set of projects that would deliver a 57% increase in environmental benefit, a 57% increase in in-kind contributions, and a 102% increase in the number of projects funded. Those results may not be realistic, however, due to uncertainty regarding project costs. This is discussed further in Issue 2 (see Section 6.2.2).

TABLE 6.1   Results of Multiple-Objective Linear Programming, Binary Linear Programming, and Benefit Targeting

	Multiple-Objective Linear Programming	Binary Linear Programming	Benefit Targeting
Money spent	$1,924,423	$2,027,195	$1,934,422
Environmental score	5,736	6,613	4,208
In-kind contributions	$640,170	$603,641	$424,141
Number of projects funded	100	119	59

6.2.1 Issue 1: How Best to Account for In-Kind Funding

On the surface, the amount of in-kind funding offered for a project is not significant because how the project is funded does not change the environmental benefit the project provides. However, the more in-kind funding a township offers, the fewer funds the county has to invest in a single project, thus allowing more projects to be funded. Townships do not necessarily have an incentive to offer large in-kind contributions, especially given constraints that limit the number of projects funded per applicant. As a result, an incentive must be established that maximizes the effectiveness of county funds spent by the program over time. The state does not require in-kind offers, so it is left to the counties to decide how to address such funding. The approach employed by Bradford County involves setting a minimum percentage of in-kind contribution and increasing the project's environmental benefit score in the ranking process for every percentage point offered beyond the minimum. While it does insert in-kind contributions into the process, this ad hoc solution lacks flexibility and is not particularly elegant. As an alternative, we propose modestly restructuring the problem as a MOLP model.

As a MOLP model, instead of maximizing only environmental benefits, the algorithm would calculate both a maximum possible environmental benefit and a maximum in-kind funding offer, and the objective is to minimize weighted percentage deviations from the two maxima with 85% of the weight placed on environmental benefit and 15% on in-kind contributions. This 85:15 weighting scheme is arbitrary but was set as an initial estimation of weights with the purpose of emphasizing environmental benefit while still considering in-kind contribution levels. Other weights are explored later.[*]

---

[*] An interesting analysis would be to determine if there is an optimal weighting scheme that would maximize benefits over time. Unfortunately, such an analysis would require data on if and how townships reacted to changes in how in-kind contributions were treated in the decision process. This type of data is not currently available.

The MOLP model can be formally stated as follows:

$$\text{Min: } Z = \frac{0.85}{E}d_e^- + \frac{0.85}{E}d_e^+ + \frac{0.15}{C}d_c^- + \frac{0.15}{C}d_c^+$$

$$\text{Subject to: } \sum_{i=1}^{n} x_i e_i + d_e^- - d_e^+ = E$$

$$\sum_{i=1}^{n} x_i c_i + d_c^- - d_c^+ = C$$

$$\sum_{i=1}^{n} x_i p_i \leq B$$

$$\sum_{i=1}^{n} x_i^j \leq 1$$

$$x_i \in \{0,1\}; \ d_e^-, d_e^+, d_c^-, d_c^+ \geq 0$$

where x_i is a binary variable indicating whether project i is chosen to be funded, x_i^j is an x_i for projects submitted by township j, e_i is the environmental score of the project, c_i is the amount of in-kind funding offered, E is the maximum level of environmental benefit obtainable, C is the maximum level of in-kind contribution obtainable, p_i is the requested grant amount for project i, B is the total budget for the year, and $d_k^{+/-}$ is the deviation from goal K. Note that, in this case, because the goals represent the maximum possible value of E and C, the positive deviations (d_k^+) (e redundant, and could be omitted). They do become relevant if there is a goal less than the absolute maximum, and are included here for completeness.

Results for both the MOLP and a model that excludes in-kind contributions are also presented in Table 6.1. They suggest that the environmental benefit offered by the MOLP with the 85:15 weighting is very close to the benefit from binary programming. MOLP decreases the environmental benefit by 0.3% and increases in-kind contributions by 10%, thus providing a much-improved benefit ranking while still incorporating an incentive for in-kind contributions.

This model can be extended by parametrically altering the weights, which can sketch out an efficiency frontier of sorts. The extended algorithm

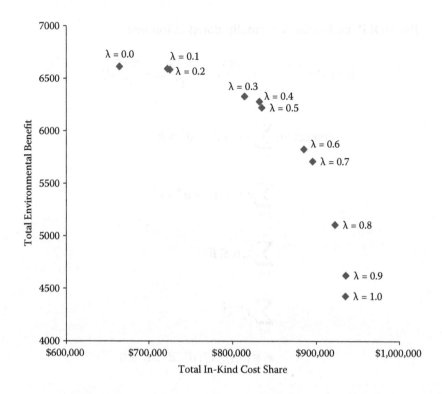

FIGURE 6.3   Benefit—In-kind frontier.

offers decision makers a menu of weighting frameworks and represents the trade-offs that exist between various objectives, as shown in Figure 6.3.

6.2.2 Issue 2: Sensitivity of Results Given the Uncertainty in Project Cost and In-Kind Contribution

A major issue that arises in comparing theoretical optimal solutions to actual project funding schedules is the accuracy of grant requestors' cost estimates. Based on the project data from Bradford County, it would appear that project expenses have historically been substantially underestimated. For 2002 through 2008, the average actual cost of projects in any given year varied from 30% under the grant request to 85% over it. The amount actually paid for an individual project by Bradford County ranged from 428% above the quote in the grant proposal to 66% below it, and averaged 54% above. There was a similar underestimation of in-kind contributions. Actual in-kind contributions provided by a contracted township ended up ranging from 738% above the original quote to 87%

below the original quote, with an average of 129% above. From a planning perspective, the potential for budget overruns is great.

Traditional sensitivity analysis is not helpful in this case because binary programming is used. Ideally, costs and in-kind contributions could be systematically varied independently over a range of percentages of over- and under-achievement and the results compared. This is not feasible, however, because 30 projects with only three such distortions would require more than 4×10^{14} separate optimizations.

As an alternative sensitivity analysis, we analyzed this situation using a bootstrap type of approach that evaluates the persistence of projects in optimal solutions over a series of random variations in price and in-kind contributions. All costs and in-kind contributions were independently varied by a factor within the 10th to 90th percentile range: −28% to +140% for costs and −57% to +307% for in-kind funding. The optimal solution was recorded for several random samples, and the "persistence" or percentage of times a particular project was recommended was calculated. This persistence score can be used to identify projects for which the expense is a "sure thing" versus those that are particularly sensitive to cost. This analysis was performed for 2002 using 55 observations. Table 6.2 offers a selection of results for projects that were actually funded. Projects that have persistence scores at or near 1.0 are very likely to be efficient in granting environmental benefits even under a fair degree of cost uncertainty. Projects with a large variance, such as A606

TABLE 6.2   Selection of Persistence Scores

Project No.	Rank	Multiple-Objective Linear Programming Value	Persistence
Z010	1	1	1.00
Z006	2	0	0.51
X313	3	1	1.00
A398	4	0	1.00
A438	5	1	0.98
A300	6	1	1.00
A872	7	0	0.65
A518	8	1	0.96
A241	9	1	0.15
X353	10	1	1.00
A606	11	1	0.07
A949	12	1	1.00

TABLE 6.3   Results of Benefit Targeting, Multiple-Objective Linear Programming, and Persistence Selection

	Benefit Targeting	Multiple-Objective Linear Programming	Persistence Selection
Money spent	$283,901	$293,962	$293,080
Environmental score	1,342	1,613	1,629
In-kind contributions	$57,549	$96,741	$110,907

in Table 6.2, however, are unlikely to be efficient if costs change substantially, although both the ranking and the MOLP processes recommend them, and should be approached more cautiously. It is worth noting that the levels of expected benefit achieved under these uncertainties is, overall, just slightly lower than the level generated by the initial specification of the MOLP model (see Table 6.3). This is under the condition of knowledge of the actual costs when making the decision.

6.2.3 Issue 3: Sensitivity of Results to State Fund Distribution Rules

Officials from Cambria and Carbon Counties have been frustrated in their efforts to develop the DGRP program in their counties because they receive such small grants, which sometimes do not even entirely cover the costs associated with one project. This raises an interesting question: What effect would different fund distribution rules have on the overall environmental benefit to the state and on county programs? To optimize the overall program, decisions on projects to fund during a given year could be made at the state level. This system, however, would reduce local involvement, which is a stated goal of the DGRP. As an alternative, we considered a state distribution mechanism that could redistribute funds from one county to another to see how the overall environmental benefit changed.

We used Bradford County's 2002 project submissions and the projects completed to date for Cambria County, which amounts to essentially one year's worth of project submissions. Under a parameter analysis, optimal fund distributions were determined by starting with each county's average DGRP budget as a baseline and varying the amount budgeted to each county symmetrically by unit changes of $10,000. With each county receiving its traditional budget allotment of *approximately* $300,000 for Bradford and $15,000 for Cambria, the total environmental benefit score for the two counties was 1,923. Figure 6.4 represents the total level of benefit achieved by redistributing some of the Bradford County budget to Cambria County. The *x*-axis represents the total annual amount shifted

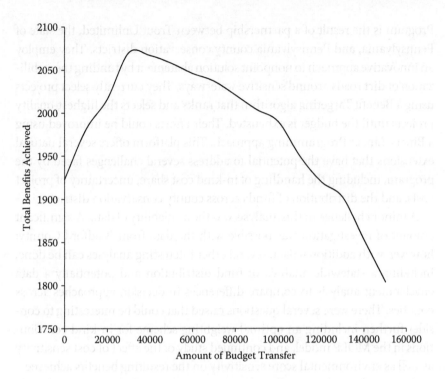

FIGURE 6.4   Intra-county fund distribution.

from Bradford County to Cambria County, while the y-axis represents the total benefit score for the two counties. The maximum occurs at an environmental benefit score of 2,070, with a \$30,000 redistribution from Bradford County to Cambria County.

At the maximum benefit level, Bradford County still receives \$270,000 (90%) while Cambria's budget grows significantly to \$45,000 (300%). The total environmental benefit, however, begins to decline steadily after that point. So while a minor redistribution to counties receiving fewer funds could have a significant advantage, the bulk of the DGRP funds should continue to go to the counties with larger dirt road systems.

6.3 CONCLUSIONS

This chapter has applied optimization through mathematical programming to techniques to the problem of water quality conservation in the state of Pennsylvania. It demonstrated how Binary Linear Programming can be extended to deal with a variety of challenges encountered in an on-the-ground conservation situation. The Pennsylvania Dirt and Gravel Roads

Program is the result of a partnership between Trout Unlimited, the state of Pennsylvania, and Pennsylvania county conservation districts. They employ an innovative approach to nonpoint solution abatement by funding the stabilization of dirt roads around sensitive waterways. They currently select projects using a Benefit Targeting algorithm that ranks and selects the highest-quality projects until the budget is exhausted. Their efforts could be improved using a Binary Linear Programming approach. This platform offers several natural extensions that have the potential to address several challenges faced by the program, including the handling of in-kind cost share, uncertainty of project costs, and the distribution of funds across county conservation districts.

A minor challenge in this analysis was the availability of data. A significant amount of investigation was possible with the data from Bradford County; however, with additional data, several other interesting analyses can be done, including a statewide analysis of fund distribution and potentially a data envelopment analysis to compare differences in decision approaches across counties. There were several questions raised that could be interesting to consider further, including an optimal weighting scheme for in-kind contributions in the MOLP model, and continued study of the effect of cost sensitivity as well as environmental score sensitivity on the resulting benefits achieved.

Despite these data challenges, optimization still shows considerable promise for gains in this program. First, there is the potential for considerable efficiency gains in larger counties from using BLP in their decision process, although this is tempered somewhat by cost uncertainties. Second, MOLP could be useful in taking in-kind contributions into account to encourage higher contribution rates by townships. Also, due to the uncertainty in project costs, it could be useful to consider the persistence of a solution under random disturbances of project costs to help identify projects most likely to be efficient regardless of actual cost. Finally, statewide efficiency could be increased by a minor redistribution of funds to counties currently receiving only limited funding, but states with larger road systems should continue to receive the bulk of the funds.

REFERENCES

Aldrich, R., and Wyerman, J. (2006). 2005 National Land Trust Census Report. Washington, DC: The Land Trust Alliance.

American Farmland Trust (2010). Status of State PACE Programs. Online at www.farmland.org (accessed on March 17, 2010).

Babcock, B.A., Lakshminarayan, P.G., Wu, J., and Zilberman, D. (1997). Targeting tools for the purchase of environmental amenities. *Land Economics, 73,* 325–339.

Baker, M., Payne, S., and Smart, M. (1999). An empirical study of matching grants: The "cap on the CAP." *Journal of Public Economics, 72,* 269–288.

Ballestero, E., Alarcon, S., and Garcia-Bernabeu, A. (2002). Establishing politically feasible water markets: A multi-criteria approach. *Journal of Environmental Management, 65,* 411–429.

Boadway, R., and Shah, A. (2007). Intergovernmental Fiscal Transfers. Washington, DC: The World Bank.

Borge, L.-E., and Rattsø, J. (2008). Local Adjustment to Temporary Matching Grant Programs: A Dynamic Analysis. Mimeo, Department of Economics, Norwegian University of Science and Technology.

Bucovetsky, S., Marchand, M., and Pestieau, P. (1998). Tax competition and revelation of preferences for public expenditure. *Journal of Public Economics, 44,* 367–390.

Center for Dirt and Gravel Road Studies, University of Pennsylvania (2009). Center for Dirt and Gravel Road Studies: Better Roads, Cleaner Streams. Website at www.dirtandgravel.psu.edu.

Chernick, H. (1995). Fiscal effects of block grants for the needy: A review of the evidence. In *Proceedings of the National Tax Association Annual Conference on Taxation,* pp. 24–33.

Claassen, R. (2009). Conservation Policy Briefing Room, Economic Research Service, U.S. Department of Agriculture. Online at www.ers.usda.gov/briefing/conservationpolicy/background.htm (accessed February 2010).

Dantzig, G.B. (1957). Discrete-variable extremum problems. *Operations Research,* 5(2), 266–288.

Drynan, R.G., and Sandiford, F. (1985). Incorporating economic objectives in goal programs for fishery management. *Marine Resource Economics,* 2(2), 175–195.

European Union Directorate-General for Agriculture and Rural Development (2009). Rural Development in the European Union: Statistical and Economic Information Report 2009. Brussels: The European Union.

Fooks, J., and Messer, K.D. (2012). Maximizing Conservation and In-Kind Cost Share: Applying Goal Programming to Forest Protection, *Forest Economics,* 18: 207–217.

Kaiser, H.M., and Messer, K.D. (2011). Mathematical Programming for Agricultural, Environmental, and Resource Economics. Hoboken, NJ: Wiley.

Kotani, K., Messer, K.D., and Schulze, W.D. (2010). Matching grants and charitable giving: Why some people sometimes provide a helping hand to fund environmental goods. *Agricultural and Resource Economics Review,* 39(2), 324–343.

Mardle, S., and Pascoe, S. (1999). A review of applications of multiple criteria decision-making techniques to fisheries. *Marine Resource Economics,* 14, 41–63.

Mardle, S., Pascoe, S., Tamiz, M., and Jones, D. (2000). Resource allocation in the North Sea demersal fisheries: A goal programming approach. *Annals of Operations Research,* 94, 321–342.

Messer, K.D. (2006). The conservation benefits of cost-effective land acquisition: A case study in Maryland. *Journal of Environmental Management,* 79, 305–315.

Messer, K.D., Allen, W.L., and Chen, C. (2011). Best Practices for Increasing the Cost Effectiveness of the Maryland Agricultural Lands Preservation Foundation. Harry R. Hughes Center for Agro-Ecology Research Report.

Neely, W.P., North, R.M., and Fortson, J.C. (1977). An operational approach to multiple objective decision making for public water resource projects using integer goal programming. *American Journal of Agricultural Economics,* 59, 198–203.

Oates, W.E. (1999). An essay on fiscal federalism. *Journal of Economic Literature,* 37, 1120–1149.

Önal, H. (1997). Trade-off between structural diversity and economic objectives in forest management with environmental impact and income distribution goals. *American Journal of Agricultural Economics,* 79(3), 1001–1012.

Önal, H., Algozin, K.A., Işik, M., and Hornbaker, R.H. (1998). Economically efficient watershed management with environmental impact and income distribution goals. *Journal of Environmental Management,* 53, 241–253.

Polasky, S., Camm, J.D., and Garber-Yonts, B. (2001). Selecting biological reserves cost-effectively: An application to terrestrial vertebrate conservation in Oregon. *Land Economics,* 77, 68–78.

Prendergast, J.R., Quinn, R.M., and Lawton, J.H. (1999). The gaps between theory and practice in selecting nature reserves. *Conservation Biology,* 13(3), 484–492.

Pressey, R.L., and Cowling, R.M. (2001). Reserve selection algorithms and the real world. *Conservation Biology,* 15(1), 275–277.

Silva, D., and Nakata, T. (2009). Multi-objective assessment of rural electrification in remote areas with poverty considerations. *Energy Policy,* 37(8), 3096–3108.

Trust for Public Lands (2009). Annual Report 2009. Online at www.tpl.org (accessed on August 10, 2010).

Underhill, L.G. (1994). Optimal and suboptimal reserve selection algorithms. *Biological Conservation,* 70, 85–87.

U.S. Department of Agriculture (2009). Agriculture Secretary Vilsack announces $1.7 billion in conservation reserve program rental payments. USDA Newsroom. Online at www.fsa.usda.gov/FSA/newsReleases?area=-newsroom&subject=landing&topic=ner&newstype=newsrel&type=detail&item=nr_20091007_rel_0497.html (accessed on July 20, 2010).

U.S. Department of Agriculture (2010). Conservation reserve program. USDA Farm Service Agency Programs. Online at www.fsa.usda.gov/FSA/webapp ?area = home&subject=copr&topic=crp (accessed on August 10, 2010).

Wu, J., Adams, R.M., and Boggess, G. (2000). Cumulative effects and optimal targeting of conservation efforts: Steelhead trout habitat enhancement in Oregon. *American Journal of Agricultural Economics,* 82, 400–413.

Xu, J., Tao, R., Xu, Z., and Bennett, M.T. (2010). China's Sloping Land Conversion Program: Does expansion equal success? *Land Economics,* 86, 219–244.

IV

**Computational Intelligent Data Analysis
for Smart Grid and Renewable Energy**

VI

CHAPTER 7

Data Analysis Challenges in the Future Energy Domain

Frank Eichinger, Daniel Pathmaperuma,
Harald Vogt, and Emmanuel Müller

CONTENTS

7.1 INTRODUCTION

THE ENERGY SYSTEM CURRENTLY undergoes major changes, primarily triggered by the need for a more sustainable and secure energy supply. The traditional system relying on the combustion of fossil sources such as oil, gas, and coal on the one side and nuclear technologies on the other side is not sustainable, for three main reasons:

1. Fossil and nuclear resources are limited, and their exploitation will become more expensive (not economically sustainable).

2. The combustion of fossil sources leads to CO_2 emissions, which drive the greenhouse effect (not environmentally sustainable).

3. Nuclear power plants bear certain risks in their operation and produce nuclear waste, which needs to be protected from unauthorized access.

Furthermore, up to now, no permanent disposal sites for nuclear waste exist, and coming generations—who will not have profited from this kind of energy source—will have to deal with it (not socially sustainable and probably not economically sustainable if all disposal costs are considered). The best way to achieve sustainability is clearly energy efficiency, that is, all forms of saving energy. A further way is renewable energy. Luckily, renewable energies are evolving rapidly, most remarkably in the form of wind energy, photovoltaic systems, water power, and biogas. In Germany, as one example, the share of renewable energies in electricity supply crossed the 20% mark in 2011 [7]. This share is forecast to quadruple by 2050 [3]. In addition to Germany, many other countries have similar plans to reduce greenhouse gas emissions and to fight climate change.

The rise of renewable energies comes along with a number of challenges regarding the electricity supply. Data-analysis techniques are a crucial building block that can facilitate these developments, as we will see later in this chapter. In particular, renewable energies challenge the electricity grid, which must be stable and should allow everybody at any point in time to consume energy. This is difficult to achieve, as the electricity systems have to permanently maintain a balance between demand and supply. Storage can help in achieving this, but geographic availability is very limited, and the economics of storage do not make it feasible for large-scale applications at the present time. Maintaining the balance is getting more difficult as the share of renewable energy sources rises, due to their unsteady and fluctuating generation. This calls for so-called *smart grids*, which are a major topic of this chapter.

In particular, the future energy system—which aims to be less dependent on fossil fuels and nuclear technology and builds on more and more renewable energies—is challenged by the following four main factors:

1. *Volatile generation.* The possibly greatest issue of renewable energies is their volatile nature. It challenges the electricity system dramatically. The production of photovoltaic or wind energy does not depend on consumer needs, but solely on external conditions that are difficult or impossible to control (e.g., general weather conditions). These do not necessarily match the energy demand patterns of consumers. In environments where renewables have a very small share of the overall production, such a natural fluctuation can be tolerated. However, the larger the share, the more effort is needed to compensate for this effect.

Compensation for the fluctuating nature of renewables can be done, for example, with flexible gas turbines that are permanently held in standby operation. They can increase production spontaneously, as for example when clouds darken the sun and less electricity is produced. However, such standby operation is highly inefficient, and it is responsible for remarkable greenhouse gas emissions [136]. An alternative to extra production of energy is to shift demands, which is targeted in more detail in the remainder of this chapter. If certain demands can be shifted to points in time where more renewable energy is available, this amount of energy can be considered a virtual production, energy storage, or buffer. Respective load-shifting programs and implementations are frequently referred to as *demand response.*[*]

In future scenarios, however, the situation can be even more severe. When large shares of electricity production come from renewable fluctuating sources, it might happen that the total production becomes larger than the total demand. If the demand (including energy storage facilities) cannot be shifted to such periods anymore, even the production of renewable energy must be stopped, which makes its generation less efficient. This furthermore brings in the potential to substantially damage the energy generation and grid infrastructure.

2. *Distributed generation.* Future energy generation will be more distributed. Today, it builds on a comparatively small number of large, central power plants. These power plants feed in energy from a higher voltage level to a lower voltage level, resulting in a unidirectional power flow. In the future, in particular due to the rise of renewable energies, the number of power-generating units is likely to rise dramatically and to be a lot more distributed. On the one side, this is due to the increasing number of photovoltaic systems installed on private and industrial buildings and also to wind turbines that are not always part of larger wind parks. On the other side, small biogas-based power plants and *co-generation units (combined heat and power units (CHP units))* are becoming more and more popular. CHP units can contribute to a more sustainable energy generation too. This is because they are more efficient compared to pure fossil-based generation of electricity, which does not make use of the waste heat. In addition, they potentially can be used to generate energy when production is low. In particular, so-called *micro-CHP units* are increasingly installed in private houses, partly triggered by incentives from government programs. These developments turn many *consumers* into so-called *prosumers*. Prosumers are consumers owning, for example, photovoltaic systems or micro-CHP units generating energy that is fed into the electricity grid if it exceeds their own demand.

---

[*] *Demand response* is considered an element of the broader field of *demand-side management*, which also includes energy efficiency measures [110].

Distributed generation challenges the electricity system, which has been designed for more central generation with a comparably small number of large power plants. Much of today's grid infrastructure is built on the understanding and technology that power flows from higher to lower voltage levels. Distributed generation units, however, will operate at different voltage levels, which can potentially result in a unidirectional power flow within the grid. Issues arise, for instance, when photovoltaic panels installed on many roofs in a certain neighborhood feed their electricity into the local low-voltage distribution grid. These grids were originally designed solely to distribute energy from higher to lower voltage levels. Massively distributed generation can therefore lead to severe grid conditions (i.e., voltage and frequency fluctuations) and, in the worst case, to power outages [81]. This happens, for instance, when transmission-system capacities are temporarily not high enough or if there is a surplus of energy in a certain grid segment that cannot be transferred to higher-level parts of the grid. Another issue can be, for example, that wind parks in remote areas generate lots of energy that cannot be consumed locally. In such cases, the electricity grid might not have enough capacity to transport the electricity to areas where it is needed. Thus, wind turbines might have to be stopped temporarily. Solving such issues by means of increased grid capacities is surely possible, but very expensive in cases where such peak situations occur very rarely. Additionally, the construction of new power lines is very often opposed by local residents. In addition to enhanced infrastructure, information technology will also play a more important role in the future.

3. *New loads.* Not only does the supply side undergo major changes, but also on the demand side new loads are arising. In particular, *air conditioning, heat pumps,* and *(hybrid) electric vehicles* become more and more popular. The latter is caused by the aim to make mobility more sustainable by driving vehicles with electric energy generated from renewable sources. It also makes countries more independent of fossil fuels. Several countries have programs to support such electric mobility. As one example, the German government has released the goal to have 1 million electric vehicles in Germany by 2020 and 6 million by 2030 [3]. This is ambitious, as by the end of 2010, only

40,000 out of 42 million registered cars in Germany were (hybrid) electric vehicles [5].

Electric mobility can only be sustainable if the consumed energy is also sustainable. As electric mobility will lead to an increased consumption of energy, even more renewable sources are needed to satisfy this new demand. Furthermore, the demand for charging electric vehicles is highly volatile, and peak demands can hardly be supplied if they are not aligned with the production and distribution of energy. In addition, charging too many electric vehicles at the same time in the same segment of the electricity grid might lead to overloads and, in the worst case, to power outages. At the same time, the typical average load of the electricity grid leaves, by far, enough capacity to charge electric vehicles. Again, tackling such peak demands with increased grid capacities is expensive, and it does not solve the issue of insufficient production of renewable electricity at certain points in time. Therefore, an intelligent control of charging is necessary to integrate electric vehicles with the smart grid.

Electric mobility should not only be seen as a challenge, but rather as a chance to realize the smart grid. For example, intelligent techniques could schedule the charging processes of electric vehicles in order to avoid electricity network issues, to realize demand response (e.g., charge when renewable production is high and further demand is low), and to fulfill user needs (e.g., have the vehicle charged to a certain level when the user needs it). In addition to smart charging, the batteries of electric vehicles might also be used as a buffer in the electricity grid. That is, energy from the vehicle might be fed into the electricity network (*vehicle to grid, V2G*) when production is low or if there are demand peaks [118]. However, as electric mobility is still in its infancy, many challenges—including data analysis—must be tackled to integrate it with the smart grid. As an example, to achieve user acceptance, intelligent systems need to capture and predict user behaviors in order to have a vehicle sufficiently charged when the user needs it.

In addition to electric mobility, *heat pumps* have become more popular in certain regions. Such devices draw thermal energy from the environment for heating and/or cooling. They, however, are a nonnegligible load on the electricity system and might be used to shift demand to a certain extent.

4. *Liberalization.* In addition to the aim for sustainability and technological developments, the energy system is also challenged by legislation [104]. While traditionally electricity generation, transition, distribution, and retail have been done by regional monopolies, the electricity market is now liberalized in many countries. Since the end of the 1990s, the mentioned tasks are separated and competition is introduced for generation and retail of electrical energy. In addition to generation and retail companies, liberalization leads to a number of other actors, such as transition and distribution-network operators, balance-responsible parties, metering operators, value-added-service providers, etc. In particular, actors related to the operation of the grid are typically regulated by governmental authorities. From a more technical perspective, a larger number of actors are involved in the electricity system. They all generate data, and this distributed data must be exchanged with other partners in order to fulfill their respective tasks. This opens up new and interesting possibilities for data analyses as well as the need for ways of treating data in a privacy-preserving way.

To wrap up the challenges, sustainable energy systems will undergo major changes in the future. Generation and production will be more volatile and the landscape becomes more fragmented, both from a technical (distributed generation, volatile generation, and consumption) and an organizational perspective (new and more specialized actors). Most important is the paradigm shift from *demand-driven generation* in the past to *generation-driven demand* in the future, triggered by renewable energy generation and new loads. Generation-driven management of energy consumption in the smart grid is a complex optimization problem [138]. It involves the operation of certain distributed energy sources and the control of energy consumption, for example, via market-based mechanisms. In the liberalized electricity market, different actors will probably contribute to the solution of the optimization problem in a distributed manner. Further, the solution will likely be hierarchical: Certain optimizations will be done on the transition grid, further optimizations at the distribution grids, the next ones might be more fine-grained consumption and generation shifting between neighbor consumers and small energy generators. At these different levels, consumption, generation, and grid-usage data will arise at different levels of aggregation and induce new challenges for data analysis.

Another rather technical development that affects current and future energy systems is *smart metering*. Smart electricity meters facilitate fine-grained measurements of energy consumption, production and quality, and the communication of the respective measurements. They are one of the technological foundations of many future energy scenarios described in this chapter. Also, from a legislative point of view, their introduction is promoted, and many countries have respective programs. As one example, the European Union wants to achieve an 80% share of smart meters by 2020 [1].

This chapter reviews, in detail, selected scenarios in the field of smart grids. Most of them contribute to the realization of the paradigm shift from demand-driven generation to generation-driven demand, or to achieving energy efficiency. These elaborations reveal a number of data-analysis challenges that must be tackled to implement the scenarios. These challenges are discussed in more detail, along with possible solutions.

The remainder of this chapter is organized as follows: Section 7.2 describes the current status of the electricity market; Section 7.3 reviews selected future energy scenarios that are building blocks of the smart grid; based on Sections 7.2 and 7.3; Section 7.4 then describes the resulting data-analysis challenges and highlights first solutions; and Section 7.5 provides conclusions.

7.2 THE ENERGY MARKET TODAY

In this section we provide a short overview of the current market for electric energy, with Europe as an example. This section is not only a basis for understanding future energy scenarios described in Section 7.3, but also bears some data-analysis challenges. In particular, the prediction of consumption and generation already plays an important role in today's energy market. In this section, we first introduce the different roles in the energy market (Section 7.2.1). Then we describe energy trading (Section 7.2.2) and energy balancing in the electricity grid (Section 7.2.3).

7.2.1 Actors in the Energy Market

As discussed in the introduction, liberalization leads to a number of new actors and roles in the energy market. Caused by regulation, this can vary in different countries, and some of the roles might be taken on by the same entity (e.g., a generator might also act as a retailer who sells energy to consumers). The number of (new) actors in the energy market is also interesting from a data-analysis point of view: Most of these actors have access to potentially interesting data or could profit from data provided by different actors. Investigating the actors and their data leads to interesting opportunities for data analysis and maybe even to new roles, such as analytic service providers. In the following, we introduce the most common actors and roles that are relevant for the remainder of this chapter [2]:

- *Generator.* A company that produces electrical energy and feeds it into the transportation or distribution grid. Generators might use conventional power plants or generate renewable energy.

- *Consumer.* An industrial or private entity or a person who consumes electrical energy.

- *Prosumer.* A consumer who also produces electrical energy. A difference from the generator is that the prosumer might entirely consume its own generation. The generation is typically done by renewable sources or micro-CHP (combined heat and power) units.

- *Distribution system operator (DSO).* Operates regional electricity distribution grids (low and medium voltage) that provide grid access to consumers, prosumers, and small generators. Historically, such grids were intended to distribute centrally produced energy to the consumers. Today, it can also happen that temporarily more energy is fed into a grid than energy is taken from the grid. The DSO also plans, builds, and maintains the grid infrastructure.

- *Transmission system operator (TSO).* Operates a transmission grid (high voltage) and transmits electrical energy in large quantities over large distances. This includes providing grid access to large generators and consumers and to the DSOs. The TSO is responsible for the overall stability of its parts of the transmission grid and for providing balancing power (see Section 7.2.3). The TSO also plans, builds, and maintains the grid infrastructure.

- *Balance-responsible party (BRP).* The BRP responsible for ensuring that the scheduled supply of energy corresponds to the expected consumption of energy in its balance area. To achieve this, the BRP eliminates upcoming imbalances using balancing power with the help of the TSOs. The BRP financially regulates for any imbalances that arise.

- *Retailer.* A company that buys electrical energy from generators and sells it to consumers. The retailer also has to interact with DSOs and possibly metering operators to provide grid access to the consumers.

- *Metering operator.* Provides, installs, and maintains metering equipment and measures the consumption and/or generation of electrical energy. The readings are then made accessible (possibly in an aggregated manner) to the retailer, to the consumer/prosumer, and/or to other actors. Frequently, the role of the metering operator is taken on by DSOs.

- *Energy market operator.* An energy market may be operated for different kinds of energy to facilitate the efficient exchange of energy or related products such as load-shifting volumes (demand response). Typical markets may involve generators selling energy on the wholesale market and retailers buying energy. Energy market operators may employ different market mechanisms (e.g., auctions, reverse auctions) to support the trade of energy in a given legal framework.

- *Value-added service providers.* Such providers can offer various services to different actors. One example could be to provide *analytic services* to final customers, based on the data from a metering operator.

7.2.2 Energy Trading

In order to supply their customers (consumers) with electrical energy, retailers must buy energy from generators. In the following, we do not consider how prosumers sell their energy, as this varies in different countries. While consumers traditionally pay a fixed rate per consumed kilowatt-hour (kWh) of energy to the retailers (typically in addition to a fixed monthly fee), the retailers can negotiate prices with the generators (directly or at an energy exchange). A procurement strategy for a retailer may be to procure the larger and predictable amount of their energy need in advance on a long-term basis. This requires analytic services and sufficiently large collections of consumption data. The remaining energy demand, which is difficult to predict in the long run, is procured on a short-term basis for typically higher prices. Similarly, generators of electricity need to predict in advance what amounts of energy they can sell.

7.2.2.1 Long-Term Trading

While electric energy has traditionally been traded by means of bilateral *over-the-counter (OTC)* contracts, an increasing amount of energy is nowadays traded at power exchanges. Such exchanges trade standardized products, which makes trading easier and increases the comparability of prices. While there are different ways of trading energy, double auctions as known from game theory [54] are the dominant means for finding the price [137].

As one example, the *European Energy Exchange AG (EEX)* in Leipzig, Germany, trades different kinds of standardized energy futures and options. These products describe the potential delivery of a certain amount of energy at certain times in the future. The delivery must be within one of the transportation grids. In addition to the traded products, they also provide clearinghouse services for OTC contracts. The volume traded at the EEX derivate market for Germany amounted to 313 terawatt-hours (TWh) in 2010, 1,208 TWh including OTC transactions [6]. The latter number roughly corresponds to two times the energy consumed in Germany in the same time frame.

7.2.2.2 Short-Term Trading

Short-term trading becomes necessary as both consumption and production cannot be predicted with 100% accuracy. Therefore, not all needs for energy can be covered by long-term trading. In particular, fluctuating renewable energies make correct long-term predictions of production virtually impossible. As one example, wind energy production can only be predicted with sufficient accuracy for a few hours in advance. Therefore, energy exchanges are used for short-term trading, again making use of different kinds of auctions. At such exchanges, retailers can buy electrical energy for physical delivery in case their demand is not covered by futures. Again, the delivery must be within one of the transportation grids.

The EPEX Spot SE (European Power Exchange) in Paris, France, trades energy for several European markets. There, trading is divided as follows:

- In *day-ahead auctions,* electrical energy is traded for delivery on the following day in 1-hour intervals [6]. These auctions take place at noon on every single day. Bids can be done for individual hours or blocks of several hours, and the price can be positive or negative. Negative prices may occur, for instance, when the predicted regenerative production is very high and the demand is low, possibly on a public holiday.

- In *intraday trading*, electrical energy is traded for delivery on the same or following day, again in 1-hour intervals [6]. Each hour can be traded until 45 minutes before delivery; starting at 3:00 P.M., all hours of the following day can be traded. Bids can also be done for individual hours or blocks of hours, and prices can again be positive or negative.

At the EPEX, 267 TWh were traded in 2010 by means of day-ahead auctions and 11 TWh during intraday trading (German, French, and Austrian market) [6]. The sum of these trades roughly corresponds to half of the electrical energy consumed in Germany in the same time frame (most of this energy is traded for the German market).

7.2.3 Energy Balancing

To ensure a reliable and secure provision of electrical energy without any power outages, the energy grids must be stable at any point in time. In particular, there must be assurance that the production always equals the consumption of energy. In practice, avoiding imbalances between generation and demand is challenging due to stochastic consumption behavior, unpredictable power-plant outages, and fluctuating renewable production [137].

On a very coarse temporal granularity, a balance is achieved by means of energy trading (see Section 7.2.2) and data-analysis mechanisms, in particular prediction and forecast: Retailers buy the predicted demand of their customers, and generators sell their predicted generation. As mentioned in Section 7.2.1, the BRPs make sure that the scheduled supply of energy corresponds to the expected consumption of energy. This expected consumption is also derived using data-analysis techniques. The TSOs are responsible for the stability of the grids. In the following, we describe how they do so.

From a technical point of view, a decrease in demand leads to an increase in frequency, while a decrease in production leads to a decrease in frequency (and vice versa for increases). Deviations from the fixed frequency of 50 Hz in electricity grids should be avoided in real time, as this might lead to damage to the devices attached to the grid.

Typically, frequency control is realized in a three-stage process: *primary*, *secondary*, and *tertiary control*. The primary control is responsible for very short deviations (15 to 30 seconds), the secondary control for short deviations (max. 5 minutes), and the tertiary control for longer deviations (max. 15 minutes) [137]. The control process can be realized by various means, for example, standby generators, load variation of power plants, or load shifting. Different measures involving different types of power plants have different reaction times and are therefore used for different control levels.

The capacities needed for balancing the grids are again frequently traded by means of auctions: Primary and secondary capacities are traded biannually, while tertiary capacity is traded on a daily basis [137]. Usually, only prequalified actors are allowed in such balancing markets, as it must be ensured that the requirements at the respective level can be fulfilled technically. Primary-control bids consist of the offered capacity and the price for actual delivery of balancing power. In contrast, bids for secondary and tertiary control consist of one price for making available a certain capacity and another price for consumed energy [137]. Thus, capacities play an important role in the balancing market, and actors are partly paid for a *potential supply*, which hinders a generator from selling this energy on the regular market.

For costs that arise from the actual energy delivered for secondary and tertiary control, the generators who caused deviations or retailers who did not procure the correct amount of energy for their customers are charged [81, 137]. Costs for primary control and for the capacities of secondary and tertiary control are paid by the corresponding grid operators [137], who earn grid-usage fees. Because costs at the balancing market are typically higher than on the normal energy market, generators and retailers are stimulated to make best-possible predictions of energy production and consumption [81].

7.3 FUTURE ENERGY SCENARIOS

In this section we describe a number of visionary energy scenarios for the future. They represent building blocks of a possible *smart grid*. We describe the scenarios from a researcher's point of view—they assume certain technical developments and may require legislative changes. We have selected scenarios that are commonly discussed in the scientific and industrial communities, either in the described form or in some variation.

Scenario 7.1: Access to Smart-Meter Data

Smart metering is a key building block of the smart grid, as many further scenarios rely on the availability of fine-grained information of energy consumption and production. For instance, smart metering can enhance load forecasting and enable demand response, dynamic pricing, etc. Some of these scenarios are described in the following. However, smart metering is not only an enabler for other scenarios. Giving users access to their energy consumption profiles can make them more aware of their consumption and improve energy efficiency. This is important as many consumers have little knowledge about their energy consumption.

For purposes of billing, smart-meter data is typically generated in 15-minute intervals. That is, the meter transfers the accumulated consumption of the consumer every 15 minutes to the metering operator. Technically, smart meters can increase the temporal resolution of consumption data, for example, measure the consumption within every second or minute. This allows one to obtain a detailed picture of the energy consumption—down to the identification of individual devices (e.g., coffee machines), as each device has its typical load curve. Such fine-grained data could also be transferred to a metering operator. In addition, metering data at any granularity can be made available within a home network, for example to be accessed via visualization tools on a tablet computer.

Access to consumption profiles for energy consumers can be more than pure numbers or simple plots. Respective visualization tools can easily show comparisons to previous days, weeks, etc. In the case of service providers, they can also provide comparisons to peer groups of consumers having similar households (in terms of size and appliances used). Furthermore, devices can be identified by their load profile [113], which can be visualized additionally. This leads to an increased awareness of the energy consumption of each single device.

A number of studies have investigated the effects of giving users access to smart-metering data. Schleich et al. [126] have carried out controlled field experiments with 2,000 consumers and came to the conclusion that giving access to detailed consumption data may lower the total energy consumption moderately, by about 4%. Other (meta) studies suggest that savings can be even a little higher [39, 45, 94].

Scenario 7.2: Demand Response with Dynamic Prices

Energy retailers procure parts of their energy needs at the spot market, where the prices reflect the actual availability of (renewable) energy (see Section 7.2.2.2). At the same time, energy consumers typically procure energy for a fixed price per kilowatt-hour, additionally to a consumption-independent monthly fee. Although this is comfortable for the consumers and the sum of the monthly or annual bill can be easily calculated if the consumption is known, there are no incentives to consume energy when large amounts are available (e.g., when wind-energy production is high) or to save energy when production is low. As discussed in the introduction, such a paradigm shift from demand-driven generation to generation-driven demand is necessary to facilitate the integration of renewable energies. One approach to realize this is dynamic pricing. In a nutshell, the retailer communicates the actual or future prices of energy per kilowatt-hour to their consumers, and they can decide if they react to such incentives or if they prefer to consume energy when they want it while tolerating possibly higher prices.

The predecessors of dynamic prices are tariff schemes where electricity is cheaper during the night, reflecting a lower average demand at that time. However, this does not consider the fluctuating production of renewable energy. Dynamic price mechanisms can take into account these fluctuations and incorporate them in the prediction of renewable generation and demand of the consumers. Dynamic price schemes mainly differ in the range of possible prices, in the resolution of time ranges in which prices are valid, and in the time spans in which the prices are communicated in advance. Very short time spans enable highly dynamic demand response, but also make it difficult to plan energy consumption. Furthermore, legislation may demand certain minimum time spans. A more detailed review of dynamic prices can be found by Jokic et al. [70].

The German research project MeRegio investigates user acceptance of so-called "energy traffic lights" (see [4] for more information). These are small devices receiving the energy tariffs for the forthcoming 24 hours via radio. The granularity of prices comprises three discrete levels: "low," "normal," and "high." Consumers can see these levels and plan accordingly. In addition, the device visualizes the three levels in different colors (e.g., red stands for "high"), which makes the consumers more aware of the current price of electricity. Of course, dynamic prices are not merely intended for human interpretation. Intelligent devices can receive such price signals and decide when a certain process should be started (e.g., a dishwasher can be started automatically when the lowest tariff starts). This automation is done to a greater extent in so-called smart homes, which are described in Scenario 7.4.

In addition to the promising approach to realize demand response, dynamic prices also bear risks. As one example, it might happen that many devices start operation when a low-price time span starts. This may challenge the distribution grid as sudden significant increases in demand can hardly be handled by energy-balancing mechanisms and should therefore be avoided. This might be realized by using individual dynamic prices for the different consumers (slight differences in order to smoothen demand curves), or by having a much finer granularity of prices. If granularity is fine enough, different user preferences might lead to a more widespread time span in which devices are started.

Many scientific studies have investigated the user acceptance and efficiency of dynamic pricing. A meta study [50] has investigated the results of 24 different pilots. The result in almost all these studies was that consumers do accept dynamic prices and adapt their behavior to a certain extent. Concretely, these studies show that dynamic pricing schemes are an efficient demand-response measure—a median peak reduction of 12% could be achieved. Naturally, user acceptance is particularly high if users are supported by intelligent technologies such as in a smart home (see Scenario 7.4) [109].

Scenario 7.3: Market-Based Demand Response with Control Signals

When energy retailers experience energy shortages during the day, they buy energy at intraday exchanges (see Section 7.2.2.2). When renewable production is low, this can be very expensive and it might be a better option to ask their customers to consume less energy within a certain time frame. Similarly, grid operators monitor the electricity grid and may want to ask consumers to temporarily reduce their consumption in order to achieve grid stability. This scenario describes an alternative to dynamic prices (see Scenario 7.2) for demand response, with a focus on solving grid issues. It requires respective contracts between the consumers and the involved parties that describe the incentives for the consumers to participate in the respective measures (e.g., reductions in the energy bill). Concretely, consumers contract with specialized demand-side management companies, which might be the local distribution system operators. Further, an infrastructure is required that can execute demand-response measures. This scenario describes market mechanisms different from dynamic prices that can be used for trading flexible loads for demand-response purposes, relying on such an infrastructure.

Energy retailers considering a demand-response measure can send their request to an electronic marketplace. As well, if overloads or voltage problems are detected, the grid operator can issue a similar request. Then, all affected demand-side management companies receive these requests from the marketplace, and each company submits an offer for resolving the issue. The marketplace selects a combination of offers that fulfills the request. If the retailer or grid operator accepts the assembly of offers (the retailer alternatively might prefer to buy energy at the exchange if this is cheaper), the respective demand-side management companies are then responsible for conducting the demand-response request. The companies then send priority signals to the smart-home control boxes of their contracted consumers. The control boxes send the signal to intelligent devices at the consumer's premises as well as the charging infrastructure of electric vehicles.

Scenario 7.4: Smart Homes

Home automation has been known under the name "smart home" for quite some time. However, until lately, this meant mainly providing comfort features such as automatically shutting window blinds, switching the lights on automatically, or controlling the house's air-conditioning system in accordance with current weather conditions. Smart homes are often equipped with some kind of energy production unit (e.g., photovoltaic or micro-CHP), and they can employ a central optimization component that controls most generation and utilization of energy in the house. Recently, the potential of home automation for smart-grid applications was recognized [17]. While control components in smart homes primarily act based on the user's presets, they could also take the current situation in the energy grid into account [23].

Some applications in a household have the potential to shift their time of operation into the future; others might run earlier than they normally would. Shifting their power consumption in time realizes demand response. Of course, not all applications in a house are suitable for such a purpose. Applications such as lighting or cooking bear no potential for a time-variable application [60, 111]. The case is different for the dishwasher or the washing machine. These appliances normally have no need for an immediate start and in that way present a potential for shifting the power demand to the future. As one example, users want to have clean dishes for dinner. Whether they get cleaned right after lunch or sometime in the afternoon does not matter.

Another possibility for shifting power demand is the variation of temperature in heating or cooling applications. Such applications include refrigerators, and air-conditioning and heating systems. They all have to maintain a temperature within a certain range. The tolerable range in a freezer would be around −18° C with a tolerance of ±2° C. In normal operation mode, the device would cool down to −20° C, then pause until the temperature reaches −16° C and then start over again. An intelligent system would be able to interrupt the cooling at −18° C or start cooling already at this temperature without waiting for a further rise, thus shifting the power demand of the cooling device. The same scheme could be applied to the room temperature, as the comfort range normally lies around 21°C. Extended knowledge of user preferences could expand this potential even further. If the resident wants the temperature to be 21°C upon return in the evening, the system could heat the house up to 25°C in the afternoon and let it cool down slowly to the desired 21°C. This would require more energy in total, but could still be feasible in a future energy system where a lot of solar energy is available (and is thus cheap) during the day [73].

Profiles of typical user behavior could improve the demand shifting capabilities of a smart home even further if they were combined with an electric vehicle (EV). Not only could the charging profile of the vehicle be matched to the user's and energy system's demands, but the battery of the EV could also be used as temporary energy storage when the vehicle is not needed. This concept is known as vehicle to grid (see Scenario 7.5) [118].

Scenario 7.5: Energy Storage

Storing electric energy becomes more important as the share of volatile energy production (such as solar or wind power) increases. Although electric energy is difficult to store, some technical solutions do exist. In the context of storage for electrical power, one has to keep in mind some key parameters of such systems. The first is the efficiency and refers to the percentage of stored energy that can be regained. It is always below 100%. Other parameters are the capacity and the peak power of a storage system, which refer to the performance of such systems.

Today, the only storage systems with the ability to store a relevant amount of energy for a reasonable price are pumped-storage water-power plants. They store energy by pumping water from a low reservoir up into high storage and regain this potential energy by letting the water run down through generators, just like in water-power plants. While this type of storage could store energy for an almost unlimited time, its land use is quite high and it requires a natural height difference, which makes it difficult to realize such storage in densely inhabited regions.

Another option is the installation of large battery-based chemical storage facilities. This is already done in some regions of Japan. Battery systems can be manufactured with almost any desired capacity and peak power. The drawback of battery systems is their relatively high price. With the anticipated rise in the market share of EVs, this could change soon. Batteries lose capacity constantly during their lifespan. At a certain point in time, their power density is not high enough to use them as batteries for EVs. However, power density is negligible in the context of immobile storage. Thus, battery storage facilities could benefit from a relevant market share of EVs by reusing their old batteries.

A further storage option would be the V2G concept [118]. As vehicles spend only about 5% of their lifetime on the road, an EV could potentially be used 95% of the time as local energy storage. Assuming 1 million EVs in one country (the German government, for instance, aims at reaching this number by 2020 [3]), this could sum up to about 15 gigawatt-hours (GWh) of storage capacity with a peak power of 3 to 20 gigawatts (GW), resembling two to five typical pumped-storage water-power plants.

The profitability of a storage system is, depending on the business model, correlated with its usage, which nowadays is proportional to the number of store-drain cycles. As battery-quality factors decrease not only with their lifetime but also with each use cycle, the utilization of such systems must be considered with reservations.

Scenario 7.6: Management Decisions Derived from Energy Data

Energy has become a major cost factor for industry, public facilities, warehouses, small and medium enterprises, and even for universities. Thus, the management in any of these organizations demands decision support based on the energy consumption of the organization. Let's take the example of a university where the data center is planning to install a new generation of servers. Not only the acquisition costs, but also cooling, space, and especially energy consumption must be considered. While for most such management decisions, IT solutions are available, yet energy consumption remains an open issue ignored by most enterprise resource planning (ERP) tools. Energy management opens up several new aspects to consider. In particular, with the availability of novel data sources, such as smart meters, we observe a high potential for such data-analysis toolkits.

Automated data analysis or semiautomated data exploration can provide an overview of the entire energy consumption of a university, a department, a single institute, or in other dimensions, detailed energy consumption for all servers, all personal computers, and many more such orthogonal views on energy consumption. It is essential to provide such a multitude of views on different aggregation levels as management decisions might demand arbitrary selections of this huge information space. They require reports for such selected views, automated detection of suspicious consumption, comparison between different views, estimation of future consumption, etc.

The essential challenge lies in the large variety of management actions that base their decisions on such energy data. Each of these decisions poses different challenges on data storage, data analysis, and data interaction. Furthermore, they address different management levels, and thus subparts of an organization. For example, individual reports might be required for each professor about the energy consumption of the institute in the past few months. Such reports must show a detailed view of the energy consumption, distinguishing between different rooms or consumer classes. Optimally, interesting views for each institute would be selected (semiautomatically). On the other side, some automated fault-detection algorithms might be required for the maintenance department of a university. Techniques require an intuitive description of failing situations in contrast to the regular behavior of the facility under observation. Going up to the dean of a department or any higher instance in the university, one requires more general and aggregated views. Typically, such information is required for strategic planning of new facilities, new buildings, or the estimation of future energy consumption.

Overall, we have highlighted several, quite different management decisions that pose novel challenges to data analysis. They could be realized by novel data acquisition with smart meters. However, neither data storage of such large data volumes nor its analysis has been tackled by recent toolkits. It is an emerging application domain in database and data-mining research.

Further scenarios are described in subsequent chapters of this book. In particular, Chapter 8 describes a scenario that deals with finding the best mix of renewable demand management and storage, and Chapter 9 focuses on a scenario that deals with real-time identification of grid disruptions.

7.4 DATA ANALYSIS CHALLENGES

With the rise of the *smart grid*, more data will be collected than ever before, and at finer granularity. This facilitates innovative technologies and better control of the whole energy system. As one example, the availability of both consumption/generation data and predictions facilitates the realization of demand-side management techniques such as demand response. Ultimately, this allows a better integration of renewables and a more sustainable energy system. The new data sources and new technologies in the *future energy scenarios* (see Section 7.3) call for more advanced data management and data analysis, as has already been used in the traditional energy system (see Section 7.2). This section describes the data-analysis challenges in the energy area and presents first solutions. In particular, we look at data management (Section 7.4.1); data preparation (Section 7.4.2); the wide field of predictions, forecasts, and classifications (Section 7.4.3); pattern detection (Section 7.4.4); disaggregation (Section 7.4.5); and interactive exploration (Section 7.4.6). Finally, we comment on optimization problems (Section 7.4.7) and the emerging and challenging field of privacy-preserving data mining (Section 7.4.8).

7.4.1 Data Management

Before addressing the actual data-analysis challenges, we present some considerations regarding data management. As motivated before, the rise of the *smart grid* leads to many large and new data sources. The most prominent sources of such data are *smart meters* (see Scenario 7.1). However, there are many more data sources, ranging from dynamic prices to data describing demand-response measures, to the use of energy storages and events in smart homes. In the following, we focus on smart-meter data. In Section 7.4.6.1 we deal with further data-management aspects in the context of the exploration and comparison of energy datasets.

As described previously, smart meters are able to measure energy consumption and/or generation at high resolution, for example, using intervals of 1 second. Figure 7.1 provides an example of such measurements

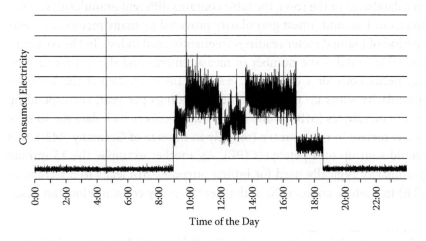

FIGURE 7.1   Typical electricity consumption in an office.

TABLE 7.1 Storage Needs for Smart-Meter Data (pure meter readings only)

Metering Granularity	No. Measurements		Storage Need			
	1 day	1 year	1 day	1 year	1 day	1 year
1 second	86.400	31,536.000	338 kB	120 MB	13 TB	4 PB
1 minute	1.440	525.600	6 kB	2 MB	215 GB	76 TB
15 minutes	96	35.040	384 B	137 kB	14 GB	5 TB
1 hour	24	8.760	96 B	34 kB	4 GB	1 TB
1 day	1	365	4 B	1 kB	153 MB	54 GB
1 month		12		48 B		2 GB
1 year		1		4 B		153 MB
			1 smart meter		40 mio. smart meters	

and shows a typical electricity-consumption curve in a two-person office with a resolution of 1 second (see Section 7.4.2 and [135] for more details on the data).

From a data-analysis point of view, storing data at finest granularity for long time periods and for many smart meters would certainly be interesting. However, in addition to privacy concerns (see Section 7.4.8), this might not be possible from a technical point of view. Therefore, one has to decide which amounts of data need to be kept for which purpose. In many cases, not the finest granularity is needed and samples or aggregations of meter data will suffice.

Table 7.1 illustrates the amounts of measurements and storage needs of smart-meter data, assuming that a single meter reading needs 4 bytes (B) in a database.* In the rows, the table contains different granularities, ranging from 1 second (finest granularity provided by many meters) to 1 year (period of manual meter readings frequently used today). In the columns, the table contains the number of measurements and the respective storage needs both for 1 day and 1 year. For instance, data at the 1-second granularity sums up to 32 mio meter readings per year, corresponding to 120 megabytes (MB). If one would like to collect such data for 40 mio. smart meters in one country (roughly in the size of Germany [143]), this would sum up to 4 petabytes (PB). As another example, the 15-minute granularity typically used for billing purposes still leads to 5 terrabytes (TB) in a whole country. Note that real memory consumption can easily

---

* This does not include metadata such as date, time, and location; Schapranow et al. [125] reports that the size including such data could be much larger, that is, by a factor of 12.

be twelve-old, as mentioned above [125]. Managing these amounts of data remains challenging.

As illustrated by Table 7.1, smart meters might lead to huge amounts of data. This is similar for other data sources in future energy systems. As mentioned previously, every actor involved in the energy system will only be responsible for certain subsets of the existing data. This might still lead to amounts of data that challenge the data-management infrastructure. Concrete challenges for the respective actors are the selection of relevant data as well as aggregation and sampling of such data without loss of important information.

Several researchers have investigated storage architectures for smart-meter data: Martínez et al. [19] has investigated centralized and distributed relational databases, key-value stores, and hybrid database/file-system architectures; Schapranow et al. [125] presents results with in-memory databases [112]; Biseiglia [26] presents experiences with the Hadoop [139] MapReduce [41] framework; and Rusitschka et al. [120] has investigated further cloud-storage techniques. Apart from that, smart-meter readings can be managed with techniques from *data streams* [10], because fine-grained readings can be seen as such a stream (see Section 7.4.4).

One approach to deal with huge amounts of data is compression. It might ease the storage using one of the architectures mentioned previously. Schapranow et al. [125], for example, reports a compression factor of 8 when using *lossless* compression techniques in database technology (on metering data including metadata). Using *lossy* compression techniques on fine-grained data (see Figure 7.1 for an example) that approximate the original data seems to make compression factors of several hundred possible, depending on the required accuracy and granularity of the data. Such an approximation of *time-series data* can be done with various *regression models*, for instance, using straight-line functions [35, 47], linear combinations of basis functions, or nonlinear functions (using respective approximation techniques, for example, described by Seidel [127] and Tishler and Zang [130]). However, the authors of this chapter are not aware of any studies that investigate the trade-off between compression ratio, computational costs, and the usefulness of lossy compressed data for different applications based on smart-meter data of differing temporal granularities. Further, lossy compression techniques would need to be integrated with data-management technology. Investigating respective techniques and validating their deployment in realistic scenarios—in particular with regard to the trade-off mentioned—is an open research problem.

Data from smart meters belongs to the group of *time-series data* [86]. In addition to compression via regression techniques and the actual storage of such data, many other data-management aspects are of importance. This includes indices and similarity-based retrieval of time series (surveys of these techniques can be found by Fink and Pratt [52], Hetland [64], and Vlachus et al. [134]). Such techniques are of importance for many analytical applications that are based on such data. For example, indexes and similarity searches can be used to retrieve consumers with a similar electricity demand, which is important in classification and clustering (see Sections 7.4.3.2 and 7.4.4.1, respectively). Investigating the usage of the mentioned techniques from time-series analysis in the context of energy data should be promising as they are rarely mentioned in the literature.

7.4.2 Data Preprocessing

Data preprocessing is an essential step in data-analysis projects in any domain [30]. It deals with preparing data to be stored, processed, or analyzed and with cleaning it from unnecessary and problematic artifacts. It has been stated that preprocessing takes 50% to 70% of the total time of analytical projects [30]. This certainly applies to the energy domain as well, but the exact value is obviously highly dependent on the project and the data. In the following, we highlight some preprocessing challenges that are specific to the energy domain. Many further data-quality issues are present in many other domains and might be important here as well (see, e.g., textbooks by Berthold et al. [24], Han et al. [61], and Witten et al. [140] for further issues and techniques).

Data from smart meters frequently contains *outliers*. Certain outliers refer to measurement errors rather than to real consumption, as can be seen in the raw data visualized in Figure 7.1: The peaks roughly at 04:30 and at 10:00 happening at single seconds are caused by a malfunction of measurement equipment. The smart meter has malfunctioned for some seconds, resulting in an accumulated consumption reported at the next measurement point. Such outliers must be eliminated if certain functions need to be applied afterward. For example, calculating the maximum consumption of uncleaned data in Figure 7.1 would not be meaningful. Other outliers might refer to atypical events or days: Consumption patterns of energy might differ significantly when there is, for example, a World Cup final on TV or if a weekday becomes a public holiday. (Figure 7.2(b) illustrates that load profiles at weekdays and weekends are quite different.) Such exceptional consumption patterns should not be used as a basis for

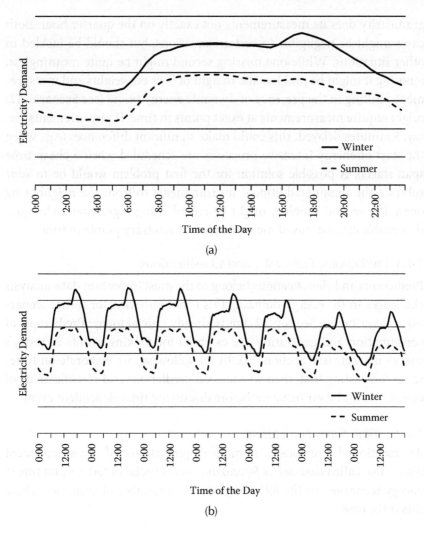

FIGURE 7.2 Typical aggregated demand curves. (Data from Metered Half-Hourly Electricity Demands[8].)

predictions of "normal" days, but analyzing them might be particularly interesting if one approaches a similar special event. We elaborate a bit more on unsupervised learning techniques for preprocessing—in particular, cluster analysis and outlier detection—in Section 7.4.4.

Another common problem with smart-meter data concerns *timing issues*. It might happen that (1) a smart meter operating at the 1-second granularity produces a few measurements too much or too little during one day (or week, month, etc.); or (2) that a meter operating at the 15-minute granularity does its measurements not exactly on the quarter hour. Both cases might be negligible in certain situations, but should be tackled in other situations. While one missing second might be quite meaningless, ignoring it might be problematic in light of laws on weights and measurements. Billing in the presence of dynamic energy prices (see Scenario 7.2) might require measurements at exact points in time. If measurements are, say, 5 minutes delayed, this could make significant differences (e.g., when the start of energy-intensive processes are scheduled when a cheap time span starts). A possible solution for the first problem would be to add/subtract the missing/additional measurements to/from the neighboring ones. The second problem might be solved using regression techniques that enable estimations of measurements at arbitrary points in time.

7.4.3 Predictions, Forecasts, and Classifications

Predictions and classifications belong to the most important data-analysis challenges in the energy domain. This is not only true for future scenarios as described in Section 7.3, but is already crucial today: Predictions of consumption and generation are essential for making profits in today's energy markets (see Section 7.2). In the following, we elaborate on time-series forecasting first; then we focus on predictions and classifications of consumers and their behavior before discussing time-dependent events.

7.4.3.1 Time-Series Forecasting

As mentioned previously, numerical predictions of time-dependent data—also called *time-series forecasting*—are crucial in today's and future energy scenarios. In the following, we list a number of scenarios where this is the case:

- *Predicting consumer demand* is needed in many different scenarios: (1) In *energy trading* (see Section 7.2.2), retailers are interested in predicting the demand of their customers. The more precise this prediction is, the more energy can be bought at potentially cheaper long-term markets instead of buying it at the intraday market or pay for energy balancing. Buying more "cheap" energy than needed is also unprofitable, as retailers have to pay for it even if their customers do not use it. (2) To realize *dynamic pricing* (see Scenario 7.2), retailers need to know the predicted consumption of their customers. This is to derive the prices in a way that the customers might shift loads to other time spans in order to align consumption with previously procured energy or predicted renewable production. (3) To *avoid grid issues*, balance responsible parties need to plan their grid capacities based on the predicted load in the respective areas. If predicted high loads (e.g., when charging electric vehicles) are supposed to cause grid issues, *demand-response scenarios* could ease the situation (see Scenarios 7.2 and 7.3). (4) *Smart homes* (see Scenario 7.4) typically plan their energy consumption and generation in advance, requiring the predicted consumption. (5) An operator of *energy-storage facilities* (see Scenario 7.5) needs to know the predicted consumption in order to plan its operation accordingly. (6) Deriving *management decisions* (see Scenario 7.6) frequently requires not only information on actual consumption, but also on the forecasts. As an example, this allows assessing if a certain unit within an organization consumes less or more than predicted.

- *Predicting renewable generation* is needed in exactly the same scenarios as predicting consumer consumption of conventional energy. This is because generation and consumption must be equal at all times. Thus, all mechanisms requiring predicted consumption also need to know the predicted generation of energy.

- *Predicting grid loads* is important in the short run and in the long run: Knowing the predicted grid load for certain segments for several hours in advance is important for planning *demand-response measures* (see Scenarios 7.2 and 7.3) and operating *energy-storage facilities* (see Scenario 7.5). Having an estimate for the grid load in several years is important for electricity grid planners (i.e., the distribution system and transmission system operator, see Section 7.2.1) who need "to guide their decisions about what to build, when to build, and where to build" [85].

- *Predicting flexible capacities* is needed in several scenarios and is related to the prediction of consumer demand, as an energy demand can only be shifted if it actually exists. Concretely, the requirements of the *demand-response scenarios* considered in this chapter are as follows: (1) To bid for demand shifting, a demand-side manager in the control-signal scenario (see Scenario 7.3) needs to know the load-shifting potential of its customers as precisely as possible. (2) A retailer who uses *dynamic prices* (see Scenario 7.2) needs to estimate the number of customers who react to price incentives, along with the respective volumes. This requires knowing how much load can potentially be shifted.

- *Predicting energy storage capacities* is helpful in *storage scenarios* (see Scenario 7.5). As storage operators typically aim to maximize profit by means of *energy trading* (see Section 7.2.2), they need to know the future capacities. This can be an input for optimization algorithms that determine the scheduling of filling-up and emptying an energy storage.

- *Predicting energy prices* is certainly not easy, but there might be some regularity in energy prices that facilitate forecasting. Concretely, the following two directions are of interest: (1) If one knows the future energy prices with a certain probability in *energy trading* (see Section 7.2.2), then one can obviously reap large benefits. For example, in the presence of *demand response* (see Scenarios 7.2 and 7.3), one can shift the loads of customers to cheaper points in time. (2) In the presence of *dynamic prices* (see Scenario 7.2) that are not known long in advance, one can make one's own predictions of the energy price and speculatively adjust the consumption. This could be done, in particular, in highly automated *smart homes* (see Scenario 7.4).

All these scenarios are different, but they deal with the same problem from a technical point of view: *time-series forecasting*. However, the different scenarios require different data. Historical generation and consumption data from smart meters—possibly aggregated from many of them—is the basis for most scenarios. Other scenarios rely on historical storage capacities, data on demand-response measures conducted in the past, or energy prices, or they require external data such as weather forecasts for predicting renewable generation. In the following, we focus on predictions of consumption. The other predictions mentioned previously can be treated in a similar way with their own specific data.

Predictions and forecasts can generally be done by learning from historical data. In the case of energy consumption, this is a promising approach, as there are certain regularities in the data: (1) The consumption within 1 day is typically similar. People get up in the morning and switch the light on, they cook at noon and watch TV in the evening. Figure 7.2(a) illustrates two typical demand curves during two different days, aggregated for all consumers in the United Kingdom (UK). (2) The consumption on weekdays is typically similar, while it is different on weekends and national holidays where, for example, factories are not running.

Figure 7.2(b) describes the typical energy consumption in the course of a week. (3) The electricity consumption in winter is different from that in the summer. This is caused by differing usages of electrical light and possibly heating. Figure 7.2 illustrates this lower demand in summer as well as different consumption patterns on winter and summer days.

Probably the easiest approach for predictions of consumption is to average the curves of a certain number of similar days in the past, days that do not refer to special events. As one example, to predict the demand of a particular Sunday, one could average the demand from the past four Sundays where no special events occurred. This could be improved by increasing the influence of Sundays having a similar weather forecast.

The different approaches for time-series forecasts differ not only in the techniques involved, but also in the time span for the predictions: Are predictions needed for the next couple of hours, for the next day, next month, or next year? In general, time-series forecast techniques can be categorized as follows [36]:

- *Auto regression* is a group of techniques using mathematical models that utilize previous values of the time series. Some of these techniques, called *moving average*, rely on sliding-window approaches using historical time series. Various enhancements are used to deal, for example, with seasonal effects in energy data.

- *Exponential-smoothing techniques* are moving-average approaches but use a weighting with factors decaying exponentially over time.

Many of the concrete approaches for auto-regression and exponential smoothing rely on parameter estimation, for which various techniques can be used.

Several techniques from *machine learning* have also been adapted to time-series forecasting. This includes *artificial neural networks, Bayesian networks,* and *support-vector machines*. See, for example, textbooks by Berthold et al. [24], Han et al. [61], Mitchell [95], and Witten et al. [140] for descriptions of these algorithms.

Dannecker et al. [36] provides an extensive review of all the previously mentioned techniques in the context of energy; Alfares and Nazeeruddir [16] is another one; and Hippert et al. [66], in particular, reviews *neural-network approaches*, which can be combined with similar-day approaches mentioned previously [93]. While a large number of papers focus on predictions of consumption of energy, many of them can also be used for other pre-dictions. In addition to more general reviews [16, 36, 66], Aggarwal et al. [14] reviews *price-forecasting techniques* in particular. Another direction of work is the forecast of wind-power production [20, 84, 89]. The application of some of the above-mentioned time-series forecast techniques has been investigated in this context for both short- and long-term predictions, based on data from wind-energy production and meteorological observations.

Dannecker et al. [37] is a study on hierarchical *distributed forecasting* of time-series of energy demand and supply. Such approaches tackle explic-itly the huge amounts of data that might need to be considered when mak-ing forecasts at higher levels, such as a whole country (see Section 7.4.1). In addition to distributed forecasting, the authors also deal with the impor-tant problem of *forecast model maintenance* and reuse previous models and their parameter combinations [38].

Time-series forecasting seems to be quite a mature field, but it is still a challenge for the future energy domain. It has been applied to forecast-ing demand, generation, and prices, but there is little literature available regarding the other future energy scenarios listed above. Particularly in light of dynamic pricing (see Scenario 7.2), other demand-response mea-sures (e.g., Scenario 7.3), energy storage (see Scenario 7.5) and distributed and volatile small-scale generation (see Section 7.1), predictions of con-sumer demand, grid usage, etc., has become much more challenging. This is because many more factors than pure historical time series are needed to make accurate predictions. Section 7.4.3.2 sheds some light on the human factor, but many further factors must be integrated in an appropri-ate way to achieve the high-quality forecasts that are needed in the smart grid. (Many future energy scenarios require extremely high accuracies of predictions; that is, even small deviations from the optimal result may cause huge costs.) This calls for more research on the question of which factors are useful in which situation and which forecast model (or ensem-ble thereof) to use for which task when certain data are available. These questions can certainly not be answered in general and must be addressed individually. However, some guidance and experience would be of high practical relevance for new smart-grid scenarios.

7.4.3.2 Predicting and Classifying User Behavior

Predicting and classifying users and their behaviors is one of the most pop-ular applications of data mining. This is also the case in the energy domain. We assemble an exemplary list of respective challenges in the following:

- Electricity retailers (see Section 7.2.1) acting in a very competitive market want to *classify customers for marketing reasons*. For example, if they would like to introduce a new tariff scheme targeting a certain group of consumers, say families living in apartments, they would like to select this target group for marketing campaigns, based on the energy consumption patterns.

- In demand-response scenarios relying on dynamic prices or control signals (see Scenarios 7.2 and 7.3), the respective parties would like to *predict which consumers will participate* in a certain demand-response measure (e.g., a price incentive) and *how much demand could be shifted* with this particular measure. Similar predictions are of relevance in smart homes.

- In smart homes (see Scenario 7.4), *user behavior classification* can decide whether a user will go to work, will stay at home, will use an EV, etc. This is important for scheduling energy generation and consumption. Similar classifications are important in the field of EVs (see the paragraph on *new loads* in Section 7.1 and Scenario 7.5). Intelligent charging and V2G mechanisms [118] need to know, for example, whether the user will behave as usual and will solely drive to work and back, or if the user might plan any longer or further trips.

Again, individual challenges require different data, ranging from general customer data and smart-meter readings to data describing demand-response measures, events in a smart home, and EV usage. As prediction and classification are very mature fields in data mining and machine learning, a large number of potentially relevant techniques is available. This includes *decision tree classifiers, neural networks, support vector machines, naïve Bayes classifiers,* and *k-nearest neighbor algorithms*. More information can be found in the relevant literature [24, 61, 95, 140]. However, such classifiers cannot be applied directly to all kinds of relevant data in order to predict behavior. If, for example, sequential data of behavioral events are available, combined approaches [29] might be needed to deal with the data. To cope with time-series data from smart meters, aggregates must be calculated to feed the data into standard classifiers. Alternatively, more specific time-series techniques [86] can be applied (see Section 7.4.1), for example, specialized *time-series classification* [56, 76].

A few works on classifying electricity consumers are available in the literature. Ramos and Vale [116] first uses clustering techniques to identify different groups of customers (see Section 7.4.4.1). Then, the authors assemble feature vectors and use a standard decision-tree classifier to learn these groups and to automatically assign new consumers to them. They assemble the features from averaged and normalized daily load profiles of the consumers by defining a number of aggregates. These aggregates include ratios between peak demand and average demand, ratios of energy consumed at lunchtime, at night, etc. [90] extracts its features differently. The authors use the average and the peak demand of a consumer, as well as coefficients from time-series forecasting techniques [36]. For classification, the authors employ linear discriminate analysis.

Predicting and classifying the behavior of customers has been an important application of data analysis in the past. Surprisingly, not that much research has been conducted in the context of energy consumer behavior. However, as more market roles are arising (see Section 7.2.1) and potentially more data will be collected, the need of such analytics will increase. Some analytic challenges can certainly be solved by means of established techniques from data mining and machine learning. Because data might be complex and come from different sources, there is also a need for further developing specific algorithms and to combine different analysis techniques [29]. Prediction and classification of energy customer behavior is therefore an important field in *domain-driven data mining* [28].

7.4.3.3 Predicting and Classifying Consumption Events

In future energy systems, there are a number of challenges involving prediction and classification of events and consumption patterns:

- Optimized control and planning in a *smart home* (see Scenario 7.4) requires the detection of load profiles and the prediction of events, together with their respective forecasts [117, 141].

- In the *smart-meter scenario* (see Scenario 7.1), the visualization could be enhanced by displaying not only a household's total consumption, but also to disaggregate the load curve into the different appliances and highlight them in the visualization. This would increase user awareness and boost energy efficiency. Pattern-recognition algorithms can be used to identify appliances within the household's load curve [63, 87].

- Another use case for load-pattern recognition are *cross-selling activities* conducted by, for example, value-added service providers. By analyzing single appliances, special sales offers could be triggered in cases where new energy-efficient appliances are available.

- *Energy-efficiency* effects become more important with the size of the loads that are considered. Therefore, identifying consumption patterns is of importance *in complex environments* as described in Scenario 7.6.

- *Charging EVs* will become a major load in electricity grids. To illustrate, driving 10 kilometers to work and back resembles four loads of a washing machine. These loads need to be predicted in a reliable way in order to allow the future energy system to make appropriate schedules both within a smart home and in the whole electricity grid [118].

- Detection and prediction of *user behavior events in electric mobility* (an event could be to start a certain trip) is quite complex, as a vehicle is often used by multiple people. Such knowledge and predictions are essential to facilitate smart charging of EVs and V2G (see Scenario 7.5).

Massively distributed generation and new loads (see Section 7.1) can lead to *problematic grid situations*. Detecting and predicting such events is a major topic in smart grids. Chapter 8 in this book elaborates this in a comprehensive way.

From a technical point of view, the mentioned challenges can be divided into two parts: (1) prediction of events and (2) classification of consumption patterns. Abundant research has been conducted in the field of pattern detection from smart-meter data. This has been published partly in the privacy domain [96, 113] (see Section 7.4.8). Pattern detection is also a basic block for *disaggregation techniques,* which we describe in more detail along with the techniques in Section 7.4.5. Early works have already shown that the electricity consumption of a whole house can be disaggregated, with high accuracy< into the major appliances [49]. Nizar et al. [108] is a survey of load profiling methods. Event prediction has received less attention in the context of energy. While traditional techniques such as *sequence mining* [62] can be used in principle to predict discrete events [46], further techniques from *machine learning* have been adapted recently. For instance, Savio et al. [124] performs event prediction in the field of electricity consumption with neural networks and support vector machines.

To summarize, there is a huge need for the prediction of events and for the classification and prediction of consumption patterns. On the one side, quite a bit of research has been conducted in pattern detection (classification of patterns), partly in the context of *disaggregation* (see Section 7.4.5). On the other side, techniques for predicting consumption patterns and events of user behavior can still be improved for application in the field of future energy. As the demand for accurate techniques becomes a given, respective research would be an opportunity to support the developments of the smart grid significantly.

7.4.4 Detection on Unknown Patterns

In many of the described energy scenarios, data analysis is needed to detect novel, unknown, and unexpected knowledge. Such knowledge is represented by hidden patterns describing the correlation of energy measurements, groups of similar consumers, or deviating objects such as a single household with unexpected energy consumption. In all these cases, no information is given about the type of pattern or its characteristics, and there are no example instances known for this pattern. Thus, this unsupervised learning is clearly different from the prediction techniques described in Section 7.4.3. In the following, we describe pattern-detection techniques focusing on *clustering, outlier mining,* and *subspace analysis.* We highlight the applicability of these techniques in the energy domain. However, we will also point out open challenges not yet addressed by these data-analysis paradigms.

We begin with a brief overview of clustering applications on energy data:

- *Unsupervised learning as preprocessing step.* In most cases, the proposed techniques, such as clustering and outlier mining, are used as preprocessing steps to other data-analysis tasks. For example, for prediction tasks (see Section 7.4.3), it is essential to know about substructures in the data. One can train specific classifiers for each individual cluster of customers. In other cases, one can extract novel features by cluster analysis and use these features for the prediction of unknown objects. Outlier analysis can be used to clean the data; it removes rare and unexpected objects that hinder the learning process. Pattern detection can assist in all of the previously mentioned scenarios (see Section 7.3) as a data preprocessing step. However, it is also of high value for knowledge discovery, as described in the following two cases.

- *Pattern detection for enhanced demand response.* In demand response (e.g., for dynamic prices in Scenario 7.2), one tries to match energy production with energy consumption, which requires a deep understanding of both sides. For the generation side, one has proposed prediction techniques that are used to forecast wind or solar energy production (see Section 7.4.3.1). For the consumption side, in addition to forecasts, one is interested in customer profiles that provide insights about their daily behavior (see Section 7.4.3.2). As behaviors change dramatically over time, one cannot always rely on historical data and learning algorithms. Thus, unsupervised methods (e.g., clustering or outlier mining) are means for this kind of data analysis. Clustering algorithms detect groups of customers showing highly similar behavior, without any prior knowledge about these groups. In particular, for demand-side management, these clusters can be used for specific strategies in each customer group. While some customers will not be able or willing to participate in some management actions, others will show high potential for shifting parts of their energy consumption. It is essential to be aware of such groupings to utilize the overall potential of demand-side management.

- *Automatic smart-home surveillance.* As one part of smart homes (see Scenario 7.4), we discussed demand response in the previous example. However, smart homes have further potential for data-analysis tasks. Having all the energy consumption data of smart homes available, one can design automated surveillance mechanisms assisting, for example, elderly people in their daily living. Energetic profiles are very detailed and reveal a lot of information about our daily behavior and can be used for tracking, warning, and assistance systems. For example, in assisted home living, it is crucial to know if elderly people change their daily habits. A youngster who typically moves around and uses many electric devices throughout the day will become highly suspicious if she or he stops this behavior for one day. Such dramatic changes can be detected as unexpected patterns and used as warnings for medical or other assistance parties. This example highlights the requirements for unsupervised learning techniques. Although some patterns might be learned with supervised techniques, most unexpected behavior will be new for the system and difficult to be learned. In particular, we observe outlier mining as one of the key techniques in the area of energy data analysis.

- *Cluster customers for marketing reasons.* Corresponding to the case of a classification of the customers (see Section 7.4.3.2), cluster analysis can detect the different groups of customers of an electricity retailer. This promises interesting insights into the customer base and is a basis for the design of tariffs.

7.4.4.1 Clustering

Let us now abstract from these individual scenarios and discuss some well-known techniques in pattern detection. Clustering is an unsupervised data-mining task for the grouping of objects based on their mutual similarity [61]. Algorithms can detect groups of similar objects. Thus, they separate pairs of dissimilar objects into different groups. A large variety of approaches have been proposed for convex clusters [43, 92], density-based clusters [48, 65], and spectral clustering [106, 107]. Further extensions have been proposed for specific data types such as time series [76, 114]. All these approaches differ in their underlying cluster definitions. However, they have one major property in common: they all output a single set of clusters, that is, one partitioning of the data that assigns each object to a single cluster [102].

We now discuss this single clustering solution for customer segmentation based on smart-meter data. One has a given database of customers (objects) that are described by a number of properties (attributes). These attributes can be various types of information derived from smart-meter measurements (see Scenario 7.1). For example, each customer has a certain set of devices. For each device, one might detect its individual energy consumption and additional information about the time points when these devices are used in the household [78] (see Sections 7.4.3.3 and 7.4.5 for further details about the identification of devices). Obviously, one can detect groups of customers owning different types of devices. This grouping can be used to separate customers into different advertisement campaigns (expensive devices, low-budget devices, energy-efficient devices, and many more). However, in contrast to this simple partitioning, one might be interested in several other groupings: Each customer is part of groups with respect to the daily profile (early leaving, home office, part-time working), or with respect to a current living situation (single household; family without children, with children, elderly people). This example highlights the need for multiple clustering solutions on a single database [102]. In particular, with the large number of attributes given, it is unclear which of them are relevant. It is an additional challenge for data analysis to select these attributes.

Dimensionality-reduction techniques have been proposed to select a set of attributes. They tackle the "curse of dimensionality," which hinders meaningful clustering [25]. Irrelevant attributes obscure the cluster patterns in the data. Global dimensionality techniques, such as *principle component analysis (PCA)*, reduce the number of attributes [71]. However, the reduction may obtain only a single clustering in the reduced space. For locally varying attribute relevance, this means that some clusters will be missed that do not show up in the reduced space. Moreover, dimensionality reduction techniques are unable to identify clusterings in different reduced spaces. Objects may be part of distinct clusters in different data projections. Our customer segmentation example highlights this property. Each cluster requires an individual set of relevant dimensions.

Recent years have witnessed increasing research in clustering in high-dimensional spaces. Projected clustering or subspace clustering aims at identifying the locally relevant reduction of attributes for each cluster. In particular, subspace clustering allows identifying several possible subspaces for any object. Thus, an object may be part of more than one cluster in different subspaces [101, 128].

For customer segmentation based on energy profiles, several open challenges arise in the detection of object groups and the detection of relevant attributes for each of these groups. Many private and public organizations collect large amounts of energy measurements; however, their relevance for individual patterns is still unclear. Neither is clustering on the full set of attributes a solution, nor is preselection of relevant attributes by dimensionality reduction techniques. Costly search in all possible projections of the data must be performed to identify multiple clustering solutions with respect to different attribute combinations. Thus, the scalability of such data-mining techniques will be a major challenge, as highlighted by a recent study [101]. As described in Section 7.4.1, smart-meter readings will provide huge databases. Only a few publications have focused recently on such scalability issues [34, 98, 99]. However, most subspace clustering models are still based on inefficient processing schemes [15, 72, 100]. Further challenges arise in the stream processing of such data [11]. It raises questions on the detection of clusters, but also on their tracking over time [59, 129]. Tracking the change of customer profiles will be an essential means for tracking the energy demands in demand-site management systems or online adjustment of energy prices in future energy markets.

The literature in the field of energy data analysis has focused only on clustering similar consumers or consumption profiles, making use of similar preprocessing techniques as in classification (see Section 7.4.3.2). Examples of such works are by Li et al. [90], Ramos and Vale [116], and Verdú et al. [132]. However, they do not address the mentioned challenges in tracing, multiple clustering solutions, and local projection of data, which leave a high potential for enhanced clustering results.

7.4.4.2 Outlier Mining

In contrast to clusters (groups of similar objects), outliers are highly deviating objects. Outliers can be rare, unexpected, and suspicious data objects in a database. They can be detected for data cleaning, but in many cases they provide additional and useful knowledge about the database. Thus, pattern detection considers outliers as very valuable patterns hidden in today's data. In our previous example, suspicious customers might be detected that deviate from the residual customers. Considering the neighboring households, one might observe very high energy consumption for heating devices. While all other households in this neighborhood use oil or gas for heating, the outlier is using electric heating. There have been different outlier detection paradigms proposed in the literature to detect such outliers. Techniques range from deviation-based methods [119], to distance-based methods [80], to density-based methods [27]. For example, density-based methods compute a score for each object by measuring its degree of deviation with respect to a local neighborhood. Thus, one is able to detect local density variations between low-density outliers and their high-density (clustered) neighborhood. Note that in our example, the neighborhood has been literally the geographic neighborhood of the household. However, it can be an arbitrary neighborhood considering other attributes (e.g., similarity to other customers with respect to the set of devices used).

Similar to the clustering task, we observe open challenges in online stream analysis for outlier detection [9], the detection of local outliers in subspace projections [12, 103], and the scalability to large and high-dimensional databases [40]. An additional challenge is the description of such outlier patterns. Most approaches focus only on the detection of highly deviating objects. Only a few consider their description [18, 79]. Similar to subspace clustering, it seems very promising to select relevant attribute combinations as descriptions. Based on this general idea of sub-space mining in arbitrary projections of the data, several preprocessing techniques for the selection of subspaces have been proposed [33, 74]. They try to measure the contrast between outliers and the clustered regions of a database. A first approach proposes a selection based on the entropy measure [33]. A subspace is selected if it has low entropy, that is, if it shows a large variation in the densities. More recent approaches have focused on statistical selection of high-contrast regions [74]. They compare the deviation of densities and utilize only the most significant subspaces. Such subspaces can be seen as the reasons for high deviation. In our example, high-contrast subspaces might be "energy consumption of heating devices" and "age of the refrigerator." This combination might be characteristic for the distinction of modern versus old households and might reveal some unexpected cases with old refrigerators (that should be exchanged) in an energy-efficient house. This example shows that it is important to detect these cases. However, it is even more important to provide good explanations of why these cases show high deviation.

Looking at the future users of such outlier-mining techniques in, for example, smart homes, we observe that most of them will be people with no background in data analysis. This will raise new visualization and explanation requirements for result presentation. It requires novel data-mining techniques that are able to highlight the differences between patterns. For instance, such techniques could reveal the reason for the high deviation of a single object or the difference between two groups of customers. First techniques in this direction have been proposed [22]. Given two different datasets, they try to measure the difference and output characteristic properties to distinguish between these sets. Very promising instantiations have been applied to emerging pattern detection or novelty detection in the context of stream data [44].

As outlier mining is an established technique in data mining, it has been used in several works in the field of energy data. To name some examples, Li et al. [90] uses outlier mining to detect abnormal energy use. Chen et al. [32] defines so-called load cleansing problems for energy data and develops techniques similar to outlier mining. Jakkula and Cook [67] presents specialized outlier detection algorithms dedicated to power data-sets collected in smart homes. All these approaches can be seen as first instantiations of simple outlier models. The further potential of energy data must be exploited by more enhanced outlier detection techniques.

7.4.5 Disaggregation

For achieving energy efficiency, deep knowledge concerning the distribution of the consumed power among the devices within a facility is important (see Scenarios 7.1 and 7.6). In practice, this is often achieved by installing metering devices directly on single devices, which is expensive, time-consuming, and usually not exhaustive. It would be easier to derive the power distribution from the metered data at the interface to the grid (see also Section 7.4.3.3).

Smart metering, that is, high-resolution metering and remote transmission of metered data, promises to provide that deep look into the infrastructure at all metering points. Techniques for achieving this are commonly called *nonintrusive (appliance) load monitoring* (*NILM*, sometimes also *NALM*) or *disaggregation* of power data. This has potential applications in achieving better energy efficiency (see Scenarios 7.1 and 7.6) and in facilitating demand response (see Scenarios 7.2 and 7.3) and load management (e.g., in a *smart home*, see Scenario 7.4). Thus, the topic has recently sparked increased interest [31, 53, 55, 78, 82, 91, 142] after further research (including, e.g., [49, 87]) has been done since the first paper was published in 1992 [63].

Common smart meters in residential and industrial environments are placed at the interface to the distribution grid. They measure the active and reactive energy used by all the devices connected to the electric circuit that originates at the meter. Additional values can be measured, such as peak loads. Multiple meters can be installed at a single facility, which is usually the case if separated billing of the consumed energy is required. For billing purposes, such meters pick up the consumed energy typically in intervals of fifteen minutes. However, an interface with a higher temporal resolution is usually provided at the meter itself, which can be accessed locally.

As these meters are increasingly available, it is tempting to also use the metered data for analytical purposes. In a residential setting, transparency of energy consumption may lead to energy conservation (see Scenario 7.1). NILM has also been proposed as a tool for verifying the effectiveness of demand-response measures. In industrial or commercial settings, an energy audit is a valuable tool for identifying potentials for energy efficiency (see Scenario 7.6). Such audits can be executed more thoroughly the more detailed information is available. The (temporary) installation of sub-meters is therefore commonly practiced and could be, at least partially, substituted by NILM.

An example of real energy data available to load disaggregation is visualized in Figure 7.1. If this load curve would represent what one has been doing throughout that day, one would be able to assign labels to certain patterns in the load curve. These labels would describe events or activities of that day. However, if somebody else looks at the load curve, they cannot directly infer information about one's daily activities. They might be able to identify certain devices, such as an oven. The lack of contextual information limits the usage of this data. This calls for automated disaggregation and visualization, as described in Section 7.4.3.3.

The load curve of a factory or a commercial building is much more complex than that of a household or an individual person (see Scenario 7.6). Many more individuals and devices are contributing to the load curve, and many of them with individual behavior. Complex industrial processes are executed at the same time. However, there is a lot of contextual information available that can be used to identify individual devices and processes.

In addition to the curve representing the real power over time, values such as reactive power, peak current, and possibly other electrical features can also be used. From these time series, a lot of higher-level information can be deduced, such as features in the frequency domain, the instantaneous admittance waveform, and more [91].

A sophisticated energy auditing system should be enabled to map process information to load patterns. It should be able to identify recurring patterns. It might be necessary to initialize this system with additional knowledge. Load disaggregation should be as accurate as possible and with a tunable relation between false positives and false negatives.

7.4.5.1 Approaches to Load Disaggregation

In the following we describe the fundamental problem of load disaggregation. Further, we describe the fundamental approach to the problem, and discuss some recent work. For a thorough description of historic and recent work in this field, we refer you to Zeifman and Roth [142] and Froehlich et al. [53] for an overview of device characteristics that can be useful for disaggregation.

A load curve is a function L that describes the complex load (real and reactive energy) over time. In each discrete time step t, the real energy consumed by all devices r_i and their respective reactive energy q_i is summed. Noise r_b and q_b are added as well:

$$L(t) = \sum_{i=0}^{N} \left(r_i(t), q_i(t) \right) + (r_b, q_b)$$

Given only the resulting sum value over time, we are looking for a state matrix that contains the state of each device at any discrete point in time. The state spaces of the devices are independent of each other. For most practical devices, there exist several constraints on the possible states and the state transitions that are caused by their internal electrical structure and their usage modes. For example, all practical devices are operating between a minimum load and a maximum load, and they have finitely many operating states.

There are two fundamental steps to be made for load disaggregation. The first step is *feature recognition*, which extracts features from the observed meter data. The second step is the application of an *optimization* algorithm that assigns values to the state matrix.

Pattern recognition is being applied to the observed values (see Section 7.4.3.3), in its simplest form to a change in the real power load. The objective of this step is to identify a set of devices that may exhibit the observed pattern. A naïve algorithm could map a load change to the device that exhibits the closest step size of the observed change. An ideal algorithm would perfectly identify the cause of an observed event as either a fluctuation not caused by a state change, or the very device and its state change that caused the change. However, no such perfect algorithm exists today and false positive matches and false negatives are unavoidable.

There are a variety of features that can be used to find a valid disaggregation. The most basic feature of a device is its load variance, which was used by Hart [63]. Based on this feature, four classes of devices can be identified: *permanent, on-off, multi-state,* and *variable*. Permanent devices are single-state and are consuming the same load at all times (e.g., alarm systems that are never switched off). On-off devices have an additional off-state, where consumption is (near-)zero. Multi-state devices have multiple operating modes that are usually executed in certain patterns; for example, a washing machine has certain modes, such as heating water, pumping, or spinning. Variable load devices expose arbitrary, irregular load patterns that may depend on their actual usage mode. It is important to note that most practical devices cannot be fully characterized by one of these classes alone. Usually, a device exhibits behavior that is a complex mixture of these classes. The challenge of disaggregating such loads is complicated by the fact that, of course, the complex load profiles of devices are superimposed on each other, which makes an accurate, nonambiguous disaggregation difficult to achieve.

Because basic features, which are also referred to as *macroscopic features*, such as consumption or real and reactive power, have their limitations, features on the *microscopic* level have been studied in order to obtain more accurate results [142]. Microscopic features refer to characteristics of the underlying electrical signal, which can be measured at frequencies of at least in the kilohertz range. This allows for identification of waveform patterns and the harmonics of the signal. Using these features yields better results than disaggregation based on basic features alone. However, such measurements require dedicated hardware and additional processing capacities, which limits their practical use.

The *optimization* step (which is a common task in data analysis; see Section 7.4.7) tries to find an assignment to the state matrix that best matches the observed values. This answers the question of which device was active during which period and at which power level.

A common approach to finding the state matrix is to create a *hidden Markov model (HMM)* of the system [31, 78, 82]. Each device is represented by an HMM, which is a flexible structure that can capture complex behavior. Roughly, a sharp change in power consumption corresponds to a state change within a device HMM. The challenge is to extract the HMM parameters from the observed meter data. This is often supported by a supervised training phase where known features are being used.

7.4.5.2 Practical Applications

Accurate load disaggregation could replace sub-metering, at least for some applications. But even with the currently available level of accuracy, useful applications seem feasible. For example, Chen et al. [31] is using meter data from water consumption to identify activities such as showering or washing. This work improves results by evaluating the specific context in which load disaggregation is being used. Usage patterns depending on the time of day, household size, and demographics help to derive statistical information about appliance use, such as the distribution of washing machine usage. Reportedly, it also helped people make decisions about more efficient resource usage, for example, by replacing appliances with more efficient ones.

It remains a challenge to improve the accuracy of NILM for practical applications. Many studies assume that the features of the involved devices are known in advance. In such *supervised* settings, it is necessary to determine the features of individual devices in a controlled environment. In contrast, *unsupervised* techniques have recently been proposed [55, 78]. This class of techniques does not rely on a given decomposition of power signals from individual devices, but instead automatically separates the different consumption signals without training. Although unsupervised techniques seem to work in practice, research shows that the quality drops when increasing the number of devices [78].

The accuracy of the existing approaches has only been tested under individual lab conditions thus far. A common methodology for evaluation is missing; for example, no systematic testing on a common dataset has been performed as yet. Only recently, a set of test data has been proposed [83] that comprises residential appliances. Similarly, test data for industrial applications are required, but are not freely available. Some notion of accuracy is usually used to assess the quality of an approach. As discussed by Zeifman and Roth [142], this might not be the desirable measure. Thus, the authors propose to use *receiver operating characteristic (ROC) curves* as a quality measure [24, 61, 140].

Notwithstanding the deficiencies of the measure itself, it is clear that none of the existing approaches are suitable to completely substitute sub-metering due to inaccuracy. Thus, disaggregation is not suitable for billing and other applications that require accurate and precise measures. It is likely that sub-metering or separate metering will be required to satisfy these demands—at least in the near future. For "soft" applications such as energy-efficiency auditing, the accuracy of load disaggregation might be sufficient in many cases. However, no evaluation in a working environment has been reported thus far. Sub-metering remains state-of-the-art when it comes to accurate load disaggregation. Research is still required to demonstrate the practicability of NILM as there seem to be no reports of large-scale field tests of NILM. Furthermore, the literature mentioned in this section employs data at 1-second granularity or at even finer temporal resolutions. Further research is needed to investigate if and under which conditions disaggregation techniques can be applied to data at the coarser granularities that are frequently available in practice.

In the future, a semiautomatic approach to load disaggregation might be practically valuable for energy audits. Graphical, interactive exploration tools could be used to validate the automatic recognition of devices and correct for errors. After the consumption patterns of individual devices (or classes of devices) are identified, the next step would be to correlate these patterns with additional data, such as operational data from production runs, working hours, or out-of-order events. By doing so, higher accuracies could be obtained.

7.4.6 Exploration and Comparison of Energy Datasets

In previous sections, the focus was on automatic learning: (1) for models in prediction tasks (Section 7.4.3), (2) extraction of unexpected and novel patterns (Section 7.4.4), and (3) disaggregation of devices by metadata extraction (Section 7.4.5). In contrast to these automatic techniques, many energy scenarios, such as Scenarios 7.1 and 7.6, require manual exploration of data. Users want to understand the underlying data and use data management and analysis techniques to get an overview of their data. In many cases, they try to derive knowledge from the data by comparing two or more different datasets. Assisting these manual or semiautomated exploration tasks will be the main focus of the following discussion.

Let us give some brief examples of semiautomated and manual tasks on energy data related to exploration and comparison:

- *Exploration of energy trades.* For the energy market, it is crucial to know about the amount of trades with specific conditions. All market participants are interested in such manual selections to understand the market. They explore the trades with respect to some manually defined condition. For example, how many trades have been made with solar energy, in the last month, overall in Germany. Others might be interested in the overall volume of energy produced in wind parks in offshore regions located around the coast of Denmark. A third example might be the average capacity of energy storage facilities in Europe and how it evolved from 2010 to 2011. All these examples are user-driven queries on aggregated subparts of the data. Human experts design these queries and data management techniques must be designed for efficient processing.

- *Comparison of different customer behaviors.* Many case studies [57] have looked at the difference in energy consumption for two or more given databases describing the energy behavior of different customers. One is interested in the characteristic behavior of one group of people (or devices, facilities, etc.) compared to a second group. These characteristic differences are used to understand the customer population. In other cases, the two contrasting data states are "before" and "after" an energy-saving campaign. Thus, comparison is required to measure the success of such a campaign. For example, semiautomated techniques can derive the reduced energy consumption for lighting and cooling devices. This energy saving can be an important result for future campaigns and might reveal some more potentials for energy savings.

- *Manual verification of unexpected events.* As discussed in Section 7.4.3, there are some rare events, such as the World Cup soccer final on TV, that dramatically affect the typical energy consumption. In simple cases, such as the World Cup final, the understanding of this event is quite easy. Experts will not need any assistance in the verification of this event. However, for both energy production and energy consumption, there are a large variety of factors influencing the system. Many of the unexpected events (e.g., the detected outliers as described in Section 7.4.4.2, or the emerging events hindering good prediction in Section 7.4.3) will require assistance in their verification. Providing a time stamp on the unexpected high energy consumption might be very limited information for the human expert. Understanding and verifying such events means that we have to enrich the set of information provided to the user.

7.4.6.1 Extending Data Management Techniques

We observe the efficient aggregation of energy data as one of the main tasks for manual exploration. Abstracting from our toy example based on energy trades, the users are interested in various aggregations of the raw production, consumption, distribution, and sales data. In general, such processing is well known in the database community as *online analytical processing (OLAP)*. Based on a user-specified hypothesis, the system must provide aggregated information with respect to a specific set of conditions. The conditions are described by the attributes (e.g., location, time, production type, etc.) and are structured based on a given hierarchy of granularities (e.g., weeks, months, years, etc.). Such OLAP systems have been proposed for sales analysis in retail companies. They provide the essential means for decision making but do not address the specific scenario of decisions based on energy data (see Scenario 7.6).

Essential properties of energy production, distribution, and consumption are missed by these techniques. Modern data management techniques (see Section 7.4.1) try to overcome these challenges. In particular, large data volumes must be aggregated in main memory. This processing can be assisted by modern column-based data storage [112, 125]. In contrast to row-based data representation, column-based storage allows for efficient aggregation over a single (or multiple) attribute without accessing the entire database. This selectivity allows for very efficient processing of OLAP queries. In addition, we can utilize automated techniques such as disaggregation (see Section 7.4.5) to enrich the set of available attributes. This results in large and high-dimensional databases, which pose novel scalability issues to both manual (and semiautomated) exploration as well as to automatic data analysis. For future energy data, we must extend traditional OLAP and data mining techniques to achieve such a scalable data analysis.

Currently, most energy case studies rely on traditional techniques in OLAP and information management [57]. They are not able to cope with the entire set of information available. They design their interactive exploration on a small subset of attributes with quite rough aggregation levels (e.g., allowing exploration of energy data only on a daily basis). Further restrictions are made for query types and visualization methods. Overall, we consider such systems only as first steps to future energy information systems. The state-of-the-art has not reached the complexity of data, user exploration, and interaction required by most of the energy scenarios envisioned.

7.4.6.2 Guided Exploration to Unexpected Patterns

One major challenge of OLAP is its manual search for interesting patterns in the data. It is highly dependent on the expert using the OLAP system. If she or he knows a lot about the energy data, it will be easy to find the right aggregation level, the appropriate set of attributes, and the conditions on these attributes. Thus, one might be able to reveal the required information out of the huge database. However, in most cases, this information is unexpected, such that even experts do not know where to search. Furthermore, if lay users are involved in the OLAP system, they do not have any idea where to start with the aggregation. Thus, it is very important to provide semiautomated techniques that guide the user through the database to the unexpected aggregates and the right attribute combinations.

In recent years, there have been some interesting approaches for the so-called discovery-driven OLAP systems. They add automatic techniques to the OLAP system, which guide the users according to unexpected data distributions [122]. Comparing the mean and variance of each column of the database, one can simply detect unexpected cells in an OLAP cube.

For example, if we look at the energy production in each month, one could detect a high peak in August, which deviates from the residual months due to some unexpected high-energy production. The same statistics can be applied for all August months over several years and highlight a specific year. This leads to a very promising selection of attribute combinations, each with a high deviation in energy production. Overall, these unexpected measures can be seen as candidates for manual exploration. One can provide some of these attribute combinations to the user, and he or she will be able to refine these selections.

Further techniques have been proposed for guided OLAP [121, 123]; they focus more on the interaction with the users and provide additional means for step-by-step processing through the OLAP cube and additional descriptions on the deviation of data. However, all these techniques are expensive in terms of computation. Similar to other automatic data-analysis techniques, they do not scale to energy databases with many attributes and millions of measurements on the very fine-grained level. Applications of such techniques are always limited by efficiency, and energy data pose one of the most problematic application areas with respect to scalability issues.

7.4.6.3 Contrast Analysis and Emerging Patterns

Another automated approach for pattern exploration is *contrast analysis*. This technique focuses on the extraction of descriptive, distinguishing, emerging, and contrasting patterns for two or more given classes in a database [22, 44, 79]. Contrast analysis techniques provide subsets of attributes (and attribute values) as contrasting patterns. For example, given a database with more than two persons living in the same household and another database of energy profiles for single households, one might be interested in comparing these two groups of customers. Such automatic comparison can provide the characteristic differences in the behavior of people. On the one side, these differences can be used as input to any learning task. On the other side, they provide the essential mean for human exploration. We focus here on the latter one and highlight the technical challenges in contrast analysis.

For human exploration it is always essential to have outputs that are easy to understand. In contrast analysis, one research direction is based on so-called contrast sets [22]. They form characteristic attribute combinations that show high deviation in the two databases. For example, the energy consumption with respect to washing machines could be one of these characteristic differences between single and family households. Contrast analysis detects such deviations and outputs a set of these contrasting properties for further investigation by the user. It is quite similar to the previous discovery-driven OLAP techniques. However, it is based on prior knowledge about the two classes, which is not given in OLAP. Hence, it is based on some prior knowledge and provides specific insight into these two classes, while discovery-driven OLAP highlights any unexpected data distribution. Further relationships can be observed with subspace analysis (see Section 7.4.4), which is quite similar to the extraction of influential attributes [79].

Overall, we observe a high demand for such exploration and comparison techniques. For energy databases with many unexpected events, it is essential to have some descriptive information about the differences among other databases or the deviation of an object inside a database. In all these cases, automatic techniques provide guidance for humans in their manual exploration. Only the combination of manual and automatic exploration seems to be able to reveal hidden knowledge out of complex databases. With many of the proposed techniques for prediction, pattern detection, and disaggregation, one can perform some fully automated data analyses. However, in most cases, users are not willing to accept these black-box techniques, in which they do not understand the derived models, patterns, and separation. Furthermore, similar to other domains, such as health surveillance, we observe many regulations by law in the energy domain. This enforces the manual verification of automatically detected patterns. Modern data-analysis techniques should be aware of this additional requirement and provide more descriptions as outputs of their algorithms. For example, it is more or less useless to detect unexpected energy consumption in a single household if one has no information about *why* this consumption profile is unexpected compared to other households.

7.4.7 Optimization

In the context of future energy and smart grids, there are a large number of different optimization problems that must be solved. As elaborating on all these problems would be beyond the scope of this chapter, we limit ourselves to highlight the most important problems.

Optimization problems in the field of electricity can be roughly partitioned in the demand side and the supply side:

- On the *demand side*, intelligent devices (e.g., in a smart home, see Scenario 7.4) need to *react to dynamic prices* (see Scenario 7.2) and optimize their demand planning accordingly. If consumers own micro-CHP units, they have to find optimized schedules for their operation. A further challenge is *charging of EVs* and possibly *V2G scenarios* (see Scenario 7.5). This is not only of importance in consumer premises, but also in so-called *smart car parks* [115]. They have a particularly high impact on the energy systems as they display high power consumption. *Disaggregation* is a further technique that makes use of optimization (see Section 7.4.5).

- On the *supply side*, probably the most prominent optimization problem is *finding dynamic prices* [70]. In scenarios with *control signals*, optimization is needed to select offers from demand-side managers (see Scenario 7.3). Another field where optimization is of relevance is the *management of energy storages* (see Scenario 7.5) where it needs to be decided when to charge and when to discharge a storage.

Many of the mentioned optimization problems can become quite complex. This, in particular, is due frequently to the many parameters to be considered:

- Planning of *micro-CHP units* has constraints concerning their profitability. This includes minimum runtime, uptime, and cycle costs. Similar constraints apply to *central storages* such as pumped-storage water-power plants.

- *Smart charging of EVs and V2G* requires one to consider user preferences (when does the car need to be charged to which level?) and economic interests of the owner or car-park operator. Furthermore, the current situation of the grid and possibly dynamic prices are also of importance [115].

- *Finding dynamic prices* aims at achieving the desired profits and realizing demand response to prevent grid issues with a low economical risk. Furthermore, the predicted generation and demand needs to be taken into account (see Section 7.4.3.1), together with the predicted willingness and ability of customers to react accordingly (see Section 7.4.3.2). Obviously, the current market prices and possibly existing long-term contracts are further parameters.

- In *control-signal scenarios*, available demand-shifting offers must be selected, taking into account that they are cost-efficient, reliable, and located in the correct grid segments.

- In *energy storages*, the operator must consider the (predicted) future generation, demand, and prices, as well as the storage-system parameters capacity and peak power.

The result of the above-mentioned conditions and constraints are often high-dimensional, multivariate optimization problems. In addition to classical solving methods [51], heuristic methods [42, 75, 88, 97] have been an important field of research in recent years. For smart-charging scenarios, for instance, multi-objective evolutionary optimization algorithms have been investigated [115].

7.4.8 Privacy-Preserving Data Mining

As discussed in this chapter, an increasing number of actors in the liberalized electricity markets (see Section 7.2.1) collect more and more data (see Section 7.4.1) when realizing the current and future energy scenarios (see Section 7.3). Many types of data can be mapped to real persons and bear potential privacy risks. Smart-meter data (see Scenario 7.1) is probably the most common example, but other types of data, such as participation in demand-response measures (see Scenario 7.3), user behavior in a smart home (see Scenario 7.4) or from an electric vehicle might disclose private data as well.

As privacy is a wide field, we concentrate on illustrating the possibilities of analyzing smart-meter data in the following discussion. Depending on the temporal resolution of such data, different user behaviors can be derived. Having smart-meter data at 1-minute granularity, for example, enables identifying most electric devices in a typical household [113]. Having data at half-second granularity might reveal whether a cutting machine was used to cut bread or salami [21]. Needless to say, disclosing such data would be a severe privacy risk as one could derive precisely what a person does at which moment. Furthermore, recent research suggests that it is even possible to identify which TV program (out of a number of known programs) someone is watching using a standard smart meter at the temporal granularity of half-seconds [58]. Interestingly—and maybe frighteningly—even data at the 15-minute granularity frequently used for billing scenarios can be a privacy threat. Such data is sufficient to identify which persons are at home and at what times, if they prepare cold or warm breakfast, when they are cooking, and when they watch TV or go to bed [96]. Jawurek et al. [69] furthermore show that consumption curves of a household are typically unique and can be used to identify a household.

There is a myriad of work that identifies the different scenarios of privacy risks and attacks in the field of energy; an overview can be found, for example, by Khurana et al. [77]. A smaller number of studies propose particular solutions, mostly for specific problems such as billing in the presence of smart meters [68]. However, this field is still quite young, and effective methods to provide privacy protection are still needed, ones that can easily be applied in the field. In addition to the privacy of consumers, such methods need to ensure that all actors in the energy market can obtain the data they need in order to efficiently fulfill their respective role in the current and future energy scenarios. This calls for further developments and new techniques in the fields of *security research* and *privacy-preserving data mining* [13, 131, 133], for which future energy systems and markets are an important field of application.

7.5 CONCLUSIONS

The traditional energy system relying on fossil and nuclear sources is not sustainable. The ongoing transformation to a more sustainable energy system relying on renewable sources leads to major challenges and to a paradigm shift from *demand-driven generation* to *generation-driven demand*. Further influential factors in the ongoing development are liberalization and the effects of new loads, such as electric vehicles. These developments in the future energy domain will be facilitated by a number of techniques that are frequently referred to as the *smart grid*. Most of these techniques and scenarios lead to new sources of data and to the challenge to manage and analyze them in appropriate ways.

In this chapter we highlighted the current developments toward a sustainable energy system. We provided an overview of the current energy markets and described a number of future energy scenarios. Based on these elaborations, we derived the data-analysis challenges in detail. In a nutshell, the conclusion is that there has been a lot of research but that there are still many unsolved problems and there is a need for more data-analysis research. Existing techniques can be applied or need to be further developed for use in the smart grid. Thus, the future energy domain is an important field for applied data-analysis research and has the potential to contribute to sustainable development.

ACKNOWLEDGMENTS

We thank Pavel Efros for his assistance, Anke Weidlich and many colleagues at SAP Research, and Acteno Energy for fruitful discussions and proofreading (parts of) the chapter.

REFERENCES

1. Directive 2009/72/EC of the European Parliament and of the Council of 13 July 2009 Concerning Common Rule for the Internal Market in Electricity. *Official Journal of the European Union*, L 211: 56–93, 2009.
2. E-Energy Glossary. Website of the DKE—Deutsche Kommission Elektrotechnik Elektronik Informationstechnik im DIN und VDE, Germany: https://teamwork.dke.de/specials/7/Wiki_EN/Wiki Pages/Home.aspx, 2010.
3. Energy Concept for an Environmentally Sound, Reliable and Affordable Energy Supply. Publication of the German Federal Ministry of Economics and Technology and the Federal Ministry for the Environment, Nature Conservation and Nuclear Safety, September 2010.
4. MeRegio—Project Phase 2. Homepage of the MeRegio project: http://www.meregio.de/en/?page=solution-phasetwo, 2010.
5. Annual Report 2010. Publication of the German Federal Motor Transport Authority, 2011.
6. Connecting markets. EEX Company and Products brochure, European Energy Exchange AG, October 2011.
7. Federal Environment Minister Röttgen: 20 Percent Renewable Energies Are a Great Success. Press Release 108/11 of the German Federal Ministry for the Environment, Nature Conservation and Nuclear Safety, August 2011.
8. Metered Half-Hourly Electricity Demands. Website of National Grid, UK: http://www.nationalgrid.com/uk/Electricity/Data/Demand+Data/, 2011.
9. Charu C. Aggarwal. On abnormality detection in spuriously populated data streams. In *International Conference on Data Mining (SDM)*, 2005.
10. Charu C. Aggarwal, Editor. *Data Streams: Models and Algorithms*, Volume 31 of *Advances in Database Systems*. Berlin and New York: Springer, 2007.
11. Charu C. Aggarwal. On High Dimensional Projected Clustering of Uncertain Data Streams. In *International Conference on Data Engineering (ICDE)*, 2009.
12. Charu C. Aggarwal, and Philip S. Yu. Outlier detection for high dimensional data. In *International Conference on Management of Data (SIGMOD)*, 2001.
13. Charu C. Aggarwal, and Philip S. Yu, Editors. *Privacy-Preserving Data Mining: Models and Algorithms*, Volume 34 of *Advances in Database Systems*. Berlin and New York: Springer, 2008.
14. Sanjeev Kumar Aggarwal, Lalit Mohan Saini, and Ashwani Kumar. Electricity Price Forecasting in Deregulated Markets: A Review and Evaluation. *International Journal of Electrical Power and Energy Systems*, 31(1): 13–22, 2009.
15. Rakesh Agrawal, Johannes Gehrke, Dimitrios Gunopulos, and Prabhakar Raghavan. Automatic subspace clustering of high dimensional data for data mining applications. In *International Conference on Management of Data (SIGMOD)*, 1998.

16. Hesham K. Alfares and Mohammad Nazeeruddin. Electric Load Forecasting: Literature Survey and Classification of Methods. *International Journal of Systems Science*, 33(1): 23–34, 2002.

17. Florian Allerding and Hartmut Schmeck. Organic smart home: Architecture for energy management in intelligent buildings. In *Workshop on Organic Computing (OC)*, 2011.

18. Fabrizio Angiulli, Fabio Fassetti, and Luigi Palopoli. Detecting Outlying Properties of Exceptional Objects. *ACM Transactions on Database Systems*, 34(1): 1–62, 2009.

19. Mariá Arenas-Martínez, Sergio Herrero-Lopez, Abel Sanchez, John R. Williams, Paul Roth, Paul Hofmann, and Alexander Zeier. A comparative study of data storage and processing architectures for the smart grid. In *International Conference on Smart Grid Communications (SmartGridComm)*, 2010.

20. Thanasis G. Barbounis, John B. Theocharis, Minas C. Alexiadis, and Petros S. Dokopoulos. Long-Term Wind Speed and Power Forecasting Using Local Recurrent Neural Network Models. *Energy Conversion, IEEE Transactions on*, 21(1): 273–284, 2006.

21. Gerald Bauer, Karl Stockinger, and Paul Lukowicz. Recognizing the Use-Mode of Kitchen Appliances from Their Current Consumption. In *Smart Sensing and Context Conference*, 2009.

22. Stephen D. Bay and Michael J. Pazzani. Detecting Group Differences: Mining Contrast Sets. *Data Mining and Knowledge Discovery*, 5(3): 213–246, 2001.

23. Birger Becker, Florian Allerding, Ulrich Reiner, Mattias Kahl, Urban Richter, Daniel Pathmaperuma, Hartmut Schmeck, and Thomas Leibfried. Decentralized Energy-Management to Control Smart-Home Architectures. In *Architecture of Computing Systems (ARCS)*, 2010.

24. Michael R. Berthold, Christian Borgelt, Frank Höppner, and Frank Klawonn. *Guide to Intelligent Data Analysis: How to Intelligently Make Sense of Real Data*, Volume 42 of *Texts in Computer Science*. Berlin and New York: Springer, 2010.

25. Kevin Beyer, Jonathan Goldstein, Raghu Ramakrishnan, and Uri Shaft. When Is Nearest Neighbors Meaningful? In *International Conference on Database Theory (ICDT)*, 1999.

26. Christophe Bisciglia. The Smart Grid: Hadoop at the Tennessee Valley Authority (TVA). Blog of Cloudera, Inc., USA: http://www.cloudera.com/blog/2009/06/smart-grid-hadoop-tennessee-valley-authority-tva/, 2009.

27. Markus M. Breunig, Hans-Peter Kriegel, Raymond T. Ng, and Jörg Sander. LOF: Identifying Density-Based Local Outliers. In *International Conference on Management of Data (SIGMOD)*, 2000.

28. Longbing Cao, Philip S. Yu, Chengqi Zhang, and Yanchang Zhao. *Domain Driven Data Mining*. Berlin and New York: Springer, 2010.

29. Longbing Cao, Huaifeng Zhang, Yanchang Zhao, Dan Luo, and Chengqi Zhang. Combined Mining: Discovering Informative Knowledge in Complex Data. *IEEE Transactions on Systems, Man, and Cybernetics*, 41(3): 699–712, 2011.

30. Pete Chapman, Julian Clinton, Randy Kerber, Thomas Khabaza, Thomas Reinartz, Colin Shearer, and Rüdiger Wirth. *CRISP-DM 1.0. Step-by-Step Data Mining Guide*, SPSS, Chicago, USA. August 2000.

31. Feng Chen, Jing Dai, Bingsheng Wang, Sambit Sahu, Milind Naphade, and Chang-Tien Lu. Activity Analysis Based on Low Sample Rate Smart Meters. In *International Conference on Knowledge Discovery and Data Mining (KDD)*, 2011.

32. Jiyi Chen, Wenyuan Li, Adriel Lau, Jiguo Cao, and Ke Wang. Automated Load Curve Data Cleansing in Power Systems. *IEEE Transactions on Smart Grid*, 1(2): 213–221, 2010.

33. Chun-Hung Cheng, Ada Waichee Fu, and Yi Zhang. Entropy-Based Subspace Clustering for Mining Numerical Data. In *International Conference on Knowledge Discovery and Data Mining (KDD)*, 1999.

34. Robson Leonardo Ferreira Cordeiro, Agma J.M. Traina, Christos Faloutsos, and Caetano Traina Jr. Finding Clusters in Subspaces of Very Large, Multi-Dimensional Datasets. In *International Conference on Data Engineering (ICDE)*, 2010.

35. Marco Dalai and Riccardo Leonardi. Approximations of One-Dimensional Digital Signals under the l^∞ Norm. *IEEE Transactions on Signal Processing*, 54(8): 3111–3124, 2006.

36. Lars Dannecker, Matthias Böhm, Ulrike Fischer, Frank Rosenthal, Gregor Hackenbroich, and Wolfgang Lehner. State-of-the-Art Report on Forecasting—A Survey of Forecast Models for Energy Demand and Supply. Public Deliverable D4.1, *The MIRACLE Consortium* (European Commission Project Reference: 248195), Dresden, Germany, June 2010.

37. Lars Dannecker, Matthias Böhm, Wolfgang Lehner, and Gregor Hackenbroich. Forecasting Evolving Time Series of Energy Demand and Supply. In *East-European Conference on Advances in Databases and Information Systems (ADBIS)*, 2011.

38. Lars Dannecker, Matthias Schulze, Robert Böhm, Wolfgang Lehner, and Gregor Hackenbroich. Context-Aware Parameter Estimation for Forecast Models in the Energy Domain. In *International Conference on Scientific and Statistical Database Management (SSDBM)*, 2011.

39. Sarah Darby. The Effectiveness of Feedback on Energy Consumption: A Review for DEFRA of the Literature on Metering, Billing and Direct Displays. Technical report, Environmental Change Institute, University of Oxford, UK, April 2006.

40. Timothy de Vries, Sanjay Chawla, and Michael E. Houle. Finding Local Anomalies in Very High Dimensional Space. In *International Conference on Data Mining (ICDM)*, 2010.

41. Jeffrey Dean and Sanjay Ghemawat. MapReduce: Simplified Data Processing on Large Clusters. In *Symposium on Operating Systems Design and Implementation (OSDI)*, 2004.

42. Kalyanmoy Deb, Samir Agrawal, Amrit Pratap, and T. Meyarivan. A Fast Elitist Non-Dominated Sorting Genetic Algorithm for Multi-Objective Optimization: NSGA-II. In *International Conference on Parallel Problem Solving from Nature (PPSN)*, 2000.

43. Arthur P. Dempster, Nan M. Laird, and Donald B. Rubin. Maximum Likelihood from Incomplete Data Via the EM Algorithm. *Journal of the Royal Statistical Society*, 39(1): 1–38, 1977.

44. Guozhu Dong and Jinyan Li. Efficient Mining of Emerging Patterns: Discovering Trends and Differences. In *International Conference on Knowledge Discovery and Data Mining (KDD)*, 1999.

45. Karen Ehrhardt-Martinez, Kat A. Donnelly, and John A. "Skip" Laitner. Advanced Metering Initiatives and Residential Feedback Programs: A Meta-Review for Household Electricity-Saving Opportunities. Technical Report E105, American Council for an Energy-Efficient Economy, Washington, D.C. June 2010.

46. Frank Eichinger, Detlef D. Nauck, and Frank Klawonn. Sequence Mining for Customer Behaviour Predictions in Telecommunications. In *Workshop on Practical Data Mining: Applications, Experiences and Challenges*, 2006.

47. Hazem Elmeleegy, Ahmed K. Elmagarmid, Emmanuel Cecchet, Walid G. Aref, and Willy Zwaenepoel. Online Piece-Wise Linear Approximation of Numerical Streams with Precision Guarantees. In *International Conference on Very Large Data Bases (VLDB)*, 2009.

48. Martin Ester, Hans-Peter Kriegel, Jörg Sander, and Xiaowei Xu. A Density-Based Algorithm for Discovering Clusters in Large Spatial Databases. In *International Conference on Knowledge Discovery and Data Mining (KDD)*, 1996.

49. Linda Farinaccio and Radu Zmeureanu. Using a Pattern Recognition Approach to Disaggregate the Total Electricity Consumption in a House into the Major End-Uses. *Energy and Buildings*, 30(3): 245–259, 1999.

50. Ahmad Faruqui and Jennifer Palmer. Dynamic Pricing and Its Discontents. *Regulation Magazine*, 34(3): 16–22, 2011.

51. Michael C. Ferris and Todd S. Munson. Complementarity Problems in Games and the Path Solver. *Journal of Economic Dynamics and Control*, 24(2): 165–188, 2000.

52. Eugene Fink and Kevin B. Pratt. Indexing of Compressed Time Series. In Last et al. [86], Chapter 3, pages 51–78.

53. Jon Froehlich, Eric Larson, Sidhant Gupta, Gabe Cohn, Matthew S. Reynolds, and Shwetak N. Patel. Disaggregated End-Use Energy Sensing for the Smart Grid. *Pervasive Computing*, 10(1): 28–39, 2011.

54. Drew Fudenberg and Jean Tirole. *Game Theory*. Cambridge, MA: MIT Press, 1991.

55. Hugo Gonçalves, Adrian Oceanu, and Mario Bergés. Unsupervised Disaggregation of Appliances Using Aggregated Consumption Data. In *Workshop on Data Mining Applications in Sustainability (SustKDD)*, 2011.

56. Carlos J. Alonso González and Juan J. Rodríguez Diez. Boosting Interval-Based Literals: Variable Length and Early Classification. In Last et al. [86], Chapter 7, pages 149–171.

57. Jessica Granderson, Mary Piette, and Girish Ghatikar. Building Energy Information Systems: User Case Studies. *Energy Efficiency*, 4: 17–30, 2011.
58. Ulrich Greveler, Benjamin Justus, and Dennis Löhr. Multimedia Content Identification through Smart Meter Power Usage Profiles. In *International Conference on Computers, Privacy and Data Protection (CPDP)*, 2012.
59. Stephan Günnemann, Hardy Kremer, Charlotte Laufkötter, and Thomas Seidl. Tracing Evolving Subspace Clusters In Temporal Climate Data. *Data Mining and Knowledge Discovery*, 24(2): 387–410, 2011.
60. Duy Long Ha, Minh Hoang Le, and Stéphane Ploix. An approach for home load energy management problem in uncertain context. In *International Conference on Industrial Engineering and Engineering Management (IEEM)*, 2008.
61. Jiawei Han, Micheline Kamber, and Jian Pei. *Data Mining: Concepts and Techniques*. Morgan Kaufmann, Burlington, USA, 2011.
62. Jiawei Han, Jian Pei, and Xifeng Yan. Sequential Pattern Mining by Pattern-Growth: Principles and Extensions. In W. Chu and T. Lin, Editors, *Studies in Fuzziness and Soft Computing*, Volume 180 of *Foundations and Advances in Data Mining*, pages 183–220. Berlin and New York: Springer, 2005.
63. George W. Hart. Nonintrusive Appliance Load Monitoring. *Proceedings of the IEEE*, 80(12): 1870–1891, 1992.
64. Magnus L. Hetland. A Survey of Recent Methods for Efficient Retrieval of Similar Time Sequences. In Last et al. [86], Chapter 2, pages 27–49.
65. Alexander Hinneburg and Daniel Keim. An Efficient Approach to Clustering in Large Multimedia Databases with Noise. In *International Conference on Knowledge Discovery and Data Mining (KDD)*, 1998.
66. Henrique Steinherz Hippert, Carlos Eduardo Pedreira, and Reinaldo Castro Souza. Neural Networks for Short-Term Load Forecasting: A Review and Evaluation. *IEEE Transactions on Power Systems*, 16(1): 44–55, 2001.
67. Vikramaditya Jakkula and Diane Cook. Outlier Detection in Smart Environment Structured Power Datasets. In *International Conference on Intelligent Environments (IE)*, 2010.
68. Marek Jawurek, Martin Johns, and Florian Kerschbaum. Plug-In Privacy for Smart Metering Billing. In *International Symposium on Privacy Enhancing Technologies (PETS)*, 2011.
69. Marek Jawurek, Martin Johns, and Konrad Rieck. Smart Metering De-Pseudonymization. In *Annual Computer Security Applications Conference (ACSAC)*, 2011.
70. Andrej Jokić, Mircea Lazar, and Paul P.J. van den Bosch. Price-Based Control of Electrical Power Systems. In Negenborn et al. [105], Chapter 5, pages 109–131.
71. Ian Joliffe. *Principal Component Analysis*. Berline and New York: Springer, 1986.
72. Karin Kailing, Hans-Peter Kriegel, and Peer Kröger. Density-Connected Subspace Clustering for High-Dimensional Data. In *International Conference on Data Mining (SDM)*, 2004.

73. Andreas Kamper. Dezentrales Lastmanagement zum Ausgleich kurzfristiger Abweichungen im Stromnetz. KIT Scientific Publishing, Korlsruhe, Germany, 2009.

74. Fabian Keller, Emmanuel Müller, and Klemens Böhm. HiCS: High Contrast Subspaces for Density-Based Outlier Ranking. In *International Conference on Data Engineering (ICDE)*, 2012.

75. James Kennedy and Russel Eberhart. Particle Swarm Optimization. In *International Conference on Neural Networks*, 1995.

76. Eamonn Keogh and Shruti Kasetty. On the Need for Time Series Data Mining Benchmarks: A Survey and Empirical Demonstration. *Data Mining and Knowledge Discovery*, 7(4): 349–371, 2003.

77. Himanshu Khurana, Mark Hadley, Ning Lu, and Deborah A. Frincke. Smart-Grid Security Issues. *IEEE Security and Privacy*, 8(1): 81–85, 2010.

78. Hyungsul Kim, Manish Marwah, Martin F. Arlitt, Geoff Lyon, and Jiawei Han. Unsupervised Disaggregation of Low Frequency Power Measurements. In *International Conference on Data Mining (SDM)*, 2011.

79. Edwin M. Knorr and Raymond T. Ng. Finding intensional knowledge of distance-based outliers. In *International Conference on Very Large Data Bases (VLDB)*, 1999.

80. Edwin M. Knox and Raymond T. Ng. Algorithms for mining distance-based outliers in large datasets. In *International Conference on Very Large Data Bases (VLDB)*, 1998.

81. Koen Kok, Martin Scheepers, and René Kamphuis. Intelligence in Electricity Networks for Embedding Renewables and Distributed Generation. In Negenborn et al. [105], Chapter 8, pages 179–209.

82. J. Zico Kolter and Tommi Jaakkola. Approximate inference in additive factorial hmms with application to energy disaggregation. In *International Conference on Artificial Intelligence and Statistics (AISTATS)*, 2012.

83. J. Zico Kolter and Matthew Johnson. REDD: A public data set for energy disaggregation research. In *Workshop on Data Mining Applications in Sustainability (SustKDD)*, 2011.

84. Andrew Kusiak, Haiyang Zheng, and Zhe Song. Short-Term Prediction of Wind Farm Power: A Data Mining Approach. *IEEE Transactions on Energy Conversion*, 24(1): 125–136, 2009.

85. National Energy Technology Laboratory. A Vision for the Modern Grid. In *Smart Grid*, Chapter 11, pages 283–293. The Capitol Net Inc., 2007.

86. Mark Last, Abraham Kandel, and Horst Bunke, Editors. *Data Mining in Time Series Databases*, Volume 57 of *Series in Machine Perception and Artificial Intelligence*. World Scientific, Singapore, 2004.

87. Christopher Laughman, Kwangduk Lee, Robert Cox, Steven Shaw, Steven Leeb, Les Norford, and Peter Armstrong. Power Signature Analysis. *Power and Energy Magazine*, 1(2): 56–63, 2003.

88. Yiu-Wing Leung and Yuping Wang. An Orthogonal Genetic Algorithm with Quantization for Global Numerical Optimization. *IEEE Transactions on Evolutionary Computation*, 5(1): 41–53, 2001.

89. Shuhui Li, Donald C. Wunsch, Edgar O'Hair, and Michael G. Giesselmann. Comparative Analysis of Regression and Artificial Neural Network Models for Wind Turbine Power Curve Estimation. *Journal of Solar Energy Engineering*, 123(4): 327–332, 2001.

90. Xiaoli Li, Chris P. Bowers, and Thorsten Schnier. Classification of Energy Consumption in Buildings with Outlier Detection. *IEEE Transactions on Industrial Electronics*, 57(11): 3639–3644, 2010.

91. Jian Liang, Simon K.K. Ng, Gail Kendall, and John W.M. Cheng. Load Signature Study. I. Basic Concept, Structure, and Methodology. *IEEE Transactions on Power Delivery*, 25(2): 551–560, 2010.

92. J. MacQueen. Some methods for classification and analysis of multivariate observations. In *Berkeley Symposium on Mathematical Statistics and Probability*, 1967.

93. Paras Mandal, Tomonobu Senjyu, Naomitsu Urasaki, and Toshihisa Funabashi. A Neural Network Based Several-Hour-Ahead Electric Load Forecasting Using Similar Days Approach. *International Journal of Electrical Power and Energy Systems*, 28(6): 367–373, 2006.

94. Friedemann Mattern, Thorsten Staake, and Markus Weiss. ICT for green: How computers can help us to conserve energy. In *International Conference on Energy-Efficient Computing and Networking (E-Energy)*, 2010.

95. Tom Mitchell. *Machine Learning*. New York: McGraw Hill, 1997.

96. Andrés Molina-Markham, Prashant Shenoy, Kevin Fu, Emmanuel Cecchet, and David Irwin. Private memoirs of a smart meter. In *Workshop on Embedded Sensing Systems for Energy-Efficiency in Building (BuildSys)*, 2010.

97. Sanaz Mostaghim and Jürgen Teich. Strategies for finding good local guides in multi-objective particle swarm optimization (MOPSO). In *Swarm Intelligence Symposium (SIS)*, 2003.

98. Emmanuel Müller, Ira Assent, Stephan Günnemann, and Thomas Seidl. Scalable density-based subspace clustering. In *International Conference on Information and Knowledge Management (CIKM)*, 2011.

99. Emmanuel Müller, Ira Assent, Ralph Krieger, Stephan Günnemann, and Thomas Seidl. DensEst: Density estimation for data mining in high dimensional spaces. In *International Conference on Data Mining (SDM)*, 2009.

100. Emmanuel Müller, Ira Assent, and Thomas Seidl. HSM: Heterogeneous subspace mining in high dimensional data. In *Scientific and Statistical Database Management (SSDBM Conference Proceedings)*, 2009.

101. Emmanuel Müller, Stephan Günnemann, Ira Assent, and Thomas Seidl. Evaluating clustering in subspace projections of high dimensional data. In *International Conference on Very Large Data Bases (VLDB)*, 2009.

102. Emmanuel Müller, Stephan Günnemann, Ines Färber, and Thomas Seidl. Discovering multiple clustering solutions: Grouping objects in different views of the data. In *Internatinal Conference on Data Mining (ICDM)*, 2010.

103. Emmanuel Müller, Matthias Schiffer, and Thomas Seidl. Statistical selection of relevant subspace projections for outlier ranking. In *International Conference on Data Engineering (ICDE)*, 2011.

104. Daniel Müller-Jentsch. The Development of Electricity Markets in the Euro-Mediterranean Area: Trends and Prospects for Liberalization and Regional Integration. Technical Paper 491, The World Bank, Washington, D.C., 2001.

105. Rudy R. Negenborn, Zofia Lukszo, and Hans Hellendoorn, editors. *Intelligent Infrastructures*, Volume 42 of *Intelligent Systems, Control and Automation: Science and Engineering*. Berlin and New York: Springer, 2010.

106. Andrew Ng, Michael Jordan, and Yair Weiss. On spectral clustering: analysis and an algorithm. In *Conference on Neural Information Processing Systems (NIPS)*, 2001.

107. Donglin Niu, Jennifer G. Dy, and Michael I. Jordan. Multiple non-redundant spectral clustering views. In *International Conference on Machine Learning (ICML)*, 2010.

108. Anisah H. Nizar, Zhao Y. Dong, and J.H. Zhao. Load profiling and data mining techniques in electricity deregulated market. In *Power Engineering Society General Meeting*, 2006.

109. Alexandra-Gwyn Paetz, Birger Becker, Wolf Fichtner, and Hartmut Schmeck. Shifting electricity demand with smart home technologies—An experimental study on user acceptance. In *USAEE/IAEE North American Conference*, 2011.

110. Peter Palensky and Dietmar Dietrich. Demand Side Management: Demand Response, Intelligent Energy Systems, and Smart Loads. *IEEE Transactions on Industrial Informatics*, 7(3): 381–388, 2011.

111. Peter Palensky, Dietrich Dietrich, Ratko Posta, and Heinrich Reiter. Demand side management in private homes by using LonWorks. In *International Workshop on Factory Communication Systems*, 1997.

112. Hasso Plattner and Alexander Zeier. *In-Memory Data Management—An Inflection Point for Enterprise Applications*. Berlin and New York: Springer, 2011.

113. Elias Leake Quinn. Smart Metering and Privacy: Existing Laws and Competing Policies. Report for the Colorado public utilities commission, University Colorado Law School (CEES), Boulder, CO, May 2009.

114. Thanawin Rakthanmanon, Eamonn Keogh, Stefano Lonardi, and Scott Evans. Time series epenthesis: clustering time series streams requires ignoring some data. In *International Conference on Data Mining (ICDM)*, 2011.

115. Maryam Ramezani, Mario Graf, and Harald Vogt. A simulation environment for smart charging of electric vehicles using a multi-objective evolutionary algorithm. In *International Conference on Information and Communication on Technology for the Fight against Global Warming (ICT-GLOW)*, 2011.

116. Sérgio Ramos and Zita Vale. Data mining techniques application in power distribution utilities. In *Transmission and Distribution Conference and Exposition*, 2008.

117. Sira Panduranga Rao and Diane J. Cook. Identifying tasks and predicting actions in smart homes using unlabeled data. In *The Continuum from Labeled to Unlabeled Data in Machine Learning and Data Mining*, 2003. Published in the "Identifying Tasks and Predicting Actions in Smart Homes Using Unlabeled Data" Workshop Proceedings.

118. Ulrich Reiner, Thomas Leibfried, Florian Allerding, and Hartmut Schmeck. Potential of electrical vehicles with feed-back capabilities and controllable loads in electrical grids under the use of decentralized energy management. In *International ETG Congress*, 2009.

119. Peter J. Rousseeuw and Annick M. Leroy. *Robust Regression and Outlier Detection*. New York: Wiley, 1987.

120. Sebnem Rusitschka, Kolja Eger, and Christoph Gerdes. Smart grid data cloud: A model for utilizing cloud computing in the smart grid domain. In *International Conference on Smart Grid Communications (SmartGridComm)*, 2010.

121. Sunita Sarawagi. User-adaptive exploration of multidimensional data. In *International Conference on Very Large Data Bases (VLDB)*, 2000.

122. Sunita Sarawagi, Rakesh Agrawal, and Nimrod Megiddo. Discovery-driven exploration of OLAP data cubes. In *International Conference on Extending Database Technology (EDBT)*, 1998.

123. Gayatri Sathe and Sunita Sarawagi. Intelligent rollups in multidimensional OLAP data. In *International Conference on Very Large Data Bases (VLDB)*, 2001.

124. Domnic Savio, Lubomir Karlik, and Stamatis Karnouskos. Predicting energy measurements of service-enabled devices in the future smartgrid. In *International Conference on Computer Modeling and Simulation (UKSim)*, 2010.

125. Matthieu-P. Schapranow, Ralph Kühne, Alexander Zeier, and Hasso Plattner. Enabling real-time charging for smart grid infrastructures using in-memory databases. In *Workshop on Smart Grid Networking Infrastructure*, 2010.

126. Joachim Schleich, Marian Klobasa, Marc Brunner, Sebastian Gölz, and Konrad Götz. Smart Metering in Germany and Austria: Results of Providing Feedback Information in a Field Trial. Working Paper Sustainability and Innovation S 6/2011, Fraunhofer Institute for Systems and Innovation Research (ISI), Karlsruhe, Germany, 2011.

127. Raimund Seidel. Small-Dimensional Linear Programming and Convex Hulls Made Easy. *Discrete & Computational Geometry*, 6(1): 423–434, 1991.

128. Kelvin Sim, Vivekanand Gopalkrishnan, Arthur Zimek, and Gao Cong. A Survey on Enhanced Subspace Clustering. *Data Mining and Knowledge Discovery*, 2012.

129. Myra Spiliopoulou, Irene Ntoutsi, Yannis Theodoridis, and Rene Schult. MONIC: Modeling and monitoring cluster transitions. In *International Conference on Knowledge Discovery and Data Mining (KDD)*, 2006. Available online: http://link.springer.com/article/10.1007/S10618-012-0258-X. DOI:10.1001/s10618-012-0258-X.

130. Asher Tishler and Israel Zang. A Min-Max Algorithm for Non-Linear Regression Models. *Applied Mathematics and Computation*, 13(1/2): 95–115, 1983.

131. Jaideep Vaidya, Yu Zhu, and Christopher W. Clifton. *Privacy Preserving Data Mining*, Volume 19 of *Advances in Information Security*. Berlin and New York: Springer, 2006.

132. Sergio Valero Verdú, Mario Ortiz García, Carolina Senabre, Antonio Gabaldón Marín, and Francisco J. García Franco. Classification, Filtering, and Identification of Electrical Customer Load Patterns through the Use of Self-Organizing Maps. *IEEE Transactions on Power Systems*, 21(4): 1672–1682, 2006.

133. Vassilios S. Verykios, Elisa Bertino, Igor Nai Fovino, Loredana Parasiliti Provenza, Yucel Saygin, and Yannis Theodoridis. State-of-the-Art in Privacy Preserving Data Mining. *SIGMOD Record*, 33(1): 50–57, 2004.

134. Michail Vlachos, Dimitrios Gunopulos, and Gautam Das. Indexing Time-Series under Conditions of Noise. In Last et al. [86], Chapter 4, pages 67–100.

135. Harald Vogt, Holger Weiss, Patrik Spiess, and Achim P. Karduck. Market-based prosumer participation in the smart grid. In *International Conference on Digital Ecosystems and Technologies (DEST)*, 2010.

136. Horst F. Wedde, Sebastian Lehnhoff, Christian Rehtanz, and Olav Krause. Bottom-up self-organization of unpredictable demand and supply under decentralized power management. In *International Conference on Self-Adaptive and Self-Organizing Systems*, 2008.

137. Anke Weidlich. *Engineering Interrelated Electricity Markets*. Physica Verlag, Heidelerg, Germany, 2008.

138. Anke Weidlich, Harald Vogt, Wolfgang Krauss, Patrik Spiess, Marek Jawurek, Martin Johns, and Stamatis Karnouskos. Decentralized intelligence in energy efficient power systems. In Alexey Sorokin, Steffen Rebennack, Panos M. Pardalos, Niko A. Iliadis, and Mario V.F. Pereira, Editors, *Handbook of Networks in Power Systems: Optimization, Modeling, Simulation and Economic Aspects*. Berlin and New York: Springer, 2012.

139. Tom White. *Hadoop: The Definitive Guide*. O'Reilly, Sebastopol, USA, 2009.

140. Ian H. Witten, Eibe Frank, and Mark A. Hall. *Data Mining: Practical Machine Learning Tools and Techniques*. Morgan Kaufmann, Burlington, USA, 2011.

141. G. Michael Youngblood and Diane J. Cook. Data Mining for Hierarchical Model Creation. *IEEE Transactions on Systems, Man, and Cybernetics*, 37(4): 561–572, 2007.

142. Michael Zeifman and Kurt Roth. Nonintrusive Appliance Load Monitoring: Review and Outlook. *Transactions on Consumer Electronics*, 57(1): 76–84, 2011.

143. Roberto V. Zicari. Big Data: Smart Meters—Interview with Markus Gerdes. ODBMS Industry Watch Blog: http://www.odbms.org/blog/2012/06/big-data-smart-meters-interview-with-markus-gerdes/, 2012.

CHAPTER 8

Electricity Supply without Fossil Fuels

John Boland, Peter Pudney, and Jerzy Filar

CONTENTS

8.1 INTRODUCTION

Aᴜsᴛʀᴀʟɪᴀɴs ɴᴇᴇᴅ ᴛᴏ ʀᴇᴅᴜᴄᴇ their per-capita greenhouse gas emissions to 5% of 2000 levels by 2050 if the international community is to stabilize the concentration of atmospheric CO_2 at 450 parts per million (ppm) [18]. Since the Garnaut report was published, it has become apparent that 350 ppm is a more realistic target if global warming is to be limited to 2°C. Either target is a huge challenge and will require unprecedented changes to the way we generate and use energy. See Figure 8.1 to get a better idea of the challenge.

Some 38% of Australia's greenhouse gas emissions are due to electricity use [11]. This proportion is high by international standards because our use of electricity is high, and because 93% of our electricity is generated from fossil fuels.

Our use of fossil fuels is unsustainable. We need to imagine, design, and transition to a future where all electricity is generated from renewable energy sources. The solution will require a mix of generation technologies, including solar thermal, solar photovoltaic, and wind. The variability of renewable energy sources will be overcome using a combination of reserve capacity, spatially diverse generator locations, energy storage, and management of demand to match supply. This chapter describes the mathematical models and methods required to design and optimize a system that can provide Australia with affordable, reliable, clean electricity.

On November 8, 2011, the Australian Senate passed the Clean Energy Futures bills, enacting legislation that will put a price on CO_2 emissions beginning July 1, 2012. Finance Minister and former Climate Change Minister

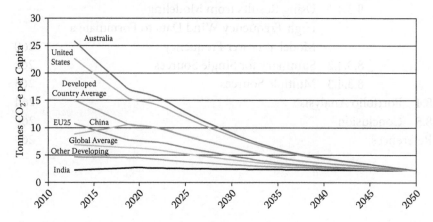

FIGURE 8.1   Per-capita CO_2 entitlements [18].

Penny Wong stated that, "We accept the science and the advice that putting a price on carbon is the best way to reduce emissions." This action sets up the environment for a transformation of the electricity supply sector in Australia. According to an article in *Climate Spectator* online on December 7, 2011:

> The government's clean energy policy is currently centred around two basic principles—the 20 per cent [large-scale] renewable energy target (LRET) is designed to deploy the cheapest available renewable technologies, while the Clean Energy Finance Corporation will support the commercialization and deployment of those technologies that are likely to be the cheapest and the most useful in the future.

The LRET requires that by 2020, 20% of electricity will be supplied from renewable sources. This can be done in an ad hoc fashion, as is the present situation, with wind farms dominating large-scale installations and an intensification of photovoltaic installations on domestic houses (so much so that in NSW, for example, there is 300 megawatts (MW) installed). This is widely purported to be driving up the costs of electricity for the remainder of the population. However, this conjecture is disputed by the Australian Energy Market Commission, who estimate that the combined costs of feed-in tariffs and renewable energy schemes will make up about 14% of future price increases, whereas the cost of reinforcing transmission and distribution systems to cope with growth in peak demand will make up 49% of electricity price rises over the next 3 years* [3]. To maximize greenhouse gas reduction, a more coordinated approach is necessary.

Maximizing the penetration of renewable energy sources for supplying electricity can be achieved through two disparate techniques: (1) building a supergrid, or (2) mixing the renewable sources with demand management and storage. In Europe, for example, there are proposals such as the Desertec initiative to create a supergrid interconnecting installations of renewable generation across Europe, North Africa, and the Middle East [21]. The underlying principle is that if you have solar farms distributed east-west along a latitude, there is an elongation of the solar day for providing

---

* Another challenge for today's grid is the growth in air-conditioning penetration. In Western Sydney, more than 80% of homes now have air conditioning. This growth is driving energy suppliers such as Integral to spend approximately $3 billion over the next 5 years on grid infrastructure, to meet the increased peak loads. But this extra infrastructure will only be needed for a few days a year; it's like building a twenty-seven-lane freeway so that we never have peak-hour traffic jams.—*The Climate Spectator,* 14 July 2010.

energy for the grid. In addition, wind farms distributed north-south along a longitude can take advantage of weather systems moving cohesively at different latitudes. This concept of using meteorological and astronomical attributes to enhance the diversity of sources requires significant augmentation of the grid, including provision of high-voltage, direct-current transmission systems to minimize distance-related losses. In this configuration, even augmented by other renewable sources, there is a necessity for some energy storage for backup and load balancing—Denmark stores excess wind power in Norway's hydroelectric dams through pumping.

An alternative approach is to develop a protocol for combining a renewable supply of diverse sources (both in technologies and locations) with sophisticated demand management (load follows the supply rather than the reverse) and energy storage to maximize the penetration of renewables. This entails a variety of supply options, more directly embedded in the transmission and distribution networks than the supergrid option, as well as a variety of storage options. The task arising from this more subtle approach is deciding on the quantities of each supply option, as well as a storage option, where they are positioned in the system, as well as how to best use the demand-side management. This results in a portfolio optimization problem.

In summary, in this chapter we present the mathematical modeling tools we argue are necessary to perform a rational, sophisticated analysis of the problem of moving to a high penetration of renewable sources in the provision of the electricity supply.

8.2 APPROACH

8.2.1 Renewable Generation

There are many renewable energy technologies that can generate electricity without consuming finite resources and without producing CO_2 emissions, including concentrating solar thermal plants, solar photovoltaic panels, wind turbines, tidal generators, and biofuel generators.

Zero Carbon Australia [41] describes an ambitious plan to meet Australia's electricity needs using a combination of 60% concentrating solar thermal power (with molten salt storage), 40% wind, and backup power from hydroelectricity and biofuels. Elliston et al. [13] have shown that it is technically feasible to supply electricity from renewables with the same reliability as the present system.

Renewable generation technologies, particularly those powered by solar radiation or wind, are often criticized as not being able to generate "baseload" power. A key objective of current and future research should be to show how a combination of renewable generation, energy storage, and demand-side management can meet our energy needs. This research should consider a wider environmental basis that also includes the effects on reducing our ecological footprint* from the use of renewable energy for electricity supply. From that we obtain an increase in available land for ecosystem enhancement, for example.

8.2.2 Overcoming Variability

The key challenge with renewable energy sources is the variability of the supply. Delucci and Jacobson [10] describe seven ways to cope with variability in an electricity grid powered from wind, water, and the sun:

1. Interconnect geographically dispersed generators

2. Use controllable sources, such as hydroelectric generation, to meet temporary shortfalls

3. Manage demand to match the available supply

4. Store energy at generator sites, using batteries, pumped hydroelectric, compressed air, flywheels, hydrogen, or thermal storage

5. Oversize generators to reduce the probability of undersupply (and generate hydrogen with excess energy)

6. Store energy at points of end use and in electric vehicle batteries

7. Forecast weather to improve the planning of energy supply.

8.2.2.1 Storage

Options for storing energy include the following:

- Molten salt reservoirs integrated with concentrating solar power plants

- Grid-smoothing stationary storage such as vanadium redox flow batteries, high-temperature liquid-metal batteries, supercapacitors, compressed air storage, pumped water storage, and flywheels

---

* Ecological Footprint accounts track our supply and use of natural capital. They document the area of biologically productive land and sea a given population requires to produce the renewable resources it consumes and to assimilate the waste it generates, using prevailing technology.

- Short-term storage in electric vehicles
- Seasonal heat storage.

Many of these technologies have been demonstrated in medium- to large-scale installations. The problem is to develop methods that can determine which combination of storage technologies and locations will be most effective for a given electricity system.

8.2.3 Demand Management

The current electricity system is designed to supply whatever power is demanded, with little or no coordination of loads. As a result, the system is sized for peak demands that occur for only a few hours each year. The mean demand for power in the Australian National Electricity Market is 70% of the peak demand; in South Australia, the mean demand is just 50% of the peak demand. Figure 8.2 shows hourly demand for power in the National Electricity Market for each day of 2010.

Appliances are becoming more efficient, but we are using more of them. Increases in peak demand require upgrades to the transmission and distribution infrastructure, which adds significantly to the cost of electricity. Furthermore, fixed retail prices isolate residential and commercial consumers from supply constraints and the associated variations in generation costs. This problem can be partly addressed by time-of-use pricing, where electricity is cheaper during periods when demand is usually low; or by critical peak pricing, where the price to consumers varies with the cost of supply. An energy price that increases with power use would

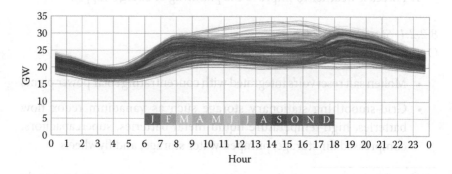

FIGURE 8.2   (*See color insert.*) Hourly demand profile in the NEM for 2010 (data from Australian Energy Market Operator [5]).

also encourage load leveling. Ultimately, however, we need appliances to respond to changing grid conditions to prevent overload. Demand management can defer the need for grid reinforcement, reduce the need for expensive generation used only during periods of high demand, and improve the quality and reliability of supply.

There is another important reason for demand management. As more energy is supplied from variable renewable energy sources, we will need to move from a system where supply follows demand to a system where demand also responds to variations in the available supply.

Over half of Australia's electricity is used in the domestic and commercial sectors. Many domestic and commercial loads—air conditioning, water heaters, clothes and dishwashers, clothes dryers, refrigerators, freezers, pool pumps, and electric vehicle chargers—could be automatically rescheduled, to varying extents, without causing inconvenience. Australian Standard AS 4755 is defining a simple interface that will allow appliances to be controlled. Home Area Networks, Building Management Systems, and Smart Grids will also allow appliances and buildings to change their power demand in response to signals, including the price of electricity and the availability of renewable power. Still needed, however, are mechanisms that will encourage participation and allow smart appliances to fairly share the power available at any instant.

8.2.4 Mechanism Design for Demand Management

Mechanism design is a branch of mathematical game theory that seeks to design the rules of a game, for self-interested players with private information, to achieve an overall desirable outcome. One must design mechanisms that allocate available power to appliances in such a way that, when feasible, each appliance will complete its task on time. Allocation mechanisms should be "incentive compatible" so that players cannot gain by misreporting their requirements. When it is not possible to complete all tasks on time, mechanisms should allocate power as fairly as possible.

The 2007 Nobel Prize for Economic Sciences was awarded to Hurwicz, Maskin, and Myerson for their work on mechanism design theory. A report from the Royal Swedish Academy of Sciences [35] gives a good overview of the topic, as does Nisan et al. [28].

A group at the University of Southampton is currently investigating the use of mechanism design for demand-side management, demand aggregation, and for pricing electric vehicle charging [19, 32, 33]. Gerding et al. [19] describe a system for allocating charging to electric vehicles so that capacity constraints in a local area are not exceeded. Each vehicle owner specifies the value they place on their first hour of charging, second hour of charging, and so on, as well as the time interval during which the vehicle will be available for charging. An online mechanism allocates charging capacity each hour to the vehicles with the greatest value. The pricing mechanism is designed so that there is no incentive for owners to misreport their values or their charging interval. Further work is required to extend the method to work with a mix of different appliances, and to compare it to other online mechanisms [29–31].

Fahrioglu and Alvarado [15] describe the use of mechanism design when designing electricity supply contracts to encourage participation in demand management programs, but do not consider how smart appliances might react to real-time demand management signals.

Closer to the supply side of the electricity system, Zou [42] discusses the two schemes commonly used to buy and sell electricity on the wholesale market: (1) *uniform pricing*, where every generator is paid the marginal market price; or (2) *pay-as-bid*, where each generator is paid what they bid. It is not clear which of these schemes is better, as the bidding behavior of generators is different for each scheme. Zou proposes a new mechanism based on the Vickrey-Clarke-Groves mechanism, which can enhance the social welfare of the electricity market by only selecting bidders whose contribution to social welfare is positive. However, it remains to be seen whether these ideas could be applied in the retail electricity market.

Finally, Rothkopf [34] gives 13 reasons why the Vickrey-Clarke-Groves mechanism, which underpins much of mechanism design theory, may not work in practice. It will be important to consider these issues when designing practical systems for demand-side management.

8.3 FORECASTING WIND AND SOLAR POWER

A key area of research, and a precursor to portfolio optimization, is the forecasting of supply from variable renewable energy sources. Recent results [1, 40] present a dramatic improvement in methods for the estimation of both the level and volatility of wind and solar farms. This is especially the case with forecasting the conditional variance of output. Renewable energy generation does not exhibit homogeneous variability, and we have devised methods of estimating this changing variability rather than using ensemble methods [1].

Our efforts to date have focused on wind farm output for specific locations. We need to investigate the accumulation of wind farm output over wide areas, considering the effects of spatial coherence. How can geographic diversity reduce variability and improve predictability? For solar energy forecasting, we have focused on global solar irradiance, and at single locations. The methods should be extended to include forecasting of direct solar irradiance, necessary for photovoltaic and thermal concentrated solar plants (CSPs). We also need to investigate the spatial diversity of solar irradiance, and the mix of solar and wind.

The Australian Energy Market Operator provides 5-minute energy generation data for each wind farm in Australia. Hourly wind speed data are available from the Bureau of Meteorology (BOM) for nearby automatic weather stations. By combining this data, we can create an empirical energy curve for the output of existing wind farms. The results can then be used to estimate power output, given the wind speed for proposed wind farms. In a similar manner, we can access solar radiation values for any location in Australia (on a 5 kilometer by 5 kilometer grid), wherein hourly irradiation is estimated from satellite images. This data can then be used to estimate the energy output from various types of solar collectors, including photovoltaic (PV) with varying orientations, concentrating PV, and concentrating solar thermal. The BOM publishes estimates of global solar irradiation on a horizontal plane and direct normal irradiation. Global solar irradiation is a combination of direct beam irradiation and diffuse irradiation. For estimating the output of concentrating PV and thermal solar plants, we need to estimate the direct beam component. This can be done by first using the BRL model [36] to estimate the diffuse irradiation on a horizontal surface. The difference between the global and diffuse irradiation gives the direct irradiation on a horizontal surface, from which a straightforward trigonometric calculation gives the direct irradiance on a surface normal to the beam. This is precisely the chain of modeling that the BOM uses to infer solar components. They will use this procedure in work for the Solar Flagships Program to inform industry on the siting of solar farms. The direct beam and diffuse components can be used to estimate the output of fixed, tracking, and concentrating solar generators.

For the purpose of determining the optimal mix of generation technologies and sites, it is not necessary to develop detailed forecast models for each generator. However, we will need to rigorously determine the stochastic nature of the output from individual sites and also of sets of spatially diverse as well as platform-diverse sources.

For individual stations, we have been developing methods for analysis of series of both wind farm output and solar energy. For forecasting, we use a combination of standard time-series techniques such as autoregressive moving average (ARMA)(p,q) models and a resonating model adapted from research into the firing of synapses in the brain. Lucheroni [26] applied the FitzHugh-Nagumo system of coupled nonlinear stochastic differential equations to create a dynamic regime called stochastically resonating spiking. The ARMA technique, on its own, cannot effectively model the spiking behavior in modeling electricity prices that was the focus of Lucheroni, nor similar spiking behavior in climate variables.

8.3.1 Estimating Hourly Solar Irradiation

When performing time-series analysis of a climate variable or a system dependent on one, the first step is to identify and model the seasonality. Several significant cycles can be identified using spectral analysis [8]. The seasonal component of solar irradiation for hour t of the year can be estimated by a Fourier series:

$$S_t = \alpha_0 + \alpha_1 \cos\frac{2\pi t}{8760} + \beta_1 \sin\frac{2\pi t}{8760}$$

$$+\alpha_2 \cos\frac{4\pi t}{8760} + \beta_2 \sin\frac{4\pi t}{8760}$$

$$+\sum_{i=3}^{11}\sum_{n=1}^{3}\sum_{m=-1}^{1}\left[\alpha_i \cos\frac{2\pi(365n+m)t}{8760} + \beta_i \sin\frac{2\pi(365n+m)t}{8760}\right]$$

Here, α_0 is the mean of the data; α_1, β_1 are coefficients of the yearly cycle; α_2, β_2 of twice yearly; and α_i, β_i are coefficients of the daily cycle and its harmonics and associated beat frequencies. An inspection of the power spectrum would show that we need to include the harmonics of the daily cycle ($n = 2, 3$, as well as $n = 1$) and also the beat frequencies ($m = -1, 1$). The latter modulate the amplitude to fit the time of year—in other words, describe the beating of the yearly and daily cycles.

Figure 8.3 shows the daily variation over the year for an example site. Figure 8.4 shows 5 days of hourly solar radiation and the Fourier series model for that variation. In Figure 8.5 we see the worth of the particular frequencies variously termed "beat frequencies" or "sidebands," which modulate the amplitude of the daily harmonic to suit the time of

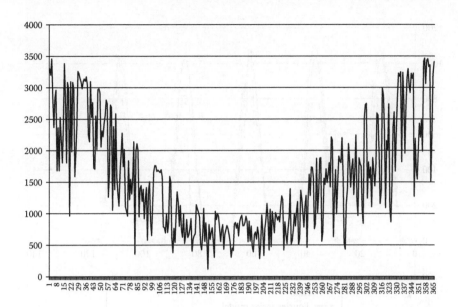

FIGURE 8.3   Daily solar radiation.

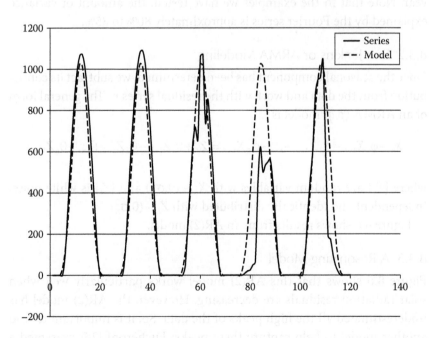

FIGURE 8.4   Five days data and Fourier series.

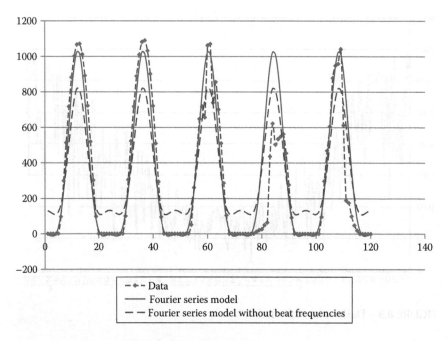

FIGURE 8.5   Effect of beat frequencies—winter.

year. Note that in the examples we have tested, the amount of variance explained by the Fourier series is approximately 80% to 85%.

8.3.2 Box-Jenkins or ARMA Modeling

Once the seasonal component has been determined, we subtract its contribution from the data and work with the residual series r_t. The general form of an ARMA (p,q) model is

$$X_t - \phi_1 X_{t-1} - \phi_2 X_{t-2} - \ldots - \phi_p X_{t-p} = Z_t + \theta_1 Z_{t-1} - \theta_2 Z_{t-2} + \ldots + \theta_q Z_{t-q}$$

where $\{X_t\}$ are random variables with $X_t \sim (0, \sigma_X^2)$ and $\{Z_t\}$ is white noise, independent and identically distributed with $Z_t \sim (0, \sigma_Z^2)$.

Figure 8.6 shows results from an AR(2) model.

8.3.3 A Resonating Model

Figure 8.6 shows that this AR(2) model works particularly well when solar radiation residuals are decreasing. However, the AR(2) model has underestimated all the high peaks of the data. So, it is important to find another model to help capture these peaks. Lucheroni [26] presented a resonating model for the power market that exploits the simultaneous

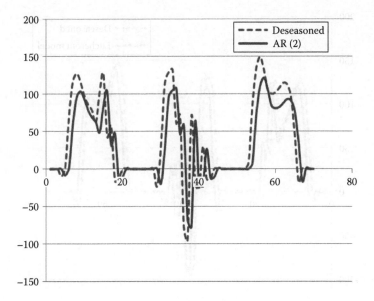

FIGURE 8.6   An AR(2) model fitted to 3 days of residuals.

presence of a Hopf critical point, periodic forcing, and noise in a two-dimensional, first-order nonautonomous stochastic differential equation system for the logarithm of the power price and the derivative of logprice. The model that originates from biophysics (known in the literature as the FitzHugh-Nagumo system, [17, 25]) performs very well for power market modeling; see Lucheroni [26].

This model (written here in its discretized form) was developed by Lucheroni [26]:

$$f_{i+1} = f_i + z_i \Delta t \tag{8.1}$$

$$z_{i+1} = z_i + \left[\kappa(z_i + f_i) - \lambda(3f_i^2 z_i + f_i^3) - \varepsilon z_i - \gamma f_i - b \right] \frac{\Delta t}{\varepsilon} \tag{8.2}$$

Here, ω_t and a_t are noise terms, and Δt is the time step. Equation (8.2) aims to exploit the fact that the current value of z_t is useful to predict the future value R_{t+1}. The parameters κ, λ, ε, γ, and b can be estimated using the method of ordinary least squares (OLS). For our deseasoned data, estimated values for the parameters are $\kappa = -2.1$, $\lambda = -6 \times 10^{-8}$, $\varepsilon = 0.09$, $\gamma = 0.5$, and $b = 2$. λ is virtually zero, which indicates that the deseasoned residuals R_t behave linearly. Further to this, a negative value of κ assures the stability of the inherent damped oscillator in Equation (8.2).

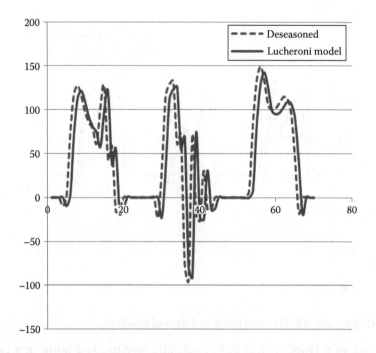

FIGURE 8.7 Lucheroni model for the 3 sample days.

The Lucheroni model (Figure 8.7) is good at picking up the peak, and the AR(2) model (Figure 8.6) is good at forecasting in the main regions of the series, because when the AR(2) model reaches the peak, it is converging to the mean faster than the Lucheroni model. Is there evidence for this other than eyeballing the graphs? Combining the AR(2) model with the Lucheroni model could solve those problems. We can also add a second derivative component (a proxy for curvature) that adds even more to the predictability (Figure 8.8).

8.3.4 Estimating Volatility

Traditional methods for forecasting volatility are indirect by necessity because the volatility is unobservable in a time series. These indirect methods include generalized autoregressive conditional heteroscedastic (GARCH) [9] and Hidden Markov Models (HMMs) [40]. We have developed a method for estimating the volatility using high-frequency data [1], and then use the resonating model [26] for forecasting the volatility at the 5-minute and 30-minute timescales required by the electricity market. These forecasting methods can also be used to delineate the level and variability of output. We are thus able to make these estimations for any proposed individual wind or solar installation.

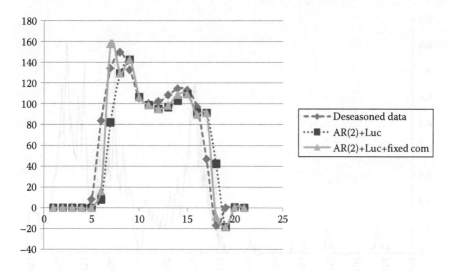

FIGURE 8.8 (*See color insert.*) When fixed components add into combination of Lucheroni and AR(2) model.

Figures 8.9 through 8.11 show wind farm output at two different time-scales and an AR(3) model fitted to the 5-minute output.

The noise is uncorrelated but dependent. This phenomenon is prevalent in financial markets—it is called *volatility clustering*. Periods of high volatility are followed by periods of low volatility. Engle [14] developed the autoregressive conditional heteroscedastic (ARCH) model to cater to this. Figure 8.11 indicates that the model will have to be a long-lag AR model. For this lack of parsimony and other reasons, Bollerslev developed the generalized ARCH (or GARCH) model, where we replace the long-lag AR model with a short-lag ARMA model. The residuals of the AR(3) model of wind farm output display this conditional volatility. Often, an ARMA(1,1) for the residuals squared is sufficient and the GARCH model is derived from that. For this example, the GARCH model for conditional volatility is $\sigma_t^2 = 0.006 + 0.122 a_{t-1}^2 + 0.821 \sigma_{t-1}^2$.

We developed a method to estimate volatility when high-frequency data follow an $AR(p)$ process [1, 2]. Many researchers have made use of high-frequency data to estimate the volatility. Their approach involved computation of covariance, etc. Our approach is different, as we use a model of high-frequency data to estimate the volatility. The following is a description of how to use 10-second wind farm output to estimate the volatility on a 5-minute timescale.

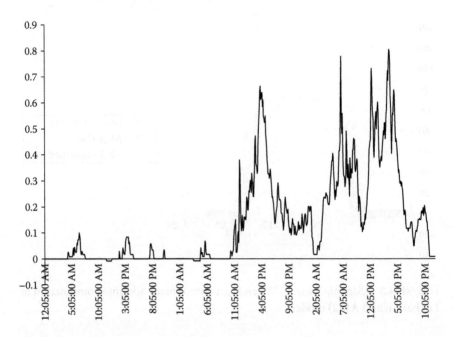

FIGURE 8.9 Five minute wind farm output.

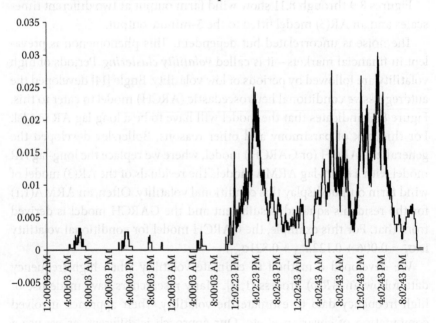

FIGURE 8.10 Ten second wind farm output.

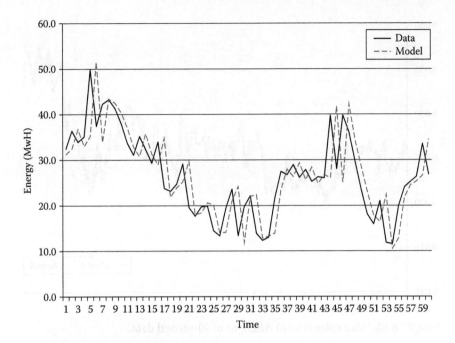

FIGURE 8.11   Five minute output and model.

Ten-second data (X_t) can be satisfactorily modeled using an AR(3) process (see Figure 8.12):

$$X_t = \alpha_1 X_{t-1} + \alpha_2 X_{t-2} + \alpha_3 X_{t-3} + Z_t$$

or equivalently,

$$\phi(B)X_t = Z_t$$

where $\phi(B) = 1 - \alpha_1 B - \alpha_2 B^2 - \alpha_3 B^3$, and B denotes the backshift operator, that is, $BX_t = X_{t-1}$.

As $\phi(B)$ is invertible, the process is equivalent to an infinite moving average process.

$$X_t = \psi(B)Z_t$$

where $\psi(B) = \psi_0 + \psi_1 B + \psi_2 B^2 + \psi_3 B^3 + \ldots$

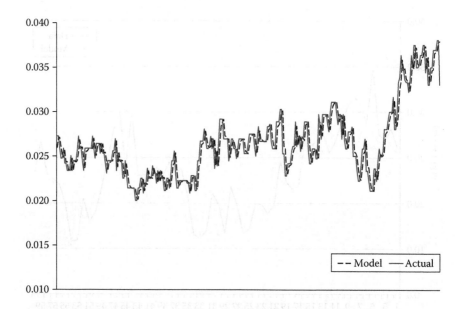

FIGURE 8.12 *(See color insert.)* $AR(3)$: fit of 10-second data.

Thus, in simple terms,

$$X_t = \psi_0 Z_t + \psi_1 Z_{t-1} + \psi_2 Z_{t-2} + \psi_3 Z_{t-3} + \dots, \tag{8.3}$$

It can be shown that

$$\psi_j = \alpha_1 \psi_{j-1} + \alpha_2 \psi_{j-2} + \alpha_3 \psi_{j-3} \tag{8.4}$$

with $\psi_0 = 1$ and $\psi_j = 0$ for $j < 0$.

8.3.4.1 Using Results from Modeling High-Frequency Wind Data to Formulate a Model at Lower Frequency

The total wind energy on a 5-minute timescale is the sum of the thirty 10-second energy totals within that 5-minute period, and so we can sum the variables on the 10-second timescale that follow an $AR(3)$ process to get a 5-minute variable. Let $\{X_t\}$ denote the time series of wind energy output at intervals of 10 seconds, and let $\{Y_t\}$ denote the time series of aggregated energy output at every 5 minutes. The 5-minute process as a sum of thirty "10-second observations" can be expressed as

$$Y_t = X_t + X_{t-\frac{1}{30}} + X_{t-\frac{2}{30}} + \dots + X_{t-\frac{29}{30}} \tag{8.5}$$

It is understood throughout that

$$X_{t-\frac{i}{30}}$$

represents the wind energy output at the i-th 10-second prior to time t, so that $t - 1$ remains the consistent notation for 5 minutes prior to t.

$$
Y_t = \psi_0 Z_t + (\psi_0 + \psi_1) Z_{t-\frac{1}{30}} + (\psi_0 + \psi_1 + \psi_2) Z_{t-\frac{2}{30}}
$$
$$
+ (\psi_0 + \psi_1 + \psi_2 + \psi_3) Z_{t-\frac{3}{30}} + \ldots
$$
$$
+ (\psi_0 + \psi_1 + \ldots + \psi_{29}) Z_{t-\frac{29}{30}}
$$
$$
+ (\psi_1 + \psi_2 + \psi_3 + \ldots + \psi_{30}) Z_{t-1} \tag{8.6}
$$
$$
+ (\psi_2 + \psi_3 + \psi_4 + \ldots + \psi_{31}) Z_{t-\frac{31}{30}} + \ldots
$$
$$
+ (\psi_{29} + \psi_{31} + \ldots + \psi_{58}) Z_{t-\frac{59}{30}}
$$
$$
+ (\psi_{30} + \psi_{32} + \ldots + \psi_{59}) Z_{t-2} + \ldots
$$

Note that in Equation (8.6), coefficients up to the 30th term have a different form than those after the 30th term.

Variance $\sigma^2(Y_t)$ in terms of ψ_i values is given below. We assume that within each 5-minute interval, the Z_t values are independent and identically distributed with zero mean. The variance of Y_t is thus

$$
\sigma^2(Y_t) = [\psi_0^2 + (\psi_0 + \psi_1)^2 + (\psi_0 + \psi_1 + \psi_2)^2
$$
$$
+ (\psi_0 + \psi_1 + \psi_2 + \psi_3)^2 + \ldots
$$
$$
+ (\psi_0 + \psi_1 + \psi_2 + \ldots + \psi_{29})^2] \sigma^2(Z_t)
$$
$$
+ [(\psi_1 + \psi_2 + \psi_3 + \ldots + \psi_{30})^2 \tag{8.7}
$$
$$
+ (\psi_2 + \psi_3 + \psi_4 + \ldots + \psi_{31})^2 + \ldots
$$
$$
+ (\psi_{30} + \psi_{31} + \ldots + \psi_{59})^2] \sigma^2(Z_{t-1}) + \ldots
$$

Rearranging gives

$$
\sigma^2(Y_t) = \left(\sum_{n=0}^{29} \left(\sum_{i=0}^{n} \psi_i \right) \right)^2 \sigma^2(Z_t) +
$$

$$
\left(\sum_{n=30}^{59} \left(\sum_{i=0}^{n} \psi_i - \sum_{i=0}^{n-30} \psi_i \right) \right)^2 \sigma^2(Z_{t-1}) + \qquad (8.8)
$$

$$
\left(\sum_{n=60}^{89} \left(\sum_{i=0}^{n} \psi_i - \sum_{i=0}^{n-30} \psi_i \right) \right)^2 \sigma^2(Z_{t-2}) + \dots
$$

The basic components in the expression for $\sigma^2(Y_t)$ are

$$
\sum_{i=0}^{n} \psi_i
$$

We are able to prove that

$$
\sum_{i=0}^{n} \psi_i = \sum_{k=0}^{n} \sum_{(n_1,n_2,n_3) \in A} \frac{(n_1 + n_2 + n_3)!}{n_1! n_2! n_3!} \alpha_1^{n_1} \alpha_2^{n_2} \alpha_3^{n_3}
$$

where the triplets (n_1,n_2,n_3) come from the set $A = \{(n_1,n_2,n_3) | n_1 + n_2 + n_3 \le k \ \& \ n_1 + 2n_2 + 3n_3 = k\}$. Using Equation 8.8 we obtain the estimated standard deviation for five minute data shown in Figure 8.13.

8.3.4.2 Summary for Single Sources

The steps needed to reliably forecast solar and wind outputs include the following:

1. Validate the mixture of autoregressive and resonating model (ARR) to representative solar datasets for climates throughout Australia.

2. Extend ARR to wind farm output series.

3. Determine what type of volatility modeling is needed for solar energy series.

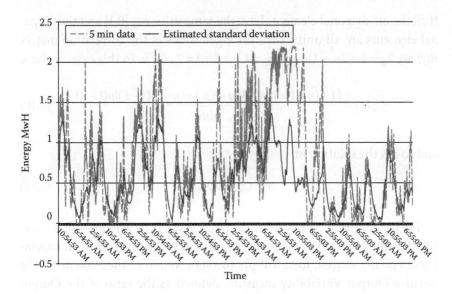

FIGURE 8.13 *(See color insert.)* Output and estimated standard deviation.

8.3.4.3 Multiple Sources

Increasing the spatial diversity of the renewable sources will help smooth the volatility of the overall input, subject to there being enough interconnectivity in the grid. One can easily compute pairwise correlation between two time series, but how does one evaluate a group connectivity? Getz [20] developed the concept of correlative coherence to analyze the overall connectedness of movements of individual elephants in a herd. A similar method can be used to determine an overall correlation between the outputs of multiple wind farms [7]. First, take the correlation matrix R containing the pairwise correlations between the n sources. Its eigenvalues λ_i, $i = 1, \ldots, n$ have the properties that $0 \le \lambda_i/n \le 1$, and

$$\sum_{i=1}^{n} \lambda_i/n = 1$$

Getz [20] presents a Shannon-Weaver measure of the diversity of eigenvalues, which gives us an idea of the degree to which the sources vary in concert with each other:

$$C(X^n) = 1 - \frac{1}{\ln(1/n)} \sum_{i=1}^{n} \left(\frac{\lambda_i}{n}\right) \ln\left(\frac{\lambda_i}{n}\right) \qquad (8.9)$$

If all the off-diagonal elements have the same value $r \in [0,1]$ and the diagonal elements are all unity, then the eigenvalues of the correlation matrix $R(r)$ are $\lambda_1 = 1 + (n-1)r$ and $\lambda_i = 1 - r$ for $i = 2, ..., n$. In this case, we have

$$C_n(r) = \frac{(1+(n-1)r)ln(1+(n-1)r)+(n-1)(1-r)ln(1-r)}{nlnn} \qquad (8.10)$$

and so r is the solution of

$$r = C_n^{-1}(C(X_n)) \qquad (8.11)$$

The other option comes from Hoff and Perez [23], who provide a measure for the short-term power output variability resulting from an ensemble of equally spaced, identical photovoltaic systems. They construct the Relative Output Variability measure, defined as the ratio of the Output Variability for the ensemble to the Output Variability of the same PV fleet concentrated in a single location. The output variability is

$$\sigma_{\Delta t}^N = \frac{1}{C}\sqrt{Var\left[\sum_{n=1}^{N}\Delta P_{\Delta t}^n\right]} \qquad (8.12)$$

where C is the total installed peak power of the ensemble and $\Delta P_{\Delta t}^n$ is a random variable that represents the time series of changes in power in the nth installation using a sampling time interval of Δt.

8.4 PORTFOLIO ANALYSIS

Delucchi and Jacobson [10] note that

> No...optimization analysis has been done for a 100% [wind, water, sun] system in a major region of the world (let alone for all regions of the world), so this clearly is a critical area for new research.

The problem of choosing an optimal mix of electricity generation, storage, and efficiency policies is not very different from a portfolio optimization problem. Each decision alternative results in more or less electricity yield, and carries more or less cost, and more or less variability.

A particular challenge is that the electricity industry requires very high levels of coordination between supply and demand at all times and at all

locations within the network. Traditional approaches to generation investment have modeled demand as an exogenous time series that needs to be
met by some mix of conventional, controllable generation technologies.
High renewable energy penetrations are not amenable to such approaches
as they are not dispatchable in the conventional sense and, as noted earlier, they have highly complex, uncertain and correlated primary energy
fluxes. Because of this, high penetrations will not only impose greater
requirements on dispatchable generation (both renewable and nonrenewable), but are also likely to require far greater demand participation
to assist in managing supply shortfalls and excess supply. Portfolio tools
for these challenges are far less advanced. There has been work on incorporating renewables into optimal generation mix tools [12, 39]. However,
there is considerable progress required in this area, particularly in the
context of optimizing the different possible mixes and locations of renewable energy resources. There are also interesting and challenging research
needs on how energy storage and controllable loads can be appropriately
integrated into these investment tools.

The problem of choosing an optimal mix of electricity generation technologies will be modeled in a manner analogous to the problem of finding
an optimal portfolio of investments. However, instead of a monetary yield
and its variability, one must consider the energy output and its variability.
The constraints of the problem will, of course, include the requirement
that the energy yield equals or exceeds the demand, in addition to many
other practical requirements.

Suppose that, during a given, fixed time interval, the demand for electricity is D megawatt-hours (MW-h) and we decide to supply a certain
proportion of the demanded electricity from $n = 4$ different sources of
energy: (ε_1) conventional, (ε_2) solar, (ε_3) wind, and (ε_4) storage. Let

$$x_r = \text{the proportion of } D \text{ allocated to source } \varepsilon_r, \text{ r} = 1, \ldots, 4$$

We require

$$x_1 + x_2 + x_3 + x_4 = 1$$

$$x_1, x_2, x_3, x_4 \geq 0$$

Without loss of generality, we can interpret the demanded proportion x_r
as corresponding to the amount $a_r := x_r D$, in megawatt-hours, of electricity

to be obtained from source ε_r, for each $r = 1, \ldots,$. However, each ε_r is a random variable whose probability distribution is not known precisely.

Suppose, however, that we have historical data for p earlier periods showing that when an amount $a_r := x_r D$ was allocated to the energy source ε_r, it yielded $x_{rk} D$ MW-h in period $k = 1, 2, \cdots, p$ in the past. We interpret this as a probability distribution.

$$\varepsilon_r: \quad x_{r1}D \quad x_{r2}D \quad \cdots \quad x_{rp}D$$

$$P(\varepsilon_r = x_{rk}D): \quad \frac{1}{p} \quad \frac{1}{p} \quad \cdots \quad \frac{1}{p}$$

A weighted distribution could also be used. In the case of uniform weights, we can estimate the expected output from source ε_r by

$$E_r := E(\varepsilon_r) = \frac{D}{p} \sum_{k=1}^{p} x_{rk} \quad r = 1, 2, 3, 4$$

Thus, if our "allocation portfolio strategy" is $x^T = (x_1, x_2, x_3, x_4)$, that means that the total energy supplied during this period is the random variable

$$\varepsilon := \sum_{r=1}^{4} \varepsilon_r x_r \tag{8.13}$$

whose expectation can be estimated by

$$E := E(\varepsilon) = \sum_{r=1}^{4} E(\varepsilon_r) x_r \tag{8.14}$$

Of course, the variability in ε is a problem and hence, by analogy to Markowitz's famous portfolio optimization problem, we may attempt to find $x^{*T} = (x_1^*, x_2^*, x_3^*, x_4^*)$ that solves

(EPVM) = energy portfolio variance minimization problem:

$$\min \text{Var}(\varepsilon)$$

subject to

$$\sum_{r=1}^{4} E(\varepsilon_r)x_r > L \quad \text{acceptable lower bound}$$

$$\sum_{r=1}^{4} x_r = 1$$

$$x_1, x_2, x_3, x_4 \geq 0$$

In the above, the variance of ε can be estimated by

$$Var(\varepsilon) = \sum_{k=1}^{p} \frac{1}{p} \left[D \sum_{r=1}^{4} x_{rk}x_r - E \right]^2 \tag{8.15}$$

Similarly, covariances of outputs from sources ε_r and ε_s, for $r \neq s$, can be estimated by

$$\sigma_{ij} = Cov(\varepsilon_r, \varepsilon_s) = \sum_{k=1}^{p} \frac{1}{p}(Dx_{rk} - E_r)(Dx_{sk} - E_s)$$

Naturally, the above can be generalized to an arbitrary n set of alternative energy sources $\varepsilon_1, \varepsilon_r, \cdots, \varepsilon_n$ with the analogous quantities:

$$E_i = E(\varepsilon_i) = \sum_{k=1}^{p} \frac{Dx_{ik}}{p}$$

$$\sigma_{ij} = Cov(\varepsilon_i, \varepsilon_j) = \frac{1}{p}\sum_{k=1}^{p}(Dx_{ik} - E_i)(Dx_{jk} - E_j)$$

$$V = \begin{pmatrix} \sigma_1^2 & \sigma_{12} & \cdots & \sigma_{1n} \\ \sigma_{21} & \sigma_2^2 & \cdots & \sigma_{2n} \\ \vdots & & & \\ \sigma_{n1} & \sigma_{n2} & \cdots & \sigma_n^2 \end{pmatrix}$$

where the estimated variance-covariance matrix V captures the correlation structure.

Now the energy portfolio variance minimization problem (EPVM) becomes

$$\min \mathbf{x}^T V \mathbf{x}$$

subject to

$$\sum_{j=1}^{n} E_j x_j \geq L \qquad \text{(EPVM)}$$

$$\sum_{j=1}^{n} x_j = 1$$

$$x_j \geq 0, \ \forall j$$

Finally, extensions of this approach to multi-period planning horizons are also possible under appropriate assumptions about interactions between successive periods.

Performance criteria other than variance minimization must be considered. The latter include other risk measures such as CVaR (conditional value at risk) and target-percentile criteria [24]. Vithayasrichareon and MacGill [39] have applied VaR techniques to generation investment, and there are obvious extensions that would strengthen the value of the tool. In addition, the stochastic and robust programming versions of the associated optimization problems [6] must be utilized.

8.5 CONCLUSION

In this chapter we canvassed a number of the tools that are needed for proper analysis of increasing the proportion of renewable energy for delivery of electricity supply. This is only for a macro-level study, as we have not investigated the power engineering aspects of the problem, nor indeed the financial questions.

The benefits of strong, early action considerably outweigh the costs. From the Stern Review [37], we have the following from the Executive Summary:

- Unabated climate change could cost the world at least 5% of GDP each year; if more dramatic predictions come to pass, the cost could be more than 20% of GDP.

- The cost of reducing emissions could be limited to around one percent of global GDP; people could be charged more for carbon-intensive goods.

- Each tonne of CO_2 we emit causes damages worth at least \$85, but emissions can be cut at a cost of less than \$25 a tonne.

REFERENCES

1. M.R. Agrawal, J. Boland, and B. Ridley, Volatility of Wind Energy Using High Frequency Data, *Proceedings of IASTED International Conference; Modelling, Identification and Control (AsiaMIC 2010)*, November 24–26, 2010, Phuket, Thailand, 1–3, 2010.
2. M.R. Agrawal, J. Boland, J. Filar, and B. Ridley, Analysis of wind farm output: Estimation of volatility using high frequency data, *Environmental Modeling and Assessment*, 2013.
3. Australian Energy Market Commission, Future Possible Retail Electricity Price Movements: 1 July 2010 to 30 June 2013, Technical Report, 2010.
4. Australian Energy Market Operator, *An Introduction to Australia's National Electricity Market*, AEMO, Melbourne, Australia, July 2010.
5. Australian Energy Market Operator, http://www.aemo.com.au, 2011.
6. A. Ben-Tal and A. Nemirovski, Robust optimization–methodology and applications, *Mathematical Programming*, 92: 453–480, 2002.
7. J. Boland, K. Gilbert, and M. Korolkowicz, Modelling wind farm output variability, *MODSIM07*, Christchurch, New Zealand, 10–13 December, 2007.
8. J.W. Boland, Time series and statistical modelling of solar radiation, in *Recent Advances in Solar Radiation Modelling*, Viorel Badescu (Ed.), Berlin and New York, Springer-Verlag, pp. 283–312, 2008.
9. T. Bollerslev, Generalised autoregressive conditional heteroskedasticity, *Journal of Econometrics*, 31: 307–327, 1986.
10. M.A. Delucchi and M.Z. Jacobson, Providing all global energy with wind, water and solar power. II. Reliability, system and transmission costs, and policies, *Energy Policy*, 39: 1170–1190, 2010.
11. Department of Climate Change and Energy Efficiency, Quarterly Update of Australia's National Greenhouse Gas Inventory, December Quarter 2010, Technical report, 2011.
12. R. Doherty, H. Outhred, and M. O'Malley, Establishing the role that wind generation may have in future generation portfolios, *IEEE Transactions on Power Systems*, 21: 1415–1422, 2006.
13. B. Elliston, M. Diesendorf, and I. MacGill, Simulations of scenarios with 100% renewable electricity in the Australian National Electricity Market, *Solar2011, the 49th AuSES Annual Conference*, 2011.
14. R.F. Engle, Autoregressive conditional heteroscedasticity with estimates of the variance of United Kingdom nations, *Econometrica*, 50: 987–1007, 1982.

15. M. Fahrioglu and F.L. Alvarado, Designing incentive compatible contracts for effective demand management, *IEEE Transactions on Power Systems*, 15(4): 1255–1260, 2000.

16. T. Farrell, Demand Response/Smart Grid Interfaces for Appliances— The Need for Global Standards, Technical report, Department of Climate Change and Energy Efficiency, 37th Expert Group on Energy Efficiency and Conservation Meeting, Washington, D.C., United States 28 February– 2 March 2011.

17. R.A. FitzHugh, Impulses and physiological states in models of nerve membrane, *Biophysical Journal*, 1: 445–466, 1961.

18. R. Garnaut, *The Garnaut Climate Change Review: Final Report*, Technical report, Garnaut Climate Change Review, 2008.

19. E.H. Gerding, V. Robu, S. Stein, D.C. Parkes, A Rogers, and N.R. Jennings, Online mechanism design for electric vehicle charging, *Proceedings of the 10th International Conference on Autonomous Agents and Multiagent Systems*, 2011.

20. V.M. Getz, Correlative coherence analysis: Variation from intrinsic sources in competing populations, *Theoretical Population Biology*, 64: 89–99, 2003.

21. H. Girardet and M. Mendonca, *A Renewable World, Energy, Ecology, Equality*, Green Books, Foxhole, Dartington, Totnes, Devon, UK, 2009.

22. J. Hansen, M. Sato, P. Kharecha, D. Beerlineg, V. Masson-Delmotte, M. Pagani, M. Raymo, D.L. Royer, and J.C. Zachos, Target atmospheric CO_2: Where should humanity aim?, *Open Atmospheric Science Journal*, 2: 217–231, 2008.

23. T.E. Hoff and R. Perez, Quantifying PV power output variability, *Solar Energy*, 84: 1782–1793, 2010.

24. B. Kang and J.A. Filar, Time consistent, dynamic, risk measures, *Mathematical Methods of Operations Research*, 63: 169–186, 2011.

25. B. Linder, J. Garcia-Ojalvo, A. Neiman, and L. Schimansky-Geier, *Physics Reports*, 392: 321–424, 2004.

26. C. Lucheroni, Resonating models for the electric power market, *Physics Review E*, 76: 1–13, 2007.

27. P.J. Lunde, *Solar Thermal Engineering*, John Wiley & Sons, New York, 1979.

28. N. Nisan, T. Roughgarden, E. Tardos, and V.V. Vazirani (Editors), *Algorithmic Game Theory*, Cambridge University Press, Cambridge (UK) and New York, 2007.

29. D.C. Parkes and Q. Doung, An ironing-based approach to adaptive online mechanism design in single-valued domains, *Proceedings of the 22nd National Conference on Artificial Intelligence*, pp. 94–101, 2007.

30. D.C. Parkes and S. Singh, An MDP-based approach to online mechanism design, *Proceedings of NIPS'03*, 2003.

31. R. Porter, Mechanism design for online real-time scheduling, *Proceedings of the Fifth ACM Conference on Electronic Commerce*, pp. 61–70, 2004.

32. S.D. Ramchurn, P. Vytelingum, A. Rogers, and N.R. Jennings, Agent-based control for decentralised demand side management in the smart grid, *The Tenth International Conference on Autonomous Agents and Multiagent Systems (AAMAS 2011)*, 2011a.

33. S.D. Ramchurn, P. Vytelingum, A. Rogers, and N.R. Jennings, Agent-based homeostatic control for green energy in the smart grid, *ACM Transactions on Intelligent Systems and Technology*, 2(4), Article No. 35, 2011b.

34. M.H. Rothkopf, Thirteen reasons why the Vickrey-Clarke-Groves process is not practical, *Operations Research*, 55(2): 191–197, 2007.

35. Royal Swedish Academy of Sciences, Mechanism Design Theory, Technical report, 2007.

36. B. Ridley, J. Boland, and P. Lauret, Modelling of diffuse solar fraction with multiple predictors, *Renewable Energy*, 35(2): 478–483, 2010.

37. N. Stern, *The Stern Review: The Economics of Climate Change*, 2010, http://siteresources.worldbank.org/INTINDONESIA/Resources/226271-1170911056314/3428109-1174614780539/SternReviewEng.pdf.

38. M.A.P. Taylor, P.J. Pudney, R. Zito, N.M. Holyoak, A.R. Albrecht, and R. Raicu, Planning for electric vehicles in Australia—Can we match environmental requirements, technology and travel demand?, *Proceedings of the 12th World Conference of the Transport Research Society*, 2010.

39. P. Vithayasrichareon and I.F. MacGill, Generation portfolio analysis for low-carbon future electricity industries with high wind power penetrations, *2011 IEEE Trondheim PowerTech*, 2010.

40. K. Ward, M. Korolkiewicz, and J. Boland, Modelling windfarm volatility using HMMs, *18th WorldIMACS/MODSIM Congress*, Cairns, Australia, 13–17 July, 2009.

41. Zero Carbon Australia, Stationary Energy Plan, Technical report, 2010.

42. X. Zou, Double-sided auction mechanism design in electricity based on maximizing social welfare, *Energy Policy*, 37: 4231–4239, 2009.

CHAPTER 9

Data Analysis for Real-Time Identification of Grid Disruptions

Varun Chandola, Olufemi Omitaomu, and Steven J. Fernandez

CONTENTS

9.1   INTRODUCTION

THE U.S. POWER GRID system comprises multiple distinct interconnections of generations, high-voltage transmission systems, and local distribution systems that maintain a continuous balance between generation and load with impressive levels of efficiency and reliability. This critical infrastructure is likely to see more changes over the next decade as a result of the proposed modernization of the grid system than it has seen over the past century. In particular, the widespread deployment of renewable generation (centralized and distributed), smart meters, synchrophasors, smart-grid controls, energy storage, and new conducting materials will require fundamental changes in grid planning and the way we run the power grid.

This modernization will lead to an explosive growth in the amount of data collected at each level of the power grid system: generation, transmission, distribution, and consumption. The data collected at these levels can be summarized into three classes: (1) field data (collected by the various devices distributed throughout the system, such as digital recorders); (2) centralized data archives (from monitoring, control, and operation systems, such as supervisory control and data acquisition (SCADA) systems); and (3) data from simulation (carried out in planning or operation environments). At the center of this data collection activity is the ability to process the information from the massive stock of data to support future decision making. It should be noted that the data cannot be left in the hands of field experts alone because of the high latency (for example, as high as sixty data points per second in case of phasor measurement units (PMU)) and the high dimensionality of the datasets. Hence, there is a need to develop algorithms capable of synthesizing structures from data.

Developing such algorithms, implementing them, and applying them to real problems are the purposes of the so-called data mining field.

Data mining is the term for a general approach that is supported to varying degrees by a set of technologies: statistics, visualization, machine learning, and neural networks. Classification, regression, clustering, summarization, dependency modeling, deviation detection, and temporal problems are expected to be solved by data mining tools. Data mining tools will be useful in a power grid system because of the characteristics of the collected data: large-scale character of the power grid (thousands of state variables), temporal (from milliseconds, seconds, minutes, hours, weeks, year) and statistical nature of the data, existence of a discrete (e.g., events such as generator trip or phase changes) and continuous (analog state variables) information mixture, necessity of communication with experts through means of visualization, online operation time restriction for fast decision making, and existence of uncertainty (noise, outliers, missing information).

This chapter presents applications of data mining tools to some of the problems in power grid systems using some of the data described earlier in this section. Section 9.2 discusses some of the identified research problems in the power grid system. Section 9.3 describes a methodology for classifying and visualizing frequency data collected using synchrophasors at the distribution level. Section 9.4 discusses a methodology for detecting and visualizing inter-area oscillatory modes from frequency data. Section 9.5 describes a spatio-temporal anomaly detection method for fast detection of grid events using a statistically principled change detection technique.

9.2 SOME RESEARCH PROBLEMS IN THE POWER GRID SYSTEM

As mentioned earlier, the modernization in the data collection capabilities within the power grid is resulting in an explosive growth in the amount of data collected at each level of the grid system—generation, transmission, distribution, and consumption. As noted earlier, we require new algorithmic approaches as well as parallel formulations to address this data explosion. One of the critical components is the prediction of changes and detection of anomalies. The state-of-the-art algorithms are not suited to handle the demands of streaming data analysis. A recent Department of Energy sponsored workshop on "Mathematics for Analysis of Petascale Data" has identified a few challenges that are important for this proposal: (1) need for events detection algorithms that can scale with the size of data; (2) need for algorithms that can not only handle multidimensional nature of the data, but also model both spatial and temporal dependencies in the data, which, for the most part, are highly nonlinear; (3) need for algorithms that can operate in an online fashion with streaming data.

As stated above, one element of the modernized power grid system is the installation of a wide-area frequency measurement system on the electric poles in the streets for conditions monitoring of the distribution lines. This would provide frequency measurements that reflect the status of the electric grid and possible information about impending problems before they occur. The timely processing of these frequency data could eliminate impending failures and their subsequent cascading into the entire system. The ability to monitor the distribution lines is just one facet of the proposed smart grid technology. Other elements include the installation of advanced devices such as smart meters, the automation of transmission lines, the integration of renewable energy technologies such as solar and wind, and the advancement of plug-in hybrid electric vehicle technology. The overall objective then is to make the electric grid system more robust in view of impending national and global operational challenges.

A wide-area frequency disturbance recorder (FDR) is already in use at both the transmission and distribution levels of the power grid system [1]. These recorders are used to monitor and record the changes in voltage frequency in real time at various locations. The FDRs perform local GPS synchronized frequency measurements and send data to a central server via the Internet, and the information management system handles data collection, storage, communication, database operations, and a Web service. There are currently more than 50 FDRs deployed around the United States. Each FDR measures the voltage phasor and frequency at the distribution level using a 110V outlet and streams ten data points per second, with future models expected to have higher streaming rates. One immediate challenge with the massive amount of data streams collected from FDRs is *how to detect and classify an impending failure of the grid from multiple high-speed data streams in real time while minimizing false alarms and eliminating missed detection, and then how to identify and evaluate the impacts of the detected failures.*

In the next three sections we describe three different applications of data mining for addressing two electric grid related problems. The first problem deals with identifying a specific type of pattern in the data (pattern discovery), while the second problem deals with identifying disruptive events from grid data. Section 9.3 addresses the first problem, while Sections 9.4 and 9.5 address the second problem.

9.3 DETECTION AND VISUALIZATION OF INTER-AREA OSCILLATORY MODES

Inter-area mode oscillations in power systems are global small-signal stability problems based on the architecture of the system. Given a specific system topology, these oscillatory modes result. Each system will have its own characteristic modes that can be excited under a various number of stress conditions. When excited, these modes create oscillations in power, generating unnecessary power flows, which serve to introduce added stress to the system. If under-damped or left unchecked, these oscillations have the potential to incite cascading blackouts.

Due to these hazards, several different control schemes have been implemented that specifically target modes of known oscillation frequencies. A major pitfall of these methods is that they rely on knowing the specific inter-area modal frequencies in advance to design the control scheme. These mode frequencies can be calculated from the system topology but in many cases the system models may be inaccurate, incomplete, or unavailable. Additionally, as the system topology changes over time, the mode frequencies will change with it. These factors can contribute to an improperly tuned control system.

With the proliferation of high time resolution power system measurement devices, it becomes possible to observe these inter-area modes as they occur. As more devices are installed across the system, a more complete picture of the different regions is achieved. The increased number of measurement vectors allows for identification of coherent generator groups and their associated geographic regions.

The work presented in this section outlines the procedures in developing a solution to extract an inter-area mode and determine its amplitude, phase, and damping at each measurement point, and it is based on the paper by Bank, Omitaomu, Fernandez, and Liu [8].

9.3.1 Signal Preprocessing

In order to provide a better fit of the oscillatory content, the measurement data needs to be properly conditioned first. An example of measured frequency data is given in Figure 9.1(a). It is desired to extract the properties of this oscillation.

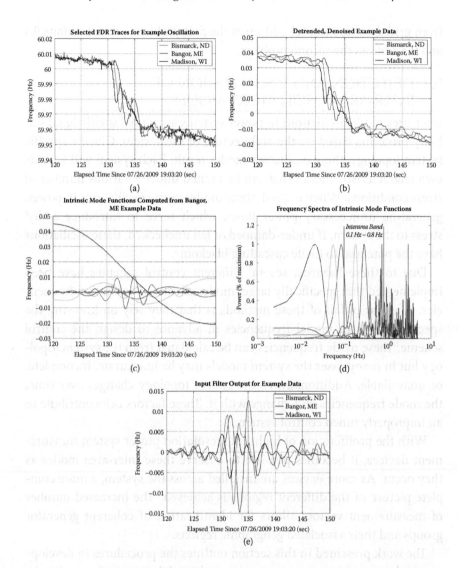

FIGURE 9.1 (*See color insert.*) Sample FDR traces and post-processing results.

The data for this example is drawn from FDR measurements that capture the system response to a generation trip. The resulting system frequency drop is seen in Figure 9.1 as a sharp decline from about 60.05 Hertz (Hz) to 59.96 Hz. During this drop period, a strong oscillation is also observed with power grid systems in Maine oscillating 180 degrees out of phase with systems in North Dakota. This example dataset will be used throughout this section to demonstrate the operation of the modal identification procedure.

Although this oscillation is easily observed by visual inspection, it is difficult to qualify numerically. The main reason for this is the high DC component that dominates the frequency spectra. The inter-area band of 0.1 Hz to 0.8 Hz is completely overshadowed by the lower-frequency components. To resolve this problem, the DC component should be mathematically removed from the signal. A simple solution to this problem is to subtract the median from the original signal; doing this detrends the data and centers the distribution of data points around zero. Although doing this removes the DC component, there are still low-frequency components overshadowing the inter-area band. These remaining unwanted components will be further attenuated by a nonlinear bandpass filter in a subsequent stage.

At this point, we consider the noise content of the input signals. Observing Figure 9.1(a), it is seen that a noticeable amount of noise is still present in the example data. From previous work [13], the nature of noise in the frequency monitoring network (FNET) system has been characterized as being Laplacian in nature. It has also been shown that a moving median filter provides an optimal filter for these noise elements. Because the inter-area oscillation components occupy the 0.1 Hz to 0.8 Hz band, the selected lowpass filter should pass these frequencies with minimal distortion. Thus, the lowpass filter used to denoise the FDR data for this application should have a break frequency greater than 0.8 Hz and less than 2 Hz. Based on this, a moving median filter with a window size of 5 points was selected to satisfy these requirements.

Application of the described detrending method and moving median filter to the example dataset yields the filtered signals of Figure 9.1(b). When compared to the original signals of Figure 9.1(a), the level to which the noise elements have been attenuated becomes obvious. Figure 9.1(b) demonstrates very little high-frequency noise content and the oscillatory content is much clearer.

The filtering process up to this point has helped to condition the input data and to isolate the oscillation frequencies of interest. Despite this, the data signal still contains a large low-frequency component that masks the inter-area band. Our interest at this point is to isolate only those frequencies within the inter-area band so that the dominant oscillation mode can be extracted. This was achieved through the implementation of a nonlinear bandpass filter. The filter would be primarily based on an Empirical Mode Decomposition (EMD) of the detrended and denoised input signal.

9.3.1.1 Signal Decomposition

Empirical Mode Decomposition is a data-driven method that decomposes a signal into a set of Intrinsic Mode Functions (IMFs). Each IMF is an oscillatory signal that consists of a subset of frequency components from the original signal. As opposed to Fourier, wavelet, and similar methods, EMD constructs these component signals directly from the data by identifying local extrema and setting envelopes around the signal in an iterative process. A fit is then performed on the local extrema to create an IMF. After the creation of an IMF, it is subtracted from the original signal and the process repeats to identify the next IMF. This identification and removal process continues until the original signal has been completely described by a set of IMFs. The output of the EMD process is the set of IMFs; generally, this set is a small number of signals (usually less than ten for the data considered here) that, when summed together, completely match the original signal. The EMD algorithm does not explicitly compute oscillation frequencies, amplitudes, or phase angles as with other signal decomposition techniques; instead, the IMFs are derived directly from the input signal based on its local extrema. A complete mathematical description of the EMD algorithm is beyond the scope of this chapter but can be found in [9–12]. The EMD and associated Hilbert-Huang Transform have also been recently proposed as methods for isolating inter-area modes in power systems [16, 17].

Performing an EMD on the Bangor trace of Figure 9.1(b) extracts the seven IMFs given in Figure 9.1(c). The first and second IMFs extracted in this process are given by the blue and green traces in Figure 9.1(c); these capture the high-frequency components and noise of the input signal. The next three IMFs given by the red, cyan, and violet traces capture the middle frequencies present in the signal. Finally, the last two IMFs extracted, those represented by the mustard and black lines, define the low-frequency components of the input, representing the event drop itself in this case.

The Fourier transform of the IMF signals in Figure 9.1(c) is given in Figure 9.1(d). The frequency variable is plotted on a log scale to better demonstrate the frequencies in the lower range. The individual Fast Fourier Transforms (FFTs) have been scaled by their maximum values so that the low-frequency components do not dominate the plot. Inspection of IMF signals confirms that each IMF is capturing one specific band of the original signal. The first IMF extracted, which is plotted in blue, is centered around 3 to 4 Hz, and each subsequent one picks up successively lower-frequency components.

Because the inter-area band is 0.1 Hz to 0.8 Hz, we would like to preserve only those IMFs that have a significant portion of their power in this band, and discard the others. The final implementation of this filter computes the IMFs and then performs a Fourier transform of each one. Using the Fourier transform results, the percentage of power within the inter-area band is computed for each IMF. If this percentage exceeds a given threshold, the IMF is retained; otherwise, it is discarded. The final filter output is the summation of the retained IMFs. Through testing on several datasets, it was determined that cut-off frequencies of 0.1 Hz and 0.8 Hz with a power percentage threshold of 0.75 provided the best response. These settings gave the best preservation of the inter-area band while removing most of the other frequency components.

The total input filtering process for this modal identification application consists of three stages: first, the median detrending stage; followed by a moving median filter; and finally the EMD-based filter. This process serves to isolate only the frequency components within the inter-area band so that further processing can extract specified modes within this region. Applying this multistage filtering process to the set of example data results in the signals presented in Figure 9.1(e). Comparing this plot with that of Figure 9.1(a), it is seen that the low-frequency trend is completely removed, leaving a zero-centered signal. Additionally, the higher frequency components and noise have also been removed from the raw data vectors. The oscillation in the inter-area band observed during the event drop is now the most prominent feature of the data, making it easier to extract from a computational viewpoint.

This filtering procedure was found to function well for several types of data. It is demonstrated here on frequency measurement derived from the FDR system but it performs similarly for angle measurements from FDR and Phasor Measurement Unit (PMU) datasets. Given any of these different types of data, the filtering process returns a zero-centered signal with the isolated inter-area modes similar to that of Figure 9.1(e). The ability of this filtering process to work for various different types of datasets makes the final modal extraction procedure compatible with all these forms of input data. The remainder of the modal extraction procedure is tuned to handle data vectors similar to those of Figure 9.1(e); thus, any dataset that the input filter can reduce to that form can be processed.

9.3.2 Identification and Extraction of Dominant Oscillatory Mode

One oscillation frequency is selected and the properties of that mode will be extracted over time for each measurement vector. For historic data analysis, this extraction will focus around some particular event containing an

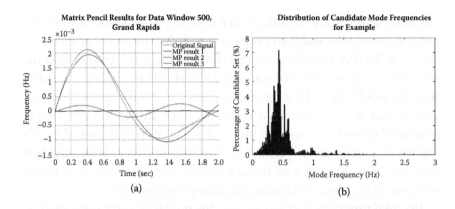

FIGURE 9.2 Matrix pencil results and analysis for one subset of the example data.

oscillation. The dominant frequency in this oscillation will be extracted and then tracked over time for a larger dataset around the event. In order to determine the dominant mode in the event, data from the corresponding time span is extracted. Once the necessary time span is determined, the data for each measurement vector are filtered and extracted into a reduced dataset. Doing this produces a set of signals that are zero centered and dominated by the oscillatory mode.

With the event data properly conditioned, the extraction of the dominant modal frequency can begin. In order to extract this mode, a Matrix Pencil [14, 15] based analysis was employed across a sliding data window. As the window is progressed across the data, an independent Matrix Pencil procedure is performed for each measurement vector and each data window. The results for one of the Matrix Pencil fits on the example dataset are given in Figure 9.2(a).

Inspection of Figure 9.2(a) shows that one of the computed modes, MP result 3, closely matches the oscillation and captures the majority of the original signal. This result is typical of all the tested cases and is primarily due to data detrending of the input filter. In all the observed cases, one of the computed modes followed the original signal very closely, with the remaining Matrix Pencil results accounting for the difference. The expression for a modal component is given by Equation (9.1), where A is the amplitude, α is the damping, f is the frequency, and θ is the phase angle.

$$y = Ae \propto t\cos(2\pi ft + \theta) \tag{9.1}$$

The power of this signal is given by Equation (9.2). Note that this equation does not give a true electrical power as it is derived from a frequency signal instead of a current or voltage.

$$Py = y^2 \tag{9.2}$$

The total energy of Equation (9.1) can then be expressed as the summation over time of the power as stated in Equation (9.3). Once again, this is not a true physical energy quantity, merely an analogous metric of the data signal.

$$Ey = \Sigma_t P_y \tag{9.3}$$

Whenever the Matrix Pencil method is performed on a measurement vector over a data window, this energy metric is assessed for each resulting mode. The mode with the largest energy value is then selected as the representative mode for that data vector and data window. This process is repeated for each vector and for each data window within the span of the oscillation event. A representative mode is then determined for each iteration, giving many possible modal frequencies.

Each of these candidates represents one oscillatory frequency that prevailed during a specific data window on one of the measurement vectors. The set of candidate modal frequencies can thus be treated as a probability distribution describing the location of the dominant mode. The distribution of candidate modes for the example dataset is given in Figure 9.2(b). This distribution represents an asymmetrical probability density function. From this data distribution, we want to determine the most likely value.

Assessing the most commonly occurring value in the candidate mode distribution gives an estimate of the most often-occurring frequency component. It is this estimate that will be taken as the dominant oscillatory mode during an event. Executing this procedure on the set of example data determined a modal frequency of 0.428 Hz. This value is within the desired inter-area band and when compared with the original data of Figure 9.1(a), it is consistent with the observed oscillation frequency.

9.3.3 Windowing Fit of Dominant Mode to Full Dataset

Now that the dominant oscillatory frequency has been determined, it will be applied across the full length of the dataset. Once again, a moving window will be employed to fit the mode across time. For each measurement vector and window instance, the damping, angle, and phase are derived, which provide a best fit to the given data. The moving window is sized such that it covers approximately one period of the dominant oscillation frequency. The data window then starts at the first data point to be included in the output. It then moves across the full dataset, shifting one time-step at a time until the end time is reached. For each instance of the window, each measurement vector is filtered according to the process of Section 9.3.1. After filtering the data, vectors are resampled to increase the discrete sampling rate. As before, this resampling serves to increase the stability and accuracy of the final fit.

Once these conditioning steps have been performed, the fit is ready to be executed. In this case, we want to fit a damped sinusoid of a specified frequency. A least squares fit of a damped sinusoid function was performed. This function is of the form in Equation (9.4). Here, the variable fit parameters are the amplitude A, the damping factor α, the phase θ, and a DC offset C. In Equation (9.4), f_0 is the dominant modal frequency determined previously.

$$y = Ae^{\alpha t} \cos(2\pi f_0 t + \theta) + C \qquad (9.4)$$

Performing this fit results in an optimal least squares solution to the four fit parameters. This solution gives the amplitude, damping, and phase for the oscillatory mode of interest. As this filtering, resampling, and fitting procedure is iterated across time and measurement vectors, an evolution of the dominant mode is captured. The amplitude, damping, and phase angles are computed with respect to a constant mode frequency. These values may then be tracked both spatially and temporally to gain an understanding of the evolution of this particular mode.

9.3.3.1 Identification of Coherent Groups

With the mode angle and phase determined for each measurement point over time, it is desired to estimate those units that form coherent groups. Given a set of phasors computed from a mode, the coherent groups can be identified by clustering the phasors according to their phase angle. As each group will be oscillating against the other group(s) in the system, the different groups should demonstrate differing phase angles. The desired cluster centroids in this case become phase angles defining the center of each coherent group.

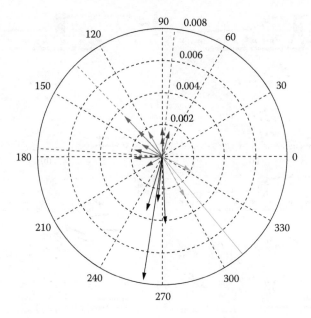

FIGURE 9.3 (*See color insert.*) Phasor clustering example.

Figure 9.3 gives the results of the clustering algorithm for a set of mode phasors drawn from the example data. Here, each measurement device yields one phasor. The clustering algorithm proceeds to identify those forming coherent groups by classifying them according to the direction in which they point. In Figure 9.3, each group is identified by a separate color, with the group centroid given by the dashed line of the same color.

9.3.4 Visualization of Modal Extraction Results

A visualization package was developed to display the results from the preceding modal identification procedure. This visualization is based on a geographic display that gives the mode amplitude and phase at each measurement point. These phasors are placed on the map so that the coherent groups can be observed spatially. This visualization architecture was used to generate movies that run across a given oscillation to present the graphics over time such that the temporal evolution can be observed in real time. One such movie is represented in Figure 9.4 by a series of frame captures. This movie was constructed from a dataset centered on the example case used throughout this section.

Figure 9.4(a) gives a movie frame from before the event and demonstrates a region with very little oscillatory content. The plot at the top of

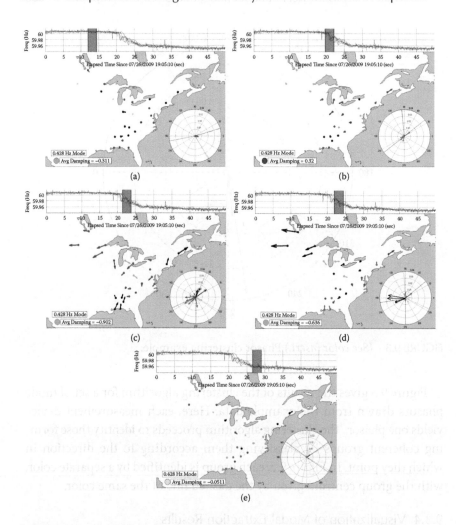

FIGURE 9.4 *(See color insert.)* Identification of a grid event using phasor visualization: (a) pre-event condition; (b) initial cycle of oscillation; (c) oscillation reaches largest magnitude; (d) damping of oscillation; and (e) system approaches steady state.

the frame gives the raw measurement data for several FDRs. The time range highlighted in red is the region to which this frame corresponds. This plot is intended to provide a timeline of the oscillation event under study, as well as give the time point currently being displayed. The main body of the frame of Figure 9.4(a) consists of geographic region spanned by the power system with each mode phasor plotted at the location of its corresponding measurement point. The phasors in this frame are also color-coded by the coherent group to which they belong. In the lower-left corner of Figure 9.4(a), the modal frequency being extracted is given along with the average damping factor seen across the measurement points of the system. To the left of the average damping is a traffic light style indicator. When the damping is greater than zero, this light turns red, specifying an alarm condition as the oscillation is growing. If the oscillation is lightly damped ($-0.1 < \alpha \leq 0$), the light turns yellow. Finally, this indicator is green when the oscillation is heavily damped ($\alpha < -0.1$). The final feature of Figure 9.4(a) is a phasor diagram in the lower right-hand corner that plots all the mode phasors on the same origin so that the clustering and relative magnitudes are better demonstrated. In this diagram, the dashed lines represent the centroids of the computed clusters. As indicated by the location of highlighted time span (red moving window), Figure 9.4(a) is drawn from a time point before the inciting event. At this stage, the system is in steady state and not experiencing an inter-area oscillation. Because of this, all the mode phasors have very small magnitude and register as nearly zero in the diagrams.

As time progresses to Figure 9.4(b), the inter-area oscillation is fully developed. Higher amplitudes are seen by FDRs around the Great Lakes as well as the FDR located in Bangor. The average damping across the system is positive, as the oscillation is growing. The clustering algorithm has identified two major coherent groups at this point: the first is the two New England FDRs in red and the second covers the Great Lakes regions in blue. For the most part, these two groups are oscillating 180 degrees out of phase.

The inter-area oscillation has grown to its largest magnitude by Figure 9.4(c); here, nearly all the measurement points are registering significant amplitude, and the phasors are all observable on the map. Also at this point, the oscillation magnitude has begun to decay, indicating damping across the system. The average damping factor is -0.902, indicating that the oscillation is decaying sharply throughout the system. Then, the two primary groups are defined by the Bangor, ME, unit and the Bismarck, ND, units, which are oscillating nearly 180 degrees out of phase.

As time progresses through to Figure 9.4(d), the oscillation continues to decay. As a result, the majority of the phasors in this capture are smaller than they were in Figure 9.4(c). The average system damping factor here has achieved -0.636. The New England units are still forming a coherent group with the southern United States, as characterized by the blue and pink groups. This group is now oscillating against the rest of the system, most notably the Northern Plains area, as seen by the black group of units.

A third group oscillating halfway between the other two has been identified by the clustering algorithm and is shown in red and green.

The oscillation has almost completely died out by the time the movie approaches the time span of Figure 9.4(e). At all the measurement points, the mode phasors have little to no amplitude. In addition, the computed dampings do not expect them to be growing substantially over the next cycle. The average system damping is still negative but approaching zero; this is not necessarily an alarm but due mainly to the fact that the system is not demonstrating any appreciable oscillation. From this it is obvious that the oscillation has run its course and the system has achieved its new steady-state value.

The visualizations and movie creation described in this section were performed in MATLAB. The individual frames are rendered as MATLAB figures and then imported into to an *.avi file to create the movie. The geographic mapping and coastlines of the displays were achieved with the use of M_Map [18], which is a set of MATLAB functions implementing a mapping toolbox. The approaches presented in this section can be used by engineers and control room operators to identify, extract, and visualize inter-area modes within the system in real time.

9.4 CLASSIFICATION OF POWER GRID FREQUENCY DATA STREAMS USING k-MEDIANS APPROACH

This section describes a k-Medians approach for clustering and identifying disruptive events in spatially distributed data streams.

9.4.1 k-Medians Approach Detecting Disruptive Events

The frequency of the power system provides a great deal of information about the health of the system and the prevailing operating conditions. The frequency trend indicates the power balance of the system. When the amount of power generated is equivalent to the amount of power consumed, the system is in steady state and the frequency remains constant. If there is an imbalance in generation/consumption, the system responds by converting some of its kinetic energy to electrical energy to make up for the power imbalance, causing acceleration toward a new operating point. This acceleration can be seen as a change in frequency. An excess of generation causes the system to accelerate, resulting in an increase in frequency. An excess of load causes the system to decelerate, depressing the frequency. This change in frequency is proportional to the magnitude of power imbalance. This concept is demonstrated in Figure 9.5(a), which

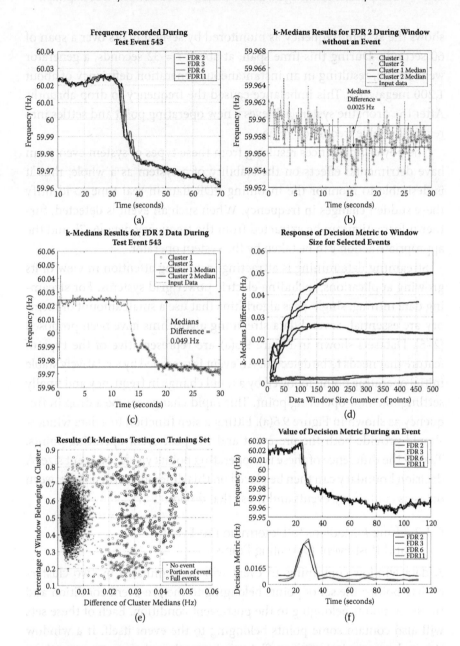

FIGURE 9.5 *(See color insert.)* Illustration of *k*-Medians-based approach for identifying events: (a) An example of frequency response to generator trip; (b) *k*-Medians result for frequency data *without* an event signature; (c) *k*-Medians result for frequency data *with* an event signature; (d) effect of window size on *k*-Medians metric for select training events; (e) *k*-Medians metric evaluated on the training data; and (f) response of decision metric during an event for selected FDRs.

shows the system frequency as monitored by several FDRs over a span of 60 seconds. During this time span, at about $t = 32$ seconds, a generator went offline, resulting in an instantaneous generation deficiency of about 1,200 megawatts. This imbalance caused the frequency to drop abruptly. After the drop, the system achieves a new operating point and settles into relatively stable frequency value.

The power imbalances resulting from these types of system events can have detrimental effects on the stability of a system as a whole; thus it is desirable to monitor the incoming FDR data in real time to identify these sudden changes in frequency. When such an event is detected, further information can be extracted from the frequency data [6, 7], and the appropriate action can be taken by the system operator.

Streaming data mining is attracting increasing attention in view of its growing applications, including electric power grid systems. For streaming data mining, single-pass algorithms that use a small amount of memory are essential. Several data streaming algorithms have been proposed [2–5]. Datasets shown in Figure 9.5(a) are representative of the type of feature that needs to be detected. An event is preceded by a relatively stable initial operating point, followed by a rapid change in frequency and finally settling to a new operating point. This rapid change can be a drop in frequency as shown in Figure 9.5(a). Fitting a step function to a data window should provide both the pre-event and the post-event operating points. Taking the difference of these two operating points yields the event size. A decision boundary can then be placed on this difference to decide between datasets containing events and those that do not.

9.4.2 Using k-Medians to Determine Pre-Event and Post-Event Operating Points

A data window containing an event will be dominated by two clusters of data points: the set of points belonging to the pre-event condition and the set of points belonging to the post-event condition. Each of these sets will also contain some points belonging to the event itself. If a window size is chosen such that it is sufficiently larger than the event region, these points will be overshadowed by the pre-event and post-event clusters. Identification of these two clusters was achieved using the k-Medians algorithm with $k = 2$. As discussed by Wang, Gardner, and Liu [7], FDR datasets naturally contain a high number of outliers and, as such, the median becomes a more appropriate estimator of position than the mean;

it is for this reason that k-Medians was chosen as opposed to k-Means. The k-Medians algorithm [4] consists of the following steps:

1. Start by assuming two clusters ($k = 2$) and selecting initial values for the centroid of each cluster, c_j.

2. For each point in the dataset, π_j, find the closest cluster, as measured using the 1-norm distance:

$$Q\left(\left\{\pi_j\right\}_{j=1}^k\right) = \sum_{j=1}^k \sum_{x \in \pi_j} \|x - c_j\|_1$$

3. Compute the new set of cluster centroids $ct_j = 1q$ by computing the median of the cluster. The median is used because it is the point that minimizes the total 1-norm distance from all points to it.

4. Repeat Steps 2 and 3 until there is no change in the cluster centroids.

Given a window of consecutive measurement points and using the frequency value of each point and a k value of 2 identifies two clusters within the input data, one being the measurements with higher frequency values and the other being those measurements with lower frequency values. Taking the difference of the two centroids of these clusters gives a robust indication of the size of a possible event within the data window. This procedure is demonstrated on two sets of data in Figures 9.5(b) and 9.5(c).

These two figures demonstrate how the k-Medians detection algorithm responds to an event. When no event is present within the data, the frequency data is relatively stable and the medians of the two clusters are close together, producing a small difference. When the source data contains an event, the data before the event are placed into one cluster with the data after the event being placed into the other cluster; as the size of the event increases, the medians of these groups will spread apart and their difference will increase. The magnitude of this difference will form the metric that determines whether an event occurred with the source data.

9.4.3 Selection of Window Data

Because the FDR measurements are sent continuously in real time, it is desirable to implement the event detector in such a way that it can be fed continuously. This was accomplished using a sliding data window approach. The k-Medians algorithm would be performed on a window of data to determine whether an event had occurred within that time span. This window would be moved across the data as it arrives from the measurement devices and be reevaluated. An optimal window size should be determined such that the decision metric provides a clear definition for event and non-event cases. In order to evaluate this, several data windows of differing sizes were tested on events from the training set. A selection of these results is presented in Figure 9.5(d). The decision metric value is plotted as a function of the data window size. The blue lines are derived from a few typical events, and the red lines are derived from datasets without events.

It is seen that as the window size increases past 50 points, there is a separation between the event and non-event cases. When the window size is small, the event drop occupies most of the data window; this pulls the group centroids together, reducing the magnitude of the decision metric. As the window size increases, more data from the stable regions are included and each centroid will be pulled toward the desired position. Increasing the size of the data window past a certain point produces diminishing returns, with the cluster centroids settling to the desired stable points. This effect is seen in the right-hand portion of Figure 9.5(d) as the traces approach horizontal. Additionally, it was observed that an excessively large window may capture slower data trends that we are not concerned with here, thus corrupting the results. Finally, a smaller window size also means that less data must be buffered in a real-time application, thereby decreasing the delay between an event occurrence and its identification.

Considering all these factors, it was determined that a 150-point (15 seconds) data window produced the best results for the training cases. In the final implementation, the data window shifts by a quarter of its width during each successive evaluation. Shifting in this manner reduced the amount of times the metric needed to be computed while ensuring that any events would be properly positioned within at least one data window.

9.4.4 Determination of Decision Boundary

A training set was compiled from 23 datasets containing events; in addition, several hours of data that contained no events was included in the training set. The 150-point sliding window was passed through this data and the metric was evaluated for each window. These results were then referenced against the known event times to evaluate the performance of the k-Medians difference metric. These results are given in Figure 9.5(e).

Each point in Figure 9.5(e) represents one window within the training set data. The blue crosses correspond to windows that contain no event. The black circles represent windows that contain a full event signature; and the red circles are windows that contain a portion of an event, but not the entire drop. The windows containing incomplete events are scattered throughout both of the other groups. These points represent a transition from a non-event case to an event case and, as such, their appearance within each group is expected. Due to the sliding nature of the data window and the width of an event signature, every event is guaranteed to appear fully within at least one window. Because of this, the red points in Figure 9.5(e) become "don't-care" situations as they represent events that have either already been detected or that will be detected by an upcoming window. An evaluation of Figure 9.5(e) to determine a decision boundary between the blue and black groups revealed that the optimal decision boundary occurs when the absolute value of the k-Medians difference metric is 0.0165 Hertz. Values less than this indicate no event, while values greater than 0.0165 Hertz indicate that an event occurred. The decision boundary determined here is specifically designed for the Eastern Interconnection in the U.S. power grid system. Other interconnections within the power grid systems will have a different decision boundary.

9.4.5 Evaluation of Decision Boundary

After constructing the event detection algorithm and setting the decision boundary for its metric, it was tested against several datasets outside the training set. For all cases, it correctly differentiates between windows that contained event signatures and those that did not. A time-based comparison of the event detection metric against the source data is presented in Figure 9.5(f). Here, the top chart gives measured data values; the bottom chart gives the corresponding values of the k-Medians difference decision metric during the event. The selected decision boundary appears as a horizontal dotted line on the decision metric plot. As demonstrated by these plots, the metric is below the decision boundary before the event, it exceeds the value during the time frame of the event signature, and finally returns below the boundary after the event has passed.

9.5 IDENTIFYING GRID DISRUPTIONS USING TIME-SERIES CHANGE DETECTION

A challenge associated with the identification of grid disruptions is to detect the events as early as possible. The k-Medians approach discussed in Section 9.3 requires data before and after the actual event to reliably identify an event. This constraint might render the approach undesirable for real-time decision-making applications. This section describes a faster method to identify grid disruptions in individual data streams that applies a time-series change detection algorithm to identify significant changes.

Time-series change detection has been a much researched area in statistics, especially in the context of *statistical quality control* [19, 20]. Recently, several data mining approaches have been proposed to identify changes in time series [21, 22]. But many of these approaches are either not online or are not scalable to the high throughput data as encountered in this domain.

An approach based on the widely used quality control method called cumulative sum control chart (CUSUM) [23] for time-series change detection is discussed here. Change detection has been extensively studied in the context of time-series analysis and forecasting. The standard approaches include various smoothing techniques, the Box-Jenkins autoregressive integrated moving average (ARIMA) modeling, innovation and outlier analysis, and more recently, wavelet-based methods.

9.5.1 A CUSUM-Based Fast Time-Series Anomaly Detection Method

In this subsection a CUSUM-based methodology to identify anomalies in a univariate time series is discussed. The exact problem can be defined as:

> Given a regularly sampled time series T, such that, each value T_t, is the measurement at time t, for a given sensor, identify *spans* of the form $[t_1, t_2]$, such that the underlying system is in an *anomalous state* from time t_1 to t_2.

While traditionally CUSUM is used to identify changes in a time series, it can be adapted for anomaly detection in time series. The core idea behind CUSUM is that one can use it to identify the start and the end of an anomalous regime in a given time series by identifying a change point.

The CUSUM approach is a sequential method that involves calculation of a cumulative sum. For a given time series, at a given time t (> 1), the following two quantities are computed:

$$S_t^+ = \max(0, S_{t-1}^+ + (T_t - \omega_t))$$

$$S_t^- = \max(0, S_{t-1}^- + (\omega_t - T_t))$$

The quantity ω_t is the weight assigned at each time instance. While this can be dependent on t, it is set to

$$\omega_t = \mu_0 + k|\mu_0 - \mu|$$

where μ_0 denotes the expected mean of the in-control distribution of T, while μ denotes the minimum shift that needs to be detected. The method has one parameter, the *allowance value k*, which is typically set to 0.5 or 1. The allowance value k governs how much deviation from the expected mean is allowed. If a process is naturally noisy, k is typically set higher, while for a relatively stable process k is set to a low value.

The process is initialized with

$$S_1^+ = \max(0, T_1 - \omega_1)$$

$$S_1^- = \max(0, \omega_1 - T_1)$$

The S^+ statistic monitors the changes in the positive direction (also sometimes referred to as "high-side" CUSUM), and the S^- statistic monitors the changes in the negative direction (also sometimes referred to as "low-side" CUSUM). For monitoring grid disruptions, the low-side CUSUM is relevant because one is interested in detecting events in which the frequency of the power falls down.

Figure 9.6 denotes a simple example that illustrates the CUSUM-based anomaly detection on a synthetically generated time-series dataset. The first 100 and last 100 points in the time series are generated from a normal distribution with mean 0 and standard deviation 1. The points from time 101 to 200 are generated from a normal distribution with mean −0.25 and standard deviation 1. It can be seen that although the anomalous region is indistinguishable to the naked eye, the CUSUM-based approach can still identify the anomalous region. During the anomalous state, the CUSUM score increases and starts falling down once the time series is in the normal state.

Computationally, this approach is fast because it requires a constant time operation at every time second, and it is also memory efficient, as we

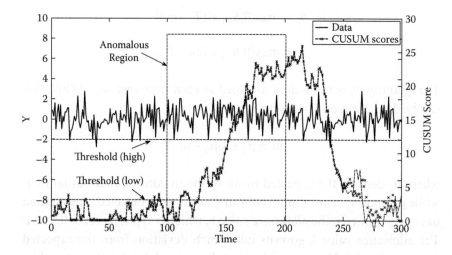

FIGURE 9.6 A random time series with anomalous region and CUSUM scores.

only need to maintain the value of the CUSUM statistic of the previous time instance.

The key issue with this approach is that the output of CUSUM requires a threshold to declare when the system is in an anomalous state. If the threshold is set very low, the false positive rate is high; and when the threshold is set high, it might result in a delay in identifying an event. To alleviate this problem, the quality control literature provides a way to set the threshold based on the *Average Run Length* (ARL) metric. Typically, the threshold is set based on the number of expected events in an in-control process.

9.5.2 Results on Grid Data

This section summarizes the performance of the CUSUM-based anomaly detector, as described in the previous section, on frequency data collected from the FDR sensors described in Section 9.3 of this chapter. The objectives of these experiments are as follows:

1. Can the CUSUM based approach identify useful events?

2. What is the typical false alarm rate?

9.5.2.1 Data Description and Algorithm Parameters

For the results shown in this section, data came from 21 FDRs located within the Eastern Interconnect (EI) of the United States. Data for 2 months (May 2008 and June 2008, total 61 days) are used. The time series are sampled at the rate of 10 Hertz. The length of the time series for each day is 864,000. The data was analyzed separately for each month. The frequency data are preprocessed using the k-Medians approach with k set to 5.

The allowance value (k) for the CUSUM algorithm is set to 1, the minimum shift (μ) to be detected is set to 0.05, and the in-control distribution mean (μ_0) is 0.[*] An anomalous event is defined as a subsequence of a month-long time series in which the CUSUM statistic is greater than zero. Based on an understanding of the domain, an anomalous event is considered *significant* if it lasts for at least 2 seconds (20 observations).

9.5.2.2 Raw Results

Table 9.1 summarizes the number of significant anomalous events identified for each of the sensors for May 2008 and June 2008. The results show that for all the FDRs, the fraction of time in which the system is in an anomalous state is a small fraction of the total time, but that fraction itself can be a large number. For example, FDR 11 in Grand Rapids, MI, was in an anomalous state, 0.0082 fraction of the total time, approximately 200,000 observations. However, the number of significant anomalous events for each sensor for a month is not more than 119.

Evaluation of the output of the anomaly detector is a challenge, given the lack of ground truth data about the grid-related events for that time period. A possibility is to examine the local news sources for the specific days of the events, although that process can be expensive, as well as not guaranteed to cover every grid event. To further consolidate the output, a *spatial co-location constraint* can be applied, as discussed below.

9.5.2.3 Incorporating Spatial Information

Electric grid events (such as outages, trips) typically have a cascading effect. Hence, a grid event must manifest itself in data collected at spatially colocated sensors. Table 9.2 shows the number of significant events identified by the CUSUM-based anomaly detection system for each sensor, while taking the spatial information into consideration. Thus, an alarm raised at a sensor is considered "true" if it was also raised by the neighboring sensors (eight for this study). The number of significant events is

---

[*] The data have already been centered using the k-Medians approach by using the medians as centers to shift the subset of data.

TABLE 9.1   Summary Statistics for CUSUM-Based Anomaly Detection Output
for Different FDRs

			May 2008		June 2008	
FDR #	Location	State	Fraction Alarms	No. Anomalous Events	Fraction Alarms	No. Anomalous Events
11	Grand Rapids	MI	0.0082	117	0.0094	115
13	Carmel	IN	0.0081	115	0.0095	113
38	Holyoke	MA	0.007	97	0.0093	106
40	St Paul	MN	0.008	116	0.0092	111
42	Tallahassee	FL	0.0081	116	0.0095	116
510	Blacksburg	VA	0.0038	64	0.0046	85
513	State College	PA	0.0082	119	0.0095	113
514	Simpsonville	SC	0.0009	16	0.0005	13
516	Rochester	NY	0.0056	88	0.009	108
519	Newport News	VA	0.0034	53	0.0034	37
521	Chillicothe	OH	0.0076	117	0.0058	71
523	Oak Ridge	TN	0.0033	43	0.0019	19
526	Birmingham	AL	0.0082	118	0.0095	113
560	Duluth	MN	0.0068	92	0.0079	90
561	Madison	WI	0.0081	119	0.0095	115
566	Gulfport	MS	0.0081	116	0.0095	113
568	Montgomery	AL	0.0082	117	0.0095	113
570	Atlanta	GA	0.0082	118	0.004	54
571	Pensacola	FL	0.0082	118	0.0095	111
596	Cookeville	TN	0.0067	93	0.0062	69
597	Cookeville	TN	0.0067	92	0.0056	66

reduced by incorporating the spatial information. While one cannot infer
that the events that are thus ignored are not useful, this approach does
allow a reduced set for further analysis.

As shown in Table 9.2, the number of significant events is sharply
reduced to 143 by taking the spatial context into account. While the real
benefit of this approach can be validated only by confirming that the
detected events are indeed beneficial in terms of identifying the actual
events, the lack of availability of reliable ground truth regarding grid
events makes the validation challenging. At the time of writing this chapter, the detected events were being validated through a manual process,
the results of which will be documented in future publications.

TABLE 9.2   Number of Significant Events for Spatially Aware
CUSUM-Based Anomaly Detection Output for Different FDRs

FDR #	Location	State	May 2008	June 2008
11	Grand Rapids	MI	8	8
13	Carmel	IN	5	6
38	Holyoke	MA	0	0
40	St Paul	MN	8	8
42	Tallahassee	FL	0	0
510	Blacksburg	VA	0	0
513	State College	PA	0	0
514	Simpsonville	SC	0	0
516	Rochester	NY	0	0
519	Newport News	VA	0	0
521	Chillicothe	OH	0	0
523	Oak Ridge	TN	0	0
526	Birmingham	AL	9	8
560	Duluth	MN	8	8
561	Madison	WI	8	8
566	Gulfport	MS	9	8
568	Montgomery	AL	9	8
570	Atlanta	GA	0	0
571	Pensacola	FL	9	8
596	Cookeville	TN	0	0
597	Cookeville	TN	0	0

9.6 CONCLUSIONS

Data mining has immense significance in terms of addressing several key power grid problems, specifically in the arena of rapid event detection, as discussed in this chapter, which have the potential of going a long way in terms of realizing the promised benefits of the smart grid. The key challenges associated with this domain, in terms of data analysis, are the massive nature of the data and the short reaction time allowed (on the order of a few seconds) for allowing adequate response. The analytic solutions proposed in this chapter focus primarily on simple analyses that can be scaled to the data sizes and the high sampling rate of the incoming power signal. In the future, as the synchrophasors become more and more advanced (both in terms of sampling rate as well as the number of deployed sensors across the country), more research will be required to make the data analysis solutions scalable.

REFERENCES

1. J.N. Bank, O.A. Omitaomu, S.J. Fernandez, and Y. Liu, Visualization and classification of power system frequency data streams, *Proceedings of the IEEE International Conference on Data Mining Workshops*, p. 650–655, 2009.

2. P. Domingos and G. Hulten, Mining high-speed data stream, *Proceedings of the Sixth ACM SIGKDD International Conference on Knowledge Discovery and Data Mining*, pp. 71–80, 2000.

3. G. Hulten, L. Spencer, and P. Domingos, Mining time-changing data streams, *Proceedings of KDD 2001*, pp. 97–106, 2001.

4. D. Kifer, S. Ben-David, and J. Gehrke, Detecting change in data streams, *Proceedings of the 30th VLDB Conference*, p. 180–191, 2004.

5. L. O'Callaghan, N. Mishra, A. Meyerson, S. Guha, and R. Motwani, Streaming data algorithms for high-quality clustering, *Proceedings of the 18th International Conference on Data Engineering*, 2002.

6. B. Qiu, L. Chen et al. Internet based frequency monitoring network (FNET), *IEEE Power Engineering Society, Winter Meeting, 2001*. Vol. 3, 28 Jan.–1 Feb. 2001, pp. 1166–1171.

7. J.K. Wang, R.M. Gardner, and Y. Liu, Analysis of system oscillations using wide-area measurements, *IEEE Power Engineering Society, General Meeting, 2007.* 25 June–28 June 2006.

8. J.N. Bank, O.A. Omitaomu, S.J. Fernandez, and Y. Liu, Extraction and visualization of power system inter-area oscillatory modes, *Proceedings of the IEEE Power & Energy Society Annual Meeting*, Minneapolis, MN, July 25–29, 2010.

9. N.E. Huang, Z. Shen, S.R. Long, M.C. Wu, S.H. Shih, Q. Zheng, C.C. Tung, and H.H. Liu. The empirical mode decomposition method and the Hilbert spectrum for non-stationary time series analysis, *Proceedings of the Royal Society of London, A454*: 903–995, 1998.

10. H. Liang, Z. Lin, and R.W. McCallum. Artifact reduction in electrogastrogram based on the empirical model decomposition method. *Medical Biological Engineering and Computing*, 38: 35–41, 2000. A.K. Jain and R.C. Dubes, *Algorithms for Clustering Data*: Prentice-Hall, Englewood Cliffs, NJ, 1981.

11. N.E. Huang, M.-L. Wu, W. Qu, S.R. Long, and S.P. Shen. Applications of Hilbert–Huang transform to non-stationary financial time series analysis, *Applied Stochastic Models in Business and Industry*, 19: 245–268, 2003.

12. S.T. Quek, P.S. Tua, and Q. Wang. Detecting anomalies in beams and plate based on the Hilbert–Huang transform of real data, *Smart Material Structure*, 12: 447–460, 2003.

13. Z. Zhong, C. Xu, et.al. Power system Frequency Monitoring Network (FNET) implementation, *IEEE Trans. on Power Systems*, 20(4): 1914–1921, 2005.

14. T.K. Sarkar and O. Pereira. Using the matrix pencil method to estimate the parameters of a sum of complex exponentials, *IEEE Antennas and Propagation Magazine*, 37(1): 48–55, 1995.

15. Y. Hua and T.K. Sarkar. Matrix pencil method for estimating parameters of exponentially damped/undamped sinusoids in noise, *IEEE Transactions on Acoustics, Speech and Signal Processing*, 36(2): 228–240, 1988.
16. D.S. Laila, A.R. Messina, and B.C. Pal. A refined Hilbert-Huang transform with applications to interarea oscillation monitoring, *IEEE Transactions on Power Systems*, 24(2): 610–620, May 2009.
17. N. Senroy. Generator coherency using the Hilbert-Huang transform, *IEEE Transactions on Power Systems*, 23(4), 1701–1708, November 2008.
18. R. Pawlowicz, M_Map: A Mapping Package for Matlab, http://www.eos.ubc.ca/~rich/map.html, Ver 1.4e, Oct 2009.
19. F. Gustafsson. *Adaptive Filtering and Change Detection*. New York: Wiley, 2000.
20. J.M. Lucas and M.S. Saccucci. Exponentially weighted moving average control schemes: Properties and enhancements, *Technometrics*, 32(1): 1–29, 1990.
21. S. Boriah, V. Kumar, M. Steinbach, C. Potter, and S. Klooster, Land cover change detection: A case study, *Proceeding of the 14th KDD*, pp. 857–865, 2008.
22. V. Chandola and R.R. Vatsavai. A scalable Gaussian process analysis algorithm for biomass monitoring, *Statistical Analysis and Data Mining*, 4(4): 430–445, 2011.
23. E.S. Page. On problems in which a change can occur at an unknown time, *Biometrika*, 44(1-2): 248–252, 1957.

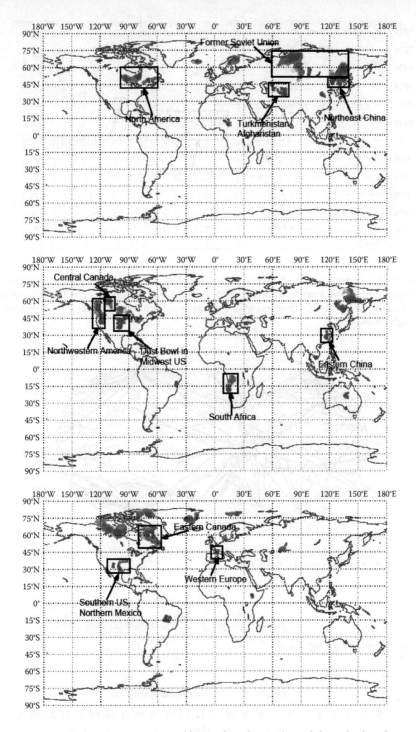

FIGURE 4.1 The drought regions detected by our algorithm. Each panel shows the drought starting from a particular decade: 1905–1920 (top left), 1921–1930 (top right), 1941–1950 (bottom left), and 1961–1970 (bottom right). The regions in black rectangles indicate the common droughts found by [63].

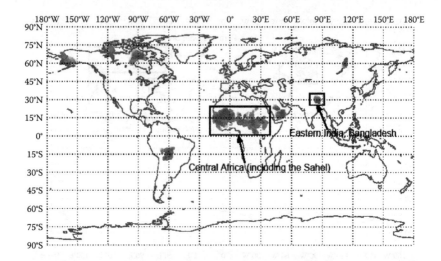

FIGURE 4.1 (continued) The drought regions detected by our algorithm. Each panel shows the drought starting from a particular decade: 1905–1920 (top left), 1921–1930 (top right), 1941–1950 (bottom left), and 1961–1970 (bottom right). The regions in black rectangles indicate the common droughts found by [63].

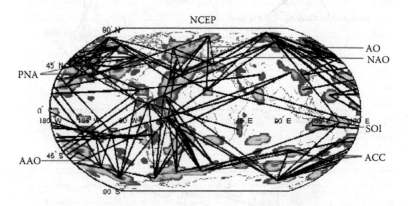

FIGURE 4.2 Climate dipoles discovered from sea-level pressure (reanalysis) data using graph-based analysis methods (see [42] for details).

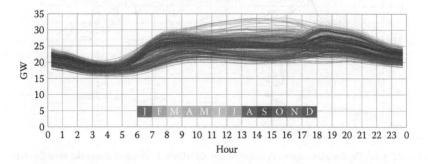

FIGURE 8.2 Hourly demand profile in the NEM for 2010 (data from Australian Energy Market Operator [5]).

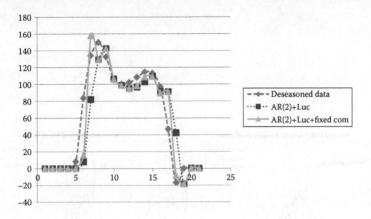

FIGURE 8.8   When fixed components add into combination of Lucheroni and AR(2) model.

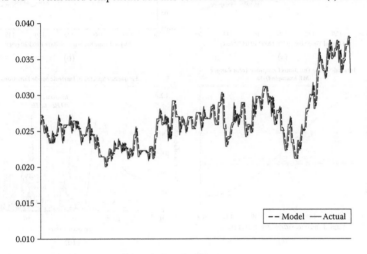

FIGURE 8.12   *AR*(3): Fit of 10-second data.

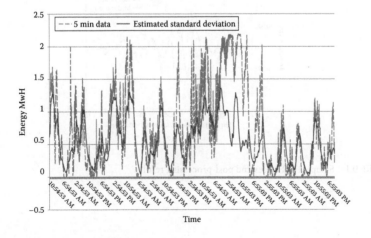

FIGURE 8.13   Output and estimated standard deviation.

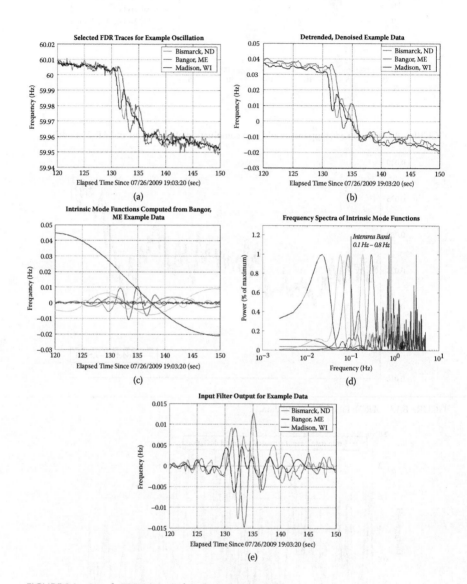

FIGURE 9.1   Sample FDR traces and post-processing results.

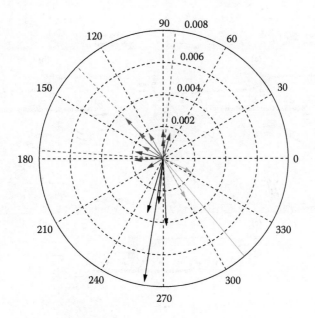

FIGURE 9.3   Phasor clustering example.

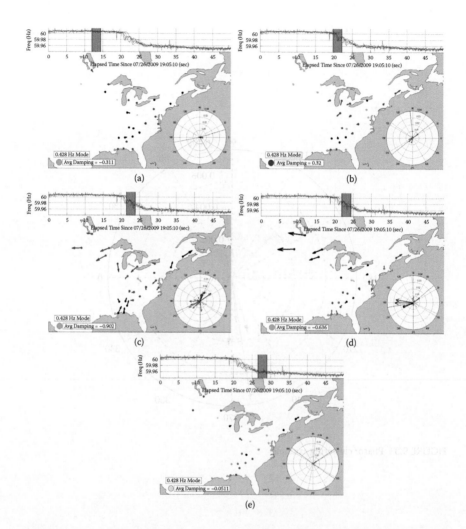

FIGURE 9.4 Identification of a grid event using phasor visualization: (a) pre-event condition; (b) initial cycle of oscillation; (c) oscillation reaches largest magnitude; (d) damping of oscillation; and (e) system approaches steady state.

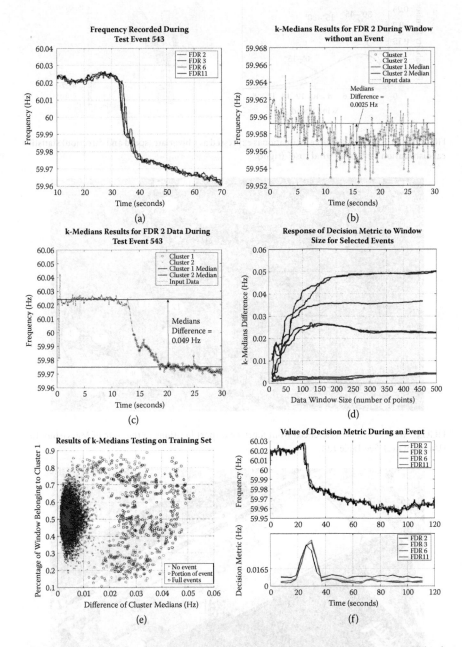

FIGURE 9.5 Illustration of *k*-Medians-based approach for identifying events: (a) An example of frequency response to generator trip; (b) *k*-Medians result for frequency data *without* an event signature; (c) *k*-Medians result for frequency data *with* an event signature; (d) effect of window size on *k*-Medians metric for select training events; (e) *k*-Medians metric evaluated on the training data; and (f) response of decision metric during an event for selected FDRs.

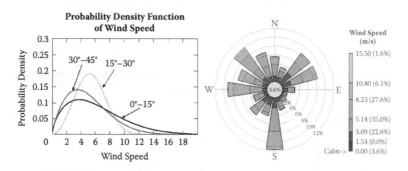

FIGURE 10.1   A wind resource estimation is expressed as a bivariate (speed and direction) statistical distribution (left) or a "wind rose" (right).

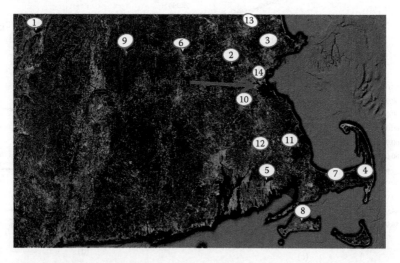

FIGURE 10.4   Data are referenced from fourteen airport locations in the state of Massachusetts (United States). See Table 10.1.

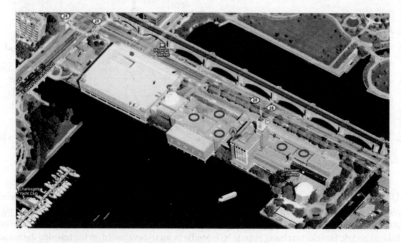

FIGURE 10.5   Red circles show location of anenometers on rooftop of Museum of Science, Boston, Massachusetts.

CHAPTER 10

Statistical Approaches for Wind Resource Assessment

Kalyan Veeramachaneni, Xiang Ye, and Una-May O'Reilly

CONTENTS

10.1 INTRODUCTION

A WIND RESOURCE ASSESSMENT IS initiated as part of the decision process leading to selecting a wind farm site. There are multiple factors that influence site selection. Among them are legal considerations, community opinion, ease of construction, maintenance, and cabling cost. Arguably, most crucial is whether there is enough wind in the ideal speed range that will endure over a long span of time, such as a generation or longer. Prediction of wind at high frequency, such as hours to days to weeks, is fraught with technical and sensing challenges—plus intrinsic uncertainty. Wind resource assessment for site selection contrasts with high frequency prediction. Its goal is to provide a general estimate that guides selection without being a precise prediction. The annual, actual wind resource of a farm would be expected to deviate from the assessment with reasonable variance. However, when the actual annual resource is averaged over a long time span, the goal is that assessment and actuality should match up. In this way, wind resource assessment helps inform the question of the production capacity of the site over its extended lifetime (which potentially includes successive upgrades of turbines and related facilities).

A wind resource assessment is presented as a set of probability distributions of wind speed for directional intervals that span 360°. An example of three distributions, for the intervals 0° to 15°, 15° to 30°, and 30° to 45° is shown on the left of Figure 10.1. Each plotted probability function is modeled with a Weibull distribution that is parameterized by shape and scale. Integrating this function (mathematically) allows one to derive the probability that the wind speed from a given direction range will be within a specific range.

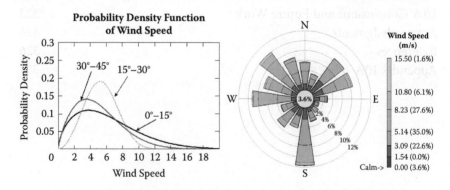

FIGURE 10.1 (*See color insert.*) A wind resource estimation is expressed as a bivariate (speed and direction) statistical distribution (left) or a "wind rose" (right).

The assessment can also be visualized via a wind rose; see Figure 10.1 (right). The span of the entire 360° is oriented in the north-south compass direction to inform its alignment to the site. Figure 10.1 (left) shows 16 direction intervals, each as a discrete "slice" with coloring that depicts wind speed. The length and width of the slice conveys probability.

There are multiple methodologies that derive a wind resource assessment. All are subject to great uncertainty. When a wind resource assessment is based upon wind maps and publicly available datasets from the closest locations, it tends to overestimate the wind speed because the maps are so macroscopic. Even when the resource estimated by the wind map for a geographical location is improved upon by utilizing a model that accounts for surface roughness and other factors, significant inaccuracies persist because specific details of the site remain neglected. Alternatively, a computational fluid dynamics (CFD) model can be used to achieve a better resource assessment. However, CFD also has limitations. It is very difficult to incorporate all the local attributes and factors related to turbulence into the simulation. While the wind industry has started to combine CFD and wind map approaches, the current methods are ad-hoc, not robust, and more expensive than desired.

In this chapter we provide new techniques for the only assessment methodology that takes into account as many years of historical data as possible (although those data are remote from the site itself), while also integrating site-specific information, albeit short term and relatively noisy. We consider the Measure-Correlate-Predict assessment methodology, abbreviated as MCP, which exploits anemometers, and/or other sensing equipment that provide site-specific data [1–4]. The Measure step involves measuring wind speed and direction at the site for a certain duration of time. In the Correlate step, these data are then associated with simultaneous data from nearby meteorological stations, so-called *historical sites* that also have long-term historical data. A correlation model is built between the time-synchronized datasets. In the Predict step, the model is then used along with the historical data from the meteorological stations to predict the wind resource at the site. The Prediction is expressed as a bivariate (speed and direction) statistical distribution or a "wind rose" as shown in Figure 10.1.

While MCP does incorporate site-specific data, these data are based upon very inexpensive sensors, that is, anemometers, which are consequently very noisy. Additionally, anemometers are frequently moved on the site and not deployed for any significant length of time. Thus, the key challenge of MCP is to accurately predict with cheap, noisy, short-term sensor measurements. We aim to address how techniques match up with data availability. Usually 8 to 10 months is considered the standard in the wind industry. However, we seek very simple modeling techniques that can reduce the amount of data required to get an accurate estimation of the long-term wind speed.

Another challenge is integrating historical site data. The best historical site (e.g., airport) to correlate wind speed with a site might be somewhat intuitive if only wind direction is considered: for example, when the wind blows from the north at the site, its speed might be best correlated with speeds from a particular airport meteorological tower immediately to the north. However, site conditions such as local terrain height variation or terrain features such as forests and large buildings make identifying the best correlation sources much more complicated. The sites' conditions cannot be observed directly in the data but influence the correlative relationships. Also, the strength of correlations may be sensitive to how the wind direction is segmented into aggregative bins and intervals. To date, the selection is done with trial-and-error modeling and ad hoc understanding of the similarity between the proposed and historical sites. Almost always, a single historical site, closest to the test site, is used to build the predictive model. Yet, for any directional bin, better accuracy is obtainable when multiple historical sites in different directions with respect to the site are candidates for integration into the estimation. In this chapter we address how to integrate the wind information from multiple historical sites and weigh each historical site according to its correlative strength.

It is not uncommon for wind farms to fall short of their expected energy output. A study performed in the United Kingdom monitored small and micro wind turbine performance and found that the wind resource was overpredicted by a factor of 15 [5]. In another example, data analysis of 19 small turbines installed in Massachusetts [6] showed, on average, turbines underperforming by a factor of 4. The capacity factor was found to be as low as 3% to −4%. Inadequate wind resource assessment was determined to be one of the major factors (20%) influencing the underperformance.

In this chapter we describe a set of computational intelligence techniques based on statistical inference. Each technique relies on estimating the joint distribution of wind speeds at the site and the publicly available neighboring sources. The accuracy of any one of these techniques is sensitive to choices in the modeling setup and/or parameterizations. We aim to assess which technique and choices are best. Our assessment will utilize anemometer

TABLE 10.1 The Boston Museum of Science Is at Position
N42.37°, W71.1°

Variable	Airport	Distance (miles)	Compass Position (Lat., Long.)
x_1	North Adams	151	(42.69°, −73.16°)
x_2	Bedford	18.7	(42.46°, −71.28°)
x_3	Beverly	20.6	(42.58°, −70.91°)
x_4	Chatham	88.5	(41.68°, −69.99°)
x_5	New Bedford	56.2	(41.67°, −70.95°)
x_6	Fitchburg	41.2	(42.55°, −71.75°)
x_7	Hyannis	72.7	(41.66°, −70.28°)
x_8	Lawrence	28.1	(42.71°, −71.11°)
x_9	Vineyard Haven	92.9	(41.39°, −70.61°)
x_{10}	Orange	84.7	(42.57°, −72.28°)
x_{11}	Norwood	23.2	(42.18°, −71.17°)
x_{12}	Plymouth	43.9	(41.96°, −70.68°)
x_{13}	Taunton	39.3	(41.87°, −71.01°)
x_{14}	Boston	4.9	(42.36°, −71.02°)

Note: Columns 1 and 2 show the airport names and their corresponding variable names in our multivariate model.
Column 3 shows each airport's line-of-sight distance (in
miles) from the Boston Museum of Science. Column 4
shows the compass position of each airport.

measurements for a site at the Boston Museum of Science when the availability of site data varies between 3, 6, and 8 months while correlating with
data from 14 airports nearby; see Figure 10.4 and Table 10.1.

We proceed as follows: Section 10.2 presents a detailed description of
MCP. Section 10.3 presents statistical techniques that can be used in an MCP
framework. Section 10.4 presents the means by which we evaluate the
techniques. Section 10.5 presents the empirical evaluation. Finally, Section
10.6 states our conclusions and outlines future work.

10.2 MEASURE-CORRELATE-PREDICT

We consider wind resource estimation derived by a methodology known
as Measure-Correlate-Predict; see Figure 10.2. In terms of notation, the
wind at a particular location is characterized by speed denoted by x and
direction θ. Wind speed is measured by anemometers, and wind direction
is measured by wind vanes. The 360° direction is split into multiple bins
with a lower limit (θ_l) and an upper limit (θ_u). We give an index value of J
$= 1 \dots j$ for the directional bin. We represent the wind speed measurement
at the test site (where wind resource needs to be estimated) with y and the

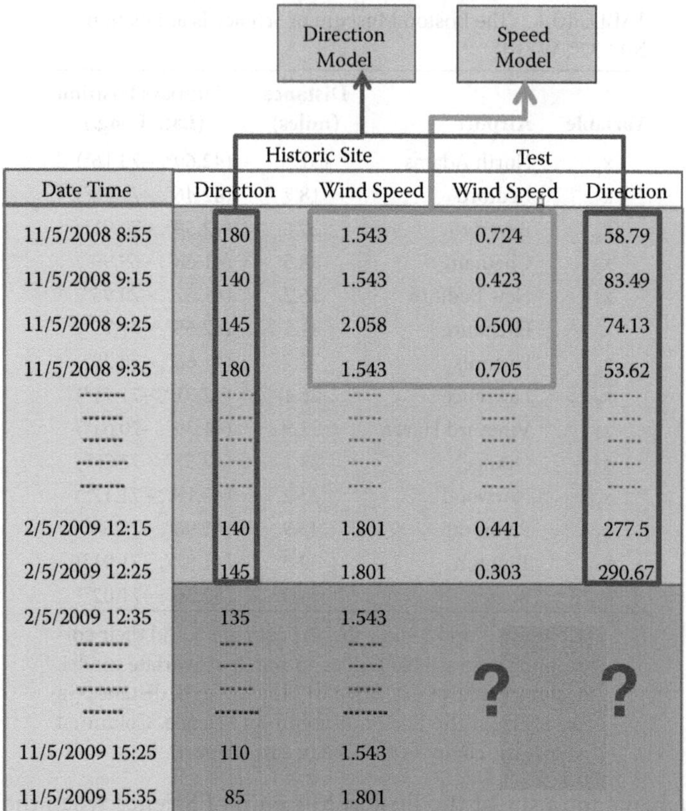

| Date Time | Historic Site | | | Test | |
	Direction	Wind Speed	Wind Speed	Direction
11/5/2008 8:55	180	1.543	0.724	58.79
11/5/2008 9:15	140	1.543	0.423	83.49
11/5/2008 9:25	145	2.058	0.500	74.13
11/5/2008 9:35	180	1.543	0.705	53.62
....	....	....	....	....
2/5/2009 12:15	140	1.801	0.441	277.5
2/5/2009 12:25	145	1.801	0.303	290.67
2/5/2009 12:35	135	1.543	?	?
....	....	....		
11/5/2009 15:25	110	1.543		
11/5/2009 15:35	85	1.801		

FIGURE 10.2 MCP generates a model correlating site wind directions to those simultaneously at historical sites. For a directional bin, it generates a model correlating simultaneous speeds.

other sites (for whom the long term wind resource is available) as x, and we index these other sites with $M = 1...m$.

The three steps of MCP are:

1. **Measure:** Short-term sensing measurements on the site are collected. This is denoted by $Y = \{y_{tk} \ldots y_{tn}\}$. Measurements can be collected using anemometers on the site, a newly constructed meteorological tower, or even remote sensing technologies such as sonar or lidar. Different measurement techniques incur different costs that dictate their feasibility for different projects. Measurements from nearby sites for the same period are gathered. These sites, called *historical sites*, have additional data for the past 10 to 20 years. These are denoted by $X = \{x_{t_k...t_n}^{1...m}\}$, where each $x_{t_k...t_n}^i$ corresponds to data from

one historical site, k and n are time indices and m denotes the total number of historical sites. Historical data that are not simultaneous in time to the site observations used in modeling will be used in the **Predict** step.

2. **Correlate:** A single directional model is first built correlating the wind directions observed at the site with simultaneous historical site wind directions. Next, for each directional interval, called a (directional) bin, of a 360° radius, a model is built correlating the wind speeds at the site with simultaneous speeds at the historical sites, that is, $Y_{t_i} = f_{\theta_j}(x_{t_i}^{1..m})$, where $k \le i \le n$. The data available from the site at this stage are expected to be sparse and noisy.

3. **Predict:** To obtain an accurate estimation of long-term wind conditions at the site, we first divide the data from the historical sites (which is not simultaneous in time to the site observations used in modeling) into subsets that correspond to a directional bin. Prediction of the long-term site conditions follows two steps:

   a. We use the model we developed for the direction f_{θ_j} and the data from the historical sites corresponding to this direction $x_{t_1...t_k-1}^{1..m} | \theta_j$ to predict what the wind speed $Y_p = y_{t_1...t_k-1}$ at the site would be.

   b. With the predictions Y_p, from Step 3a above, we estimate parameters for a Weibull distribution. This distribution is our answer to the wind resource assessment problem. We generate a distribution for each directional bin. A few example distributions for different bins are shown in Figure 10.1 (left). Alternatively, these distributions can be summarized via a wind rose also shown in Figure 10.1 (right).

The goal is to generate a predicted long-term wind speed distribution in each direction that will be as close as possible to the real (as yet unexperienced) distribution. The result from MCP—the statistical distribution in each bin—is then used to estimate the energy that can be expected from a wind turbine, given the power curve supplied by its manufacturer. This calculation can be extended over an entire farm if wake interactions among the turbines are taken into account. See Wagner et al. [7] for more details.

Note that distribution not only captures the mean, but also the variance in this speed. This is critical for assessment of long-term wind resource and the long-term energy estimate.

A variety of methods are developed by Rogers et al. [8] to evaluate the accuracy of the predicted wind speed distribution. One method measures the accuracy in terms of ratios between true and actual parameters of the Weibull distribution: that is, true shape versus estimated shape and true scale versus estimated scale. To completely capture any possible inaccuracy in the predicted distribution, we measure a symmetric Kullback-Leibler (KL) distance. It is important to note that this measure is different from the mean-squared error or mean-absolute error, which measure the accuracy in terms of difference between each predicted value and the true observation. Methods that minimize these errors would not necessarily accurately express how close the approximation is to the true distribution.

We now proceed to describe the set of statistical approaches we introduce for deployment within the MCP framework.

10.3 METHODOLOGY FOR WIND SPEED ESTIMATION

Notationally, we refer to a training point as $l \in \{1...L\}$ and a point for which we have to make a prediction as $k \in \{1...K\}$. We drop the notation for time after having time-synchronized all the measurements across locations. We also drop the subscript for directional bin. From this point onward, when we refer to a model, it is the model for a particular bin j. Then, $f_Z(z)$ refers to a probability density function of the variable (or set of variables) z. $F_Z(z)$ refers to a cumulative distribution function for the variable z such that

$$F_Z(z = \alpha) = \int_{-\inf}^{\alpha} f_Z(z)$$

for a continuous density function.

Our methodology for MCP has four steps:

Step 1: To start, we build a multivariate distribution with the probability density function $f_{X,Y}(x,y)$, where $x = \{x_1...x_m\}$ are the wind speeds at the historical sites and y is the wind speed at the site. To do this, we employ likelihood parameter estimation. The model building process is similar for all the bins, and only the data need to be changed.

Step 2: Given the joint distribution from Step 1, we predict the probability density of y that corresponds to a given test sample $x_k = \{x_{1_k}...x_{m_k}\}$ by estimating the conditional density $f_Y(y|x_k)$. The conditional can be estimated by

$$f_{Y|X=x_k}(y|x_k) = \frac{f_{X,Y}(x_k,y)}{\int_y f_{X,Y}(x_k,y)dy} \qquad (10.1)$$

Step 3: We now can make a point prediction of $\hat{y}_k$ by finding the value for y that maximizes the conditional:

$$\hat{y} = \underset{y \in Y}{\arg\max}\, f(y|X=x_k) \qquad (10.2)$$

Step 4: All the predictions for $\hat{y}_{1...K}$ are estimated to a Weibull density function, which gives an estimate of the long-term wind resource at the test site.

The methodology implies two design decisions:

1. *Choosing a model*: A key decision is which density function should be used to model the univariate densities $f_{Xi}(x_i)$ and the choice of the joint density function. A simple and straightforward choice is univariate and multivariate Gaussians. This is because Gaussian density functions have closed-form analytic equations for estimation of parameters and evaluating conditionals that are readily computed. Unfortunately, in many cases, this choice could lead to inaccuracies. Individual variables may not fit a Gaussian density function without significant error—for example, when they have significant tail properties or bimodal distribution. A joint Gaussian density function only captures the linear correlation between the variables. If we choose non-Gaussian univariate densities for x_i, then we must employ *copulas* to construct a multivariate joint density function.

2. *Assumptions regarding variable dependency structure*: Parametric estimation of a joint density function is expensive to compute and requires a large amount of data. Inference from the joint is also expensive. Assuming conditional independency among some variables offers efficiency in all three respects because it allows the density function to be factored. As an example, Figure 10.3 shows two different possible dependency structures for the variables and the

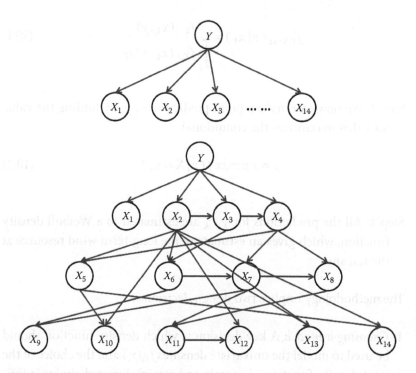

FIGURE 10.3 Top: Naive Bayes structure. This structure is assumed and no learning is required. $x_1...x_{14}$ represents the 14 variables from the airports and y represents the variable at the test site in Boston. Bottom: Structure is learned using the K2 algorithm. A maximum of two parents is specified. x_2 emerges as a parent for most of the nodes.

output variable y. Above is the simplest structure, which assumes independence among the input variables given the output variable. Below shows a possible structure that could be learnt from the data.

In wind resource assessment, a primary advantage of learning the dependency structure is the reduction in prediction time despite incorporating more airports into a model while not requiring more site data. Herein, we will evaluate whether the structure should be learned from the data or predefined.

Each of our statistical techniques for wind resource assessment follows these steps. Each is distinctive in terms of Step 1 and how it estimates the joint multivariate density function. We now proceed to describe each of them.

10.3.1 Multivariate Normal Model

Here, a multivariate normal model $N(\mu,\Sigma)$ is assumed for the joint density $f_{X,Y}(\mathbf{x},y)$ given by

$$f_Z(\mathbf{z}) = (2\pi)^{-(m+1)/2} \det(\Sigma)^{-1/2} \exp\left(-\frac{1}{2}(\mathbf{z}-\boldsymbol{\mu})^\mathsf{T}\Sigma^{-1}(\mathbf{z}-\boldsymbol{\mu})\right) \quad (10.3)$$

where $z = \{\mathbf{x},y\}$ and *det* represents determinant of a matrix. The multivariate Gaussian density function has two parameters $\{\boldsymbol{\mu},\Sigma\}$. We estimate these parameters by maximizing the likelihood function given a set of L *i.i.d* observations. The greatest advantage of this model is the ease with which the model can be built as the maximum likelihood estimates (MLEs) simply are given by closed-form analytic forms. The MLE for the mean vector $\boldsymbol{\mu}$ for the variates $\mathbf{z}$ is simply the sample mean. The MLE of the covariance matrix Σ is given by

$$\hat{\Sigma} = \frac{1}{n}\sum_{i=1}^{n}(\mathbf{z}_i - \bar{\mathbf{z}})(\mathbf{z}_i - \bar{\mathbf{z}})^\mathsf{T} \quad (10.4)$$

Once we estimate the parameters for the joint density given the training data, using closed-form expressions, we use the joint density function to derive the conditional density for y given $\mathbf{x}_k$ samples in the testing data. This density is also Gaussian and has a mean $\mu_{y|\mathbf{x}_k}$ and variance $\sigma_{y|\mathbf{x}_k}$. The value $\mu_{y|\mathbf{x}k}$ is used as the point prediction for $\widehat{y_k}$ for the given $\mathbf{x}_k$. The variance $\sigma_{y|\mathbf{x}_k}$ provides the uncertainty around the prediction. If $\sigma_{y|\mathbf{x}_k}$ is high, the uncertainty is high.

10.3.2 Nonparametric Multivariate Model

Our second model is adapted from Chan et al. [9], in which the authors employ a multivariate kernel density estimator. A Gaussian kernel is chosen and the density is estimated using all the data $\mathbf{x}_{1...L}$. The multivariate kernel density function is given by

$$f_{X,Y}(\mathbf{x},y) = \sum_{l=1}^{L}\prod_{j=1}^{m}K(x_j - x_{j,l})K(y - y_l) \quad (10.5)$$

For a test point $\mathbf{x_k}$, for which we do not know the output, a prediction is made by finding the expected value of the conditional density function $f_Y(y|\mathbf{x_k})$ given by

$$E(Y\,|\,\mathbf{X}=\mathbf{x_k})=\int_y y.f_Y(y\,|\,\mathbf{x_k})dy \tag{10.6}$$

$$=\int_y y.\frac{\dfrac{1}{L}\sum_{i=1}^{L}\prod_{j=1}^{m}K(x_{j,k}-x_{j,i})K(y-y_i)}{\dfrac{1}{L}\sum_{i=1}^{L}\prod_{j=1}^{m}K(x_{j,k}-x_{j,i})K(y-y_i)}dy \tag{10.7}$$

$$=\frac{\sum_{i=1}^{L}y_l.\prod_{j=1}^{m}K(x_{j,k}-x_{j,i})}{\sum_{i=1}^{L}\prod_{j=1}^{m}K(x_{j,k}-x_{j,i})} \tag{10.8}$$

In this model there are no parameters and there is no step for estimation. Although Equation (10.5) presents the density function, it is not evaluated unless we see a new testing point. For us to be able to evaluate the expected value of the wind speed at the test site, we need to store all the training points and use them in Equation (10.8) to make predictions. In Equation (10.8), given a test point $\mathbf{x_k} = \{x_{1,k}...x_{m,k}\}$, the kernel value is evaluated for difference between a training point $\mathbf{x_l}$ and this test point. This value is multiplied with the corresponding value of y_l. This is repeated for all the training points 1...L and summed. This forms the numerator. The summation, when done without the multiplication of y_l, forms the denominator in Equation (10.8). This approach has a few drawbacks. The designer must choose the kernel. Then the parameters for the kernel should be tuned via further splitting of the training data. It also requires retaining all the training data in order to make predictions. The evaluation of the kernel is done for L times for each test point.

10.3.3 Graphical Model with Naive Structure

This technique uses a multivariate Gaussian model assuming independent, variable dependency structure. We model the joint density function as a Bayesian network with independent variables $x_{i...m}$, that is,

$$f_{\mathbf{X},Y}(\mathbf{x}, y) = \prod_{i=1}^{m} f_{X_i}(x_i \mid y) f_Y(y) \tag{10.9}$$

A Bayesian network $\mathcal{B} = \langle \mathcal{G}, \theta \rangle$ is a probabilistic graphical model that represents a joint probability distribution over a set of random variables $X_1, \ldots, X_n$. The Bayesian network representation has two components. A directed acyclic graph (DAG) $\mathcal{G}$ encodes independence relations between variables. Each variable is a node in this graph. A set of local probability models θ defines the conditional probability distribution of each node given its parents in the graph. Let Pa $_X$ denote the parents of node X in $\mathcal{G}$. Then the network $\mathcal{B}$ encodes the following probability distribution:

$$P(X_1, \ldots, X_n) = \prod_{i=1}^{n} P(X_i \mid \mathrm{Pa}_{X_i})$$

In comparison, the multivariate model previously introduced assumes the same naive Bayes structure but uses kernel density estimators for each individual variable.

Estimation: Given this structure, also shown in Figure 10.3, we estimate the parameters at each node in Figure 10.3 (left) for the bivariate Gaussian density function $f_{X_i,Y}(x_i, y)$. We use maximum likelihood estimation and employ similar analytical expressions employed in Section 10.3.1 but this time for each pair x_i, y individually. Parameters for $f_Y(y)$ are estimated directly using the training data for y.

Prediction: For a test point $\mathbf{x_k}$, we derive the following conditional:

$$f_{Y \mid \mathbf{X} = \mathbf{x_k}}(y \mid \mathbf{x_k}) = \frac{\prod_{i=1}^{m} f_{X_i}(x_i \mid y) f_Y(y)}{\int_y \prod_{i=1}^{m} f_{X_i}(x_i \mid y) f_Y(y) dy} \tag{10.10}$$

If we were to minimize the mean squared error, the optimal prediction is the mean of the conditional density function above. If we were to minimize the mean absolute error, the optimal prediction is the median of the conditional density function [10]. Because we assume a Gaussian model for the joint density function, this also results in a Gaussian model for the conditional; the mean and median for $y|\mathbf{x}_k$ are the same. This is also the value that maximizes the conditional. Hence, $\hat{y}_k$ is

$$\hat{y}_k = \int_y y f_{Y|\mathbf{X}=\mathbf{x}_k}(y|\mathbf{x}_k)dy \tag{10.11}$$

10.3.4 Graphical Model with Structure Learning

In the model of Section 10.3.3, we assume a naive structure. By contrast, in this technique we learn the variable dependency structure (i.e., Bayesian network) given the site data. Many structure learning algorithms are available in literature and can be readily employed [11–13].

Estimation: Our estimation has two steps. First, we learn the network structure $\mathcal{G}$ and then estimate parameters for the conditional probability distribution at each node in $\mathcal{G}$. In our experiments, we employ a heuristic called K2 [13]. The algorithm takes the order of the variables and attempts to learn a dependence structure [11]. We then estimate the parameters at each node for the conditional joint density via likelihood parameter estimation.

Prediction: Given a new test point, multiple inference techniques are available to predict the value of $y_k|\mathbf{x}_k$ [11].

We refer the reader to Koller and Friedman [11] for a thorough introduction to Bayesian networks and a well-known, publicly available MATLAB-based tool for $K2$, likelihood parameter estimation, and inference [14].

10.3.5 Multivariate Copulas

Our previous modeling techniques assume a Gaussian distribution for all variables and a Gaussian joint for the multivariate. It is arguable, however, that Gaussian distributions do not accurately represent the wind speed distributions. In fact, conventionally, a univariate Weibull distribution [15] is used to parametrically describe wind sensor measurements. A Weibull distribution is likely also chosen for its flexibility because it can express any one of multiple distributions, including Rayleigh or Gaussian.

To the best of our knowledge, however, joint density functions for non-Gaussian distributions have not been estimated for wind resource assessment. In this chapter, to build a multivariate model from marginal distributions that are not all Gaussian, we exploit *copula* functions. A *copula* framework provides a means of modeling a multivariate joint distribution from training data. It is then possible to proceed with inference from the copula function.

Because copula estimation is less well known, we now briefly review copula theory. We will then describe how we construct the individual parametric distributions that are components of a copula, and then how we couple them to form a multivariate density function. Finally, we present our approach to predict the value of y given $x_{1...m}$.

A copula function $C(u_1,...u_{m+1};\theta)$ with parameter θ represents a joint distribution function for multiple *uniform* random variables $U_1...U_{m+1}$ such that

$$C(u_1,...u_{m+1};\theta) = F(U_1 \leq u_1,...U_{m+1} \leq u_{m+1}) \qquad (10.12)$$

Let $U_1...U_m$ represent the cumulative distribution functions (CDFs) for variables $x_1,...x_m$ and U_{m+1} represent the CDF for y. Hence, the *copula* represents the joint distribution function of $C(F(x_1)...F(x_m),F(y))$, where $U_i = F(x_i)$. According to Sklar's theorem, any *copula* function taking marginal distributions $F(x_i)$ as its arguments defines a valid joint distribution with marginals $F(x_i)$. Thus, we are able to construct the joint distribution function for $x_1...x_m,y$ given by

$$F(x_1...x_m,y) = C\big(F(x_1)...F(x_m),F(y);\theta\big) \qquad (10.13)$$

The joint probability density function (PDF) is obtained by taking the $m + 1th$ order derivative of the Equation (10.13):

$$f(x_1...x_m,y) = \frac{\partial^{m+1}}{\partial x_1...\partial x_m \partial y} C\big(F(x_1)...F(x_m),F(y);\theta\big) \qquad (10.14)$$

$$= \Pi_{i=1}^{m} f(x_i)f(y)c(F(x_1)...F(x_m),F(y)) \qquad (10.15)$$

where $c(.,.)$ is the *copula* density. Thus, the joint density function is a weighted version of independent density functions, where the weight is derived via *copula* density. Multiple copulas exist in the literature. In this chapter we consider a multivariate Gaussian copula to form a statistical model for our variables given by

$$C_G(\Sigma) = F_G(F^{-1}(u_1)\ldots F^{-1}(u_m), F^{-1}(u_y), \Sigma) \tag{10.16}$$

where F_G is the CDF of the multivariate normal with zero mean vector and Σ as covariance, and F^{-1} is the inverse of the standard normal.

Estimation of parameters: There are two sets of parameters to estimate. The first set of parameters for the multivariate Gaussian copula is Σ. The second set, denoted by $\Psi = \{\psi, \psi_y\}$, consists of the parameters for the marginals of $\mathbf{x}, y$. Given N *i.i.d* observations of the variables $\mathbf{x}, y$, the log-likelihood function is

$$L(\mathbf{x}, y; \Sigma, \Psi) = \sum_{l=1}^{N} logf(\mathbf{x}_l, y_l \mid \Sigma, \Psi) \tag{10.17}$$

$$= \sum_{l=1}^{N} log\left\{\left(\prod_{i=1}^{m} f(x_{il}; \psi_i) f(y_l; \psi_y)\right) c\big(F(x_1)\ldots F(x_m), F(y); \Sigma\big)\right\} \tag{10.18}$$

Parameters Ψ are estimated via Iyengar [16]:

$$\hat{\Psi} = \tag{10.19}$$

$$\underset{\Psi \in \psi}{\arg\max}\left\{\sum_{l=1}^{N} log\left\{\left(\prod_{i=1}^{m} f(x_{il}; \psi_i) f(y_l; \psi_y)\right) c\big(F(x_1)\ldots F(x_m), F(y); \Sigma\big)\right\}\right\}$$

A variety of algorithms are available in the literature to estimate the MLE in Equation (10.19). We refer users to Iyengar [16] for a thorough discussion of estimation methods. For more details about the *copula* theory, readers are referred to Nelsen [17].

Predictions from a copula: For a new observation $\mathbf{x}$, we have to predict y. For this, we form the conditional first by

$$P(y \mid \mathbf{x}) = \frac{P(\mathbf{x}, y)}{\int_y P(\mathbf{x}, y) dy} \tag{10.20}$$

Our predicted $\hat{y}$ maximizes this conditional probability:

$$\hat{y} = \arg\max_{y \in Y} P(y \mid \mathbf{x}) \tag{10.21}$$

Note that the term in the denominator of Equation (10.20) remains constant; hence, for the purposes of finding the optimum, we can ignore its evaluation. We simply evaluate this conditional for the entire range of Y in discrete steps and pick the value of $y \in Y$ that maximizes the conditional.

10.4 EVALUATION SETUP

To evaluate and compare our different algorithms, we acquired a variety of wind data from the state of Massachusetts. We downloaded the data from the ASOS (Automated Surface Observing System) airport database, which is public and has wind data from 14 airports in Massachusetts collected over the past 10 to 20 years. These data are frequently used by the wind industry. The airports' locations are shown in Figure 10.4. We then acquired data from an anemometer positioned on the rooftop of Boston's Museum of Science where a wind vane is also installed. These anemometers are inexpensive and, consequently, noisy. The museum is located among buildings, a river, and is close to a harbor as shown in Figure 10.5. This provides us with a site that is topographically challenging. At this location

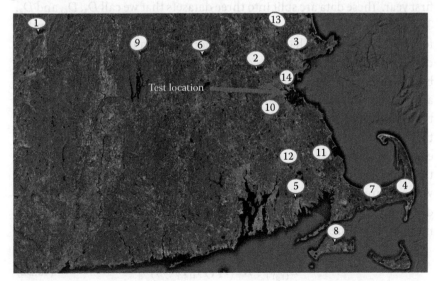

FIGURE 10.4 (*See color insert.*) Data are referenced from fourteen airport locations in the state of Massachusetts (United States). See Table 10.1.

FIGURE 10.5 *(See color insert.)* Red circles show location of anenometers on rooftop of Museum of Science, Boston, Massachusetts.

we have approximately 2 years' worth of data collected at a frequency of 1 sample/second with 10-minute averages stored in a separate database.

To derive the wind resource assessment, we train using data from the first year. These data are split into three datasets that we call D_3, D_6, and D_8. The split D_3 has data for 3 months. The split D_6 has 3 additional months, for a total of 6; and D_8 has yet 2 more months, for a total of 8. We further divide each dataset and the second year's dataset into twelve directional bins of equal size, starting at compass point north (0°). We assume that a linear regression model can be used to identify the wind direction at the Museum of Science. The second year's dataset becomes our "ground truth"—the true wind resource assessment of the site—and allows us to evaluate and compare the different techniques. We estimate a Weibull distribution model of it for this purpose. As a measure of predictive accuracy, we compare the final estimated Weibull distribution to the ground truth distribution using Kullback-Leibler divergence. The lower this value, the more accurate the prediction:

$$D_{(Y\|\hat{Y})} = KL\left(P_Y(y)\,\|\,P_{\hat{Y}}(\hat{y})\right) \qquad (10.22)$$

KL divergence derives the distance between two probability distributions:

$$D_{KL}(P_Y(y))(P_{\hat{Y}}(\hat{y})) = \sum_i P_Y(y=i)\ln\frac{P_Y(y=i)}{P_{\hat{Y}}(\hat{y}=i)} \tag{10.23}$$

For baseline comparison, we also developed a linear regression model that is used quite extensively in wind resource assessment [2, 8].

10.5 RESULTS AND DISCUSSION

In this section we present the results of comparing the described wind resource assessment techniques on data acquired from the rooftop anemometers at the Boston Museum of Science. We also examine the improvement in performance of each of the algorithms as more data are made available to each one in the forms of increasing training data from 3 to 6 to 8 months.

10.5.1 Comparison of Algorithms

First we compare algorithms when the same amount of data is available to each one of them for modeling. Results are presented in Figure 10.6 through Figure 10.8 for datasets D_3, D_6, and D_8, respectively. Each plot shows the KL distance between the ground truth distribution and the distribution estimated based on the predictions provided by each technique for the Year 2 dataset per bin. We plot the KL distance for all 12 bins.

We notice that the copula modeling technique consistently performs better than the other four techniques. The graphical model technique that assumes a naive variable dependency structure performs second best, although it demonstrates poor performance on the first bin. Its performance on this bin, however, improves as we increase the size of the dataset. One would expect the graphical model, which has a learned variable dependency structure, to outperform the one with naive structure assumptions. Here, except for the first bin, it does not. This may imply that a better structure learning algorithm is necessary, or that the one used needs further fine-tuning. The latter possibility is likely because the structure learning algorithm K2 only looks at a fraction of all possible structures when it references an order of the variables. A more robust structure learning algorithm that does not assume order could potentially yield improvements.

Linear regression is the worst performer of all, but performs well when 8 months of data are available. This is consistent with many studies in the

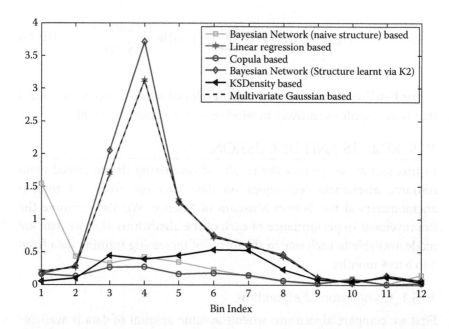

FIGURE 10.6 Comparison of different techniques when 3 months' worth of data is modeled and integrated with longer-term historical data from 14 airports. These results were derived using D_3 and are compared with KL divergence distance to the Weibull distribution estimate of the second year of measurements at the Boston Museum of Science.

wind energy area, where it has been found that for an accurate estimation of long-term distribution, 8 months worth of data is needed.

10.5.2 Increasing the Data Available for Modeling

We now examine how each technique approaches robustness when less data are made available to it for modeling. Figure 10.9 plots each technique in isolation when it is modeled using 3, 6, or 8 months of data (datasets D_3, D_6, and D_8), respectively.

We observe that not only was the copula modeling technique superior overall, but its performance did not suffer greatly with decreasing amounts of data available for modeling. The graphical model with naive variable structure overcame its weak performance, predicting the first bin as more data was made available to it. Both linear regression and the graphical model with learned variable structure improved significantly as more data were made available to them.

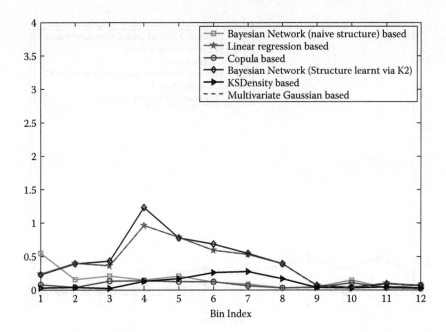

FIGURE 10.7   Comparison of different techniques when 6 months' worth of data is modeled and integrated with longer-term historical data from 14 airports. These results were derived using D_6 and are compared with KL divergence distance to the Weibull distribution estimate of the second year of measurements at the Boston Museum of Science.

10.6 CONCLUSIONS AND FUTURE WORK

In this chapter we provided a set of techniques for building a statistical model for wind resource assessment. Our goals with these techniques were to

- Estimate the wind speed density with as minimal site collected data as possible.

- Estimate as accurately as possible with minimal cost to support inexpensive site sensing.

The ability to generate accurate estimates with as minimal data as possible and with as cheap sensing as possible is critical for wind resource assessment during the initial phases of wind farm planning. For community or urban wind energy projects, anemometer sensing provides a cost-effective way to estimate wind resources.

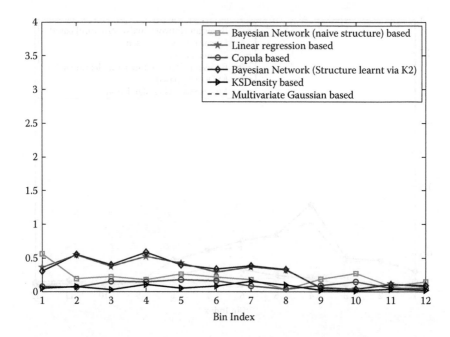

FIGURE 10.8 Comparison of different techniques when 8 months' worth of data is modeled and integrated with longer term historical data from 14 airports. These results were derived using D_8 and are compared with KL divergence distance to the Weibull distribution estimate of the second year of measurements at the Boston Museum of Science.

By definition, the techniques are different in terms of whether or not they are parametric, and whether or not they incorporate all variables into the joint distribution. This seems to have an effect on the accuracy of the model in wind resource assessment. The copula modeling is more accurate than all other techniques.

We further analyzed the performance of the techniques when different amounts of data are made available to the modeling step. The technique based on Copula theory performs well even when only minimal data (3 months) are available. Another, much simpler technique based on graphical models produces competent results as well.

Throughout this chapter we emphasize the need for exploration of a variety of statistical modeling techniques. A variety of additional advances can be made for each of the techniques presented in this chapter. These include but are not limited to the following:

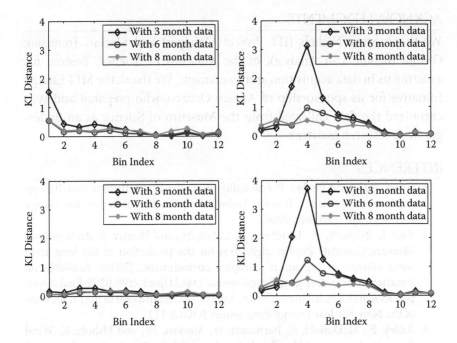

FIGURE 10.9 Top (left): Estimation accuracy using graphical models with naive structure. Top (right): Estimation accuracy using linear regressions. Bottom (left): Estimation accuracy using copulas. Bottom (right): Estimation using Bayesian networks where structure is learned.

- *Copula-based functions:* One can estimate the marginals using non-parametric kernel density functions to prepare input to a *copula*. One can also explore systematically which *copula* is better; however, the extent to which tail behavior needs to be accurately modeled is open to debate. A variety of *copulas* are documented in the statistics literature, thus opening up opportunities for further study.

- *Bayesian network functions:* A more advanced structure learning algorithm can be used to estimate the Bayesian network structure. Different parameter estimation techniques can be explored.

- *Copula Bayesian networks:* The network structure can be sought while forming the conditional at each node via a copula-based multivariate density function. This concept has been recently explored for classification problems in machine learning [18]

ACKNOWLEDGMENTS

We thank Steve Nichols (IIT Project Manager) and Marian Tomusiak (Wind Turbine Lab Analyst), of the Museum of Science, Boston, for assisting us in data acquisition and assessment. We thank the MIT Energy Initiative for its sponsorship of Adrian Orozco, who prepared and synchronized the data collected from the Museum of Science as an undergraduate research assistant.

REFERENCES

1. Gross, R.C., and Phelan, P. Feasibility Study for Wind Turbine Installations at Museum of Science, Boston. Technical report, Boreal Renewable Energy Development (October, 2006).
2. Bass, J., Rebbeck, M., Landberg, L., Cabré, M., and Hunter, A. An improved Measure-Correlate-Predict algorithm for the prediction of the long term wind climate in regions of complex environment. (2000). Available on Internet at www.res-group.com/media/234621/jor3-ct98-0295-finalreport.pdf. Research funded in part by The European Commission in the Framework of the Non-Nuclear Energy Programme JOULE 111.
3. Bailey, B., McDonald, S., Bernadett, D., Markus, M., and Elsholz, K. Wind Resource Assessment Handbook: Fundamentals for Conducting a Successful Monitoring Program. Technical report, National Renewable Energy Lab, Golden, CO; AWS Scientific, Inc., Albany, NY, (1997).
4. Lackner, M., Rogers, A., and Manwell, J. The round robin site assessment method: A new approach to wind energy site assessment. *Renewable Energy,* 33(9), 2019–2026, 2008.
5. Encraft: Warwick Wind Trials Final Report. Technical report, p. 28, Encraft (2009). Available at www.warwickwindtrials.org.uk/resources/Warwick+Wind+Trials+Final+Reports.pdf.
6. Shaw, S. Progress Report on Small Wind Energy Development Projects Receiving Funds from the Massachusetts Technology Collaborative (MTC). Cadmus Group Inc., Waltham, MA, USA. (2008).
7. Wagner, M., Veeramachaneni, K., Neumann, F., and O'Reilly, U. Optimizing the layout of 1000 wind turbines. In *Scientific Proceedings of European Wind Energy Association Conference (EWEA 2011)* (2011).
8. Rogers, A., Rogers, J., and Manwell, J. Comparison of the performance of four measure-correlate-predict algorithms. *Journal of Wind Engineering and Industrial Aerodynamics,* 93(3), 243–264, 2005.
9. Chan, C., Stalker, J., Edelman, A., and Connors, S. Leveraging high performance computation for statistical wind prediction. In *Proceedings of WINDPOWER 2010* (2010).
10. Frank, E., Trigg, L., Holmes, G., and Witten, I. Technical note: Naive Bayes for regression. *Machine Learning,* 41(1), 5–25, 2000.
11. Koller, D. and Friedman, N. *Probabilistic Graphical Models: Principles and Techniques.* The MIT Press, Cambridge, MA (2009).

12. Heckerman, D., Geiger, D., and Chickering, D. Learning Bayesian networks: The combination of knowledge and statistical data. *Machine Learning,* 20(3), 197–243, 1995.

13. Cooper, G.F. and Herskovits, E. A Bayesian method for the induction of probabilistic networks from data. *Machine Learning,* 9(4), 309–347, 1992.

14. Murphy, K. et al. The Bayes net toolbox for MATLAB. *Computing Science and Statistics,* 33(2), 1024–1034, 2001.

15. Burton, T., Sharpe, D., Jenkins, N., and Bossanyi, E. Wind Energy: Handbook. Wiley Online Library (2001).

16. Iyengar, S. Decision-Making with Heterogeneous Sensors—A Copula Based Approach. Ph.D. dissertation (2011). Syracuse University, Syracuse, NY, USA.

17. Nelsen, R. *An Introduction to Copulas.* Springer Verlag, Berlin and New York (2006).

18. Elidan, G. Copula Bayesian networks. Ed. J. Lafferty, C.K.I. Williams, J. Shawe-Taylor, R.S. Zemel and A. Culotta. *Advances in Neural Information Processing Systems,* 24, 559–567, 2010.

19. Eaton, M., Euclid, P., Library, C.U., and Press, D.U. *Multivariate Statistics: A Vector Space Approach.* Wiley, New York (1983).

APPENDIX 10A

Below we describe how to derive the conditional density function parameters for y given $\mathbf{x}_k$ under the assumption that the joint is modeled as a normal. We first partition the mean and the covariance matrix for the joint distribution of $\mathbf{z}$ as follows:

$$\boldsymbol{\mu} = \begin{bmatrix} \boldsymbol{\mu}_y \\ \boldsymbol{\mu}_x \end{bmatrix} \tag{10A.1}$$

with sizes

$$\begin{bmatrix} 1 \times 1 \\ m \times 1 \end{bmatrix} \tag{10A.2}$$

$$\Sigma = \begin{bmatrix} \Sigma_{yy} & \Sigma_{yx} \\ \Sigma_{xy} & \Sigma_{xx} \end{bmatrix} \tag{10A.3}$$

with sizes

$$\begin{bmatrix} 1 \times 1 & 1 \times m \\ m \times 1 & m \times m \end{bmatrix} \tag{10A.4}$$

Then, the distribution of y conditional on $\mathbf{x} = \mathbf{x_k}$ is multivariate normal with [19]

$$\overline{\boldsymbol{\mu}_{y|\mathbf{x_k}}} = \boldsymbol{\mu}_y + \Sigma_{yx}\Sigma_{xx}^{-1}(\mathbf{x_k} - \boldsymbol{\mu_x}) \tag{10A.5}$$

and covariance matrix

$$\overline{\sigma_{y|\mathbf{x_k}}} = \Sigma_{yy} - \Sigma_{yx}\Sigma_{xx}^{-1}\Sigma_{xy} \tag{10A.6}$$

V

Computational Intelligent Data Analysis for Sociopolitical Sustainability

V

CHAPTER 11

Spatio-Temporal Correlations in Criminal Offense Records

Jameson L. Toole, Nathan Eagle, and Joshua B. Plotkin

CONTENTS

11.1 INTRODUCTION

AN ENORMOUS AMOUNT OF behavioral data is now being generated and stored by billions of individuals across countries and cultures. The ubiquity of mobile sensors from laptops to cellular phones has ushered in a new age of digital data storage and management. It is now possible to measure social systems on a massive scale. Mobility patterns of city dwellers can be inferred from mobile phone use [4], epidemics can be modeled across distances of many orders of magnitude [20], and the diffusion of information can be measured for large populations [10]. Armed with this flood of data, there are very real and important opportunities to study and ultimately facilitate sustainability in human-built systems. Insight into these systems can help inform the social sciences from economics to sociology as well as provide policy makers with critical answers that may be used to better allocate scarce resources or implement beneficial social programs.

In order to generate these new and hopefully better solutions, however, it has become necessary to use broader combinations of tools to analyze the immense and rich stream of information. The goal is to use this data to gain a better understanding of the systems that generate it. In this chapter we present a novel application of tools and analytical techniques developed from a variety of disciplines that identify patterns and signals that capture fundamental dynamics of a social system. To explore relationships in both space and time, cross- and auto-correlation measures are combined with autoregressive models and results from random matrix theory to analyze patterns in behavioral data. Similar techniques have been applied recently to partition space based on patterns observed in mobile phone data or Wi-Fi activity [2, 14]. We show that these techniques can also be applied to criminal activity.

The dataset used for this study consists of criminal events within the city of Philadelphia from the year 1991 through 1999. It contains nearly 1 million individual criminal offense reports detailing the time, place, and police response to theft, robbery, and burglary-related crimes. In addition to these minor offenses, for the year 1999, the dataset includes major offenses as well, covering crimes from petty theft through homicide. With these reported crimes, we examine spatial, temporal, and incident information. The goal of our analysis is to explore the spatio-temporal dynamics of criminal events with the hope of identifying patterns that may be useful in predicting and preventing future criminal activity. Beyond applications to criminology, however, we feel that these techniques can be applied to a wide range of systems that exhibit complex correlations in many dimensions and on multiple scales.

Early work in criminology, sociology, psychology, and economics explored relationships between criminal activity and socioeconomic variables such as education, community disorder, ethnicity, etc. [8, 21]. Constraints on the availability of data limited these studies to aggregate statistics for large populations and vast geographic regions. Wilson and

Kelling's article in the March 1982 edition of *The Atlantic* popularized "Broken windows" and "social disorganization" theories that, for the first time, explicitly introduced flow and system dynamics into crime research. These theories proposed that crime was a consequence of urban decay and lack of community ownership in neighborhoods and that these processes worked on a local level [7]. Neglected areas not only attract criminals (the neglect is a sign of low police presence), but also act as a feed-forward mechanism by damaging community morale. Recent experimental work provides more evidence of such dynamics at work in neighborhoods [6].

Following the introduction of more local theories, attempts have been made to study crime on the neighborhood level and explore crime "hotspots" [15]. More recently, analytic and numerical models of crime hotspots have been proposed. These apply nonlinear dynamics systems approaches such as reaction-diffusion equations that give rise to behavioral regimes resembling hotspots. Suppression terms (corresponding to police interventions) are then introduced, and the stability of hotspot dynamics is assessed. Interestingly, in some cases, police suppression is able to effectively tame a hotspot without inducing crime in other regions, while under other conditions, new hotspots simply pop up elsewhere [17]. Other attempts to explain the existence and persistence of hotspots has focused on the combination of propensity and ability to commit crime. Based on socioeconomic characteristics, researchers have looked at the temporal and mobility budget constraints faced by potential criminals. This work shows significant correlations between access and exposure to the potential to commit crimes and actually doing so [22].

In this chapter we address a gap. Statistical methods have been used to characterize large, aggregate datasets over long periods of time, while sociological studies have been performed at micro scales. There remains a need for high-resolution quantitative analysis of large crime datasets. Using offense reports generated by a police department, we explore how crime here and now affects crime there and then, while also focusing on building a general set of tools to analyze behavioral datasets for spatio-temporal systems. More generally, we hope this multidisciplinary approach utilizing massive digital datasets provides inspiration for future work looking to create and optimize sustainable social systems.

11.2 DATA

The dataset is analyzed in two parts. The first contains nearly 1 million theft-related crimes from the year 1991 through 1999, while the second consists

TABLE 11.1   A Typical Offense Report

Attribute	Data (%)
Offense number	0000010
Date and time	Saturday, September 12, 1996, 1 p.m.
Address	1700 McKean
Latitude	39.926152
Longitude	−75.17267917
Description of crime	Theft of car contents, valued at more than $200.
Place of event	Automobile
Police district	District 11, Sector B
Outcome	The reported crime was confirmed. The case was closed without investigation or was not solvable.

of almost all 200,000 reported crimes within the city of Philadelphia during 1999 across all types, from petty theft to homicide. In total, crimes were reported at 42,000 unique locations across the city and were time stamped with the hour they occurred. In addition to time and place, a detailed description of the crime (e.g., theft under $200, aggravated assault with a handgun, etc.) is provided. Table 11.1 shows an example of one such report (note that these data have been generated randomly for anonymity purposes and are not actual reports). With this data, the primary goal of this research is to better understand the spatio-temporal structure of criminal events.

The spatial resolution of this data is high enough that a block/neighborhood analysis of crime is possible. Plotting the geocoded events reveals features of the city such as the street-grid, parks, bridges, rivers, etc. (Figure 11.1). While the time of each report is known to within the hour, offenses within a geographic area are generally aggregated to daily, weekly, or monthly counts, ensuring that time series are sufficiently populated. A time series displaying citywide theft-related crimes for different levels of aggregation and time windows reveals features on multiple scales. Seasonal trends, such as increases in crime during hot summer months as well as singular events such as holidays, are visible (Figure 11.2). Finally, when applicable, offense reports are aggregated by type (Figure 11.3) so relationships between crimes can be tested. Although data on crime other than theft are only available for 1999, the 200,000 crimes reported that year still represent a very rich and detailed dataset with which we can examine interactions between different types of crime.

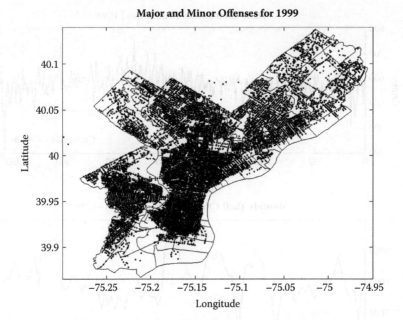

Major and Minor Offenses for 1999

FIGURE 11.1   All crimes, major and minor, are plotted on an overlay of census tracts in Philadelphia county during the year 1999. Geographic features of the city such as rivers, parks, bridges, etc., are immediately visible.

11.2.1 Conditioning the Data

Behavioral information must be transformed into variables that can be manipulated numerically. While time and place readily lend themselves to such analysis, the type of crime being reported must be inferred from its police description. While the first part of the dataset contains theft-related crimes only, for richer 1999 data, crimes are aggregated into six broader categories by parsing police descriptions for keywords as described in Table 11.2. Aggregation ensures that there are sufficient numbers of events to populate time series, while still making use of nearly 75% of the data available in that year.

We measure crime densities with two different methods of spatial aggregation. In the first, a lattice is laid over a map of the city, and crimes are aggregated to the nearest grid point. In general, any mesh size can be used, but our analysis suggests that a grid producing 50 to 100 locations across the city provides good noise reduction without obscuring patterns.

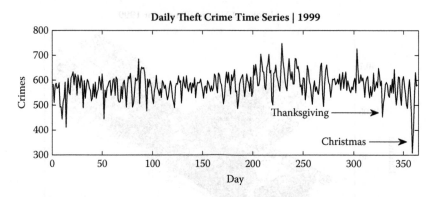

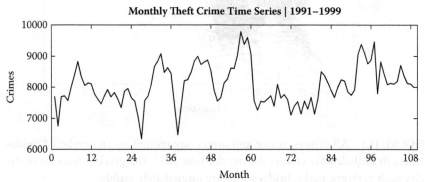

FIGURE 11.2 A time series plot of citywide theft-related crimes at different time scales. The top figure shows daily theft crimes for the year 1999 where individual events such as holidays are visible. The bottom figure aggregates further into monthly counts, revealing seasonal trends such as increases in thefts during the hot summer months.

The flexible mesh grid allows us to use larger spatial bins for rarer crime types, such as those that are drug related. The second spatial aggregation used were the 381 census tracts from the 2000 U.S. Census for the City of Philadelphia. Census tracts have the nice feature of scaling inversely with population density; thus, areas of the city with small numbers of people (and similarly small amounts of crime) will not be washed out by much higher crime counts in the more dense city center. In addition to convenient scaling properties, the use of census tracts also allows us to incorporate various socioeconomic and demographic data that might be related to crime. Finally, census tracts provide an immediately recognizable unit of analysis for policy makers.

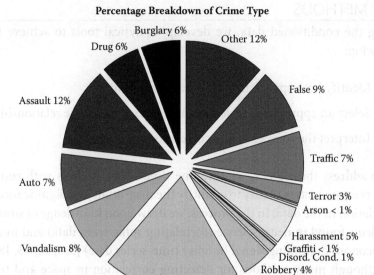

Percentage Breakdown of Crime Type

FIGURE 11.3 A percentage breakdown of different crimes based on incident reports.

TABLE 11.2 Categorical Groupings of Different Crime Types for the 1999 Data

Category	Offenses Included	Crimes (%)
All	All reported offenses	211,606 (100%)
Automobile	Auto theft, major traffic	16,005 (7.6%)
Theft	Burglary, robbery, auto	80,290 (38%)
Violent	Assault, homicide, gun	29,908 (14%)
Vandalism	Vandalism, graffiti	17,880 (8.5%)
Drug	Possession, sale, DUI	11,642 (5.5%)

For each spatial unit, be it on a grid or census tract, a time series is constructed for each category of crime for which data are available. With nearly 10 years of data available, time scales from hours to years are examined. These time series are normalized to have zero mean and unit variance to make use of various statistical tests and to capture changes in crime rates rather than the absolute number of incidents. Overall, the time series produced are mostly stable and stationary, having roughly constant mean and variance. Those that have obvious serial correlations are removed from analysis.

11.3 METHODS

Using the conditioned data, we develop analytical tools to achieve the following:

1. Identify both spatial and temporal relationships.

2. Select an appropriate scale on which to examine these relationships.

3. Interpret the sources of any correlation structure.

To address these goals, we combine time-series analysis with results from random matrix theory to quantify the magnitude and significance of correlation in the data. In the process, we draw upon knowledge of similar problems found in neuroscience (correlating spike-train data) and financial economics (finding signal in noisy time-series data) [5, 9, 12, 13, 18].

Although many methods for detecting correlation in space and time exist, the nature of criminal acts and the type of data being used lent itself to the particular tools used in this chapter. For example, while we are looking for correlations in space, it is important that techniques are able to detect nonlocal correlations, wherein two neighborhoods, on opposite sides of the city, have similar crime profiles because of socioeconomic reasons. With this in mind, we rule out models that can capture only local diffusion. Multivariate auto-regressive (MVAR) models that regress time series of a particular location onto other locations and across many lag periods can detect such a structure, but given the extremely large number of spatial locations and the length of time series, these models quickly become large and intractable [11, 23].

We also would like our analysis to speak of specific details of the correlation structure rather than just the distribution of crimes in space or time. While models concerned with speciation in heterogeneous landscapes may provide insight into properties of the distribution of phenomena or events in nonlinear environments (population density, socioeconomic factors, etc.), they have more difficulty telling stories of particular realizations of these distributions in the real geographic space of a city.

Finally, there is also the problem of noise. Our dataset, while large, is very noisy, and any tools and methods used must be able to find and separate signal with confidence. The methodology that follows has the advantage of providing both analytic and computational null models. Random matrix theory presents analytic results for the limiting distributions and statistics of covariance matrices, while artificial crime data can reliably be simulated using a Poisson process in order to achieve a computational null model. With these considerations in mind, the following algorithms and methodology were combined to satisfy our modeling and statistical requirements.

11.3.1 Basic Analysis and Statistics

We begin by using basic data analysis techniques and statistics to better understand the data. In general, crime is not distributed uniformly across the city. Instead, the spatial structure is consistent with descriptions of crime "hotspots." These hotspots are small regions within the city that regularly experience high levels of crime. Characterizing the nonuniform spatial distribution of crime is important when attempting to find relationships between types of crime. For example, Figure 11.4 shows the center of drug-related crimes occupies northwestern Philadelphia, while theft is more prevalent in downtown Philadelphia. We wish to use quantitative tools to measure interactions between these locations.

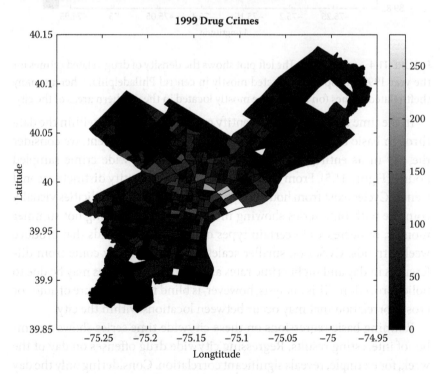

FIGURE 11.4 The left plot shows the density of drug-related crimes for the year 1999. Hotspots are located mostly in central Philadelphia, whereas many theft-related crimes (on the left) are mostly located in the southern areas of the city.

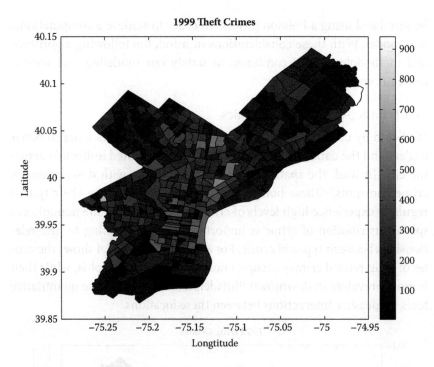

FIGURE 11.4 (continued) The left plot shows the density of drug-related crimes for the year 1999. Hotspots are located mostly in central Philadelphia, whereas many theft-related crimes (on the left) are mostly located in the southern areas of the city.

In the time domain, we can identify general periodicities within the data through basic Fourier analysis. Ignoring space for a moment, we consider the city in its entirety, creating a time series of citywide crime sampled hourly (Figure 11.5). From these methods we can quantify distinct seasonal trends. Cycles exist from hourly to yearly scales. These periodicities visually coincide with time series showing increases in crime during hot summer months, or decreases in certain types of crime on weekends that produce weekly trends. Cycles on smaller scales such as days may come from differences in day and night crime rates and hourly frequencies may be due to police procedure. This analysis, however, is blind to any measure of auto- or cross-correlation that may occur between locations within the city.

Running basic regressions on these citywide time series shows a number of interesting results. Regressing citywide drug offenses on day of the week, for example, reveals significant correlation. Considering only the day of the week, we are able to account for nearly 60% of the variance in daily drug offenses (Table 11.3). With Sunday being the omitted group, coefficients on dummy variables corresponding to Monday through Saturday

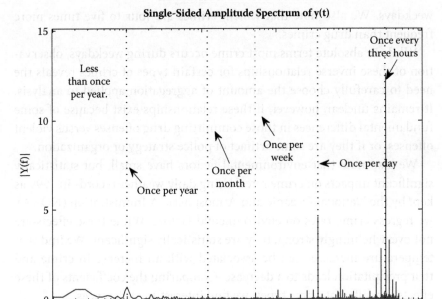

FIGURE 11.5 The frequency spectrum of the citywide theft crime time series sampled hourly from 1991 through 1999. Many periodicities appear on time scales ranging from just a few hours to years.

TABLE 11.3 Regression of Citywide Drug and Violent Offenses on Day of the Week

Day	Drugs	Violence
Sunday	16.55[a]	76.87[a]
Monday	4.61[b]	−13.20[a]
Tuesday	22.52[a]	−10.63[a]
Wednesday	23.99[a]	−10.71[a]
Thursday	21.63[a]	−11.70[a]
Friday	15.52[a]	−4.47[b]
Saturday	8.08[a]	2.57

Note: (R^2_{drug} = .59, R^2_{viol} = .30).
[a] pval < 0.001, [b] pval < 0.05, [c] pval < 0.1.

are interpreted as the change in criminal activity between Sunday and that particular day of the week. Thus, we conclude that Sundays have the lowest drug-related crime rates while the middle of the week (Tuesday, Wednesday, and Thursday) show the highest. This is in sharp contrast to violent crimes, which show an increase on weekends, dropping during weekdays. We also note that violent crimes are four to five times more frequent than drug crimes.

While in absolute terms most crime occurs during weekdays, observation of these inverse relationships for certain types of crimes reveals the need to carefully choose the amount of aggregation applied to analysis. It remains unclear, however, if these relationships exist because of some fundamental differences in those committing drug offenses versus violent offenses, or if they are some artifact of police strategy or organization.

We also note that environmental factors have small, but statistically significant impacts on crime rates. Using daily weather records in 1999 as kept by the National Oceanic and Atmospheric Administration (NOAA), we regress crime rates on environmental factors. While these effects are not overwhelmingly strong, they are statistically significant. We find that temperature increases can be associated with an increase in crime and that precipitation leads to a decrease. Comparing the coefficients of these effects for different crime types, we find interesting differences.

To compare coefficients between crimes that occur with differing frequency, we regress the log of occurrences on both temperature and precipitation. The coefficient then represents the percentage change in crime rates due to an increase of 1°F or 1 inch of precipitation, respectively. Table 11.4 shows the results of this regression. We find that drug-related crimes, which may be driven by psychological or physiological needs, are not affected by weather, while violent crimes, which are more likely to be driven by passion and environment, respond significantly to increases in temperature or precipitation.

Although these basic statistics provide insight into the types of relationships that exist within the data, they remind us that complex relationships exist on multiple scales in both space and time. We continue with more advanced methods, capable of teasing out these relationships despite noisy data.

TABLE 11.4   Impact of Environmental Factors on Crime Occurrence

	All	Auto	Drug	Theft	Vandal	Violent
Constant	6.23[a]	3.74[a]	3.30[a]	5.37[a]	3.76[a]	4.23[a]
Temperature (°F)	0.0014[a]	—	—	—	0.0018[b]	0.0026[a]
Precipitation (in)	−0.03[a]	—	−0.078[c]	−0.03[b]	−0.11[a]	−0.053[b]

[a] pval < 0.001, [b] pval < 0.05, [c] pval < 0.1, — Insignificant.

11.3.2 Auto- and Cross-Correlation

In order to perform higher-resolution analysis, we make use of the scalable lattice and census tracts as described in previous sections. Regardless of the spatial unit used, we create a time series for each point. The time series are then normalized to have zero mean and unit variance so that we may compare locations across the city regardless of the absolute number of crimes. We select two time series, y_1 and y_2, from the conditioned data and look for correlations between them.

The cross-correlation, $r_{1,2}$, is a measure of similarity between a pair of time series. Mathematically, this quantity is defined as the expectation of the inner product between the two time series:

$$r_{1,2} = E[\langle \mathbf{y}_1, \mathbf{y}_2 \rangle] = \sum_{t=1}^{n} y_1(t) y_2(t)$$

Similarly, it is possible to determine lagged correlation by shifting one series by a number of lags, m. The lagged cross-correlation, $r_{1,2}(m)$, is given by modification of the previous formula,

$$r_{1,2}(m) = \sum_{t=1}^{n} y_1(t+m) y_2(t)$$

The cross-correlation values are then normalized to lie between -1 and 1, where $r_{1,2} = 1$ corresponds to exact correlation between two time series. A cross-correlation sequence is defined as the sequence of cross-correlation values over a range of lags. Examining the cross-correlation sequence for two time series, we can identify the existence of a significant relationship as well as quantify its power over a number of lags. Not only can these measures detect the flow of crime from one area to another, but they can also quantify its speed and direction.

We must also define a plausible test for significant correlations to differentiate between real and random connections. To achieve this, we create a null model for each pair of time series. Each series is randomly permuted, preserving the mean and distribution of counts, but scrambling the order and removing any correlations in time. The new cross-correlation value is then computed. Repeating this process a large number of times, we construct a distribution of random cross-correlation values from which confidence intervals can be constructed. If the cross-correlation between the original time series deviates from the random distribution at a given confidence level, we consider it significant.

These cross-correlation methods may be used to look for relationships between crimes. We may ask if an increase in theft-related crimes leads to violent crimes in the future. For a given node, we create a time series of daily crime rates for each type of crime for the year 1999. Next, we construct the cross-correlation sequence for this pair of series across a number of lags (in most cases, lags up to 30 days were included). To visualize these correlations, we create a matrix where each column represents the cross-correlation sequence for a given location (Figure 11.6).

As an example, we have included automobile thefts in both the "Thefts" category and the "Automobile" category. Not surprisingly, we see

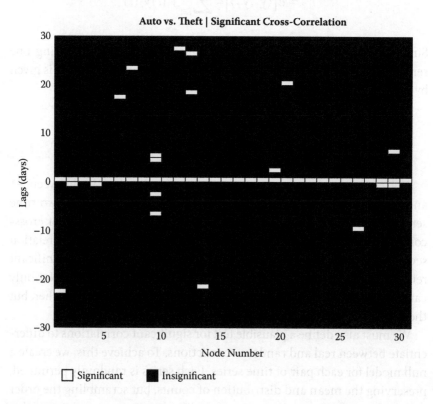

FIGURE 11.6 A matrix displaying significant lagged cross-correlations between automobile crimes and theft crimes. Because automobile crimes are counted in both categories, we find correlation at zero lag, but almost no other significant relationships.

significant correlation between the two crime types at exactly zero lag. The lack of significant correlation for other time lags indicates no other significant relationships where theft in one location leads to violence in that same location at a later time. We find very little significant correlation between the two types of crime, suggesting that, at the very least, types of crime are not related on temporal scales of less than a month.

11.3.3 Correlation Matrices

Having established a measure of correlation and corresponding null model to assess significance, we seek to couple this analysis with spatial dimensions. We would like to detect correlations not only in time, but also in space.

To do this, we form a $K \times T$ matrix, $\mathbf{Y}$, where K is the number of locations across the city and T is the length of each time series. Keeping track of which location each time series corresponds to, we can associate real city locations with correlations. The delayed correlation matrix for a specific lag m, $\mathbf{C}(m)$, is then constructed by matrix multiplication

$$\mathbf{C}(m) = \frac{1}{T}\mathbf{YY}^T(m)$$

where ^{T} is a regular matrix transposition. The elements of $\mathbf{C}$ are given by

$$C_{ij}(m) = \sum_{t=1}^{T} y_i(t)y_j(t+m)$$

Note that $m = 0$ corresponds to zero lag.

To illustrate this procedure, we test for correlations in drug-related offenses between different neighborhoods across time over the year 1999. Conditioning the data as described above, time series are constructed for 35 lattice points. These points are neighborhoods with enough crime to sufficiently populate daily time series. The zero-lag cross-correlation, measuring real-time correlation is displayed in Figure 11.7(a).

Entry C_{ij} of this matrix represents the cross-correlation between the time series of drug-related crimes from locations i and j. In examining this matrix, no strong patterns or regions of high correlation are immediately visible. It should be noted that the numbers i and j correspond to time series labels and not actual location coordinates, but the labeling

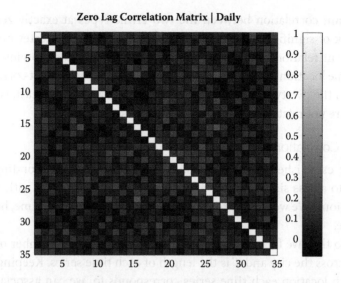

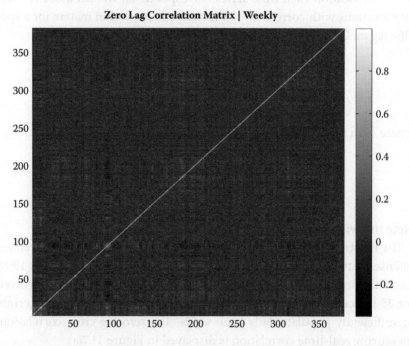

FIGURE 11.7 (a) The zero-lag correlation matrix for drug-related crimes aggregated to a spatial lattice. There appears to be little spatial correlation and a lack of high correlated locations. (b) Display of zero-lag correlation matrix showing theft-related crimes sampled weekly from 1991 through 1999, aggregated by census tracts. A stronger correlation signal is seen.

of neighborhoods is such that locations i and $i + 1$ are usually close spatially. When random permutation is again used to test significance, we find that very few of these correlations can be deemed different from random correlation.

The unstructured correlation matrix suggests that daily neighborhood crime rates may not be highly correlated spatially. This example, however, does not consider any lagged correlations that may exist between locations. Constructing matrices for lagged cross-correlation of up to 30 days (1 month), however, reveals similar results. We do not find any immediate spatial correlation structure or flows across space and time for daily drug-related crime levels.

The lack of correlation structure only shows an inability to visually identify correlation structure in daily time scales, but says nothing of correlation structure on the scale of weeks and months. Performing the same analysis using weekly theft crime rates from 1991 through 1999 (aggregated to the census tract level), Figure 11.7(b) reveals more significant correlation. When comparing lagged cross-correlation matrices over a number of lags, cycles of high correlation match yearly seasonal trends seen in a Fourier spectrum, but with added spatial resolution.

Even on short time scales, however, the data are noisy enough that identifying significant patterns may be difficult given a largely random background.

11.3.4 The Eigenvalue Spectrum and Comparison to Random Matrices

To quantify the varying degrees of correlation in the above matrices, we enlist solutions to similar problems found in fields such as financial economics (markets, stocks, equities, etc.) and climate forecasting [9, 18]. Work in these areas suggests that the correlation structure of systems can be characterized by examining the eigenvalue spectra of correlation matrices. Much success has been found in testing the significance of these metrics using results from random matrix theory (RMT).

To test for nonrandom structure in our correlation matrices, we consider two related groups of matrices: Gaussian and Wishart. Entries of a Gaussian matrix, **G**, are drawn from a standard normal, and a Wishart matrix, **W**, is formed by matrix multiplication of a Gaussian matrix and its transpose, $\mathbf{W} = \mathbf{G}\mathbf{G}^T$ [3]. The key observation is the direct analogy between formulation of the Wishart matrix and cross-correlation matrix. We use these random Wishart matrices as null models to our cross-correlation measures.

Various analytical results for the distribution of eigenvalues of a random Wishart matrix can be found by Edelman [3], Sengupta and Mitra [16], and Utsugi et al. [19]. The eigenvalue density, $\rho(\lambda)$, is defined as the fraction of eigenvalues below some value, λ. Given a random correlation matrix whose entries are drawn from the standard normal distribution, the eigenvalue density as K and T go to infinity is given by the Marcenko-Pastur law:

$$\rho(\lambda) = \frac{Q}{2\pi} \frac{\sqrt{(\lambda_{max} - \lambda)(\lambda - \lambda_{min})}}{\lambda} \tag{11.1}$$

where $Q = T/K \geq 1$ and $\lambda_{min}^{max} = 1 + 1/Q \pm 2\sqrt{1/Q}$ [9].

That is, we can establish significant correlation structure by comparing eigenvalue spectra from the data to those of a random null model. If we find eigenvalues significantly outside theoretical thresholds, we conclude there is signal buried in the noise. The eigenvectors associated with these significant eigenvalues are then interpreted as individual factors contributing to the correlation structure of the system. For example, the largest eigenvalue (and corresponding eigenvector) in the case of financial data is identified as the "market" factor, having equally weighted components. Mayya et al. have obtained similar analytical results for lagged cross-correlation matrices [12].

11.3.5 Daily Drug-Related Crime Rates in 1999

Examining the eigenvalue spectrum of our daily drug data from 1999, we find a weak signal. The spectra corresponding to the correlation matrix of drug-related crimes are shown in Figure 11.8(a). While the majority of eigenvalues cannot be distinguished from noise, there does exist a large significant eigenvalue.

Next, we examine the spectra for a series of lagged correlation matrices. Plotting the magnitude of the largest eigenvalue for each lagged correlation matrix and comparing this to the largest value expected from random data, we see a strong cyclic signal with a period of 7 days (Figure 11.8). This analysis suggests that significant correlation structure is present on a weekly cycle. We also note that this signal does not decrease in intensity over time. This suggests we are detecting some persistent periodic element that is not the result of some one-time event.

In addition to the magnitude of eigenvalues, we also examine the distribution of components within each eigenvector. Again borrowing from

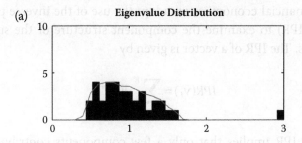

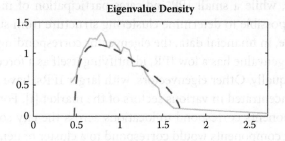

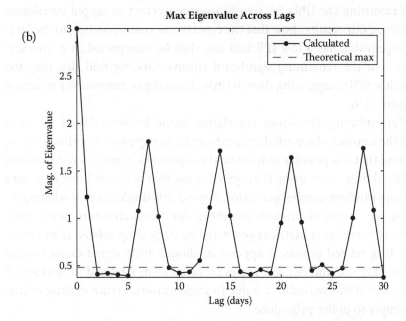

FIGURE 11.8 (a, top) Only one eigenvalue, $\lambda_1 = 3$, can be differentiated from the noise indicated by the solid line. (a, bottom) The solid curve is the eigenvalue density of the actual matrix spectra, while the dashed curve is the theoretical prediction from Equation (11.1). (b) We plot the maximum eigenvalue of the delayed correlation matrix for each of 30 lags. For drug-related crimes, we see a very clear periodicity at a frequency of 7 days (1 week).

results in financial economics, we adopt the use of the inverse participation ratio (IPR) to examine the component structure of the significant eigenvectors. The IPR of a vector is given by

$$IPR(\vec{v}_i) = \sum_{j=1}^{K} |u_{ij}|^4$$

[1]. A large IPR implies that only a few components contribute to the eigenvector, while a small IPR indicates participation of many components. It is possible to determine clustering structure from such analysis. For example, in financial data, the eigenvector corresponding to the large "market" eigenvalue has a low IPR, identifying itself as a force that affects all stocks equally. Other eigenvectors, with larger IPRs, have components that are concentrated in various sectors of the market [1]. For crime data, these components correspond to locations across the city so a cluster of eigenvector components would correspond to a cluster of neighborhoods.

Examining the IPRs for significant eigenvectors in lagged correlation matrices, our results show that the eigenvector corresponding to the largest eigenvalue has a low IPR and can thus be interpreted as a "market" force. For the remaining significant eigenvectors, we find that they too have low IPRs, suggesting there is little clustering or community structure (Figure 11.9).

Remembering the strong correlation found between day of the week and the number of reported crimes from basic regressions outlined above, we find that it is possible to recreate this eigenvalue signal by constructing artificial time series using the regression coefficients from Table 11.3 and a Poisson random number generator. Beyond this single, large market eigenvalue, we cannot distinguish any other significant structure in the spectrum of correlation matrices generated by daily drug-related crime rates. For drug-related crimes, it appears as though little signal exists beyond the weekly rise and fall of offenses reported from weekend to weekday. It is unclear if this periodicity is due to some universal truth of drug crimes or simply to police procedure.

11.3.6 Weekly Theft-Related Crime Rates from 1991 to 1999

Having identified only a small correlation structure occurring on the scale of days, we next look at crime on a weekly scale. As shown in Figure 11.7(b), a more pronounced correlation exists. For these data, we construct 381 time series, one for each census tract in the city. Examining

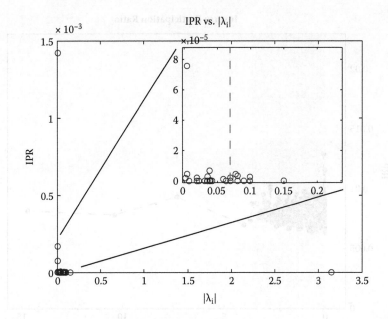

FIGURE 11.9   A plot of the IPR of the eigenvectors of the delayed correlation matrix for drug crimes with a 7-day lag.

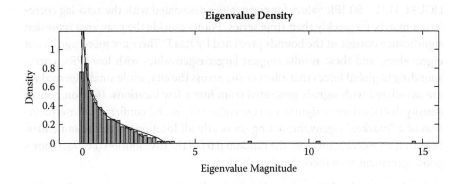

FIGURE 11.10   The eigenvalue spectrum of the zero-lag correlation matrix from weekly counts of theft-related crimes, aggregated at the census tract level. The solid line represents the RMT prediction, while the dashed line is a fit to the actual distribution using the min and max eigenvalues as fitting parameters.

the eigenvalue spectrum for the zero-lag correlation matrix of weekly theft data from 1991 to 1999, we find more significant eigenvalues than in the daily drug data (Figure 11.10). Some blocks of high or low correlation values can be seen, suggesting there is some spatial structure to theft crimes.

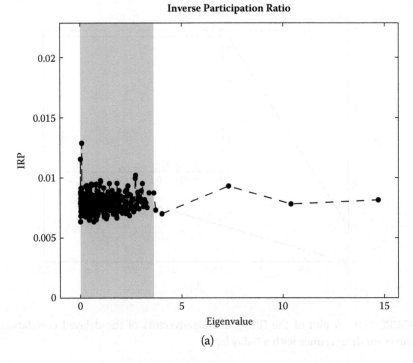

Inverse Participation Ratio

(a)

FIGURE 11.11 (a) IPR values for eigenvalues associated with the zero-lag correlation matrix for weekly theft time series. Points outside the gray area represent significance outside of the bounds predicted by RMT. There are more significant eigenvalues, and these results suggest larger eigenvalues with low IPRs, corresponding to global forces that affect crime across the city, while small eigenvalues are associated with signals generated from just a few locations. (b) Component density distributions of significant eigenvalues (λ_1, λ_2, λ_4) confirm our interpretation of a "market" eigenvalue acting on nearly all locations with the same bias. Selecting an eigenvector from the random part of the distribution (i.e., λ_{87}) shows good agreement with theoretical predictions.

Looking at the IPR values for theft-related eigenvectors, we find that the large market eigenvalue is much less pronounced. This is likely due to using sparser time series at the census tract level rather than a larger mesh grid. Now, however, there are other significant eigenvectors (both above and below the predicted min and max) that tell different stories. Figure 11.11(a) shows that eigenvectors associated with large eigenvalues generally have lower IPRs that correspond to factors that influence more spatial regions, while significant small eigenvalues have the highest IPRs, suggesting they are generated by acting on only a few components (locations around the city).

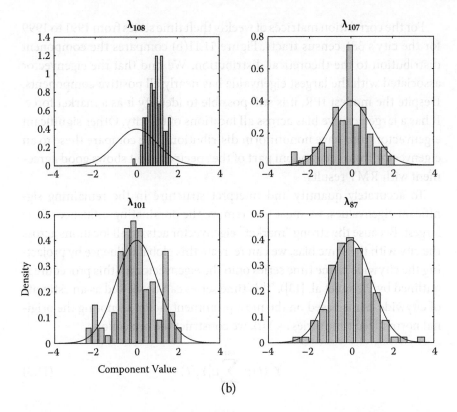

(b)

FIGURE 11.11 (continued). (a) IPR values for eigenvalues associated with the zero-lag correlation matrix for weekly theft time series. Points outside the gray area represent significance outside of the bounds predicted by RMT. There are more significant eigenvalues, and these results suggest larger eigenvalues with low IPRs, corresponding to global forces that affect crime across the city, while small eigenvalues are associated with signals generated from just a few locations. (b) Component density distributions of significant eigenvalues (λ_1, λ_2, λ_4) confirm our interpretation of a "market" eigenvalue acting on nearly all locations with the same bias. Selecting an eigenvector from the random part of the distribution (i.e., λ_{87}) shows good agreement with theoretical predictions.

Looking more closely at the eigenvectors that contribute to the signal contained in our correlation matrices, we examine the components of each, $\mathbf{u}_i = (u_1, u_2, \ldots, u_k)$. The theoretical distribution of components as derived from RMT is a normal distribution with zero mean and unit variance [13].

$$\rho(u) = \frac{1}{\sqrt{2\pi}} e^{-u^2/2} \tag{11.2}$$

For the correlation matrices of weekly theft time series from 1991 to 1999 for the city's 381 census tracts, Figure 11.11(b) compares the component distribution to the theoretical distribution. We find that the eigenvector associated with the largest eigenvalue has nearly all positive components. Despite the modest IPR, it is still possible to identify it as a market force. It has a large positive bias across all locations of the city. Other significant eigenvectors also have nonuniform distributions. We compare these to an eigenvector from the random part of the spectrum that shows good agreement with RMT results.

To accurately quantify and interpret structure in the remaining significant eigenvalues, we must first remove the dominating influence of the largest. Because the strong "market" eigenvector acts on all locations across the city with the same bias, we can recreate this global influence by projecting the citywide crime time series onto the eigenvector $\mathbf{u}^1$ (this procedure is outlined by Plerou et al. [13]). This time series can be viewed as an estimate of citywide crime based on the most prominent factor. Denoting the original normalized time series as $Y(t)$, we construct the projection

$$Y^1(t) = \sum_{j=1}^{381} u_j^1 Y_j(t) \tag{11.3}$$

Comparing this time series with the original weekly citywide crime, we find strong agreement over nearly 10 years of weekly data with the correlation coefficient of $\langle Y(t)\, Y^1(t) \rangle = .95$.

Having established a reasonable proxy for the market forces acting on crime rates at all locations, we regress the location time series on this global force and use residuals that are free from its influence. For the time series associated with each location $y_i(t)$, we perform the following regression:

$$Y_i(t) = \alpha_i + \beta_i Y^1(t) + \varepsilon_i(t) \tag{11.4}$$

where α_i and β_i are location-specific fit parameters. The residual time series $\varepsilon(t)$ are then used to compute the same correlation matrices and spectral analysis as described previously, but this time with the absence of global trends.

We now take the significant eigenvectors of the residual correlation matrices and examine their component structure. Large components of specific eigenvectors correspond to locations across the city that are all similarly biased by whatever force is associated with the vector. When we plot the largest 10% of components for the remaining significant eigenvectors geographically, we find that large components of each vector are strongly correlated spatially.

Figure 11.12 shows the spatial distribution of the largest components for different residual eigenvectors. The vector associated with larger eigenvalues act primarily on neighborhoods in high crime areas near central Philadelphia. Other eigenvalues produce similar spatial clusters, although interpretation of why these locations are clustered is left as an open question. This analysis suggests that weekly time scales reveal much richer spatial structure. We found that performing similar procedures using monthly time series reduces the amount of correlation, suggesting that the weekly time scale is the correct choice for analysis of neighborhood crime trends.

The problem of scale selection is one that can be dealt with naturally given the algorithms applied in this chapter. While Fourier analysis, regressions, and cross-correlation measures all give indications as to the amount of signal in the data, none provided our analysis with a satisfactory selection of scale. For example, the largest frequency in the Fast Fourier Transform (FFT) (Figure 11.5) of citywide theft counts is found at once-per-3-hours. This result most likely has something to do with police procedures such as shift changes, but selecting the hourly scale for all subsequent analysis would surely return time series too noisy and unpopulated for use.

By using results from Random Matrix Theory as a null model, we can easily measure how much signal can be distinguished from noise by observing eigenvalues above predicted maxima. Furthermore, changes in both spatial and temporal scales affect this spectrum in the same way—increasing or decreasing the number and magnitude of significant eigenvalues. Thus, we can select an appropriate scale by sweeping over time from hours to months, and space from a small lattice to a large one. Selecting the combination that maximizes these deviations allows us to extract the most signal from noisy data, aggregating as much, but not more, than necessary.

We can refine these statements even further by noting that whatever social phenomena are behind these significant eigenvectors (or principle factors), they are independent in some way. Whatever force is driving crime rates in the locations corresponding to large components of the second eigenvector is separate enough either in cause or manifestation from the force behind the third vector. This is a level of interpretation currently not offered by the majority of tools aimed at explaining causal relationships. The underlying social dynamics of these factors still remain

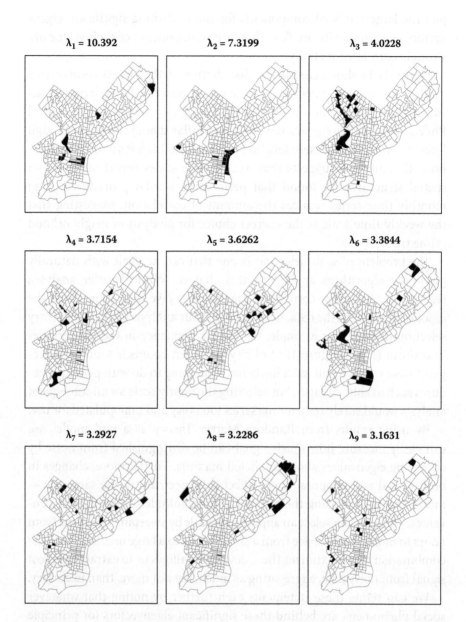

FIGURE 11.12   Plotting the geographic location of the largest 10% of components for the first nine significant eigenvectors reveals strong spatial correlation. We conclude that these eigenvectors correspond to neighborhoods or sets of neighborhoods and represent the forces that affect crime rates there.

unknown, a point we hope to address in future work. What is important, however, is that this analysis suggests that there is good reason to treat crime differently within different neighborhoods, and policing strategy may be improved by introducing more local autonomy into strategy.

11.4 SUMMARY AND CONCLUSION

In this chapter we presented a novel application of quantitative tools from fields such as mathematics, physics, and signal processing that can be used to analyze spatial and temporal patterns behavioral datasets. Basic analytic and statistical techniques revealed periodicities and cycles within the data that were then explored further by higher-resolution techniques. Due to a low signal-to-noise ratio, we adopted results from Random Matrix Theory as a suitable null model to construct significance tests. These tests revealed definite structure in the eigenvalue spectra of our correlation matrices.

Given the large portion of daily crime rates that can be explained by regressing data onto the day of the week, it is possible that these results reflect police procedures such as scheduling more officers on Mondays than Sundays. Differences in high crime days across types of crime, however, may suggest that different types of crime may represent unique aggregate behaviors. Another interesting result from our analysis is the lack of correlation between these different crime types. Broken windows and social disorganization theories postulate that an influx of minor offenses such as graffiti and vandalism might lead to an increase in more serious crimes such as assaults or gun violence. We find no evidence of this for short time scales. This is not to say, however, that no relationship exists. Due to data constraints, we have only looked for interaction on time scales of up to 30 days. It may be that these types of flows happen on the monthly or yearly time scale.

With 10 years of theft crime data, we are able to look for correlations on a weekly scale. Examining the eigenvalue and eigenvectors of correlation matrices, we perform a type of Principle Component Analysis where significance is determined by comparison to results from Random Matrix Theory. We find that the largest eigenvalue and corresponding eigenvector can be interpreted as a citywide force that acts on all locations equally.

Removing the influence of this dominating factor, we found a number of significant eigenvalues and vectors. Examining the component structure of these eigenvectors, we showed that they correspond to neighborhoods or sets of neighborhoods that share correlated crime rates. We drew an analogy to similar methods used in the analysis of finance markets where the eigenvalue spectrum also contains a "market" influence, and other significant eigenvalues are associated with specific industries and market sectors. The added value in this type of analysis is the ability to identify correlations due to different eigenvectors as representing independent forces.

We believe there is valuable policy and prevention insight to be gained from this work that might be applied to many facets of sustainable societies. We have demonstrated that daily crime rates are of little use when attempting to find significant correlation structure, while weekly crime rates may be a much richer choice. Along with the selection of a proper time scale, we have identified sets of neighborhoods whose crime rates are driven in sync. These connections are not entirely visible to simple correlation measures and may include neighborhoods at opposite ends of the city. They can also be attributed to different forces, suggesting policy that works in certain areas may not be relevant in other areas. Adoption of police procedures that take these relationships into account may lead to more effective law enforcement.

Aside from the results gained by using these techniques on crime data, we hope that they can and will be put to use in more situations calling for multiscale analysis. Not only do they prove reliable even given very noisy data, but also there are strong theoretic and experimental null hypotheses to verify the significance of results. Already, these methods have been shown capable of performing reliable factor analysis of financial markets and crime rates, two very complex behavioral systems.

ACKNOWLEDGMENTS

The authors would like to thank the Santa Fe Institute and the wonderful community of people that has helped us with their thoughts and ideas. We would also like to thank NSF Summer REU program for partially funding this research.

REFERENCES

1. Christoly Biely and Stefan Thurner. Random matrix ensembles of time-lagged correlation matrices: Derivation of eigenvalue spectra and analysis of financial time-series. *Quantitative Finance*, 8(7): 705–722, October 2008.
2. Francesco Calabrese, Jonathan Reades, and Carlo Ratti. Eigenplaces: Segmenting space through digital signatures. *IEEE Pervasive Computing*, 9(1): 78–84, January 2010.

3. Alan Edelman. Eigenvalues and condition numbers of random matrices. *SIAM J. Matrix Anal. Appl.*, 9(4): 543–560, 1988.

4. Marta C. Gonzalez, Cesar A. Hidalgo, and Albert-Laszlo Barabasi. Understanding individual human mobility patterns. *Nature*, 453(7196): 779–782, June 2008.

5. Maciej Kamiński, Mingzhou Ding, Wilson A. Truccolo, and Steven L. Bressler. Evaluating causal relations in neural systems: Granger causality, directed transfer function and statistical assessment of significance. *Biological Cybernetics*, 85(2): 145–157, August 2001.

6. Kees Keizer, Siegwart Lindenberg, and Linda Steg. The spreading of disorder. *Science*, 322(5908): 1681–1685, December 2008.

7. George L. Kelling and James Q. Wilson. Broken windows. *The Atlantic Monthly*, March 1982. 249(3): 29–38.

8. Gary Lafree. Declining violent crime rates in the 1990s: Predicting crime booms and busts. *Annual Review of Sociology*, 25(1): 145–168, 1999.

9. Laurent Laloux, Pierre Cizeau, Jean P. Bouchaud, and Marc Potters. Noise dressing of financial correlation matrices. *Physical Review Letters*, 83(7): 1467–1470, August 1999.

10. Jure Leskovec, Lars Backstrom, and Jon Kleinberg. Meme-tracking and the dynamics of the news cycle. In *Proceedings of the 15th ACM SIGKDD International Conference on Knowledge Discovery and Data Mining*, KDD '09, p. 497–506, 2009, New York, NY: ACM.

11. Helmut Lütkepohl. *New Introduction to Multiple Time Series Analysis*. Springer, Berlin and NY. *1st ed.* 2006. corr. 2nd printing edition, October 2007.

12. K.B.K. Mayya and M.S. Santhanam. Correlations, delays and financial time series. *Econophysics of Markets and Business Networks*, 69–75, 2007.

13. Vasiliki Plerou, Parameswaran Gopikrishnan, Bernd Rosenow, Lu'is A. Nunes Amaral, Thomas Guhr, and H. Eugene Stanley. Random matrix approach to cross correlations in financial data. *Physical Review E*, 65(6): 066126+, June 2002.

14. J. Reades, F. Calabrese, and C. Ratti. Eigenplaces: Analysing cities using the space–time structure of the mobile phone network. *Environment and Planning B: Planning and Design*, 36(5): 824–836, 2009.

15. Robert J. Sampson, Stephen W. Raudenbush, and Felton Earls. Neighborhoods and violent crime: A multilevel study of collective efficacy. *Science*, 277(5328): 918–924, August 1997.

16. A.M. Sengupta and P.P. Mitra. Distributions of singular values for some random matrices. *Physical Review E*, 60(3): 3389–3392, September 1999.

17. Martin B. Short, P. Jeffrey Brantingham, Andrea L. Bertozzi, and George E. Tita. Dissipation and displacement of hotspots in reaction-diffusion models of crime. *Proceedings of the National Academy of Sciences*, 107(9): 3961–3965, March 2010.

18. Michele Tumminello, Fabrizio Lillo, and Rosario N. Mantegna. Correlation, hierarchies, and networks in financial markets. *Journal of Economic Behavior & Organization*, 75(1): 40–58, July 2010.

19. Akihiko Utsugi, Kazusumi Ino, and Masaki Oshikawa. Random matrix theory analysis of cross correlations in financial markets. *Physical Review E*, 70(2): 026110+, August 2004.

20. Duncan J. Watts, Roby Muhamad, Daniel C. Medina, and Peter S. Dodds. Multiscale, resurgent epidemics in a hierarchical metapopulation model. *Proceedings of the National Academy of Sciences of the United States of America*, 102(32): 11157–11162, August 2005.

21. David Weisburd, Gerben J.N. Bruinsma, and Wim Bernasco. Units of analysis in geographic criminology: Historical development, critical issues and open questions. In David Weisburd, Wim Bernasco, and Gerben J.N. Bruinsma, Editors, *Putting Crime in its Place: Units of Analysis in Geographic Criminology*. New York: Springer, 2009.

22. Per-Olof Wikstrm, Vania Ceccato, Beth Hardie, and Kyle Treiber. Activity fields and the dynamics of crime. *Journal of Quantitative Criminology*, 26: 55–87, 2010. 10.1007/s10940-009-9083-9.

23. Jeffrey Wooldridge. Introductory Econometrics: A Modern Approach (with Economic Applications, Data Sets, Student Solutions Manual Printed Access Card). South-Western College Publishing, Mason, Ohio, 4th edition, March 2008.

CHAPTER 12

Constraint and Optimization Techniques for Supporting Policy Making

Marco Gavanelli, Fabrizio Riguzzi,
Michela Milano, and Paolo Cagnoli

CONTENTS

SYMBOL DEFINITIONS

A	Vector of activities. For energy sources, it is measured in megawatts (MW).
N_a	Number of activities: $N_a = |A|$.
a_i	Element of the A vector: $i \in \{1, ..., N_a\}$.
P	Vector of pressures.

N_p Number of pressures: $N_p = |\mathbf{P}|$.

p_i Element of the $\mathbf{P}$ vector: $i \in \{1, ..., N_p\}$.

$\mathbf{R}$ Vector of receptors.

N_r Number of receptors: $N_r = |\mathbf{R}|$.

r_i Element of the $\mathbf{R}$ vector: $i \in \{1, ..., N_r\}$.

$\mathbf{O}$ Vector of the outcomes.

o_i Outcome of the activity $\mathbf{A}_i$. For activities that are energy sources, it is the energy (in TOE) produced in 1 year by a plant of 1 MW.

T^b Total outcome of the regional plan. It is the sum of the outcomes of the single activities.

$\mathcal{M}$ Matrix defining the relation between activities and pressures.

m_j^i Element of the matrix $\mathcal{M}$. Dependency of activity a_i on pressure p_j.

$\mathcal{D}$ Matrix defining the dependency between primary and secondary activities.

d_{ij} Element of the matrix $\mathcal{D}$. It measures the dependency of (secondary) activity a_j on (primary) activity a_i.

$\mathcal{N}$ Matrix defining the relation between pressures and receptors.

n_j^i Element of the matrix $\mathcal{N}$. It is the effect of pressure p_i on receptor r_j.

$\mathbf{C}$ Vector of costs: $|\mathbf{C}| = N_a$.

c_i Element of the $\mathbf{C}$ vector. Unit cost of activity a_i.

A^P Set of the indexes of the primary activities; if $i \in A^P$, then $\mathbf{A}_i$ is a primary activity.

A^S Set of indexes of the secondary activities; if $i \in A^S$, then $\mathbf{A}_i$ is a secondary activity.

A_{ren}^P Set of indexes of those primary activities that provide renewable energy.

G Vector of magnitudes.

B Total available budget.

U_i Maximum energy that can be produced by energy source a_i in the Region.

L_i Minimum energy that must be produced by energy source a_i in the Region.

F_i Minimum fraction (percentage) of energy that should be produced by energy source a_i in the Region.

12.1 THE PROBLEM

PUBLIC POLICY ISSUES ARE extremely complex, occur in rapidly changing environments characterized by uncertainty, and involve conflicts among different interests. Our society is ever-more complex due to globalization, enlargement, and the changing geopolitical situation. This means that political activity and intervention become more widespread, and so the effects of its interventions become more difficult to assess, while at the same time it is becoming ever-more important to ensure that actions are effectively tackling the real challenges that this increasing complexity entails. Thus, those responsible for creating, implementing, and enforcing policies must be able to reach decisions about ill-defined problem situations that are not well understood, have no single correct answer, involve many competing interests, and interact with other policies at multiple levels. It is therefore increasingly important to ensure coherence across these complex issues.

In this chapter we consider, in particular, policy issues related to regional planning, the science of the efficient placement of activities and infrastructures for the sustainable growth of a region. Regional plans are classified into types, such as Agriculture, Forest, Fishing, Energy, Industry, Transport, Waste, Water, Telecommunication, Tourism, Urban Development, and Environment, to name a few. Each plan defines activities that should be carried out during the plan implementation. On the regional plan, the policy maker must take into account impacts on the environment, the economy, and the society. The procedure aimed to assess the impacts of a regional plan is called Strategic Environmental Assessment (SEA) [14] and relates activities defined in the plan to environmental and economic impacts. This assessment procedure is now manually implemented by environmental experts, but it is never applied during the plan/program construction. In addition, this procedure is applied on a given, already instantiated plan. Taking into account impacts *a posteriori* enables only corrective interventions that can, at most, reduce the negative effect of wrong planning decisions.

One important aspect to consider when supporting policy makers with Computational Intelligence approaches is the definition of formal policy models. In the literature, the majority of policy models rely on agent-based simulation [9, 12, 17], where agents represent the parties involved in the decision-making and implementation process. The idea is that agent-based modeling and simulation is suitable for modeling complex systems. In particular, agent-based models permit carrying out computer experiments to support a better understanding of the complexity of economic, environmental, and social systems, structural changes, and endogenous adjustment reactions in response to a policy change.

In addition to agent-based simulation models, which provide "individual-level models," we claim that the policy planning activity needs a global perspective: in the case of regional planning, we need "a regional perspective" that faces the problem at a global level while tightly interacting with the individual-level model. Thus, rather than proposing an alternative approach with respect to simulation, we claim that the two approaches should be properly combined as they represent two different perspectives of the same problem: the individual and the global perspective. This integration is the subject of our current research activity. In this setting, regional planning activities can be cast into complex combinatorial optimization problems. The policy maker must take decisions satisfying a set of constraints while at the same time achieving a set of (possibly conflicting) objectives such as reducing negative impacts and enhancing positive impacts on the environment, the society, and the economy. For this reason, impact assessment should be integrated into the policy model so as to improve the current procedure performed *a posteriori*.

In previous work [7] we experimented with two different technologies to address the Strategic Environmental Assessment of a regional plan, that is, assessing the effects on the environment of a given plan. The technologies we applied were Constraint Logic Programming (CLP) [11] and Causal Probabilistic Logic Programming [18]. Gavanelli et al. [8] proposed a fuzzy model for the SEA. While being far more expressive than a traditional CLP approach, it is less usable within a regional planning decision support system. We evaluated a previous regional plan with the two models, and proposed the outputs to an environmental expert. The expert compared the two outputs and chose the CLP model as closest to a human-made assessment.

In this work we extend the CLP model used for the assessment and apply it to the planning problem—that is, deciding which actions should be taken in a plan. In the model, decision variables represent political decisions (e.g., the magnitude of a given activity in the regional plan), potential outcomes are associated with each decision, constraints limit possible combinations of assignments of decision variables, and objectives (also referred to as criteria) can be used either to evaluate alternative solutions, or be translated into additional constraints. The model has been solved with Constraint Logic Programming [11] techniques, and tested on the Emilia-Romagna regional energy plan. The results have been validated by experts in policy making and impact assessment to evaluate the accuracy of the results.

Further constraint-based approaches have been proposed for narrower problems in the field of energy, such as locating biomass power plants in positions that are economically affordable [2, 5, 6] and environmentally sustainable [4]. Other approaches have been applied to wind turbine placement [10]. The problem faced in this chapter is much broader, as the region should decide which strategic investments to perform in the next 2 to 3 years (with a longer vision to 2020) in the energy field. All specific details are left to the implementation of the plan, but are not considered at the Regional Planning stage. To the best of our knowledge, this is the first time that constraint-based reasoning has been applied to such a wide and strategic perspective.

12.1.1 Regional Planning and Impact Assessment

Regional Planning is the result of the main policy-making activity of European regions. Each region has a budget distributed by the Operational Programme (OP); an OP sets out each region's priorities for delivering the funds. On the basis of these funds, the region has to define its priorities: in the field of energy, one example of priority is increasing the use of renewable energy sources. Then, a region should decide which activities to insert in the plan. Activities may be roughly divided into six types:

1. Infrastructures and plants

2. Buildings and land use transformations

3. Resource extraction

4. Modifications of hydraulic regime

5. Industrial transformations

6. Environmental management

Also, a magnitude for each activity should be decided, describing how much of a given activity is performed.

Each activity has an outcome (such as the amount of energy produced or consumed) and a cost. We have two vectors, $\mathbf{O} = (o_1, ..., o_{N_a})$ and $\mathbf{C} = (c_1, ..., c_{N_a})$, where each element is associated to a specific activity and represents the outcome and cost per unit of an activity.

There are constraints linking activities: for example, if a regional plan decides to build three biomass power plants (primary activities for an energy plan), each of these plants should be equipped with proper infrastructures (streets, sewage or possibly a small village nearby, power lines), also called *secondary activities*. We thus have a matrix of dependencies between activities. In particular, we have an $N_a \times N_a$ square matrix $\mathcal{D}$ where each element d_{ij} represents the magnitude of activity j per unit of activity i.

Taking as an example the Emilia-Romagna Regional Energy Plan approved in 2007, some objectives of the policy makers are the production of a given amount of energy (400 additional megawatts from renewable energy sources), while reducing the current greenhouse gas emission percentage by 6.5% with respect to 2003. In addition, the budget constraint limiting the amount of money allocated to the energy plan by the Regional Operational Programme was 30.5M€ in 2007.

The policy maker must also take into account impacts on the environment, the economy, and the society, as defined by a Strategic Environmental Assessment that relates activities defined in the plan to environmental and economic impacts. In fact, each activity has impacts on the environment in terms of positive and negative pressures. An example of positive pressure is the increased availability of energy, while an example of a negative pressure is the production of pollutants. Pressures are further linked to environmental receptors such as the quality of the air or of surface water. On both pressures and receptors, there are constraints: for example, the maximum amount of greenhouse gas emissions of the overall plan.

One of the instruments used for assessing a regional plan in Emilia-Romagna are the so-called *coaxial matrices* [3], a development of the network method [16].

One matrix $\mathcal{M}$ defines the dependencies between the above-mentioned activities contained in a plan and *impacts* (also called *pressures*) on the environment. Each element m_j^i of the matrix $\mathcal{M}$ defines a qualitative dependency between the activity i and the impact j. The dependency can be *high, medium, low,* or *null*. Examples of negative impacts are energy, water, and land consumption; variation of water flows; water and air pollution; and so on. Examples of positive impacts are reduction in water/air pollution, reduction in greenhouse gas emission, reduction in noise, natural resources saving, creation of new ecosystems, and so on.

The second matrix $\mathcal{N}$ defines the dependencies between the impacts and environmental receptors. Each element n_j^i of the matrix $\mathcal{N}$ defines a qualitative dependency between the impact i and an environmental receptor j. Again, the dependency can be *high, medium, low,* or *null.* Examples of environmental receptors are the quality of surface water and groundwater, the quality of landscapes, energy availability, wildlife wellness, and so on.

The matrices currently used in Emilia-Romagna contain 93 activities, 29 negative impacts, 19 positive impacts and 23 receptors, and assess 11 types of plans.

12.2 WHY CONSTRAINT-BASED APPROACHES?

The regional planning activity is now performed by human experts who build a single plan, considering strategic regional objectives that follow national and EU guidelines. After devising the plan, the agency for environmental protection is asked to assess the plan from an environmental point of view. Typically, there is no feedback: the assessment can state that the devised plan is environmentally friendly or not, but it cannot change the plan. In rare cases, it can propose corrective countermeasures, which can only mitigate the negative impact of wrong planning decisions. Moreover, although regulations state that a significant environmental assessment should compare two or more options (different plans), this is rarely done in Europe because the assessment is typically manual and requires a long effort. Even in the few cases in which two options are considered, usually one is the plan and the other is the absence of a plan (i.e., do nothing).

Constraint-based modeling overcomes the limitation of a handmade process for a number of reasons:

- First, it provides a tool that automatically performs planning decisions, considering both the budget allocated to the plan by the Regional Operative Plan as well as national/EU guidelines.

- Second, it takes into consideration environmental aspects during plan construction, thus avoiding trial-and-error schemes.

- Third, constraint reasoning provides a powerful tool in the hand of a policy decision maker as the generation of alternative scenarios is extremely easy and their comparison and evaluation come with no cost. Adjustments can be performed on-the-fly in case the results do not satisfy policy makers or environmental experts. For example, in the field of energy regional planning, by changing the bounds on the amount of energy each source can provide, we can adjust the plan by considering market trends and also the potential receptivity of the region.

12.2.1 A CLP Model

To design a constraint-based model for the regional planning activity, we have to define variables, constraints, and objectives. Variables represent decisions that must be taken. Given a vector of activities $\mathbf{A} = (a_1, \ldots, a_{N_a})$, we associate to each activity a variable G_i that defines its magnitude. The magnitude can be represented either in an absolute way, as the amount of a given activity, or in a relative way, as a percentage with respect to the existing quantity of the same activity. In this chapter we use the absolute representation.

As stated above, we distinguish primary from secondary activities: let A^P be the set of indexes of primary activities and A^S the set of indexes of secondary activities. The distinction is motivated by the fact that some activities are of primary importance in a given plan. Secondary activities are those that support the primary activities by providing the needed infrastructures. The dependencies between primary and secondary activities are considered by the following constraint:

$$\forall j \in A^S \quad G_j = \sum_{i \in A^P} d_{ij} G_i$$

Given a budget B_{Plan} available for a given plan, we have a constraint limiting the overall plan cost as follows:

$$\sum_{i=1}^{N_a} G_i c_i \leq B_{Plan} \tag{12.1}$$

Such a constraint can be imposed either on the overall plan or on parts of it. For example, if the budget is partitioned into chapters, we can impose Equation (12.1) on the activities of a given chapter.

Moreover, given an expected outcome o_{Plan} of the plan, we have a constraint ensuring to reach the outcome:

$$\sum_{i=1}^{N_a} G_i \, o_i \geq o_{Plan}$$

For example, in an energy plan, the outcome can be to have more energy available in the region, so o_{Plan} could be the increased availability of electrical power (e.g., in kilo-TOE, Tonnes of Oil Equivalent). In such a case, o_i will be the production in kTOE for each unit of activity a_i.

Concerning the impacts of the regional plan, we sum up the contributions of all the activities and obtain an estimate of the impact on each environmental pressure:

$$\forall j \in \{1,\ldots,N_p\} \quad p_j = \sum_{i=1}^{N_a} m_j^i \, G_i \tag{12.2}$$

In the same way, given the vector of environmental pressures $\mathbf{P} = (p_1, \ldots, p_{N_p})$, one can estimate their influence on the environmental receptor r_i by means of the matrix $\mathcal{N}$ that relates pressures with receptors:

$$\forall j \in \{1,\ldots,N_r\} \quad r_j = \sum_{i=1}^{N_p} n_j^i \, p_i \tag{12.3}$$

Moreover, we can have constraints on receptors and pressures. For example, "greenhouse gas emission" (that is, a negative pressure) should not exceed a given threshold.

Concerning objectives, there are a number of possibilities suggested by planning experts. From an economic perspective, one can decide to minimize the overall cost of the plan (that is, in any way subject to budget constraints). Clearly, in this case the most economic energy sources are preferred, despite their potentially negative environmental effects (which could be anyway constrained). On the other hand, one could maintain a fixed budget and maximize the produced energy. In this case, the most efficient energy sources will be pushed forward. Or the planner might prefer a *green* plan and optimize environmental receptors. For example, one can maximize, say, the air quality, or the quality of the surface water. In this case, the produced plan decisions are less intuitive and the system we propose is particularly useful. The link between decisions on primary and secondary activities and consequences on the environment are far too complex to be manually considered. Clearly, more complex objectives can be pursued by properly combining the above-mentioned aspects.

12.3 THE REGIONAL ENERGY PLAN

We can now describe how to cast the general model for regional planning described above into the model for designing a regional energy plan. The first step is to identify primary and secondary activities. In the context of a regional energy plan, the environmental and planning experts made the following distinction. Primary activities are those capable of producing energy, namely renewable and nonrenewable power plants. Secondary activities are those that support energy production, such as activities for energy transportations (e.g., power lines) and infrastructures supporting the primary activities (e.g., dams, yards).

One important aspect to account for when designing a regional energy plan is the energy source diversification: this means that the trend to allocate funds should not be directed toward a single energy source, but should cover both renewable and nonrenewable energy sources. This requirement comes from fluctuations of the price and availability of the various resources. For this reason, we have constraints on the minimal fraction F_i of the total energy produced by each source i:

$$\forall i \in A^P \ \ G_i o_i \geq F_i T^o$$

where the total outcome T^o is simply obtained as

$$T^o = \sum_{j \in A^P} G_j o_j$$

In addition, each region has its own geophysical characteristics. For instance, some regions are particularly windy, while others are not. Hydroelectric power plants can be built with some careful consideration of environmental impacts, the most obvious being the flooding of vast areas of land. This poses constraints on the maximum energy U_i that can be produced by a given energy source i

$$\forall i \in A^P \; G_i o_i \leq U_i$$

Finally, the region priorities should be compliant with European guidelines, such as the 20-20-20 initiative that aims at achieving three ambitious targets by 2020: reducing by 20% greenhouse gas emissions, having a 20% share of the final energy consumption produced by renewable sources, and improving by 20% its energy efficiency. For this reason, we can impose constraints on the minimum amount of energy L_{ren} produced by renewable energy sources whose set of activities is referred to as A^P_{ren}. The constraint that we can impose is

$$\sum_{i \in A^P_{ren}} G_i o_i \geq L_{ren}$$

12.4 THE REGIONAL ENERGY PLAN 2011–2013

The constraint-based model described in previous sections has been used in the planning of the regional energy plan for 2011–2013. The system is implemented in the Constraint Logic Programming language ECL^{i}PS^e [1], and in particular uses its Eplex library [15], which interfaces ECL^{i}PS^e with a (mixed-integer) linear programming solver. The computation time is not an issue in this application, and it was hardly measurable on a modern computer.

The regional energy plan had the objective of paving the way to reach the ambitious goal of the 20-20-20 directive, in particular having 20% of energy in 2020 produced by renewable sources. This amount considers not only electric power, but the entire energy balance in the region, including thermal energy and transports.

Transports can use renewable energy by using renewable fuels, such as biogas (methane produced from the fermentation of vegetable or animal wastes) or oil produced from various types of crops. Currently, we do not consider this issue.

Thermal energy can be used, for example, for home heating; renewable sources in this case are thermal solar panels (that produce hot water for domestic use), geothermal pumps (that are used to heat or to refresh houses), and biomass plants (that produce hot water used to heat neighboring houses during winter).

The considered electric power plants that produce energy from renewable sources are hydroelectric plants, photovoltaic plants, thermodynamic solar plants, wind generators and, again, biomass power plants.

For each energy source, the plan should provide the following:

- The installed power, in megawatts
- The total energy produced in a year, in kTOE
- The total cost, in M€.

The ratio between installed power and total produced energy is mainly influenced by the availability of the source: while a biomass plant can (at least in theory) produce energy 24/7, the sun is available only during the day, and the wind only occasionally. For unreliable sources an average for the whole year is taken.

The cost of the plant, instead, depends mainly on the installed power: a solar plant has an installation cost that depends on the square meters of installed panels, which on their turn can provide some maximum power (peak power).

It is worth noting that the considered cost is the total cost of the plant for the regional system, which is not the same as the cost for the taxpayers of the Emilia-Romagna region. In fact, the region can enforce policies in many ways, convincing private stakeholders to invest in power production. This can be done with financial leverage, or by giving favorable conditions (either economic or other) to investors. Some power sources are economically profitable, so there is no need for the region to give subsidies. For example, currently in Italy, biomass is economically advantageous for investors, so private entities are proposing projects to build biomass plants. On the other hand, biomass also produces pollutants; they are not always sustainable (see [4] for a discussion) so local committees are rather likely to spawn against the construction of new plants. For these reasons, there is a limit on the number of licenses the region gives to private stakeholders for building biomass-based plants.

Technicians in the region estimated (considering current energy requirements, growth trends, foreseen energy savings) the total energy requirements for 2020; out of this, 20% should be provided by renewable sources. They also proposed for this amount a percentage to be provided during the plan 2011 to 2013: about 177 kTOE of electrical energy and 296 kTOE of thermal energy.

Starting from these data, they developed a plan for electrical energy and one for thermal energy.

TABLE 12.1   Environmental Assessment of a Plan Using Only Biomass

Subsidence limitation	25.4475793911422
Embankments stability	−696.277574714292
Stability of coasts or seafloor	−21.4612152513278
Stability of river banks and beds	−267.844653150394
Soil quality	−732.083075332985
Quality of seawater	−343.348156768071
Quality of inland surface waters	−669.53249452972
Groundwater quality	−1242.58982368129
Air quality	−897.397559402556
Quality of climate	−189.576828693382
Wellness of terrestrial vegetation	−1531.95274530939
Wellness of wildlife	−2156.42423356061
Wellness of aquatic plants	−1732.32367634811
Wellness and health of mankind	204.340731338623
Quality of sensitive landscapes	−2175.66773468984
Cultural/historical heritage value	−1547.2098822988
Recreation resources accessibility	−64.6744331658445
Water availability	−1163.25455176302
Availability of agricultural fertile land	−827.660112502349
Lithoid resource availability	287.089994706276
Energy availability	57.450758535756
Availability of productive resources	3204.83984275847
Value of material goods	2469.68141448106

We used the model presented in Section 12.3, considering initially only "extreme" cases, in which only one type of energy source is used.

The application provides the optimal plan, together with its environmental assessment—namely, an evaluation of the environmental receptors used by the Environmental Protection Agency (Table 12.1).

To understand the individual contributions of the various energy forms, we plotted all the plans that use a single type of energy in Figure 12.1, together with the plan developed by the region's experts. On the x-axis, we chose the receptor *Air quality* because it is probably the most sensitive receptor in the Emilia-Romagna region. On the y axis, we plotted the cost of the plan. As explained previously, all plans provide the same energy in kTOE, while they may require different installation power (in megawatts).

First of all, we notice that some of the energy types improve the air quality (positive values on the x-axis), while others worsen it (negative values). Of course, no power plant can improve the air quality by itself (as it cannot remove pollutants from the air). The point is that the plant

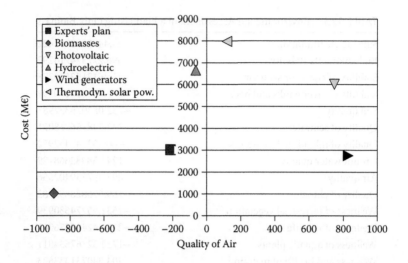

FIGURE 12.1 Plot of the *extreme* plans using only one energy source, compared with the plan by the region's experts.

provides electrical energy without introducing new pollutants; if such energy would not have been provided to the electrical network, it would have been imported from neighboring regions. In such a case, the required energy would be produced with the same mixture of energy sources as in the national production, including those emitting pollutants, so the net contribution is positive for the air quality. Note also that the different energy sources have different impacts on the air quality—not only due to the emissions of the power plants, but also to the impact of the secondary activities required by the various sources.

Finally, note that the "extreme" plans are usually not feasible, in the sense that the constraint on the real availability of the energy source in the region was relaxed. For example, wind turbines provide very good air quality at low cost, but the amount required in the corresponding extreme plan is not possible in the region considering the average availability of wind and of land for installing turbines.

The plan proposed by the region's experts is more *balanced*: it considers the real availability of the energy source in the region and provides a mixture of all the different renewable types of energy. This is very important in particular for renewable sources, which are often discontinuous: wind power is only available when the wind is blowing at a sufficient speed, solar power is only available during sunny days, etc., so having a mixture

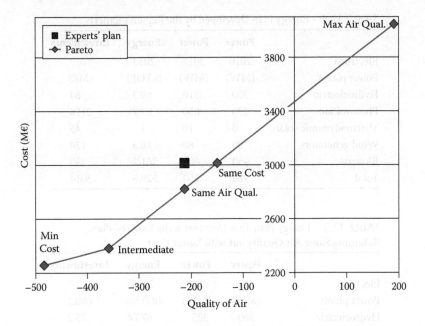

FIGURE 12.2 Pareto frontier of air quality against cost.

of different sources can provide an energy availability more continuous during the day.

In addition to assessing the plan proposed by the experts, we also provided new, alternative plans. In particular, we searched for optimal plans, both with respect to the cost and to the *air quality*. Because we have two objective functions, we plotted the Pareto-optimal frontier: each point of the frontier is a point such that one cannot improve one of the objectives without sacrificing the other. In our case, the air quality cannot be improved without raising the cost; and vice-versa, it is impossible to reduce the cost without sacrificing the air quality. The Pareto frontier is shown in Figure 12.2, together with the experts' plan. The objective function is a weighted sum of single criteria, so our formulation of the problem is linear and we can compute the Pareto frontier by changing coefficients in the weighted sum.

Figure 12.2 shows that although the plan devised by the experts is close to the frontier, it can be improved. In particular, we identified on the frontier two solutions that dominate the experts' plan: one has the same cost but better air quality, while the other has the same air quality but a lower cost.

TABLE 12.2   Energy Plan Developed by the Region's Experts

Electrical Power plants	Power 2010 (MW)	Power 2013 (MW)	Energy 2013 (kTOE)	Investments (M€)
Hydroelectric	300	310	69.3	84
Photovoltaic	230	850	87.7	2170
Thermodynamic solar	0	10	1	45
Wind generators	20	80	10.3	120
Biomass	430	600	361.2	595
Total	980	1850	529.5	3014

TABLE 12.3   Energy Plan That Dominates the Experts' Plan, Retaining Same Air Quality but with Lower Cost

Electrical Power plants	Power 2010 (MW)	Power 2013 (MW)	Energy 2013 (kTOE)	Investments (M€)
Hydroelectric	300	303	67.74	25.2
Photovoltaic	230	782.14	80.7	1932.51
Thermodynamic solar	0	5	0.5	22.5
Wind generators	20	140	18.03	240
Biomass	430	602.23	362.54	602.8
Total	980	1832.37	529.5	2823

Table 12.2 contains the plan developed by the region's experts, while Table 12.3 shows the plan on the Pareto curve that has the same air quality as the plan of the experts. The energy produced by wind generators is almost doubled (as they provide a very convenient ratio (air quality)/cost; see Figure 12.1); we have a slight increase in the cheap biomass energy, while the other energy sources reduce accordingly.

Concerning the environmental assessment, we plot in Figure 12.3 the value of the receptors in significant points of the Pareto front. Each bar represents a single environmental receptor for a specific plan on the Pareto frontier of Figure 12.2. In this way it is easy to compare how receptors are impacted by different plans. In the figure, the white bar is associated to the plan on the frontier that has the highest air quality, while bars with dark colors are associated to plans that have a low cost (and, thus, a low quality of the air). Notice that the receptors have different trends: some of them improve as we move in the frontier toward higher air quality (like *climate quality, mankind wellness, value of material goods*), while others

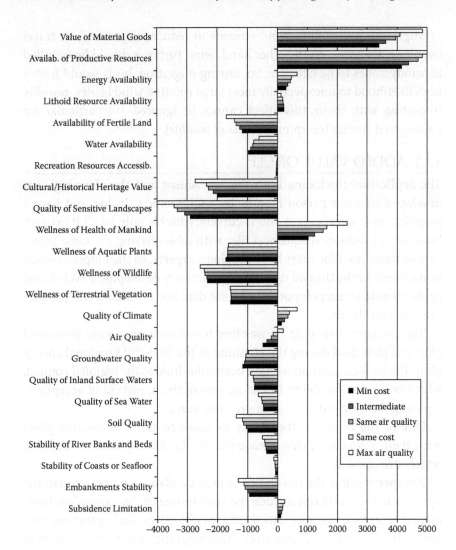

FIGURE 12.3   Value of the receptors on the Pareto front.

improve when moving to less expensive solutions (like *quality of sensitive landscapes, wellness of wildlife, soil quality*). This is due to several reasons, depending both on the type of power plants installed and on the secondary activities.

For example, wind turbines have a good effect on the air quality, but they are also considered aesthetically unpleasant, so they cannot be installed in sensitive zones, such as on hilltops, without having protests from the residents (receptor *quality of sensitive landscapes*). Unluckily, the hills are also the most windy zones in Emilia-Romagna.

Migratory birds follow wind streams to reduce fatigue in their travel over long distances; on the other hand, wind turbines should be installed in windy zones to be effective. So, during migration, birds would have a high likelihood to unexpectedly meet large rotating wind blades, possibly impacting with them; this effect cannot be ignored—in particular for endangered species (receptor *wellness of wildlife*).

12.5 ADDED VALUE OF CLP

The application (including both the assessment and the planning) was developed in a few person-months by a CLP expert. It does not have a graphical user interface yet and is currently usable only by CLP experts; however, it produces spreadsheet files with tables having the same structure as those used for years by the region's experts, so the output is easily understandable by the end user. We are currently developing a Web-based application to let users input the relevant data and try themselves producing plans on-the-fly.

The assessment module [7] was first tested on a previously developed plan and then used during the planning of the 2011–2013 regional energy plan. The various alternatives have been submitted to the regional council, which will have the ability to choose one of them, instead of accepting/rejecting the only proposal, as in previous years.

One of the results is the ability to generate easily alternative plans with their assessment; this is required by the EU regulations, but it is widely disregarded.

Another result is the possibility to provide plans that are optimal; the optimization criteria can include the cost, or one of the various environmental receptors. The user can select two objectives, and in this case the application generates a Pareto front. This helps the experts or the regional council in making choices that are more grounded.

We still do not know which plan the regional council will choose; neither do we know if and how the directives given in the regional plan will be implemented. More refined plans (at the province or municipality level) should follow the guidelines in the regional plan, but it is also possible to introduce modifications during the plan execution. However, in a perfect world in which everything is implemented as expected, the added value of CLP in monetary terms could be the difference of the *investment* columns in the plans in Tables 12.2 and 12.3: 191 M€ saved (by the various actors, public and private, in the whole region) in 3 years.

Finally, the choice of Constraint Programming greatly enables model flexibility. In discussions with experts, it is often the case that they change their minds on some model constraints or on objectives. Therefore, flexibility in dealing with side constraints and in dealing with nonlinear constraints facilitates knowledge acquisition making Constraint Programming the technique of choice for the problem and its future extensions.

12.6 CONCLUSION AND FUTURE OPEN ISSUES

Global public policy making is a complex process that is influenced by many factors. We believe that the use of constraint reasoning techniques could greatly increase the effectiveness of the process by enabling the policy maker to analyze various aspects and to play with parameters so as to obtain alternative solutions along with their environmental assessment. Given the amount of financial, human, and environmental resources that are involved in regional plans, even a small improvement can have a huge effect.

Important features of the system are its efficiency, as a plan is returned in a few milliseconds; and its wide applicability to many regional plans, to provincial and urban plans, and also to private and public projects. The system was used for the environmental assessment of the regional energy plan of the Emilia-Romagna region of Italy. In addition to performing automatically the assessment (that was performed manually in previous years), the assessment for the first time includes the evaluation of alternative plans: this is a requirement of EU regulations that is largely disregarded in practice. Moreover, the alternative plans were produced by optimizing the quality of the environmental receptors, together with the cost for the community of the plan itself.

This work is a first step toward a system that fully supports the decision maker in designing public policies. To achieve this objective, the method must be extended to take into account the individual level, by investigating the effect of a policy over the parties affected by it. This can be achieved by integrating constraint reasoning with simulation models that reproduce the interactions among the parties. In our current research, we are studying how the region can choose the form of incentives and calibrate them in order to push the energy market to invest in the directions foreseen by the Regional Energy Plan [13].

In turn, these models can be enriched by adopting e-Participation tools that allow citizens and stakeholders to voice their concerns regarding policy decisions. To fully leverage e-Participation tools, the system must also be able to extract information from all the available data, including natural language. Thus, opinion mining techniques will be useful in this context.

At the moment, the system can be used only by IT expert people. In order to turn it into a practical tool that is routinely used by decision makers, we must equip it with a user-friendly interface. In particular, we are in the process of developing a Web interface to the constraint solver in order to make it easy to use and widely accessible.

Finally, economic indicators will be used to assess the economic aspect of the plan. Up to now, only budget and a few economic pressures and receptors are considered. We believe that a comprehensive system should fully incorporate this aspect. We will integrate a well-established approach (UN and Eurostat Guidelines) and robust data from official statistics into the system to combine economic accounts (measured in monetary terms) and environmental accounts (measured in physical units) into a single framework useful for the evaluation of the integrated economic, environmental-social performance of regions.

ACKNOWLEDGMENTS

This work was partially supported by EU project ePolicy, FP7-ICT-2011-7, grant agreement 288147. Possible inaccuracies of information are the responsibility of the project team. The text reflects solely the views of its authors. The European Commission is not liable for any use that may be made of the information contained in this chapter.

REFERENCES

1. Krzysztof R. Apt and Mark Wallace. *Constraint Logic Programming Using Eclipse*. Cambridge (UK) and New York: Cambridge University Press, 2007.
2. Maurizio Bruglieri and Leo Liberti. Optimal running and planning of a biomass-based energy production process. *Energy Policy*, 36(7): 2430–2438, July 2008.
3. Paolo Cagnoli. *VAS Valutazione Ambientale Strategica*. Dario Flaccovio, Palermo, Italy, 2010.
4. Massimiliano Cattafi, Marco Gavanelli, Michela Milano, and Paolo Cagnoli. Sustainable biomass power plant location in the Italian Emilia-Romagna region. *ACM Transactions on Intelligent Systems and Technology*, 2(4), article 33, 1–19, July 2011.
5. Damiana Chinese and Antonella Meneghetti. Design of forest biofuel supply chains. *International Journal of Logistics Systems and Management*, 5(5): 525–550, 2009.

6. Davide Freppaz, Riccardo Minciardi, Michela Robba, Mauro Rovatti, Roberto Sacile, and Angela Taramasso. Optimizing forest biomass exploitation for energy supply at regional level. *Biomass and Bioenergy*, 26: 15–24, 2003.

7. Marco Gavanelli, Fabrizio Riguzzi, Michela Milano, and Paolo Cagnoli. Logic-based decision support for strategic environmental assessment. *Theory and Practice of Logic Programming, 26th Int. Conference on Logic Programming (ICLP'10) Special Issue*, 10(4-6): 643–658, July 2010.

8. Marco Gavanelli, Fabrizio Riguzzi, Michela Milano, Davide Sottara, Alessandro Cangini, and Paolo Cagnoli. An application of fuzzy logic to strategic environmental assessment. In R. Pirrone and F. Sorbello, Editors, *Artificial Intelligence Around Man and Beyond—XIIth International Conference of the Italian Association for Artificial Intelligence*, Volume 6934 of *Lecture Notes in Computer Science*, pp. 324–335, 2011. Berlin/Heidelberg: Springer.

9. Nigel Gilbert. *Computational Social Science*. Thousand Oaks, CA: Sage Publications, 2010.

10. S.A. Grady, M.Y. Hussaini, and Makola M. Abdullah. Placement of wind turbines using genetic algorithms. *Renewable Energy*, 30(2): 259–270, 2005.

11. Joxan Jaffar and Michael J. Maher. Constraint logic programming: A survey. *Journal of Logic Programming*, 19/20: 503–581, 1994.

12. Robin B. Matthews, Nigel G. Gilbert, Alan Roach, Gary J. Polhill, and Nick M. Gotts. Agent-based land-use models: A review of applications. *Landscape Ecology*, 22(10), 1447–1459, 2007.

13. Michela Milano, Marco Gavanelli, Barry O'Sullivan, and Alan Holland. What-if analysis through simulation-optimization hybrids. In *Proceedings of European Conference on Modelling and Simulation (ECMS)*, 2012.

14. Barry Sadler, Ralf Aschemann, Jiri Dusik, Thomas Fischer, Maria Partidario, and Rob Verheem (Eds.). *Handbook of Strategic Environmental Assessment*. Earthscan, London and Washington, D.C. 2010.

15. Kish Shen and Joachim Schimpf. Eplex: Harnessing mathematical programming solvers for constraint logic programming. In P. van Beek, Editor, *Principles and Practice of Constraint Programming—CP 2005*, Volume 3709 of *Lecture Notes in Computer Science*, pages 622–636, 2005. Berlin/Heidelberg: Springer-Verlag.

16. Jens C. Sorensen and Mitchell L. Moss. Procedures and Programs to Assist in the Impact Statement Process. Technical report, University of California, Berkeley, 1973.

17. Klaus G. Troitzsch, Ulrich Mueller, G. Nigel Gilbert, and Jim Doran. Social Science Microsimulation. *J. Artificial Societies and Social Simulation*, 2(1): Berlin: Springer Verlag, 1996.

18. Joost Vennekens, Sofie Verbaeten, and Maurice Bruynooghe. Logic programs with annotated disjunctions. In Bart Demoen and Vladimir Lifschitz, Editors, *International Conference on Logic Programming*, Volume 3131 of *Lecture Notes in Computer Science*, pages 195–209, 2004. Heidelberg, Germany: Springer.

Index

3D tensor, 35
20-20-20 initiative, 371
50 Hz frequency, 192

A

Abnormal energy use, detecting through outlier mining, 219
Abrupt changes, 91–94
  with spatial and temporal persistence, 92
Acceleration, with excess generation, 288
Actionable insights, 102
  on climate extremes and uncertainty, 127–128
Activity cost, 366
Activity magnitude, for regional planning, 365
Activity outcome, 366
Adaptive anisotropic deterministic sampling methods, 144
Adaptive mechanisms, 6
Advanced Reasoning using Knowledge for Typing of Sea ice (ARKTOS), 110
AEROCOM, 85
Aerosol data, 85
Agent-based modeling and simulation, 363–364
Aggregated demand curves, 205
Aggregated sectors, 61
  confidence intervals, 65
  error rates, 64, 65
  positive mean values, 65

Aggregation bias, 55
  effects on aggregated *versus* unaggregated sectors, 68
Aggregation effects
  in carbon footprint accounting using MRIO, 53–56, 55
  on environmental analysis, 55
  error rates, aggregated sectors, 64
  factors influencing, 65–66
  magnitude, 61–65
  procedure 1, 59
  procedure 2, 59–60
  test of, 56–60
Aggregation errors, 60
  carbon intensity, Leontief multiplier, and final demand influences, 68
  of small sectors, 60
  top 30 ranking, 73–77
Aggregation level, 54
  method sensitivity to, 55
  variation increases with, 54
Aggregation matrix, 58
  randomly determined, 60
Aggregation problem, 54
  in environmentally extended IOA, 55
Aggregation units, 13
AI56O 2000 database
AIO 2000 database
  aggregation effects on CF accounting, 62–63, 68
  sector classification, 71–73
Air conditioning, 185

For Product Safety Concerns and Information please contact our
EU representative GPSR@taylorandfrancis.com Taylor & Francis
Verlag GmbH, Kaufingerstraße 24, 80331 München, Germany